CW00520779

ROCHDALE AFC

A Who's Who
1999 to 2016

Steven Phillipps

A *SoccerData* Publication

Published in Great Britain by Tony Brown,
4 Adrian Close, Toton, Nottingham NG9 6FL.
Telephone 0115 973 6086. E-mail soccer@innotts.co.uk
www.soccerdata.com

First published 2016

Cover design by Bob Budd. The author is grateful to Mark Wilbraham for the use of the
club photographs of the players used in the book.

Printed and bound by 4Edge, Hockley, Essex
www.4edge.co.uk

ISBN: 978-1-911376-01-9

PREFACE

As of May 2016, Rochdale have completed 109 seasons, all of them as a professional club, and in that time 1864 players have appeared in the first team in competitive games. Of those 1247 of them have played in Football League matches, an additional 40 have been unused substitutes in the league and six saw their only league matches for the club expunged. This fourth volume of the Who's Who covers those who have played in the 17 years since 1999. After years of gloom for Dale supporters, this period saw the club reach the play-offs on three occasions, play at Wembley for the first time and – after a remarkable 36 years in the fourth tier - twice win promotion, even if the second was required after a catastrophic relegation season in between. Although the players from this era are largely well known, some have had long non-league careers, some details of which are uncertain. As with the previous volumes, I have therefore included details which, while likely true, are not completely certain (and are clearly marked as such). Also continuing the style of the earlier volumes, the players appear in the text in the order in which they made first team appearances for Rochdale, so that there is also an underlying narrative history of the club over the years in question. A total of 315 players are included in the present volume (taking the overall tally to the aforementioned 1864), and as in the previous books, these range from future full internationals to local juniors with just the odd senior appearance to their credit. All players chosen among the (ever increasing number of) substitutes are included, even if they never left the bench.

Steven Phillipps
June 2016

ACKNOWLEDGEMENTS

The details contained within these pages have been acquired over a period of many years with the help of many Rochdale followers and statisticians of other clubs. Special thanks go to Mark Wilbraham for the use of his archive of official Rochdale AFC photographs and Tony Brown for readily agreeing to publish these volumes.

Dale at Wembley, 2008

ROCHDALE AFC HISTORY 1999-2016

MILLENIUM

The 1998-99 season had ended with Graham Barrow sacked a week short of three years in charge and with Dale completing a 25th consecutive season in the fourth tier. A fortnight later, despite his side just missing the play-offs, Mansfield boss Steve Parkin quit at Field Mill, and he and his assistant, Tony Ford, the longest serving player in the Football League, were quickly installed as the new management team at Spotland. They were joined by physio Andy Thorpe, the former Stockport stalwart, while David Hamilton remained in charge of the reserves.

With the 'any three from five' substitutes rule from the Premier League and the FA Cup extended to the Nationwide Football League, larger squads would be required by the smaller clubs. However, despite Robbie Painter leaving to join Halifax, apart from Ford, only three major signings were included on what became a regular pre-season tour to Scotland during Parkin's time with the club (Dale overcoming Stenhousemuir, Berwick Rangers and Raith Rovers during their week north of the border). The newcomers were Wayne Evans, a right back from Walsall, Chester midfielder Dave Flitcroft, and winger Graeme Atkinson from relegated Scarborough, a former loanee at Spotland. Squad numbers also became compulsory for the first time and when Walsall youngster Clive Platt joined them on loan on the eve of the season, Dale began with numbers 1 to 21.

The opening day of the 1999-2000 campaign saw Dale become the first Football League visitors to Cheltenham Town, and the 40 year old Ford scored in a 2-0 win over the newcomers. Dave Flitcroft made a different sort of impression when he rugby tackled the unsuspecting home mascot before the game! Clive Platt then netted in a similar success against Southend (despite Flitcroft being sent off), and Dale went top of the table when they won 3-0 at York. However, they lost both legs of the League Cup tie against Chesterfield, scoring own goals in each of them.

They slipped up at home a couple of times, but ran up further away wins at Chester, Rotherham and Northampton, all without conceding a goal, by far the best start to a season away from home that the club had ever enjoyed. Remarkably the win at Millmoor – where Atkinson scored a memorable last minute solo goal, after Monington had been sent off against his former club for the second year running – was Dale's first since 1931. The team even managed some good publicity, with Neil Edwards making the news as perhaps the league's shortest 'keeper but the one with the best record, conceding only 4 goals in 12 games. Platt, too, had been in tremendous form and Dale moved rapidly to make his transfer permanent, for a new club record fee of £100,000. However, on the day he signed, the story the press went with was that of a 'dust-up' between Dale mascot Desmond the Dragon and his Halifax counterpart, Freddie the Fox!

The run ended with a 1-0 defeat by leaders Barnet and Dale – with the injury prone Lancashire out already – surprisingly failed to score in any of the next six games either. Indeed, they had not scored at Spotland since the first home game of the season, and were back down in 16th place before a cup replay against Burton Albion gave them the break they needed, Platt netting to end a goalless home run of 688 minutes. Former fitness instructor Julian Dowe, who had played for Ayr United and for Marbella in Spain, also netted his only senior goal in the 3-0 win. In the original game, Graham Hicks, son of former player and current School of Excellence chief Keith, made the second appearance of a much briefer career than his father's.

Parkin had by now recruited the veteran striker Tony Ellis from Blackpool to partner Platt - neither of the previous term's leading scorers, Andy Morris and Michael Holt netted a single league goal this time around – and both Ellis and Platt scored in a 2-1 victory over the boss's former club Mansfield. Remarkably, after 17 games, this was the first time all season that both sides had scored in a Dale league match. After three fairly uninspiring draws – Ellis missing a penalty against Cheltenham – Rochdale then travelled to Brighton. A 2-0 lead was frittered away and Albion led 3-2 with 10 minutes left, but the lanky Platt then popped up with a brace of headers to earn what, amazingly enough, was Dale's first ever 4-3 away win in the FL.

A seventh away win, at Carlisle, and a rarer home success against Shrewsbury put Dale right back in contention, but a vital match at Hartlepool – the first of Year 2k - went against them 3-2.

Completely overturning their previous form, Dale now won six out of seven at home in the league and also got through the first two rounds of the Auto Windscreens Shield, coming from two down to beat Macclesfield via Monington's extra time 'golden goal' (his second of the match) and winning a penalty shoot-out against Hull. Remarkably, the former match was the first time Dale had won after trailing 2-0 for 30 years, but in the very next match the boot was on the other foot as Southend salvaged a point after Dale had led 3-0 at the interval.

The restored Lancashire's eighth goal in ten games helped Dale to another away win, at Halifax, but he was injured later in the game and crucially missed the next six, only one of which was won. The victory was at Carlisle in the AWS, a match which saw Tony Ford – awarded an MBE in the New Year's Honours List – reach the phenomenal milestone of 1000 senior games (or even a few more, counting minor cup ties), the first outfield player to do so. Richard Bott, Dale's new director with responsibility for publicity, and a journalist himself, had been hoping to interest Sky TV etc, but a Tuesday night game in the AWS was hardly prime material to work with. Having reached the Northern Final of the competition for the second time, unfortunately Dale found themselves three down to Stoke within the first half hour and eventually lost 4-1 on aggregate.

Gary Jones had become a fixture in midfield since November and scored twice at Hull to scrape a point against 10 men, in between heavy defeats by promotion contenders Darlington and strugglers Orient. However, three wins and three draws from late March closed the gap again, the 4-2 success at Shrewsbury looking likely to put the Shrews down in the process. Having fought out a 3-3 draw at Peterborough, thanks to Neil Edwards' penalty save, Dale were unable to prevent the Posh winning at Spotland, but top scorer Tony Ellis headed an injury time equaliser at Plymouth after Jones and the Argyle goalscorer were sent off.

Though they had signed former Scotland under-21 left back Sean McAuley, Dale had recently been playing a wing back system, with the veterans Ford and Atkinson on the flanks, but both were ruled out through injury when new front runners Northampton visited Spotland, and Dale old boy Keith Welch had an easy time as his side cruised to a 3-0 win. Nevertheless a rare goal by Wayne Evans eked out a 2-1 win at Macclesfield, Dale's tenth away victory of the campaign, to keep alive an outside chance of making the play-offs until the final day.

Needing to win well and hope that Cheltenham, Hartlepool and Torquay lost, in the event Dale could manage only a draw with Barnet, and it was Hartlepool – the only winners on the day – who claimed the last playoff-place. Dale finished 10th with 68 points (their best since three points for a win was introduced), four behind them. Reversing the narrow defeat at the Victoria Ground back in January would have been sufficient to put the Dale in 7th position instead. Nevertheless – and despite Total Football magazine voting Spotland the best ground to visit for a match in the FL - the attendance for the late season game against Torquay was the lowest anywhere that year, just 1529.

Rochdale scored more away goals than anyone in the Nationwide League except Charlton and Barnsley in Division 1 and Preston in Division 2, but netted only 21 in 23 home games, less than anyone else in Division 3 apart from Chester, who went down, and Shrewsbury, who made a last day escape. For once Dale had had a fairly settled side with six of them playing at least 40 games, though the only ever-present was Wayne Evans, who was also voted player of the year. Off the field, in a classic `poacher turned gamekeeper' move, Francis Collins, one-time editor of the satirical Dale fanzine, became the club's chief executive, while elsewhere, Stephen Bywater's full debut for West Ham triggered the next substantial instalment of his transfer fee. (A few months later he also made his debut for England under-21s).

Acquisitions in the close season of 2000 included midfielder Michael Oliver from Darlington and the former Welsh international winger Simon Davies from Macclesfield. After the pre-season tour to Scotland, these were joined by Bradford City's Lee Todd, who had played for City in the first round of the European Intertoto Cup earlier in the summer. On the way out, again, was Jason Peake – scorer of the Dale's 'goal of the season', with a spectacular bicycle-kick against Halifax - who turned down new terms to sign for Plymouth, while Graeme Atkinson was put out of action – eventually for the whole of the coming season - by cruciate ligament damage. Former player of the year and cult hero Alan Johnson was finally forced to quit the game after another attempted comeback towards the end of the season.

Dale opened 2000-01 with a home draw against Darlington and then lost 2-1 at Brighton (future England international Bobby Zamora netting both the home goals), after Ellis and an Albion defender were sent off following a scuffle. The veteran striker atoned in the next game, a Worthington Cup tie against Premier League Blackburn Rovers, when he netted a last minute equaliser in what was billed as the battle of the Flitcrofts, Dale's Dave facing his brother Gary. In the second leg Rovers were awarded no less than three penalties (all converted by Damian Duff) and won 6-1. Ellis had been suspended and on loan Gary Hamilton ineligible against his own club, so 16 year-old YTS striker David Walsh got a surprise run out as substitute against their multi-million pound opponents. Hamilton actually made an international appearance while at Spotland, as he played for Northern Ireland under-21s one night and for Dale the next.

Meanwhile, Dale had obtained their first victories of the season, at home to Scunthorpe and away at Halifax. Another youngster, Phil Hadland came on as substitute at Cardiff and grabbed the equaliser. As at the start of the previous term, Dale were in great form away from home, adding victories at Carlisle, York and Shrewsbury, Platt netting his sixth in eight games and centre half Monington his third in successive games in the 4-0 demolition of the Shrews.

Dale were now second in the table, but with Lancashire injured again, Steve Parkin had been attempting to sign Southend's Martin Carruthers. However a change in management at Roots Hall led to a recall for Carruthers and he inevitably scored the only goal when the sides met. Nevertheless, Dale dispatched fellow contenders Hartlepool and Cheltenham, defender Monington taking his tally to a remarkable six in eight games (including two on his birthday), and played out a superb 2-2 draw with leaders Chesterfield, a match which saw the opening of the new Willbutts Lane stand. A sixth away win in seven games came at Exeter, Platt's last minute header earning Rochdale's first win there since 1963. As in the previous year's AWS game, Dale came from two down at Macclesfield, the goals coming from substitutes Paul Ware, against his former club, and the on loan Christian Lee.

Mansfield ended Dale's run, and defeats were also suffered in the remaining cups (losing to a golden goal at non-league Doncaster in the LDV Vans Trophy), but single strikes from Gary Jones accounted for both Blackpool and Hull in the league, the latter game attracting Spotland's best Boxing Day crowd for 40 years, over 4300. Just before the `real' millennium on 1st January 2001 (most people having celebrated it a year too early), Tony Ford, at 41 years and 6 months, passed Jack Warner's record as Rochdale's oldest Football League player (thus justifying younger supporters' chants of "He's big, he's bad, he's older than my Dad"). A fluke by Wayne Evans defeated Darlington and despite a slip-up at home to Halifax, a superb 3-1 victory over fellow challengers Leyton Orient in a Sky TV live game kept Dale 4th with 47 points from 25 games. Unfortunately, bad weather and the state of the Spotland pitch then conspired to cause several postponements; there were ten before the end of the season.

Goalless draws at Cardiff – themselves on the back of a record-breaking winning sequence – and Scunthorpe looked to be points well won, but in fact were the beginning of another goal drought, as had afflicted the side the year before. Struggling Torquay and York both beat Dale 1-0, and with Platt and Ford injured Steve Parkin changed his defence to try and help out his attack, bringing in the potentially more constructive Simon Coleman in place of Keith Hill, to play in a back three. Coleman had been signed from Southend the previous summer but in an injury wrecked season had played only once. The experiment backfired spectacularly as Shrewsbury, down in the bottom half, inflicted Rochdale's worst ever home defeat, by seven goals to one. Dale had conceded only eight goals in their previous 14 league games put together.

In the aftermath, they also went down badly at Southend, Flitcroft ending up in goal when Edwards was sent off for handling outside his area; after losing only 4 games in 27, they had now lost four in a row. Four draws steadied the ship, and it could have been so much better had both Hartlepool and leaders Chesterfield not grabbed late equalisers. It was particularly cruel on YTS goalkeeper Matt Gilks who had a superb debut at Chesterfield in place of the suspended Edwards and also played part of the following game when Edwards went off injured.

After missing out on other possibilities, Steve Parkin had by now got the striker he wanted in Stoke's Paul Connor, a new record signing at £150,000. Connor scored in three successive games but Dale still lost at Hull, who had come from nowhere to move into the play-off places, despite being in receivership and not having paid their players for some time. Lee Todd scored a dramatic last minute free-kick equaliser against champions-to-be Brighton, but even so Dale had now picked up only five points from ten games and had not won in 12.

However, just when it looked all over, Dale suddenly annihilated Carlisle 6-0 (their first six goal victory since the 1968-69 promotion season), with Connor grabbing that rarity, a Dale hat-trick. After a draw at Macclesfield , when veteran ex-Rochdale reserve Lee Martin saved Jones's penalty (he had been sent off in the previous season's fixture), Connor scored two more as Rochdale beat Exeter over Easter. Though still only 10th, Dale had another six games to play at this point, compared to the three or four of their rivals. Unfortunately they blew the first one, losing 3-0 at Barnet (and not for the first time presenting a club with their last success before exiting the FL), but did beat Lincoln to reclaim a top eight spot.

Chesterfield had been under investigation for some time for numerous alleged illegalities involving payments to players and fake accounting, so although they still headed the table, it was widely assumed that, having been found guilty on several counts, they would be docked sufficient points to prevent their promotion (as had happened to Swindon some years earlier), in which case 8th place would be good enough to make the play-offs.

Regardless of that, Dale would go a long way towards guaranteeing a place if they could get a result at Blackpool, their closest rivals. However, the Seasiders won 3-1 and Edwards was sent off again for a professional foul. Celebrating Steve Parkin's award as manager of the month, his side got back on course by beating Mansfield (thus avoiding the usual manager of the month 'curse') and, dramatically, Plymouth, coming back from a goal down at half-time. The latter was the final mid-week game of the season, having been one of the numerous postponed matches fitted into the final weeks of the season, and coincidentally the last game of the season would be against the same opponents.

Meanwhile, the commission investigating Chesterfield had amazingly decided that they would be docked so few points that they wouldn't even drop out of the automatic promotion places, merely moving down from 2nd to 3rd. The Football League, concerned at the apparent leniency, then asked the (same!) panel to reconsider the punishment, but they refused to change their verdict, and with only two days of the season left, the League acquiesced. (A less gullible Serious Fraud Office investigation subsequently saw the former Chesterfield chairman sentenced to four years in jail).

Thus, Dale now had to win their final game – or at least do as well as Blackpool – to stay in 7th place. Just after half-time, they were still in pole position as Darlington pegged back an early Blackpool goal. However, the Tangerines soon retook the lead while Dale battled to break the deadlock at Plymouth. Twice, defenders hacked the ball off the line, but the ball wouldn't run Dale's way and Argyle's 17-year old debutant 'keeper kept out everything else the Dale could throw at him and the match ended scoreless. Dale were therefore condemned to finish 8th, despite their best ever points tally of 70. They could also boast their best average gate for 30 years, at 3248.

However, to rub in Dale's disappointment, it was Blackpool who then went on to gain promotion through the play-offs, at the start of a remarkable rise which saw then reach the Premier League nine years later. (By which time, coincidentally, their goalkeeper was Dale's Matt Gilks).

Dale had again fielded a consistent line-up throughout most of the season, with nine players appearing at least 38 times in the league, including Wayne Evans, who had missed only one FL game in two seasons, Lee Todd (the supporters' player of the year) and Gary Jones (the players' player of the year). In the game at Kidderminster, Tony Ford had set yet another milestone when he played on his 100th different FL ground.

Manager Parkin decide to release several of the older players, notably centre backs Keith Hill and Mark Monington and strikers Tony Ellis and the injury prone Graham Lancashire, to give himself room for manoeuvre in the transfer market, but he quashed rumours linking Clive Platt and Paul Connor with a £600,000 move to Grimsby. His first move of the summer, though, was to give Matt Gilks a professional contract, while another youngster who had made his debut late in the season, striker Kevin Townson, was selected for the England under-18s squad for a match in Italy. Back in March in a friendly for a Rochdale XI against Castleton Gabriels (which, uniquely for Dale featured the father and son duo of Keith and Graham Hicks), a young Irish trialist, Pat McCourt, had scored the only goal and he was also added to the staff.

Newcomers over the summer included the expected two new centre backs, Gareth Griffiths from Wigan and Northampton's Richard Green, who had had a successful loan spell at Spotland in 1999. Unfortunately Green suffered a pre-season back injury and never actually figured in the first team. Macclesfield's former Republic of Ireland under-21 international Keiron Durkan and Chester youngster Matt Doughty also joined Dale. Former player Alex Russell joined the squad for the tour to Scotland, but subsequently signed for Torquay.

Dale started the 2001-02 season at the new Kassam Stadium, and ruined Oxford's party by winning 2-1 with goals from debutant Matt Doughty and the unlikely hero Simon Coleman, 'Homer' deflecting it in off his knee for his only Dale goal. Indeed, Dale got off to a cracking start away from home for the third year in a row, winning all their first four games, including a Worthington Cup giant killing of Huddersfield, thanks to a diving header from the 42 year old Tony Ford, and a first victory at Plymouth for 32 years. They also took seven points from their first three home games to establish themselves at the top of the table.

Dale also took Premier League Fulham to extra time in the Worthington Cup, and led through young substitute Kevin Townson's second goal of the night until the 119th minute, a lengthy penalty shoot-out eventually going against Dale, despite Matt Gilks keeping out three Fulham efforts. However, their heroics were totally overshadowed by the unfolding events on the other side of the Atlantic, forever known as "9/11".

Hampered by an increasing list of injuries, Dale lost their next two away games, Shrewsbury knocking them off top spot with a late winner from Luke Rodgers (who had netted a hat-trick in the infamous 7-1 game). Steve Parkin acted quickly to sign veteran centre back Richard Jobson and Dale went on a run of seven matches without defeat. American international goalkeeper Marcus Hahnemann also arrived on loan from Fulham, figuring in the game between the top pair, which Dale won 1-0 at Luton, oddly enough, the first match between the sides since they met as the top two in the old Division 3 back in 1969.

A controversial game against close rivals Cheltenham saw Dale come from a goal down to take the lead, despite the dismissal of on-loan striker Paul Wheatcroft, one of the scorers, only for the referee to award Cheltenham a goal when McAuley looked to have cleared the ball well before it could cross the line. A bad day at one of their least favourite grounds then saw Dale four down to Orient before Kevin Townson scored his sixth and seventh goals of the season, all of them when coming on as substitute.

Dale beat Torquay to reclaim second spot with 34 points from 17 games, but Spotland was then rocked by the resignations of Steve Parkin and Tony Ford to take over at first division strugglers Barnsley. Dale later received £131,500 in compensation, a sizeable fraction for Tony Ford as he also had a playing contract, surely making his the most expensive transfer of a 42 year old ever! (They certainly needed the money, they were reported to be losing £25,000 a month – wages were about three times the gate money over the year, despite an improved average attendance of 3488).

With David Hamilton in caretaker charge, Dale travelled to Bristol Rovers where a tremendous team performance was capped by a memorable breakaway goal from skipper Jones. This was Hahnemann's last appearance of a spell in which he impressively kept four clean sheets in five league games and became an iconic figure despite the brevity of his connection to Dale.

After just four substitute appearances for the first team (and a hat-trick in an 8-0 win in the Youth Cup), Pat McCourt was selected to play in a practice game for Northern Ireland. Remarkably, Dale's other hat-trick scorer in the Youth Cup, Rory Patterson, though having little impact at Spotland, also later played for Northern Ireland.

The next six games only brought one victory - in the FA Cup against Tamworth - Dale losing to a controversial penalty at Darlington (referee Uriah Rennie also dismissing Kevin Townson), and inexplicably conceding twice after leading Lincoln 2-0 going into the 90th minute. Dale also lost Gary Jones, who joined his former boss at Barnsley for a fee of £215,000, and Dave Bayliss, after a reputed falling-out with David Hamilton, moving to rivals Luton. A brief and rather bizarre arrival was that of 44 year old goalkeeper Vince O'Keefe, a one time Blackburn colleague of Hamilton's, who was on the bench for the FA Cup defeat at Blackpool, nine years after his previous senior involvement

Although David Hamilton had been keen to carry on in charge, the board appointed the much more experienced and well-known figure of John Hollins, the former Chelsea player and manager, as the new boss at Spotland, with the brief to continue the push for the play-offs begun by Steve Parkin. (Hamilton became first team coach). Hollins' first move was to bring in Bolton 'keeper Steve Banks on loan, but his new charges lost at home for the first time in 10 months when yet more contentious refereeing led to a 1-0 defeat by Southend, despite the visitor's 'keeper being sent off.

Hollins quickly added Burscough striker Lee McEvilly (for £15,000) and former Irish international Alan McLaughlin (on trial from Wigan) to his squad and also gave a first start to Paddy McCourt, but Dale slumped to a 4-1 defeat at Kidderminster. However, goals from the youngsters Townson and McCourt earned five points from the next three games and Matt Gilks won the Nationwide League save of the month with a spectacular effort in a goalless game at York when he also saved a penalty and Platt was sent off.

Indeed a 2-1 reverse at Mansfield (which later turned out to be particularly significant) was Dale's only loss in 10 games. The highlights of this run were an amazing McCourt inspired 5-4 victory over York – their first such scoreline for 45 years – and a vital 1-0 success against rivals Luton, Paddy McCourt's effort looping into the net off former team mate Dave Bayliss (who was later sent off), though 'keeper Banks was the real star.

A few days later Paddy's **meteoric rise continued** when he figured for N. Ireland under-21s against Germany, while 'Super Kev' Townson appeared for England under-19s, also against the Germans. Also on the international front, Rory Patterson was on standby for the Irish under-19s, while youth team 'keeper Jamie Coates was in the Welsh under-17 squad.

After a setback at Scunthorpe, Dale went another five games unbeaten, conceding only two goals, McEvilly and McCourt turning round the game at Halifax with a goal each in the last few minutes. Veteran winger Paul Simpson from Blackpool netted on his debut, just a couple of days after playing in the LDV Vans Trophy Final, but champions-to-be Plymouth came back to win 3-1. A surprising 3-0 defeat at Torquay spoilt a run of three wins in four games, but against Hull a piece of sublime skill from McCourt brought a second equaliser for Dale and he then set up Townson for the winner to guarantee a play-off place for the first time ever.

A draw at Lincoln in their penultimate game, coupled with results elsewhere left Dale two points behind Cheltenham in 3rd place and one behind Mansfield, but Cheltenham then extended their lead with a point from a game in hand. Before the final games, Dale gained their first ever full internationals when both Lee McEvilly and Paddy McCourt came on as substitutes for N. Ireland against a Spanish side containing the likes of Raul. Dale managed to overcome Bristol Rovers thanks to a rather fortunate penalty five minutes from time, scored at the second attempt by Alan McLaughlin, but in another twist it was Mansfield who edged out Cheltenham for third spot. The Stags finished a single point ahead of Dale, who obtained a new club record of 78 points in finishing 5th.

The play-off semi-final set Dale against Rushden & Diamonds and the away leg followed the two regular league games between the sides in ending in a draw, after Dale had twice led through tremendous strikes from McEvilly and Simpson. Unfortunately they were without the injured Clive Platt for the second leg and soon lost defender Richard Jobson during the game. Despite being gifted the lead when Diamonds' 'keeper Turley let a back pass roll under his foot, Dale never looked settled and were beaten by goals from Jamaican internationals Lowe and Hall.

The most regular performers during a season which had brought Dale closer to promotion than at any time in the last 33 years were Wayne Evans, Gareth Griffiths (the player of the year) and Richard Jobson at the back, Michael Oliver in midfield and Clive Platt up front, plus Matt Doughty who alternated between midfield and left back. In fact, these were the only ones to start more than half the games and the success had come despite lengthy absences of players who would have been expected to be key members of the side, particularly Neil Edwards, Lee Todd and Paul Connor. Kevin Townson top scored with 14 league and 3 cup goals and was voted young player of the season.

Sean McAuley had already left to coach in the USA and John Hollins, whose contract had strictly run out when the season ended, released a number of players including Lee Todd and Simon Coleman. However, a little over a week later the Board abruptly announced that they had withdrawn the offer of a new contract for Hollins as they couldn't come to a financial agreement.

Over the next couple of weeks, the usual selection of names were rumoured to be interested in the manager's job (chairman David Kilpatrick revealed that there had been 45 applications), but it was soon announced that Paul Simpson would become player-manager, assisted by Jamie Hoyland, previously the youth team coach. Existing assistant manager David Hamilton was sacked to make room for Hoyland and another ex-Blackpool man Colin Greenall came in as youth team manager. On the playing front, Chris Beech arrived from Huddersfield and Dale fans were excited by the signing of Scunthorpe winger Lee Hodges. Supporter Dave Edwards won an auction for a Dale squad number (30) for the coming season.

Dale had been invited to compete in the annual Isle of Man football tournament, and as the first (reasonably) competitive games thus occurred at the end of July in 2002, team building was still underway and the squad included several youth teamers and trialist centre half Eddie Loewen, a German beach football international (and later the author of FIFA's definitive manual on the sport!). On returning home, they suffered probably their earliest ever postponement (also in July), when a friendly at Halifax was cancelled because of torrential rain. More productive, at least financially, was a friendly against Manchester City which attracted a crowd of almost 9000 to see City win 6-0.

The real season kicked off with a 1-0 victory over Orient, substitute Paul Connor netting the goal two minutes into stoppage time, but they then went down 2-0 at Lincoln. A much better day saw Dale triumph at Bristol Rovers with the manager netting the winner, though an odd turn of events – the car carrying their kit got stuck in holiday traffic – saw them do so wearing Rovers spare (and rather odd, beige quartered) shirts.

A spectacular away performance brought a 5-2 victory at Wrexham, Paul Simpson netting a hat-trick including two penalties, and after Dale also gave a trial to his old Manchester City colleague Ian Bishop, the two veterans starred in a victory at Carlisle (coincidentally their home town club). This moved Dale into the top three and a remarkable come-back from 3-1 down to defeat Cambridge 4-3 thanks to stoppage time goals from Townson and Oliver saw them go second, a place they reclaimed when they beat Macclesfield at the end of September. Remarkably, considering his hugely promising first season, this was Townson's first, and indeed only, goal of a season in which he was allowed just 6 starts. On the other hand, Paul Simpson had netted seven times in ten league games, giving him 13 from his first 20 games for the club.

A name from their past, referee Rob Styles (who Dale had apparently requested should not referee any more of their games after the debacle at Orient in 1997) came back to haunt them when he sent off Clive Platt in a draw at Swansea, and Dale then lost four games in a row. Indeed, they went nine games without a league victory, but they did knock Division 2 Peterborough out of the FA Cup.

With injuries affecting the squad and other players apparently out of favour (including star signing Lee Hodges, who only ever played three games, and Michael Oliver, reportedly after a disagreement with the manager when dropped from the starting eleven), youngsters such as Lee Duffy, Simon Grand and Scott Warner were drafted in. They were joined by McCourt and McEvilly's Irish under-21 colleague Gavin Melaugh, on loan from Aston Villa and giving an even more international flavour were Australian defender Shane Cansdell-Sheriff, on loan from Leeds, and Spanish trialist 'Chus' Fernandez from Real Zaragoza.

By now playing a wing-back system, and with Platt in a withdrawn role behind two other strikers, Dale halted the slide down the league with a remarkable 4-0 win against leaders Hartlepool (aided, it must be admitted, by some dodgy goalkeeping) and three successive draws. They also beat Bristol Rovers in a cup replay, substitute Paddy McCourt – who had started only three games so far, despite becoming a regular for the Irish under-21's – netting a spectacular winner after Platt had scored in the third cup tie in a row.

In round 3, Dale met first division neighbours Preston and two sensational free-kicks, a thunderbolt from Lee McEvilly and one swerved in from an acute angle by Paul Simpson after he brought himself on as substitute, gave them their first ever away FA Cup victory against a side two divisions above them (Dale fans aiming a chant 'Are you Scotland in disguise' at their former Scotland boss Craig Brown).

Off the field (but not off the pitch!), a long running dispute between Hornets – said not to have paid any rent for the last 10 months because of their financial problems – and the stadium company came to a head when, after both Dale and Hornet had home games postponed on successive days because of the waterlogged ground, Hornets players reputedly trained on the Spotland pitch after their game was called off. Earlier Spotland had been officially valued at £4.3M and Hornets were reported to be considering selling some of their 45% share.

Back at the football club, some fans had already protested about the lack of playing success during the earlier run without a league victory, and a particularly dire performance in a home defeat by Lincoln led to the players, and more particularly the manager, being jeered off the field. Simpson also made well publicised comments about 'terrorists' in the background at Spotland.

Meanwhile, Division 1 Coventry had won their cup replay to set up a repeat of the famous 1971 game. With Doughty missing, Dale brought in youngster Stephen Hill for his debut at left back and again defied the odds to defeat their favourite higher league victims (they also beat them in 1920 and in one leg of a League cup tie in 1991). In front of a crowd of 9,156, Paul Connor scored in the first half, before skipper Gareth Griffiths netted with a towering header, reminiscent of Dave Cross' winner, thirty two years earlier. Dale subsequently drew Wolves at Molineux in the last 16 of the competition and the BBC decided to televise the game live, adding £265,000 to the monies already garnered during the run to date. (It was later reported that Dale made around £700,000 in total, though the profit on the season was only £253,000).

Dale also won their next two league games, that at Darlington despite a number of injuries and the absence of McCourt, McEvilly and Melaugh on international duty. Dale could have had the game postponed due to the international calls, but wanted Dave Flitcroft's suspension (for accumulating 10 yellow cards) out of the way before the big cup game. Dale did later have two games put back because of international calls on their players, certainly a first for the club.

In the event, Wolves won 3-1 fairly comfortably, though Dale gave them a fright when Melaugh deflected Simpson's long range strike into the net to level the score and there was more than a suspicion of offside about the goal which settled the tie after Matt Gilks, in for the injured Edwards, had made a number of excellent saves. The crowd was 23,921 while the television audience was reported as 3.8 million viewers. By contrast, attendances at several Dale home league games had slipped below the 2000 mark.

A surprise 1-0 win at Orient with a squad including 12 players aged 21 or younger, their first success at Brisbane Road after 34 years of trying, and a similar scoreline in a dour match against Boston helped earn 8 points from the next 6 games, but Dale then failed to win any of the next 10. From a neutral perspective, the best of these would have been the 3-3 draw at Rushden & Diamonds, when Simon Grand, just a month after his 19th birthday, skippered the side and netted one of the goals, Gilks also saving a penalty against the champions-to-be.

Another draw, at York, also proved eventful as Gilks had to be replaced in goal by Lee McEvilly after crashing into a goalpost, and 'Evil' subsequently claimed the honour of being the first Dale 'goalkeeper' to score a league goal when he netted the rebound after his penalty was saved (Connor having earlier also had a spot-kick saved).

Fortunately, even with two teams to be demoted to the Conference for the first time, Dale had managed to stay just above the relegation battle and despite losing at home to Swansea at the end of April, other results guaranteed their safety with two games left. Indeed, after beating Hull, a win in their final game at Macclesfield would have elevated them to 14th spot. The match saw Richard Jobson, a week short of his 40th birthday, play the 588th FL game of a 21 year career before retiring to take up a position with the PFA. However, in keeping with their miserable end to the campaign, even after McEvilly had scored twice (giving him 17 for the season, equal to Paul Connor) and Gilks (voted the players' player of the year) had pulled off another penalty save, they still conspired to concede twice in the last two minutes to lose 3-2. They finished 19th with 52 points, four more than relegated Exeter. The last 34 games had produced just 30 points.

Four days later, after discussions with the Board, Paul Simpson resigned as manager and Jamie Hoyland also left the club.

At the beginning of June, former Grimsby boss Alan Buckley was appointed as the new manager, though he was about to take a holiday in the USA. With no sign of a new contract – he was apparently offered a pre-season trial to earn one – Dave Flitcroft, the Dale's most influential player in the past season and the supporters' player of the year, agreed a move to Macclesfield, while Clive Platt had decided to move on at the end of his contract, eventually joining Notts County.

With Tony Ford re-installed as assistant manager, close season signings consisted of experienced central defender Daryl Burgess, a team mate of Ford's at West Brom when Buckley was manager at the Hawthorns, former Dale loanee Sean McClare from Port Vale, Cardiff fullback Michael Simpkins and New Zealander Leo Bertos.

Dale completed their 2003 pre-season programme with a 4-0 defeat by a very strong Manchester City side (Anelka and Wright-Phillips were among the scorers). The game again attracted a sizeable crowd in excess of 5000 and City generously allowed Dale to keep all the proceeds. They also loaned them the scorer of the final goal, Chris Shuker.

Although Kevin Townson had played in all the pre-season games, scoring five times, Shuker's arrival relegated him to the bench for the league opener against new boys Yeovil, which the latter won 3-1 at Spotland, with a little help from the referee who allowed them to roll a free-kick into the net while Gilks was still lining up his wall. A goal from Townson, reprising his super-sub role of two years earlier, looked to have earned Dale extra-time at Division 1 Stoke in the League Cup, but the home side sneaked a winner in stoppage time.

After coming back from two down to draw with Cambridge, despite a red card for Shuker, the first win came at Torquay thanks to a brace from former Coventry junior Robert Betts, though Simpkins was sent off this time. Dale also won the next two, to rise as high as 4th in the table. McEvilly netted penalties in three successive games, but Connor's dismissal for squaring up to a York defender was the third in four games.

The next match was at Carlisle, who had taken a solitary point from six games and just appointed Paul Simpson as caretaker manager. All too predictably, Dale lost. (Apart from a LDV Vans Trophy game – also against Dale - Carlisle did not win again until December). Dale didn't win any of the next four games, either, but Paul Connor did manage a goal after just 18 seconds in the draw with Huddersfield, and temporary signing Mickael Antoine-Curier netted after just four minutes of his debut. The Frenchman (who later became an international for Guadaloupe) had already played for Oldham and Kidderminster and was eventually with eight different clubs in 2003-04, appearing in the FL for a record six of them.

Away from the playing side, the main talking point was again the amount of money owed by Hornets to the stadium company, after revelations that a cheque sent to Hull KR for their share of the gate money had 'bounced'. Hornets' directors subsequently stated that at a meeting back in March, Messrs Kilpatrick and Morris had offered £110,000 for Rochdale Hornets Football Club, including their holdings in Denehurst Park (Rochdale) Ltd, but that the offer that had been rejected. Hornets' officials also claimed that they had given "huge financial subsidy" to Rochdale AFC back in the early 'nineties, which was not now being reciprocated.

Dale did beat Scunthorpe and Cheltenham (leading to the resignation of the Robins' manager Bobby Gould), with Bertos celebrating his call up to the New Zealand team with goals in each game. However, either side of a 2-1 victory at Bury in the FA Cup (with Townson grabbing the winner), they then lost six league games in succession. A particularly low point was a 4-0 defeat at managerless strugglers Southend, McEvilly missing a penalty and McClare being sent off to add to their discomfort. After the home defeat by Luton in the second round of the cup, director Jim Fagan stated that Michael Simpkins – never a favourite with the fans – had been disciplined for reacting angrily to comments from Dale supporters. Simpkins also collected 10 yellow cards in the first half of the season, more than anyone else in the division.

Fortunately, with former midfielder Gary Jones back on loan from Barnsley, they beat Bury for a second time (Townson again being on target, his 8th of the season despite only seven league starts) and also beat Boston. Two more defeats saw them slump to 20th in the table, though, and at this point the axe fell on Alan Buckley's short tenure.

The following day, New Year's Eve, former boss Steve Parkin returned to the fold, with a contract for the remainder of the season and a remit to keep Dale in the league. Though many Dale fans were happy to see their former successful manager back, others were still unwilling to forgive him for walking out on the club two years earlier. In fact, his new side carried on exactly where he had left off, by again defeating Torquay, but with Bertos away with New Zealand in the Olympic qualifying competition, the next four games brought only two points.

Bertos' return coincided with Dale's best result of the season, 3-0 against 4th placed Mansfield, with goals from Bertos himself, new skipper Jones (who re-signed permanently the following week) and Grant Holt, a reserve centre forward signed from Sheffield Wednesday for £25,000. The squad also contained two loanees from Bolton, centre back Danny Livesey and Kangana Lord N'diwa, whose previous senior games had been in the African Cup of Nations for the Democratic Republic of Congo and whose entire Dale career was fitted into the four minutes of stoppage time!

Though Dale lost only twice, the next half dozen games were less productive, Jones being sent off in a defeat at Northampton - though the referee rescinded one of the yellow cards, saving him from suspension – and Livesey seeing red at Boston. Indeed, Dale had racked up 69 yellow and six red cards by this point, and suffered from 15 separate suspensions during the course of the season.

It was supporters who were missing at Swansea, though, when the old joke about the crowd being announced to the players finally came true; the Rochdale Observer and the club website listed the names of the 45 Dale fans present at the game! (At the other end of the scale, matches at Huddersfield and Hull attracted gates just short of 11,000 and just over 16,000, respectively). A few days later, Paul Connor, who would have been out of contract at the end of the season, joined the Swans for £35,000.

Steve Parkin drafted in two veteran defenders, Shaun Smith of Hull and Orient's Greg Heald to add their experience to Dale's relegation battle and they were then joined by the oldest outfield player in the FL, Boston's Neil Redfern who was given the squad number 38 to match his age! Adding further competitiveness to the side, Desmond the Dragon was voted one of the 'hardest' mascots in the league!

Dale put significant distance between themselves and bottom club Carlisle when they gained revenge for the early season embarrassment, Jones and Holt again being on target after the Cumbrians had their 'keeper sent off. However, after a good point against leaders Doncaster, Dale lost comprehensively to Lincoln to slump back to 21st, with only six points covering 13th to 23rd in the table.

By the time Dale lost to a controversial penalty against Macclesfield, with only four games left, they stood just a point better off than York, and only two ahead of a reviving Carlisle. Fortunately they then met an out of form Orient side and two goals from Holt and one from McCourt earned a convincing victory which they followed up by winning 1-0 at Kidderminster. The final point to guarantee survival came when Gary Jones netted the rebound when his penalty was saved by the Southend 'keeper. This game was the last one covered by veteran journalist Jack Hamil after a remarkable 67 years reporting on Rochdale games. A 2-0 defeat at Oxford in the final game became immaterial and Dale finished a difficult season in 21st place, with just 50 points.

Wayne Evans had again missed only one match and was voted player of the year for a second time, but Leo Bertos, the only one of Buckley's signing to make a positive impact, was the only other player, of the 37 selected, to make 40 appearances (and shared the players' player of the year award with Evans). Over the summer he became the first Dale player to appear in a World Cup tie when he was selected for the 'All Whites' against rivals Australia. Top scorer was Kevin Townson with 12 (10 in the league), but only three of these were in the second half of a season in which Townson had again not convinced his managers that he should have a regular starting spot.

McCourt and McEvilly had also been challenged by Steve Parkin to improve their fitness levels to reclaim a place in the side, and 'Evil' was one of ten players released, as was the injury plagued Chris Beech and the relatively long serving Matt Doughty. Steve Parkin himself soon signed a new contract and set about recruiting for the new season which, after another name change, would see Dale in League 2.

Principal signings for 2004-05 were Neil Brisco from Port Vale, Mansfield's Jamie Clarke and Bristol Rovers' top scorer Paul Tait, and these were soon joined by Alan Goodall from Bangor and former Grimsby full-back Tony Gallimore. However, the decision which would have by far the greatest long term impact was to appoint former player Keith Hill as director of youth football.

After Parkin's customary training camp in Scotland, where they put seven past Stenhousemuir, Dale lost the revived Rose Bowl game to Oldham and also the first two league games.

Gary Jones' first game of the season provided the first success, courtesy of two goals from the skipper himself against Southend, and Dale followed this up with a 3-0 win at Wycombe.

Dale had again drawn Wolves in a cup competition and their Carling Cup tie was a live game on Sky. A fine performance saw Holt and Tait score early on, but Wolves came back to win 4-2.

Only two of the next eleven league games resulted in victories – one of them against league leaders Yeovil - and this unproductive spell saw Dale down in 21st place with 15 points from 15 games. The last game of this run had seen a 5-1 drubbing in a catastrophic match at Northampton. Burgess scored an own goal and was then sent off conceding a penalty with, as the FA later ruled, a perfectly good tackle, before Edwards also put the ball in his own net. On a lighter note, on-loan debutant Tai Atieno had to borrow an XXL shirt from a fan, as the Dale didn't have a spare shirt in his size with them!

Six changes for the next game sparked a remarkable revival, with the 3-0 defeat of Macclesfield launching a sequence of seven straight victories in the FL and FA Cup. Grant Holt, in particular, was in tremendous form, netting nine times in eight games, including two goals in each of the cup ties. On the receiving end were Oxford, who were beaten by last minute goals on successive Saturdays in league and cup, their manager Graham Rix being the latest in a long line of bosses to lose their jobs after a defeat by 'lowly Rochdale'. With the BBC owning the rights to all FA Cup games, the club were unable to put the highlights on their DaleWorld web site, so press officer Stuart Ashworth recreated them with a 'cast' of supporters, groundsman Phil Collinson getting to play Grant Holt!

The run ended, typically for Dale, with defeat at bottom club Kidderminster, though this had more to do with an awful performance by the referee, rather than by the players. The club were later warned by the FA for failing to control its players. The next five games, going into the New Year, saw one win, three draws and one washout, against Grimsby, when torrential rain turned Spotland into a lake. The point at Notts County was particularly hard earned when referee Boyeson reduced Dale to nine men by red carding Griffiths and recent signing Ernie Cooksey.

Meanwhile yet another row broke out about the state of the pitch. The Dale board accused Hornets of ruining it by playing a friendly against the wishes of the groundsman, while Hornets counter-claimed that the damage was done during the abandoned Grimsby match. Whichever was the case, Dale decided to suspend payments to the stadium company until a new framework for the use of Spotland was put in place.

Dale put up a spirited performance against Premier League Charlton in the third round of the cup, with Holt's goal just after the break making it 2-1, before the Addicks eventually ran out 4-1 winners. It also made Holt the leading scorer in the Cup up to this point, and the club subsequently turned down an optimistic bid of just £75,000 for him from Swansea.

Three further draws – making six in the last seven league games – followed by two wins and two defeats kept Dale just below the play-off places. The 2-2 draw at leaders Yeovil was an excellent result, the goalless affair at Chester less so, as the home side were reduced to nine men, ex-Dale man Paul Carden being one of those dismissed. Yet another controversial decision, in the defeat at Cheltenham, also saw Wayne Evans sent off and suspended for the first time in a career of over 500 games.

New signing from Stockport Rickie Lambert scored in three consecutive home games, while Matt Gilks kept four clean sheets in five as Dale held onto 10th place in the league going into the last eight games. An eventful game at Swansea saw Holt score at both ends and Trundle and Tait get sent before Lambert netted a last gasp equaliser. Trundle's red card was later rescinded by the Welsh FA, but the English FA upheld Tait's, even though Swans fans and officials agreed that it merely looked like the referee evening things up after a hasty decision moments earlier.

A defeat at second placed Southend set Dale back and though unbeaten in the remaining games, too many draws again prevented them breaking into the play-off places. The game at Cambridge in late April was drawn 0-0, with Dale keeping their 21st clean sheet of the season, but the result did neither side any good, as it left Dale seven points short of the play-offs with only two games to go and relegated Cambridge.

The last home game saw Dale cruise to their biggest win of the season, 5-1 against Oxford and a point in the last game saw then finish in 9th with 66 points, a huge improvement on the previous two campaigns. The last 31 games had produced 51 points, Dale losing only four times during that run.

Grant Holt - despite numerous yellow cards and suspensions - was easily top scorer with 17 in the league and 7 in cup ties, the best tally for some years. Most of these goals came in a mid-season run during which he netted 21 in 30 appearances. Holt was the players' player of the year, but it was Gareth Griffiths who won the supporters player of the year trophy. Earlier in the campaign, the big central defender had scored a remarkable hat-trick in the LDV Vans Trophy game against Scarborough, rushing upfield to grab the ball when Dale were handed a late penalty.

The most notable name amongst the end of season departures was Wayne Evans, after 299 games in six years, 259 of them in the league. Paddy McCourt had left during the season, returning to Ireland to play for Shamrock Rovers, and Dale's other most promising young star of the previous few years, Kevin Townson, now followed him out of Spotland. McCourt subsequently came good with Derry City and earned a sensational transfer to his boyhood heroes Celtic in 2008, by which time Townson was in minor non-league football. Leo Bertos was also released, and he too flourished in a different scene, starring in the Australian A-League and figuring regularly for New Zealand, most notably when they drew with Italy in the 2010 World Cup finals.

A new crop of hopefuls had a big moment at the end of the season when the youth team (doubling as the reserves) defeated Bury in the Lancashire Cup Final, collecting probably the oldest trophy in world football, first played for in 1880, thanks to Clive Moyo-Modise's spectacular goal. The young squad which claimed the trophy won by the first team in 1949 and 1971 was: Danny Woodhall, James McDonagh, Michael Murray, Ben Kitchen, Krystian Liptrot, Kristian Bowden, Tony Barry, Nicky Allen, Andy Mangan, Clive Moyo-Modise and Joe Thompson, with substitutes Matt Williams, Dennis Greenwood, Matty Kay and Kyle Buckley. Moyo-Modise, while never becoming a league regular, later played for the South Africa under-21s side, the 'Amaglugglug'. Mangan, a trialist from Blackpool, later a FL regular, also appeared on the international stage, playing for the England non-league side while with Wrexham.

In preparation for the new campaign, Dale signed Jon Boardman, rated one of the best centre backs in the Conference, from Woking, Northampton's Tommy Jaszczun and former Preston stalwart Lee Cartwright. With Matt Gilks now established as the number 1, Neil Edwards decided to sign for Bury, but Gareth Griffiths agreed to postpone his retirement and sign up for another season. Finally, Plymouth's Blair Sturrock (son of Argyle boss Paul) and Sheffield Wednesday loanee Rory McArdle joined Dale for their training camp at Gloucester University, during which Rickie Lambert netted a hat-trick against neighbouring Gloucester City.

Dale kicked off 2005-06 with a 1-0 win at Shrewsbury but then lost their unbeaten home record, which had lasted since the previous December, against Wycombe. However, the topsy-turvy results continued when Dale ended Orient's 100% home record by beating them 4-1, with Holt and Lambert continuing to be amongst the goals. Interest in the League Cup was abruptly ended, though, as Bradford City won 5-0 at Spotland, Gary Jones getting himself sent-off for a wild challenge.

With the club giving up on the training facilities at Bowlee promised by the Council the previous year, they decided to use the facilities at Salford University. This at least kept the squad out of the way when there was a bomb scare at Spotland because of a suspicious package – local humorists suggested that it was actually a trophy, but no-one at the club had ever seen one before!

Three straight home wins moved Dale up to second place, and three more wins on the bounce took them back to that position in mid-October when they had 26 points from 13 games, Grant Holt scoring in six successive games (seven in the league), the best run since Jimmy Wynn back in the 1930s. He also scored in a rather odd LDV Vans Trophy game where Dale overcame Stockport thanks to two own goals and a penalty.

Crowds had remained fairly low, though, and one week local North West Counties League Division 2 side Castleton Gabriels attracted almost as large a gate as the Dale, when they met the newly formed 'protest club' FC United of Manchester. Steve Parkin also criticised a minority of the fans who did turn up, for continually having a go at his players even when they were in the top four.

Three defeats, including in the first round of the FA Cup, halted their good run, but they bounced back with victory at Bristol Rovers - the Memorial Ground becoming one of Dale's favourite trips - and another remarkable game against Shrewsbury when Dale came back from 3-1 down at half-time to win 4-3 despite young fullback Gary Brown being sent off. Holt and Lambert scored two each in that game (past a young Joe Hart), giving them a joint total of 26 for the season by the end of November.

Half time of the game at Grimsby saw Dale leading 1-0 but premature chants of "top of the league" brought the wrath of the 'football gods' and Dale inexplicably conceded four times. Things went from bad to worse in a 3-0 defeat at Wycombe when both Holt and new South African full back Warren Goodhind were sent off (the latter for pulling his winger back by his pony-tail!) but it was more bad luck and refereeing decisions that led to three further defeats to end the year.

Despite earlier statements that Dale intended to keep their major assets, the January transfer window saw Grant Holt – 35 goals in 75 FL games - sold to Nottingham Forest for £300,000. (Subsequent moves and promotions would eventually see him reach the Premier League with Norwich before a return to Spotland ten years on). Coming in was young Tranmere striker Chris Dagnall for £25,000, and experienced Blackpool midfielder John Doolan, who had been a Dale target on several occasions in the past.

After just one point from eight games, Dale won at Torquay and Macclesfield and picked up a string of draws, despite injuries to three right backs in the space of four games, leading to the signing of Grimsby's Simon Ramsden. Dale had been badly affected by injuries generally – Alan Goodall played with a mask covering a fractured cheek bone at one point - and borrowed former regular Dave Bayliss from Wrexham, though he was bizarrely sent off in a defeat by his own club. Rory McArdle missed the draw with Bury in more propitious circumstances, when he was selected for Northern Ireland under-21s.

As Dale slid down the table, most of the scoring burden had passed to Rickie Lambert, and after Ramsden had scored a first league goal against his former club, Lambert managed to net a last gasp equaliser direct from a corner. Lambert also rescued Dale from two-down to promotion favourites Northampton, but Dale still found themselves in 17th, just two points ahead of Rushden in 23rd. When the two sides met in the middle of April, Rushden looked likely to take the points before Chris Dagnall curled in a superb injury time equaliser, vital not just for the point it earned Dale but for the deflating effect it had on the opposition, who lost all their remaining games before dropping out of the league.

Dale on the other hand, then won their first home game since November and, indeed, lost only one of their final eight games, and that against champions Carlisle. A last weekend draw at Lincoln sent everyone home happy, as the Imps made the play-offs while Rickie Lambert's 22nd strike of the season made him the division's joint leading scorer with Carlisle's Karl Hawley. Lambert played in every game, as did Matt Gilks, and unsurprisingly won both player of the year awards.

Dale finished a variable season back up in 14th place with 56 points, seven above the drop zone and ten short of the play-offs for which had they looked on target in the early part of the season. Some players had already moved on and several more were released at the end of the season, though this still left 14 senior players. Most prominent of the players leaving was Gareth Griffiths who retired after just over 200 games in which he netted 18 goals, a pretty good return for a centre half.

LEGENDS AND HEROES

Despite an input from the commercial side of over half a million pounds, finance was in short supply and recruitment was difficult for Steve Parkin over the summer of 2006. Indeed, new chairman Chris Dunphy – David Kilpatrick had finally managed to retire after several previous attempts! - announced that the priority was to pay off the £200,000 owed to the Inland Revenue and that the manager would have to continue operating on a reduced budget which he admitted had been unworkable. Thus the only new faces added to the squad were Darlington winger Adam Rundle, long serving Scunthorpe defender Nathan Stanton and former Manchester City man Lee Crooks, the latter two only signing on the eve of the new season.

Life was made even more difficult before the start of the season by a succession of injuries, and after losing the Rose Bowl on penalties after a goalless draw, Dale also lost the first four league games, all by the identical score of 0-1, their only contribution to the goalscoring coming at Swindon when Goodall put a far post header past Gilks. This must have been particularly galling for the 'keeper as he saved two penalties in that game.

They did manage to draw the next three league games, but on transfer deadline day, Rickie Lambert was sold to Bristol Rovers for £200,000 (to keep the tax man happy, at least). Several players were drafted in on loan or short contracts, the most noticeable the 6'7" Frenchman Morike Sako (who soon became firm friends with diminutive kitman Jack Northover).

It was Sako who netted to give Dale their first win, against Grimsby, and he might have repeated this against Wycombe had he not been stopped by a high challenge outside the area by their 'keeper, who remarkably stayed on the pitch - the offence being so blatant that the substitute goalkeeper started to prepare to come on!

Dale regained their momentum with victories at Boston and Wrexham (Dagnall scoring twice in each) and then annihilated Darlington 5-0 (Sako netting twice), their first away win by five clear goals since a match at Crewe exactly 40 years earlier.

However, the boot was firmly on the other foot just a fortnight later when Lincoln hit Dale for seven at Sincil Bank. In the aftermath, despite the arrival of Carlisle striker Glenn Murray – who had had the misfortune to make his debut at Lincoln - Dale lost four of the next five games, including a Johnson's Paint Trophy game when they contrived to miss all four of their penalties in the shoot-out.

With Rory McArdle coming in on loan for a second time, they did manage to draw twice with Hartlepool in the FA Cup but again went out on penalties in a match screened by Sky. A sole success against Mansfield was followed by three more 1-0 reversals (including Gary Jones 300th game for the club), and that at Hartlepool was in turn followed by the departures of Steve Parkin and Tony Ford. Coincidentally, this was almost exactly 12 years after Dave Sutton was sacked as a result of an identical scoreline at the Victoria Ground.

Youth team boss Keith Hill was placed in caretaker charge and had a tough start with a visit to third placed Milton Keynes two days before Christmas. Unfortunately ill luck remained despite the change at the top, as Stanton's interception of a through ball two minutes from time looped it over Gilks for the Dons winner. Things looked pretty bleak just after half time in the next game, too, as Wrexham led 2-0, but Hill then decided to go for broke with a 4-4-2 system with two wingers, the on-loan Frenchman William Mocquet and youth team product Joe Thompson, and his side responded with two goals of their own.

It was rumoured that a decision on the new manager would be made over the New Year, but Keith Hill effectively took the decision out of the chairman's hands by sending out his side to grab remarkable back-to-back 4-0 victories, at home to Boston and away at Grimsby. In the latter, fullback Ramsden showed that it is not just strikers who go back to haunt their previous clubs, when he netted two of the goals. Two days later Keith Hill was confirmed as manager. Gareth Griffiths had been assisting him in a temporary capacity (though still strictly on Northwich Victoria's playing staff) but Hill now appointed his former team mate Dave Flitcroft as assistant manager, with Griffiths returning to his various interests outside the game. (As he had always relished reminding his colleagues, he had a first class degree in Business Studies).

There was also considerable activity on the playing front, with several players released and former loanees returning to their own clubs, but Murray and McArdle signed permanent deals. Postponements and a 1-0 defeat by Bristol Rovers, Lambert inevitably netting - but not celebrating – left Dale in 23rd position, albeit with games in hand and they also lost Chris Dagnall who broke a metatarsal in training. With three new signings in the squad – Adam Le Fondre on loan from Stockport, Rory Prendergast from Blackpool and David Perkins who had played with Hill at Morecambe - they bounced back to trounce 3rd placed MK Dons 5-0, Le Fondre netting twice and Prendergast also grabbing a debut goal.

Dale also looked like inflicting a rare defeat on leaders Walsall, until defender Dann ran the length of the field to score an amazing stoppage time equaliser. Dale did win their next two games, another on loan debutant Ben Muirhead scoring at Notts County, to move seven points clear of the drop zone. With Perkins replacing Jones, out for the rest of the season with a fractured bone in his knee, Dale kept their unbeaten run going and put four past Accrington before a truly remarkable

game at Stockport. Dale cruised into a four goal lead in just 17 minutes and though County then pulled two back, they piled in three more after half time to run up a 7-2 victory,
To top off Dale's grand day out, the final strike was notched by the returning Dagnall who had only been back in training for four days; for the record, the others had gone to Murray (2), Goodall, Rundle (pen) and Muirhead (2).

The run ended at nine games, but two goals in the last two minutes saw off further promotion contenders Lincoln and a draw with Swindon saw Dale pass the 52 point mark to ensure safety with six games to go. Their unlikely pursuit of a play-off place was effectively ended by a 2-0 home defeat by Barnet, when they had no less than three goals disallowed in the final 15 minutes. However, they won on their next three outings, smashing five past Macclesfield, with a Chris Dagnall hat-trick and two for Glenn Murray (the League 2 player of the month for March). Having taken up the mantle from Holt and Lambert, Dagnall and Murray ended the season with 18 and 16 goals respectively. (Murray had also netted three for Stockport).

Dale closed the season with a 3-3 draw at Peterborough, though John Doolan's season had ended the previous week as he was sent off and suspended for exacting retribution following a high challenge on Glenn Murray, Hartlepool ending with only 9 men and losing top spot in the division.

Their amazing second half of the season saw Dale reach 9th place with 66 points, five points behind Shrewsbury in the last play-off place, and a remarkable 30 points clear of relegated Boston (though this would have 'only' been 20 without a points deduction). They had picked up 46 points from the last 23 games, of which they had lost just three. In a season of many changes – only six of a record 42 players started more than 30 games - Alan Goodall and Matt Gilks were ever-present, the latter being voted the players' player of the year for a second time. Nathan Stanton won the supporters player of the year award.

A week after the campaign ended, Rochdale AFC marked its Centenary with a Gala Dinner to which a large number of Dale legends were invited, from Stan Milburn and Stan Hepton of the League Cup final team and promotion heroes like Reg Jenkins and Steve Melledew, through Dave Cross to more modern favourites such as Lyndon Simmonds, Alan Reeves, Steve Whitehall and current manager Keith Hill. A couple of weeks later, Reg was back in action, making the presentations to the winners of the Rochdale Football Club Centenary Stakes during a race meeting at Pontefract.

Unsurprisingly, the players involved during the second half of the season were all retained or offered new deals, but Gilks – who had played in all of Dale's last 136 games - and Goodall were out of contract and decided to move on, joining Norwich and Luton, respectively. However, after several bids had been turned down, persistence paid off and Stockport agreed to sell Adam Le Fondre to Rochdale for £25,000 and Keith Hill also managed to sign the other most successful loanee from the previous term, Bradford City's Ben Muirhouse.

A busy summer also saw the arrival of Stockport goalkeeper James Spencer – with Darlington's Sam Russell as his backup - full back Tom Kennedy, who had turned down an offer to stay at Bury, and Oldham junior Kallum Higginbotham (later joined by Latics team mate Marcus Holness). Several youngsters – including Joe Thompson, who had won the Football League's apprentice of the year award for League 2 – also signed professional contracts. In addition, former players Chris Beech and Tony Ellis were appointed the head of youth development and the head of the school of excellence, respectively.

A new departure (literally!) saw the squad fly off to Cadiz for a training camp and play their second 'international' (having previously played the Isle of Man!) when they beat the Gibraltar national XI 3-1. Back home, a 1-0 friendly victory at Rossendale saw the first appearance of the Dale's centenary season kit, a reversion to the black and white stripes of 1907-08 (this actually being the club's 101st season, despite it Centenary tag). To match the new colours, Dale also gained a new mascot, 'Spotty the Dalemation' joining Desmond the Dragon. The following week saw the release of centenary anthem "Rochdale Heroes" by local band the Permanent Smilers, and Dale got their season off on the right foot by claiming the Centenary Rose Bowl against Oldham in a rerun of their first ever match.

The first league game ended 3-0 to Peterborough, but Dale knocked Championship side Stoke out of the Carling Cup in a penalty shoot-out, before going out in the same fashion themselves to Norwich. (Norwich's scorer in normal time was Dion Dublin, who had made his full debut against Rochdale back in 1988).

The first league victory came at the fourth attempt, in dramatic circumstances when Le Fondre equalised against MK Dons in the last minute and there was still time for Dagnall to net a winner. The match at Wrexham was then postponed because both sides had players away on international duty, Rory McArdle having become a regular for N. Ireland under-21s since signing for Dale. Youth team 'keeper Danny Hanford also received an international call-up, joining the Wales squad for the UEFA under-17 championships. (Though never making the Dale first team, after a spell at the Glenn Hoddle Academy in Spain he played in the league for Carlisle). Spotland, too, joined the international theme, hosting a European under-19 championship game between Belgium and Iceland.

Despite having lost Chris Dagnall to a long term cruciate ligament injury, Dale's next league victory was, if anything more remarkable than the first. With Dale again 2-1 down with time running out, Murray and Jones turned the match around and Shrewsbury then levelled matters two minutes from time, only for Le Fondre to win it at the death. Although another late goal, from Rory Prendergast, rescued a point at Darlington, a bad week for Dale fans saw local rivals Bury win twice at Spotland, in the league (leaving Dale with ten points from nine games) and the Johnstone's Paint Trophy, to continue an unbeaten run that dated back to 1993.

Two wins and two draws were followed by an undeserved defeat by Stockport, Dale having two goals mysteriously disallowed and even County boss Jim Gannon admitting his side had been outplayed. With injuries and the ineligibility of several loan players, Keith Hill had to make seven changes for the FA Cup tie at League 1 Southend, and his scratch side conceded after just 24 seconds .However, a spirited performance saw them lose only 2-1, with Russell saving one of two penalties awarded to the Shrimpers.

Back in the league, Dale now really got into the groove with four victories and two draws up to the end of the year, the pick of them probably the 4-2 win at Rotherham. Indeed, Murray's injury time equaliser at Macclesfield preserved a long unbeaten run away from home and meant that Dale had been beaten on the road only twice in league games in the whole of 2007.

The New Year started equally fruitfully, Murray, who had suffered something of a loss of form earlier in the season, netting for the fifth game in succession to overcome Darlington and move Dale up to 9th, four points short of the play-off places. Although finding life more difficult at home, Dale also won the next four away games, all of them notable for various reasons. A last minute penalty from Tom Kennedy won it at Wycombe and a hat-trick from midfielder David Perkins (who had netted just once in his senior career to that point) clinched a 4-3 victory at Chesterfield. The 1-0 victory at Milton Keynes came with 10 men after an early red card for Stanton for disputing a penalty, which Sam Russell then saved, while Chester were demolished 4-0 as Dale moved into the top seven for the first time. The unbeaten away run ended after 14 games (easily a club record, beating the nine games in 1923-24), Lincoln ruining Gary Jones' 300th FL match for the club.

Meanwhile, at a Fans' Forum, Keith Hill – the League 2 manager of the Month - and Dave Flitcroft outlined their seven year plan to get the club into the Championship. However, in the short term they had to cope with Glenn Murray moving to Brighton for £300,000. Brentford's Lee Thorpe, on a permanent contract, and Rene Howe, on loan from Peterborough, arrived as possible replacements.

Despite five successive home defeats and a number of postponements, the amazing away form resumed with Le Fondre's stoppage time winner at Bradford City in front of a crowd of over 14,000, five times what was usual at Spotland, while Gary Jones scored two of Dale's four at Mansfield on the day that he broke the club's overall appearance record.

Stockport again halted the progress, winning 2-0 at Edgeley Park, but Dale immediately bounced back with a Le Fondre hat-trick against Accrington, while a more remarkable treble saw off Rotherham; Chris Dagnall, back in training for only a few days after a five month lay-off, was thrown on for the last ten minutes and turned a 1-1 scoreline into a 4-1 victory.

With both their 'keepers out for the season, Dale brought in Tommy Lee on loan from Macclesfield and following defeat on his debut, he played his part in a ten match unbeaten sequence until the end of the season. Victory against Bradford City on April 1st had carried Dale into the top seven again and victories were also gained in the next two games, Howe grabbing a hat-trick against Grimsby and Dale beating Notts County 4-2 with something of a reserve line-up when their Yorkshire based players were stuck in traffic on the M62. Finally, Rene Howe's goal against Morecambe made it seven wins out of eight and guaranteed a play-off place with two games to spare. Indeed, Dale were only one point behind Hereford in 3rd place, but the latter had a game in hand which they duly won. Two draws saw Dale finish 5th with a new season's best tally of 80 points, 45 of them from the last 24 games. (Their success even saw the invention, by local celebrity chef Andrew Nutter, of a black and white striped 'Up the Dale' pie!).

The first leg of the play-off semi final saw Dale travel to Darlington without the suspended Nathan Stanton, while a bizarre accident on the way saw the already injured Thorpe break his arm when arm wrestling with Howe on the coach! A Jason Kennedy strike for the home side was cancelled out by Chris Dagnall, but a free-kick in stoppage time gave the Quakers the edge in the tie.

Back at Spotland, in front of a crowd of 9870, Keltie extended Darlington's lead following the softest of penalty awards, but Dagnall again pulled a goal back just before half time. With time running out, Dale levelled the tie with a magnificent strike from David Perkins, but in extra time, Perkins was red carded for a challenge on Ravenhill, mainly due to the intervention of Darlington skipper Foster, himself sent off in the league game at Spotland earlier in the season.

With the match going to penalties, Dagnall, Tom Kennedy, Le Fondre and Jones all converted safely, as did their Darlington counterparts, before Tommy Lee pulled off the vital save, deflecting Jason Kennedy's shot away with his legs. The final responsibility lay with Ben Muirhead and he fired his penalty home to take Rochdale, in their Centenary season, to Wembley for the first time ever.

After the game the club lodged an appeal against Perkins' red card, but referee Richard Beeby refused to change his decision and the panel upheld it despite clear video evidence that Perkins had not connected with Ravenhill. Chairman Chris Dunphy said "I am personally outraged because anyone who saw that on television could see that there was no contact. We felt confident that the decision could be overturned and we are all stunned." Keith Hill added "Video evidence showed the referee's made a mistake in his assessment and his evaluation contradicted what actually happened. I don't know who the panel of judges were but I wouldn't want them representing me in a trial". Perkins was handed a five match ban.

For the final against Stockport County, Keith Hill decided to move Simon Ramsden into midfield to replace Perkins, with Nathan D'Laryea coming in at right back after just three FL stars. Local youngster Will Buckley, who had only ever started one senior game was amongst the substitutes. For the record, the squad which represented Rochdale on their 'grand day out' was: Lee; D'Laryea, McArdle, Stanton, Kennedy; Higginbotham, Ramsden, Jones, Rundle; Dagnall, Le Fondre; substitutes Muirhead, Howe, Buckley, Doolan and Holness.

The club had sold 17,000 tickets for the big day, and a crowd of 35,715 assembled at a wet Wembley Stadium. County had the better of the opening exchanges, but on 25 minutes a towering header from Rory McArdle from a corner gave Dale the lead. Sadly, just six minutes later, a cross deflected off Stanton past his own 'keeper and County went ahead just after half time. A third from the dangerous Liam Dickinson, who had also scored in Stockport's two league victories over Dale, looked to have wrapped it up, but a sensational volley from Adam Rundle gave Dale hope with 13 minutes to go, though despite frantic efforts an equaliser didn't arrive. Nevertheless, the team fully deserved their civic reception at Rochdale Town Hall two days later.

Dale had managed to come so close to the long awaited promotion despite using a substantial number of players, only Kennedy, McArdle, Jones and Perkins starting 40 FL games, though Adam Le Fondre played some part in all 53 senior games. 'Alfie' was also easily the leading scorer with 16 in the league and 18 overall. Gary Jones, voted player of the year, became the first Dale midfielder to top 50 career goals. Rested for the final regular league game of the season, Jones remained level with Graham Smith on 317 FL appearances for Rochdale.

Immediately after the end of the season John Doolan left to become assistant manager at Southport, while penalty hero Ben Muirhead was freed. Then, over the summer, Dale also lost David Perkins who reportedly activated a clause in his contract allowing him to move on in the event of a bid of at least £150,000 and joined Colchester. In a perhaps even more remarkable £50,000 deal, 15 year-old Matty Hughes exchanged a place in Dale's youth team for one with Glasgow giants Celtic.

A number of new players joined Dale's summer training camp in Marbella including Clark Keltie and Scott Wiseman who had played in the Darlington side beaten by Dale in the play-offs, former N. Ireland international Ciaran Toner from Grimsby and Halifax's England 'C' international Jon Shaw, for a reputed fee of £60,000.

At a pre-season Fans' Forum, chief executive Colin Garlick reported that overall turnover in the past season had been £2.6M and that injuries had cost £165,000 in wages for injured players and extra loan signings. Director Andrew Kelly stated that £95,000 would be used to revise the contracts of current players so that situations like Gilks and Goodall leaving on frees the previous summer would not be repeated.

Dale's first two games of the 2008-09 season remained goalless, the Carling Cup tie against Oldham being a particularly poignant occasion, coming as it did just after the death of former player Ernie Cooksey at the age of only 28. Both sides wore training tops bearing the words "4 Ernie". Tragically, the club also lost one of their backroom team, sports scientist Paul Conway, shortly afterwards.

Dale got off the mark by beating Barnet 3-1, but after six league games, they still had only that one success. They should have won at Rotherham, but after taking a two goal lead, Dale had substitute Thorpe sent off only moments after coming on; McArdle then headed over his own 'keeper and the Millers eventually equalised in the 95th minute. The next two games were won, though, Ipswich loanee Jordan Rhodes – a Scottish international only three years later, while with Huddersfield – and Will Buckley netting five goals between them in the three games. The Chesterfield victory was notable for one of their players being sent off for delaying the free kick from which Kennedy scored a stoppage time winner.

In October, the club was awarded the Freedom of the Borough, Graham Morris receiving an inscribed scroll on their behalf. Mr Morris and colleague Rod Brierley stood down at the AGM after almost 60 years of combined service on the Board of Directors.

Progress remained muted, however, until Dale hit Chester for six, Dagnall netting three, and went on to win their next three league games, as well, with young Buckley continuing to shine and Thorpe netting a brace at Notts County. Indeed, Dale went ten games unbeaten in the league – five wins and five draws - to move into the play-off places and even, briefly, the top three. Nevertheless, the match against Bournemouth in December attracted only 2285 fans. (A defeat at Bradford City had attracted over 13,000 to Valley Parade). Keith Hill was also disturbed by the negativity of some fans, considering the league position.

In the FA Cup, Dale came back from two down to beat Barnet thanks to a Le Fondre hat-trick (the first FA Cup treble since Reg in 1965), but then went out to Conference side Forest Green Rovers. 'Alf' continued this goal scoring form, netting seven in the next ten league games.

The unbeaten league run ended with a 4-1 defeat at Exeter when Wiseman was sent off, but the Boxing Day fixture with Shrewsbury saw the return of two old faces end in Dale's favour. Grant Holt unsurprisingly netted against his old club, but Lee McEvilly, back for a third time, trumped that with two goals after coming on as substitute, celebrating by diving into a large pile of snow behind the goal.

Over the previous few months, Hornets financial problems had periodically come to the fore, and following the issuc of a winding-up order by the Inland Revenue, for an unpaid tax bill, it was reported that the clubs had discussed a possible merger at a meeting of the stadium committee. In the event, Hornets, formed back in 1871, went into administration, wiping out their debts and allowing a new club to be organised to carry on playing at Spotland the following season. Subsequently, two consortia, one of supporters and one involving Dale directors, bid to acquire Hornets' assets and the supporters' co-operative were successful. The question of the old club's shares in the ground (assets taken over by the Rugby Football League) remained murky.

The New Year saw the arrival on loan of Blackburn's England under-21 international goalkeeper Frank Fielding and former transfer target Nicky Adams, from Leicester, the latter scoring on his debut. Following some mixed fortunes, another good run saw four consecutive victories edge Dale back up to 4th with 51 points from 29 games, Joe Thompson becoming Dale's third youngest hat-trick scorer with a quick-fire treble in just 17 minutes against Aldershot. (Coincidentally, the following week, youth team captain George Bowyer was nominated for the Apprentice of the Year award which Joe had won a couple of years earlier).

Former loanee Rhodes scored against Dale when they lost at Brentford (later being voted League 2 player of the year), but Dale responded by winning the next two, despite an injury to skipper Jones, moving up to 2nd place in the table. Despite some mixed performances, results for the other contenders meant that Dale regained second place with victory at long time leaders Wycombe towards the end of March, though only three points separated them from 6th place Exeter with eight games left.

A couple of heavy defeats followed, 3-0 at Chesterfield – the first time Dale had failed to score for 29 league games - and 4-0 at Bournemouth, who were themselves battling the drop. These sandwiched a draw against Exeter when Stanton conceded a late penalty just moments after Le Fondre had netted from one at the other end (his seventh goal in nine games). This left Dale with an uphill struggle to make the top three, but still well in the play-off hunt. The last chance to put pressure on the leading sides disappeared when Darlington gained revenge for the previous year's play-off semi-final by winning at Spotland in front of the Sky tv cameras.

With Jones back in the side, Dale claimed the necessary point at Luton to guarantee a play-off place and for the last game of the regular season, coincidentally against play-off opponents Gillingham, Keith Hill rested most of his first team players, Dave Flitcroft making his first league appearance for two and a half years (and first for Dale since 2003) and putting in some characteristically hefty challenges, much to the annoyance of Gills' boss Stimpson.

Dale's 1-0 defeat meant that Gillingham finished 5th to Dale's 6th so that the first leg of the play-off semi-final would be at Spotland. A cagey affair saw Dale, with only one win in their last eight games, unable to recapture their form from earlier in the campaign and the game ended goalless, though Buckley did have one effort disallowed for offside. In the away leg, Dale could count themselves somewhat unlucky when an attacker blocked McArdle's clearance with his arm on the way to the first goal, and McArdle then conceded a penalty after Dagnall had put Dale back on level terms.

Due to various injuries and changes of personnel, Dale had again made the play-offs despite only a couple of players, Tom Kennedy and Rory McArdle, starting 40 or more league games, with 13 others starting at least 20. Though quite often a substitute (he and fellow striker Chris Dagnall rarely started together), Adam Le Fondre was again easily top scorer with 17 in the league plus his cup hat-trick (and won the player of the year), while Will Buckley, in his first full season, netted 11.

Although keeping the majority of the squad, Keith Hill released or transfer listed several fringe players. Scott Wiseman was also initially not offered a new contract, but after fellow right back Simon Ramsden decided to join Bradford City, Wiseman was quickly re-signed. The first incoming player of the summer was Darlington's Jason Kennedy who had scored key goals against Dale in each of the last two seasons (but had had his penalty saved by Tommy Lee in the famous shoot-out for a place at Wembley) and he was joined by Accrington's Scottish 'keeper Kenny Arthur in time for the annual Spanish training camp.

With due respect to the unfortunate player involved, arguably the key moment of the 2009-10 season – indeed of the last 36 seasons – came in the first friendly, against Radcliffe Borough when Rory McArdle dislocated his shoulder. For the first league game of the season, Dale thus had to give a debut to young centre back Craig Dawson, ironically a former Radcliffe Borough player, alongside Nathan Stanton.

However, as one player started to make his mark, another was leaving, Adam Le Fondre agreeing a £145,000 move to Rotherham, as with Rickie Lambert the money being needed to pay Dale's tax bill. The fact that Rotherham had previously gone into administration but could now spend this kind of money was not lost on Keith Hill, an outspoken critic of clubs who lived beyond their budget. ('Scrutator', writing in the Dale programme, neatly summarised Dale's historic money troubles: "Dale kept going with the famous ritual of the cap being passed around the boardroom ... It was a practice that lasted for years until they had to stop when they couldn't afford a cap.")

A winning start had been denied Dale by a linesman's decision to award a penalty to Port Vale when the ball struck Stanton and, missing several senior players, they went down 3-0 at

Sheffield Wednesday in the Carling Cup. However, despite Stanton's early dismissal, the luck turned Dale's way for once, as they defeated Aldershot via a dubious penalty converted by Tom Kennedy in the 93rd minute. Fortunes reversed again, though, when Cheltenham beat them 1-0, netting from virtually their only chance, again in stoppage time.

Another inspired move by Keith Hill saw striker Chris O'Grady arrive on loan from Oldham, but unsurprisingly it was former hero Le Fondre who was on the scoresheet – and the winning side – when Dale travelled to Rotherham. The main talking point, though, was the dreadful state of the Don Valley Stadium pitch after a U2 concert the day before, Dale lodging an official complaint with the referee and subsequently the Football League.

Keeping to the theme of alternating fortunes, Dale then dispatched Bury 3-0, their first home victory over their neighbours for 16 years. The final goal, from the spot, was extravagantly celebrated by Tom Kennedy in front of his former supporters, drawing disapproval from the BBC's Football League Show, but inspiring Dale fans' chants of 'he's not a Bucket any more', in reference to their version of the visitors' nickname, viz. 'bucket shakers', following Bury's financial problems a few years earlier.

Despite another comeback by **Dave Flitcroft** (which did prove his last appearance, though he was on the bench once the following season), Dale quickly exited the Johnstone's Paint Trophy. In the league, they came back from three down to Morecambe to grab an unlikely point but even so, eight points from six games saw them only in 13th place.

At this point the Dagnall - O'Grady partnership started to hit top form and Dale recorded four straight victories to move through the pack into 2nd place and earn Keith Hill the manager of the month award. The usual curse saw Dale beaten in a game at Burton put back until Sunday because Derbyshire police said they could not deal with this game (attendance a shade over 3000) as well as Derby County's.

They bounced back to beat fellow pace setters Barnet, though Keith Hill was again moved to criticise 'the same old moaners' for inducing negativity and tension in the last few minutes when the visitors mounted a late rally. Injuries also began to beset the squad, with Wiseman, Buckley, Jones and then 'keeper Arthur missing out, the latter with a slipped disc. Nevertheless, after a defeat at Accrington, Dale produced a tremendous performance at Bournemouth, demolishing the league leaders 4-0 thanks to goals from Dagnall, O'Grady 2, and on-loan Norwich man Simon Whaley, the only blot on their day being another red card for Nathan Stanton for a rash challenge.

Joe Thompson scored twice in the last seven minutes to rescue a draw at Luton in the FA Cup and earn the club some extra cash with the replay being televised by ITV. With Arthur and reserve Matty Edwards both injured, and the on loan Josh Lillis ineligible, 16 year old Danny Taberner became Dale's second youngest 'keeper after Stephen Bywater, and schoolboy Jordan Andrews was on the bench, the first 15 year old to make Dale's first team squad. Despite Taberner's best efforts, Dale went out to the non-league side and less than 2000 fans came to watch in person.

Keith Hill brought in Manchester United's England under-21 'keeper Tom Heaton for the next game, but another old boy ruined his debut when David Perkins netted Chesterfield's winner. (Craig Dawson had earlier recorded Dale's 3000th FL goal at Spotland). However, with two more loanees added to the squad, Hull's Will Atkinson and Rotherham's Jason Taylor, Dale then launched into another tremendous run of success, starting with a 2-1 victory at leaders Dagenham thanks to centre back Dawson's third goal in four games. They also dispatched Sven Goran Erikson's big-spending Notts County, County subsequently being found not to actually have the money they had been spending and to have thereby broken the salary cap for League 2 clubs, though a change of ownership allowed them to continue to compete towards the top of the table. Dale finally moved to the top of the league themselves with a 3-0 win at Bradford (in front of a crowd in excess of 11,000), Chris Dagnall and Chris O'Grady taking their joint tally to 20 goals.

Chairman Chris Dunphy admitted that one of Dale's stars would probably have to be sold in January, with Dagnall, Buckley and Tom Kennedy who were all out of contract in the summer being potential sales. In the meantime, the goals continued to flow, ten more flying into opponents' nets in the next three games, with only one in reply. Both O'Grady and Dawson netted twice against Shrewsbury, the latter's amazing run seeing the defender notch seven in ten games.

A brace for Atkinson completed another four goal haul against Morecambe and ensured that Dale would go into the New Year top of the table for the first time in their FL history, having already topped the 50 point mark from just 24 games. Unsurprisingly Keith Hill won the manager of the month and Craig Dawson the player of the month awards for League 2.

Although several games were postponed, Dale maintained the feel good factor by finalising Chris O'Grady's permanent transfer for a fee of around £65,000. After a draw at Aldershot, Dale overpowered Cheltenham thanks to an O'Grady hat-trick and a draw at Port Vale meant that, apart from his first game, Dale had remained unbeaten throughout Tom Heaton's three month loan spell, conceding just 8 goals in the last 11 games. Indeed, with Jason Taylor having signed a week later, the Rotherham man could claim the remarkable record of being unbeaten in the first 11 games of his Dale career.

Will Buckley, who had actually missed much of the good run through injury, proved to be the player to move on, attracting a £300,000 bid from Championship side Watford, while Adam Rundle also left at the end of January, joining Chesterfield after just short of 150 senior games for Dale. Coming in to replace Heaton was another England under-21 'keeper, Frankie Fielding arriving on loan from Blackburn for a second time.

February started with an unfortunate 1-0 loss at Bury in front of the Sky cameras, but Dale bounced back to win the next two games, Jones bagging his first goal for two years in the defeat of challengers Dagenham to make it ten wins in 14 games and to keep Dale five points clear at the top. Again a defeat was followed by two victories, Dale trouncing one of their main rivals Rotherham 4-0, with their main men Dagnall, Dawson and O'Grady all on target.

After winning at Shrewsbury, Dale found themselves two down mid-way through the second half at Accrington but a Gary Jones inspired comeback – 'Jonah' netting twice himself and 'COG' hitting his 20th of the season – saw them end up 4-2 winners, Kallum Higginbotham's outrageous volley from virtually on the half-way line capping a memorable afternoon.

Dale hit four more against Grimsby, Chris Dagnall this time hitting a treble to take his season's tally to 20 and Dale's points total to 78, virtually guaranteeing a place in the top three. Beaten by two penalties at Chesterfield, Dale played out a goalless draw with third placed Bournemouth in front of Spotland's first 5000 crowd of the season. However, true to tradition of never making anything easy for their fans, hundreds of whom had travelled to the English Riviera for the weekend, Dale were trounced 5-0 at Torquay, their worst result under Keith Hill. Even a trip to Darlington failed to produce the required outcome, Dale losing 1-0 despite 17 attempts on goal and 16 corners, though the result was not enough to prevent the Quakers' relegation to the Conference being confirmed.

Dale finally got over the line to earn their first promotion in 41 years and escape 'the Rochdale division' at the 36th attempt on April 17th when Chris O'Grady's goal proved decisive against Northampton and inspired a mass pitch invasion at the final whistle.

Notts County had meantime won a string of games which they had had in hand due to a long cup run and went a point ahead of Dale before the likely title decider at Meadow Lane. The game itself could have gone either way but was settled by a single goal from County's Lee Hughes and Dale went on to lose their remaining three games by the odd goal, too, a goal by Barnet in the last minute of the final game meaning that Dale also finished behind Bournemouth. The last nine games had produced just four points, but Dale still equalled their third place from 1969 and finished with a best ever total of 82 points. They also scored 82 goals.

The day after the season ended, Dale's team and management celebrated their promotion with an open top bus ride and civic reception at the town hall. The local council also agreed to help aid Dale's coming League 1 campaign by writing off a long term debt owed by the stadium company. To further add to the celebrations, kitman Jack Northover honoured a promise to do a skydive in just his boxer shorts if Dale were promoted!

Although Dale used 32 players – twice as many as in their 1968-69 promotion season – nine of them played at least 34 times, the regular back four of Wiseman, Stanton, Dawson and Tom Kennedy, Jason Kennedy and Jones in midfield, forward Thompson and the strike force of Dagnall and O'Grady, with the goalkeeping and other midfield/wing positions being shared between several players. Chris O'Grady netted 22 league goals and Chris Dagnall 20, the first time that two Dale strikers had both reached the 20 mark in the same season. Possibly more remarkably, young centre back Craig Dawson, in his first season, scored 11 goals, 9 in the league, beating John Bramhall's previous best for a defender from 1986-87.

Promotion celebrations, 2010

At the PFA awards night Dawson, Jones and Tom Kennedy were all named in the League 2 team of the season. Old boy Adam Le Fondre was also included, while Grant Holt and Rickie Lambert were in the League 1 selection. Boss Keith Hill also won the League 2 manager of the year award. At club level, Dawson won the player of the year award, the young player of the year and the most improved player of the year, while Chris O'Grady picked up the Supporters' player of the year award and Jason Kennedy was the players' player of the year.

Although only Kallum Higginbotham of the regular squad players was released (subsequently signing for Falkirk in the Scottish first division), along with Ciaran Toner who had spent most of the season out injured, Dale were resigned to losing some of their out of contract stars. First to go was Rory McArdle, immediately after winning his first full cap for N. Ireland, who signed for Aberdeen – a move which particularly annoyed Keith Hill as a loophole in transfer regulations with the Scottish Premier League allowed the Dons to sign him without paying the compensation that would have been due if he had joined an English club. He was soon followed by Chris Dagnall and Tom Kennedy who joined Championship sides Scunthorpe and Leicester, respectively. Finally, Nathan Stanton decided to accept a two year deal to stay in League 2 with Burton Albion, leaving just seven first team players. On the other hand, Middlesbrough had a £400,000 bid for Craig Dawson turned down and Scott Wiseman and Joe Thompson signed new two year contracts.

Incoming were Bury's experienced Irish midfielder Brian Barry-Murphy plus fullback Joe Widdowson and French striker Jean-Louis Akpa Akpro, both from relegated Grimsby, while Kenny Arthur moved the other way. Dale old boy Alan Goodall and Hereford winger Matty Done were among trialists to join Dale on their 2010 summer camp in Spain, along with Josh Lillis returning on a six month loan from Scunthorpe. An eve of season move saw former Stockport striker Anthony Elding obtained from Hungarian side Ferencvaros for £20,000.

With nine new players in the squad, Dale's first game in the third tier for 36 years ended in a nervy 0-0 draw with familiar opponents Hartlepool, but in front of a slightly disappointing crowd of 3706, less than the last five home games of the promotion campaign. Gary Jones then netted twice at promotion favourites Brighton, lobbing the 'keeper for a last minute equaliser, but Dale were beaten at home by Colchester.

Dale had defeated Barnsley in the League Cup, thanks to a goal from Elding, their first win in normal time in the competition for nine years, and only their eighth away from home in the 51 years of the competition. In the second round they had a televised game at Birmingham and Dale led briefly before a dubious penalty gave the home side the initiative, though Jones' second goal to make it 3-2 gave the Premier League side a nervous last few minutes.

The first league victory of the season came at Brentford, despite Jason Kennedy being sent off for celebrating his winning goal with the Dale fans. A couple of days later West Brom won the race to sign Craig Dawson with a deal worth around £600,000 plus add-ons. Just as importantly as the cash, the Baggies also agreed to loan him back to Dale for the rest of the season. (Dawson subsequently, and unsurprisingly, won the North West League 2 player of the year award).

The next league game saw the side visit St Mary's Stadium for the first time and they exceeded all expectations by defeating the Saints 2-0 with goals from O'Grady and Jones, Dawson and Holness keeping ex-Dale star Rickie Lambert – and 18,000 home fans - quiet. They also beat Walsall, on loan Celtic defender Josh Thompson scoring on his full debut and Jones netting the winner from the spot to give him six goals in six games.

A sixth game unbeaten saw Dale overcome Huddersfield, another of the promotion contenders, 3-0 and amazingly rise to 4th in the table. Characteristically they then lost the next three games against more modest opposition, only netting once – and that an own goal. Dale did beat Dagenham, but highly contentious penalties that had manager Hill fuming at "sub-standard" officials led to successive away defeats.

This was compounded when Dale drew minnows FC United of Manchester in the FA Cup. After fighting back from an embarrassing 2-0 deficit, they were beaten in the last minute when the referee allowed the FCUM centre forward to kick the ball out of Lillis' arms. The attendance, against a side four divisions below them, was over 7000.

After six defeats in seven games, Dale stopped the rot with three successive draws, that against neighbours Oldham (originally abandoned because of a flooded pitch a few weeks earlier) attracting a crowd of 6483. Following a defeat at Peterborough, Dale were without a game for nearly a month, due to the weather, but started 2011 with victory over Tranmere, skipper Jones netting his fourth brace of the season including Dale's 5000th league goal. Another landmark was chalked up when Dale played Sheffield Wednesday, their 100th opponents in the FL.

It was former Oldham man Chris O'Grady who scored twice when Dale gained their first league victory at Boundary Park for 50 years, despite Wiseman's harsh red card, and O'Grady scored again in their third win in a week, at Dagenham. The next five games produced another win and four draws, new 'keeper Owain fon Williams from Stockport keeping a clean sheet at Yeovil on his debut. In other Stockport related business, Anthony Elding left to join them on loan while his former strike partner Liam Dickinson arrived (from Barnsley) on the same terms, while left backs Alan Goodall and Robbie Williams exchanged clubs. January also saw Dale make permanent Nicky Adams' loan from Brentford and Will Atkinson repeat his loan move of the previous season.

Two home wins in early February saw Dale move to within a point of the play-off places and for once defy the curse of the manager of the month award for Keith Hill, Matty Done making scoring contributions from the bench each time; Done subsequently gained a more regular place in a floating role behind lone striker O'Grady. Hill's side made it 11 without defeat before being well beaten at home by MK Dons. They also lost, despite an excellent performance, at Huddersfield, though the result was overshadowed by a serious injury to Town's Anthony Pilkington.

Only 2019 fans turned up to see Dale beat Notts County 1-0, yet over 8000 saw them record the same scoreline away to bottom club Plymouth in their next game. (There had been 12,000 in attendance at Huddersfield). Further victories over Hartlepool and Charlton, with Dawson on the scoresheet each time, gave fon Williams four clean sheets in a row, last achieved by Neil Edwards in 1999.

Jones' 19th goal of the season, and third against Brighton, helped take another point off the runaway leaders (who had won all their previous eight games) and Dale completed the double over Notts County, Dawson netting for the seventh time in 13 games. After Colchester became the first side to do the double over them, a fantastic night at Spotland saw Dale beat Southampton for the second time, goals from Joe Thompson and O'Grady lifting them into the play-off places with just five games to go.

Unfortunately Dale ran out of steam at this point, losing three times in 10 days, but still ended the season by drawing with promotion bound Peterborough – Akpa Akpro scoring after just 14 seconds and Craig Dawson celebrating his final game at Spotland with a late equaliser – and beating Bournemouth, who had just pipped them for the last play-off spot, thanks to a first goal for youngster Reece Gray. With 68 points, just three behind the Cherries, Dale thus finished 9th matching their highest ever finish in the national third tier from 1969. Brighton's promotion success (despite Dale's best efforts!) earned Dale £100,000 as part of the terms of Glenn Murray's sale to the Seagulls, and they made another £150,000 sell on fee when Brighton bought Will Buckley from Watford. Meanwhile, the next generation of players, in Chris Beech's youth team, won the Alliance League (North West) after being runners-up the previous year.

Skipper and player of the year Gary Jones top scored with an amazing tally for a midfielder of 17 league goals, plus 2 in cup ties, and was followed by Craig Dawson with an equally remarkable 11 strikes from centre back. This gave Dawson a total of 22 goals in just two seasons, the most ever by a Dale defender, beating the previous best of Gareth Griffiths. Jones had played in every game, as had Holness – voted most improved player of the year - and O'Grady, while Dawson and Jason Kennedy both missed only the final game. Owain fon Williams, the regular keeper in the second half of the season, was one of just three players released.

In April, the club's financial report had shown that during the promotion campaign, turnover had increased to £2.7M, with a minimal loss of £27,000 compared to £260,000 the year before. The sales of Le Fondre and Buckley and sell-on fees for the likes of Rickie Lambert had brought in £480,000. Just before the end of the season, the club signed a deal with the Co-op to be the main sponsors in 2011-12.

BACK DOWN AND BACK UP

Within a couple of weeks of the end of the season Keith Hill was linked with managerial vacancies at Sheffield United and Barnsley, and the board reluctantly gave him permission to talk to the latter. Hill initially turned down the Tykes' offer and claimed that it was business as usual at Spotland, but further talks saw him quit Spotland for the other side of the Pennines, the manner of his departure unfortunately somewhat souring his reputation with some fans. Dave Flitcroft and most of the backroom staff also moved to Oakwell, leaving youth team coach Chris Beech to hold the fort.

Beech was suggested as a likely contender for the manager's job, while the names of former players Ronnie Moore, an experienced lower league manager, Dave Bayliss, the manager of Barrow, John Pemberton and Sean McAuley were soon added to the list, the latter pair being the academy directors at the two Sheffield clubs. Within a week, chairman Chris Dunphy reported that he had received numerous high quality applications, including some from former Premier League managers. One was rumoured to be ex-West Brom boss Roberto de Mateo who, it was claimed, had been seen filling his car at Tesco in Rochdale! If true, he subsequently had a lucky escape in not being appointed, as he took over at Chelsea half way through the following season and took them to the Champions League final!

In the event, the board settled on Manchester City academy coach Steve Eyre, son of well known former player and football pundit Fred Eyre, but who had had no senior playing experience himself. (Indeed, his level of responsibility for the older age groups in City's youth set-up also soon became a contentious question among Dale fans). Frankie Bunn, the ex-Oldham player, moved from Newcastle's coaching staff to become assistant manager.

Over the summer, Scott Wiseman and Matty Done had joined the exodus to Barnsley and Craig Dawson finally linked up with West Brom, but ten of the previous season's senior squad were still available, with Gary Jones agreeing a new two year deal, though this reduced to nine on the eve of the season when Elding signed for Grimsby. (Recall that Hill had only had seven of his promotion winning squad left at the start of the previous term). The first new arrivals were ex-City youngsters Ashley Grimes from Millwall and Andrew Tutte, who had spent some time on loan at Spotland before joining Yeovil.

The main new defensive signings were Stephen Darby on loan from Liverpool, Neil Trotman from Preston and Falkirk left back Marc Twaddle, who was somewhat surprisingly recruited to play in central defence. As it turned out, this idea lasted just one pre-season game and the unfortunate Twaddle was hardly seen again, defensive frailties evident in pre-season unfortunately sign-posting things to come. Jake Kean arrived on loan from Blackburn as number one 'keeper with the experienced David Lucas signed as both cover and goalkeeping coach.

The 2011-12 league season started with a defeat at Sheffield Wednesday, who then bought Chris O'Grady for £350,000 after earlier bids had been turned down. However, Dale came from behind to beat Chesterfield 3-2 in extra-time in the Carling Cup, Grimes scoring twice After two draws, a disastrous day for Trotman against his old club Oldham saw him concede a penalty and receive two yellow cards before half-time, Dale losing 2-0.

Remarkably, though, Dale then beat Premiership side QPR - in fact largely QPR reserves, though this still included several internationals - their manager Neil Warnock claiming after the match that he was glad they had been knocked out. This put Dale in the third round of the League Cup, under its various guises, for the first time since making it to the final in 1962. They subsequently wasted the opportunity for further glory by losing to League 2 strugglers Aldershot.

Meantime, back in the league, Dale lost twice more – leaving them with two points from six games - before grabbing the first two FL victories of the season, the first a stunning 4-2 victory over neighbours Bury, where they had Adams sent off for two yellow cards, the first for taking his shirt of in celebrating his goal against his former team. (Even then, manager Eyre's quote that "we stumbled across 4-4-2 when we played Bury" did little to dispel the aura of disorganisation). A couple more defeats followed, but Dale did beat Wycombe, Grimes getting another brace to take his tally to eight, and drew three of the next four, goals from skipper Jones rescuing them on each occasion.

However, lack of continuity - Dale had made 14 new signings by the time they played their 13th match - and lack of defensive organisation led to a run of eight games without a win, including defeat in Gary Jones 500th senior game for the club and a second loss to a side struggling in League 2, Bradford City knocking them out of the FA Cup.

Even more new faces had arrived by this point, Chesterfield's Dean Holden swapping clubs with Neil Trotman after the latter's reputed disagreements with the management, while Jake Kean returned to Blackburn rather than complete his loan spell, following a loss of form and confidence. When Roland Bergkamp – nephew of Arsenal's famous Dutch striker Dennis - was signed on loan he was the 30th player used in the first team squad by Steve Eyre by mid-November, supporters questioning the logic of signings such as the loans of Manchester City youngster Ahmad Benali, who figured just twice from the bench in half a season at Spotland (but later made the grade in Italy), and Matthew Barnes- Homer who hadn't been able to get in the first team at Conference side Luton. (At times Dale had seven simultaneous loan signings when only five were allowed in a matchday squad).

A rare bright spot saw Dale triumph 1-0 at Preston, which at least gave everyone a lift before Gary Jones' testimonial dinner. They then lost at home to Brentford, despite Marcus Holness' third goal of the season, were swamped 3-0 by Sheffield Wednesday, Lucas also suffering concussion after a collision with Holden, and were held 0-0 at home by ten-man Yeovil.

At this point, with four league victories in 21 games, one win in the last 12 matches and the worst goal difference in the division, chairman Chris Dunphy came to the same conclusion that most of the fans had reached some time earlier, that Steve Eyre was out of his depth, and relieved him of his position, along with his assistant Frank Bunn. (Eyre had recently disparaged his own side, after signing Stephen Jordan, noting that he would be in the team "for the way he organises and talks, but mostly for the fact that he passes the ball to another Rochdale player"). The chairman was also left bemoaning that the club had, this season, had its largest ever squad and biggest ever budget.

Youth team boss Chris Beech was placed in caretaker charge again and drafted in former Barnsley coach Ryan Kidd to help him. Their first game, on New Year's Eve, ended goalless at Walsall and Dale should have taken three points from the next game, when on loan Blackpool (and Malta) striker Daniel Bogdanovic scored on his debut and set up what would have been the winner for Grimes only for it to be controversially chalked off for a push on the goalkeeper that only the referee saw. Sadly the side then reverted to its previous form, culminating in one of Rochdale's worst ever home defeats, 5-1 by Stevenage.

After six games, there was therefore another change in the hot seat as the long serving Accrington boss John Coleman and his number two Jimmy Bell moved in. They had a dream start, Dale totally outplaying Bury to win 3-0, only the second victory in 17 league games. Despite a narrow defeat by Scunthorpe after a couple of postponements, which dropped them to the foot of the table, Dale also beat Bournemouth thanks to a stoppage time Jones penalty and picked up two useful away points, including one at runaway leaders Charlton.

Peter Kurucz, a Hungarian under-21 international signed on loan from West Ham by Chris Beech, had conceded only twice in five games since Coleman's arrival, but in the next game, a 1-0 defeat by Notts County, Kurucz was put out of action for the rest of the season by a challenge from Dale's arch-nemesis Lee Hughes, who was sent off. Dale were still in the fight at this point, though, and had the chance to beat 3rd placed Sheffield Wednesday to get to within two points of escaping the bottom four, but this time Jones scuffed his late penalty against the outside of the post. Even so, another draw with promotion contenders Huddersfield and a 3-2 victory over Oldham, thanks to a hat-trick from on-loan Bournemouth striker Michael Symes, meant that Dale had picked up 13 points in the last 10 games. Symes was one of five players, four with Accrington connections, who Coleman was able to recruit following his January arrival.

Two further defeats left Dale on the brink ahead of a crunch game against Walsall who were just above the relegation line. Dale looked dead and buried when they went 2-0 down in the first half, but a spirited comeback saw them take the lead through Jean-Louis Akpa Akpro's second goal of the afternoon in the 93rd minute, only to concede an equaliser straight from the kick-off. Dale conceded five at home for the second time in the season when Sheffield United won 5-2 at Spotland, but Dale did delay the inevitable by coming from two-down to beat Exeter with three goals in the last 11 minutes. The following week it was all over, though, as this time Dale conceded twice in the last 10 minutes to lose to Chesterfield (who, like Exeter, finally went down with Dale). Defeats in the last two games, as well, saw Dale finish bottom of the pile with only 38 points, 12 short of safety. They had won just eight games (four each under Eyre and Coleman) and were both the second lowest scorers (with 47) and had the second worst defence (conceding 81), not a good combination.

Dale used a massive 44 players in their first team squad (despite the temporary reduction to only five subs), 41 of them actually making appearances. Gary Jones missed only one game – reputedly after a fall-out with management as the season neared its end – and Jason Kennedy only two, but of the others only four started even 30 games. Jones had now completed a mammoth 470 FL games for the Dale and 535 matches in all competitions. Kennedy and Akpa Akpro won the player of the year and club player of the year awards. Long standing reserve Matty Edwards, signed in 2009, had finally managed a few starts in goal and was called up for the Scottish under-21 squad, winning a cap against Italy in slightly bizarre circumstances when the substitute goalkeeper himself had to be substituted. Indeed, amongst all the signings, Rochdale remarkably fielded players of ten different nationalities.

At the season's close John Coleman released just three of the fairly regular performers and offered new contracts to four, the rest of the squad already being contracted for another season. However, this was just the beginning of the changes as none of the four accepted the deals offered, both the long-serving Joe Thompson and Jean-Louis Akpa Akpro signing for League 1 Tranmere, and several others moved on over the summer. Foremost of these was club legend Gary Jones who elected to sign for Bradford City, whose assistant manager was his old Dale boss Steve Parkin. Nicky Adams had already moved on to Crawley, while Marcus Holness joined his former centre-back partner Nathan Stanton at Burton Albion.

The main arrivals for 2012-13 were former loan keeper Josh Lillis from Scunthorpe, striker George Donnelly from Macclesfield, young defenders Rhys Bennett from Bolton and Joe Rafferty from Liverpool, and several players with Accrington connections, most notably Phil Edwards, Peter Cavanagh and Kevin McIntyre. Meantime, Rochdale old boy Craig Dawson, a regular for England under-21s, figured for Great Britain at the Olympics. (The Olympic torch also passed Spotland on its way around the country).

Pre-season was a bit of a disaster. Two games were cancelled because of the wet weather both in England and in Austria where Dale travelled for their summer camp and another was abandoned because of floodlight failure. A behind closed doors friendly at Liverpool, arranged to cover the shortfall in game time, was also abandoned after it cost Dale the services of young striker Reece Gray, expected to be a key part of the first team in the coming season, with a badly broken ankle.

The season itself started with the Capital One (i.e. League) Cup, which brought Keith Hill's Barnsley to Spotland. Remarkably, apart from two former loanees, only four of the Dale's 18-man squad had played for them before, whereas five of the visitors had! The game went to extra time when an off the ball incident in the last minute saw Barnsley keeper Alnwick sent off and Jason Kennedy given the opportunity to make it 2-2 from the spot, but Chris Dagnall then scored twice to take the Tykes through 4-3.

League action started with a goalless affair against Northampton, but there was much more action when Dale visited Torquay. Dale scored first but then conceded four – two of them to another former player, Rene Howe - before a late comeback when the Gulls went down to 10 men, Kennedy this time missing a penalty as the game ended 4-2.

The first victory came against Barnet in the fourth game and Dale subsequently hit an excellent run of form; not having won away since the previous November they won four away games in succession, inflicting a first defeat of the season on runaway leaders Gillingham. They were also the first away side to win at Rotherham's new New York stadium thanks to a late strike from full back Kevin McIntyre.

John Coleman had added the veteran striker Dele Adebola to his squad on the eve of the season and he had been joined upfront by Bobby Grant from Scunthorpe. A six match unbeaten run, Grant scoring in four of them, propelled the side up to fifth place when they beat Coleman's old club Accrington and despite a couple of slip-ups they again hit fifth spot, with 30 points from 18 games, just three fewer than 2nd placed Port Vale, after beating Bristol Rovers in mid-November (the visitors ending with only nine men).

This was only Dale's third home win of the season, compared to five away, and the lack of home form had caused friction between the management and some fans, despite the side's lofty placing in the league. In a defeat by Morecambe this had escalated into a verbal battle between fans critical of Kennedy being left out of the side to accommodate players they saw as Coleman's favourites and the manager himself who suggested they should ask themselves why the team played better away from Spotland. In fact, only just over 1600 fans had turned up to watch Dale beat Oxford in October and a similar number saw then knocked out of the FA Cup in a replay against Morecambe. Dale took the lead in the second half at Southend but then conceded three, much to the frustration of the manager who was furious with his experienced defenders for leaving huge gaps at the back. Three more went into the Dale net in the first 35 minutes against York and they found themselves three down at the interval again the following week against Exeter, each time coming up just short with late revivals, new signing Terry Gornell being sent off after netting twice against the Grecians. Bouncing from one extreme to another, Dale conceded four to struggling Aldershot, but scored four against promotion contenders Cheltenham and Bradford City (who had just beaten Arsenal in the League Cup), a run of seven games producing an aggregate score of 17-19.

Even when the goal scoring returned to normal proportions Dale were on the wrong end of further defeats, two of them from winning positions, and sank into the lower half of the table with two wins and eight defeats in the last ten games. Adding to the misery, Dale had suffered disciplinary problems with a string of red and yellow cards - five players had been sent off and nine suspensions been served by Christmas - while against Dagenham, Bobby Grant was accused of racially abusing an opponent. (He was found not guilty when the case went to court the following summer).

Mid-January saw the players drafted in to clear snow off the pitch, but the game against Gillingham was postponed anyway and during the enforced lay-off the Board acted to sack Coleman and Bell. The previous month, Coleman had invited fans to drop in to his office and discuss the situation, several taking him up on his offer. Nevertheless, there had been a growing feeling that the side no longer represented a 'Team Rochdale' that the fans could feel part of.

The following day, to the amazement (and rejoicing) of most fans (though some hadn't forgiven him for the way he had left the club), Keith Hill, himself recently fired by Barnsley, was reinstated in his old job. Chris Beech, whose youth side had reached the 4th round of the FA Youth Cup, was appointed as his number two.

The second coming began with a hard earned point at Cheltenham on a Friday night in atrocious weather conditions, but it wasn't until Hill's fourth game back that he was able to celebrate a victory, 1-0 against Torquay, by which point Dale were 16th in a remarkably congested league table. After a dour stalemate at Barnet, now managed by former Holland star Edgar Davids, Dale had conceded only four times in five games and another 0-0 looked on the cards until Accrington substitute full back Molyneux (later briefly with Dale), with no previous career league goals, twice netted from 30 yards in the last 15 minutes. A second successive 3-0 defeat left Dale just 6 points above the drop zone, Hill admitting it was a harder job than he had expected.

Fortunately things did then turn around with an excellent 4-1 victory over Wycombe, and an unlucky reverse at Bristol Rovers was the only defeat in the next nine games. These included draws with the division's two best sides Gillingham and Port Vale, and three wins in a row against play-off contenders, the first, at Exeter, thanks to goals in the last three minutes from Grant and new signing Ian Henderson. Dale also scored late against Port Vale; an 89th minute goal looked to have secured the visitors' promotion but there was still time for a bandaged Kennedy to head an equaliser. Even a disappointing end-of-season performance at Oxford did not affect them too much and Dale finished on a high, beating relegation threatened Plymouth 1-0 thanks to a goal from 18 year old debutant Joe Bunney with his first touch after coming on as substitute. (Argyle survived by a point, as Barnet failed to win either).

Dale's final day success secured a place in the top half of the table, in fact just eight points shy of Bradford City in the final play-off place. Bradford, skippered by former Dale hero Gary Jones, and with three other ex-Dale players in their side, had earlier memorably reached the League Cup Final, matching Dale' run to the final as a side from the fourth tier 51 years earlier. They also won the play-off final, Rory McArdle scoring at Wembley as he had for Dale in 2008.

Josh Lillis and Jason Kennedy had appeared in every league game (and shared the player of the year awards between them), but the second mid-season managerial change in a row meant that another 36 players had been utilised at some point, though six had only been unused substitutes. Continuing the changes he had instigated since taking over, Keith Hill released 12 players and offered new contracts to six, including ex-Colchester pair Michael Rose and Ian Henderson who had become important members of the side since signing in February. Ashley Grimes was among those released meaning that after just 18 months, Andrew Tutte was the only one of Steve Eyres' signings remaining at the club. (Tutte himself departed the following January).

Further moves occurred over the summer with top scorer Bobby Grant – he had scored 15 league goals in 35 games, but on the down side had been sent off twice - asking for a transfer and being sold to Championship side Blackpool. Fans were surprisingly unmoved at the loss of their main goal scorer, who many felt was too closely linked to the previous management regime. After some indecision, Jason Kennedy decided to join Bradford City after 177 league games for Dale, while Phil Edwards turned down a new contract and joined Burton Albion. This left only nine senior pros on the books – including Brian Barry-Murphy who became player-coach - with Hill happy to go with his younger players if necessary. Reserve 'keeper Steve Collis became goalkeeping coach. Rick Ashcroft, already part of the backroom staff became full time youth team manager with the remit to continue Chris Beech's production line of talent for the first team. Indeed, the youth team had just lifted the Lancashire Youth Cup, trouncing Wigan 5-0, with full back Scott Tanser netting a hat-trick, including two penalties. Tanser was one of eight members of the youth team squad who would subsequently play in the first team.

Two of the new recruits for 2013-14 were returning for second spells with the club, Matty Done back from Barnsley and ex-youth team player Scott Hogan after a couple of years in non-league football, and both quickly made a mark with hat-tricks in pre-season games. Other new signings included Olly Lancashire and Peter Vincenti from relegated Aldershot, Ashley Eastham from

Blackpool and Stoke reserve Matty Lund. Jack O'Connell arrived on a season's long loan from Blackburn immediately after playing in a friendly against Dale. Former PSG junior Bastien Hery joined the club from Sheffield Wednesday's development squad.

The season kicked off with a special match against Hartlepool for the Football League's 125th anniversary, this being the most played fixture amongst current fourth tier sides. Ten new players were in the squad which convincingly won 3-0, Scott Hogan getting off the mark after just 11 minutes. The next four league and cup games included three 1-0 defeats, with skipper Cavanagh sent off after just seven minutes at Burton. Dale's sole point came against title favourites Chesterfield when Dale were awarded two penalties in a matter of seconds; former Dale hero Tommy Lee saved the original one but then brought down Hogan when the ball was played back in. Elsewhere, Rickie Lambert, now in the Premier League with Southampton, scored with his first touch for England against Scotland, while current Dale youngster Callum Camps was selected for the N. Ireland under-19s. Lambert later donated the England shirt he wore against Germany to a charity auction to raise funds for assistant manager Chris Beech's son Brandon's medical treatment.

Dale drew at leaders Oxford but were down in 17th at the end of August. The following month saw them come good, though, with four successive victories - two of them with ten men after red cards for Vincenti against Bury and Donnelly at Accrington - to move rapidly up to 5th place. Scott Hogan was named League 2 player of the month but the 'curse' following Keith Hill's manager of the month award brought a 3-0 defeat at struggling Portsmouth in front of a crowd of 15,000. However, with youngster Jamie Allen making his first starts, Dale then won another four in a row – making it seven wins in the last eight league games - to go top of the table. Even so, the attendance in the game against Northampton, which Dale rescued with two goals in the last two minutes after conceding in just 40 seconds, was only 2362. At the end of October, Dale lost their club president when Mrs Lillian Stoney passed away at the age of 95.

Unsurprisingly Dale were unable to keep this form up indefinitely and results became patchier. A home defeat by Wimbledon was spectacular by any standards, a massive lightning strike hitting a floodlight pylon and putting the lights out temporarily; unfortunately it was the visitors who then struck when play resumed. The visit of fellow promotion hopefuls Scunthorpe was dramatic in other ways, the Iron winning 4-0 after centre backs Lancashire and O'Connell were both sent off. Keith Hill, who had regularly complained about refereeing standards, claimed that "we have not been thrashed, we have been denied an opportunity". Indeed, after Dale lost to a controversial Fleetwood penalty, Hill received an apology from the Referees' Association chief. Even so, Dale remained in the top five at the end of December, Scott Hogan taking his tally of league goals into double figures in the victory over Bristol Rovers. Dale had also reached the third round of the FA Cup with late goals away to both Torquay and League 1 Rotherham.

The New Year began with another bad day against Scunthorpe, Rose being sent off this time and Dale again conceding twice late on to lose 3-0. However, in the cup, Leeds came up against Dale at their best, goals from Hogan and Henderson – the latter a sublime cushioned first time volley over the keeper – dispatching the Championship side (and contributing to their manager losing his job soon afterwards). Henderson's strike was chosen as goal of the round and inspired tv pundit and Scotland manager Gordon Strachan to jokingly enquire whether 'Hendo' was Scottish! (In fact, though born in Suffolk, he had been in the Scottish under-19 squad back in 2003).

Five wins and five clean sheets in six games carried Dale back to second spot before a remarkable match against fellow front runners Chesterfield; 2-0 down going into the 90th minute, Henderson netted from the spot before Vincenti scored a stoppage time leveller. Dale were narrowly beaten 2-1 by another Championship side, Sheffield Wednesday, in the FA Cup fourth round, though Michael Rose did emulate Ian Henderson by scoring the goal of the round. The gates for both cup ties against Championship sides were over 8200.

Scott Hogan had recently been left out due to a loss of form through distractions during the transfer window – he had turned down a move to Peterborough – but once the deadline passed he was restored to the eleven and responded with one of the fastest hat-tricks of recent years, just 17 minutes covering his three strikes against Wimbledon.

Dale continued to stay the pace at the top, though only 2092 supporters saw the draw with fellow contenders Burton when Donnelly (somewhat fortuitously) equalized late on against a side which had previously held on for ten 1-0 wins. Scott Hogan's second hat-trick in three weeks (making him the first Rochdale player since Reg Jenkins to score two in one season and the first to get two league hat-tricks since Jim Dailey in 1957-58) put daylight between Dale and their fourth placed opponents Oxford. However, in the nil-nil draw with neighbours Bury, now managed by Hill's former assistant Dave Flitcroft, Hogan suffered a nasty injury and Henderson was sent off for two dubious yellow cards, Josh Lillis' point blank save in the final minute preserving Dale's point.

Without their main strikers, Dale lost to bottom side Torquay (and had Lancashire sent off again), though former youth team midfielder Jamie Allen completed an unusual treble by scoring against all three Devon clubs in the space of two months. However, they then came from behind to beat Accrington with two goals by Matt Lund, the first coming when a clearance hit him in the face, and a 3-0 victory at Northampton - despite Lund being sent off for celebrating another goal with the fans – took Dale to the top of the table, and more importantly six points clear of Fleetwood in 4th place.

Two further victories and a crucial goalless draw at Fleetwood kept Dale in control of their own destiny with six games to go, but after two unexpected 3-0 defeats (Lillis having kept clean sheets in all the previous five games, and in eight of the last ten), a key moment came when Joe Bunney equalised at Bristol Rovers just 20 seconds into the second half and Dale went on to win. Dale then defeated Cheltenham, and confirmation that Fleetwood had only drawn at Southend guaranteed a second promotion under Keith Hill in the space of four years.

With the title still a possibility if the results on the final day went their way, Dale fans were encouraged to emulate Keith Hill, who had worn pink chinos at the crucial game at Bristol Rovers, and enter into the celebration of 'pink pants day' at the final game against Newport. George Donnelly's goal and scores elsewhere gave Dale a glimpse of the trophy, but Lund's 83rd minute penalty was saved and it was 10-man County who grabbed the winner. Dale thus finished in 3rd place again; as Chesterfield won in the end, Dale would not have taken the title whatever their result at Newport. Dale had won more games (24) than anyone else in the division and were second highest scorers behind the Spireites.

The club could therefore celebrate with another civic reception and open top bus parade – now becoming a common occurrence after the 41 years between their previous promotions! Keith Hill revealed that the basis of the success went back to the pre-season training camp - "at a meeting of senior players, the chairman, the chief exec and one of the directors in Tenerife; the intention was to plan for promotion and there was a great intensity to the debate as to how we were going to do it".

Dale had used 33 players, with Josh Lillis, who kept 21 clean sheets, midfielder Matt Lund, forward Ian Henderson and Michael Rose, who figured at left back and midfield, all starting at least 40 times. The other most regular performers were Joe Rafferty, skipper Olly Lancashire and Jack O'Connell in defence, Peter Vincenti and the up and coming Jamie Allen in midfield, Matt Done who had switched to left back for the second half of the season, and Scott Hogan up front. Top scorer, in his first season as a league pro, Hogan hit 17 in the league (in just 29 starts) and 19 in all, making him third highest scorer in the division. Ian Henderson netted 12. Unusually, none of Dale's 69 goals was scored by a central defender. With the turnover of players in the period between Keith Hill's two spells in charge, only two players had played a part in both promotions, and even then only because of spells on loan; Lillis had figured once on loan in 2009-10, while Jason Kennedy had reappeared from Bradford City for a time in the current campaign. Of the front line players, only the veteran Peter Cavanagh was released. Just four of the senior squad remained from when Keith Hill had returned sixteen months previously (and one of those, George Donnelly, left before the window closed in August). Off the field, the saga of the club's attempts to buy Hornets' shares in the stadium company rumbled on, the local council (the other co-owners) at one point claiming never to have heard about it despite frequent press coverage.

Promotion celebrations, 2014

There was little transfer activity over the summer of 2014, with the rest of the squad agreeing new or extended current contracts. Dale, though, continued to make money from previous transfers when sell on clauses were triggered by Rickie Lambert's £4M move to Liverpool and Adam Le Fondre's transfer to Cardiff.

Dale had turned down earlier offers for Scott Hogan, but at the end of July a fee rumoured to be around £700,000 took him to Brentford. He was replaced in the squad for the opening fixture by well-travelled target man Calvin Andrew, the only new face in the side. Soon after the season started, Keith Hill added Tom Kennedy (again) and another former Barnsley player Stephen Dawson to his squad and took Jack O'Connell on loan for a second time.

All the first three games of 2014-15 ended in defeat and the game at Chesterfield – when all three goals came from the penalty spot - also cost Dale the services of Matty Lund with a dislocated shoulder and Josh Lillis with an ankle injury, 16 year old scholar Johnny Diba Musungu having to make his debut as his replacement. Dale quickly signed up experienced Leicester reserve 'keeper Conrad Logan as cover for Lillis.

To try to solve the goal shortage, Matt Done was switched to play as a central striker for the first time in his career and the gamble paid off handsomely with a hat-trick in a 5-2 demolition of Crewe at Gresty Road. They would also have beaten title favourites and eventual champions Bristol City but for a remarkable save by former loanee Frank Fielding from Ian Henderson.

They did record another victory at Crewe in the JPT and won 4-0 at Crawley, but home form remained indifferent until a 4-0 success against Walsall. Victories in the next two games as well – coming from behind to win 3-2 at Orient with only ten men after Logan saved a penalty from former Dale striker Chris Dagnall - moved Dale up to 5th. One point accrued from the next two home games but victories at Swindon – Bastien Hery netting the stoppage time winner - and at Yeovil (their sixth in seven games on the road) emphasised the disparity in home and away form. However, they did then trounce ultimately promoted Preston 3-0 at Spotland. Home comforts were in the news, too, a BBC survey showing that a day out at Spotland was the best value anywhere in Leagues 1 and 2.

With a number of injuries and Henderson sent off, Dale were happy to take League 2 Northampton to an FA Cup replay which was won with two last gasp goals at Spotland (though in front of a crowd of just 1717). Scorer of the first was loan signing Reuben Noble-Lazarus, famous for having made his Barnsley debut at the age of just 15. With a virus sweeping through the camp, the second round tie against Aldershot followed the same pattern, Dale having Logan to thank for a string of saves in the first match, though the replay was much more decisive this time, with Done netting a hat-trick in a 4-0 win. (The youth cup team did even better, beating Nantwich 9-0 with Billy Hasler-Cregg netting four and Nyal Bell three.

Despite three further home defeats, including a depressing 0-3 scoreline against neighbours Oldham, when the attendance was 7269, a 4-1 success at Colchester, with centre back O'Connell netting for the third time in seven league games, kept Dale in an excellent 8th place at the half way point of the season. Matt Lund received personal recognition, with his first call-up for the senior N. Ireland squad, but then suffered a repeat of his shoulder injury and missed virtually all of the remainder of the campaign. Conrad Logan, who had made a big impression since his arrival, was injured against Notts County and he, too, was ruled out for the season. (Indeed, his next match was for Hibs in the Scottish Cup semi-final 14 months later). County also scored a highly controversial equaliser in the sixth minute of an announced four minutes of stoppage time, while the returning Lillis was laid out in the penalty area after an unpenalised challenge.

The other half of Nottingham fared less well when they turned up at Spotland in the third round of the cup. Already under pressure after a poor run in the Championship, Forest went the same way as Leeds a year earlier, Peter Vincenti's early penalty settling the tie. Particularly pleasing for the Dale management team was the fact that six of the squad had featured in Chris Beech's youth team in the FA Youth Cup three years before, including Callum Camps who made his full debut. Following time honoured tradition, Forest boss Stuart Pearce lost his job shortly afterwards. In the fourth round, Dale met Stoke and after fans spent the weekend clearing the pitch of snow ahead of the televised game on the Monday, Premier League class told in a 4-1 victory for the Potters, despite a brave performance from Dale, Rhys Bennett netting their goal.

In the league, Dale's form picked up again with seven points from three games, Dale again netting four against Crawley. Calvin Andrew recorded a first for Rochdale when he scored when coming on as substitute in three consecutive league games, including a winner deep into injury time at Bradford. Dale's first goal had come in a slightly odd manner, when Henderson's penalty came back off the woodwork and he had the presence of mind to duck out of the way to allow Vincenti behind him to convert the rebound.

At the end of January, Matt Done, scorer of 14 goals by this point, was transferred to fellow League 1 (but considerably wealthier) Sheffield United for an undisclosed fee (possibly around £700,000). Oddly, O'Connell returned to Blackburn to be sold to Brentford, but the latter then loaned him to Dale again.

Dale lost four of their next five games (they were actually 15th at this point, six points above the relegation places, though with games in hand), but starting with another hammering of Crewe – the 4-0 scoreline making it 12-2 on aggregate over the season - they bounced back with four wins out of five to regain their 8th spot and reach the 50 point mark with still 11 games to go. Henderson had taken over the main striking role from Done and netted five times in the five games.

Dale subsequently hovered just outside the play-off places, goals from defenders Bennett and O'Connell beating Yeovil and Calvin Andrew netting another last gasp winner against Port Vale, but on the other side Dale again going down 3-0 against Oldham, when four players had to go off injured. In fact, they still had an outside chance of making the play-offs until the penultimate game, but actually lost four of the final five matches. Dale had two players sent off at Gillingham including Lund in his first game back after his injury, while Barnsley remarkably netted five times in the last half hour of the season.

Nevertheless, Dale finished in 8th spot, their best ever in the third tier since the old northern and southern sections were merged. They won 19 games, notably 16 of them after scoring first, while conversely conceding first in 20 of their 21 defeats. Reversing the form from the first half of the season, they had won eight of the last eleven home games. In all, 31 players appeared in the league side, injuries and illness meaning that only Ian Henderson and Ashley Eastham, now a regular at centre back, topped 40 league appearances. On the other hand, this had allowed Keith Hill to introduce youngsters like Scott Tanser, Callum Camps and Andy Cannon into the side. Calvin Andrew came on as substitute no fewer than 34 times in all games, netting 6 goals in the process. Top scorer was Henderson with 22 while Peter Vincenti and Matt Done had 16 and 14 to their credit, the latter in the space of 23 games. Henderson and Done (including goals for Sheffield United) were the division's joint third highest scorers. Remarkably, the side scored more goals (72) in League 1 than when winning promotion in League 2 the year before and hit four or more in a game seven times. Keith Hill's "no fear" football had resulted in the fifth most wins and fifth most goals in the division, and there were more goals in total in Dale's games than in those of anyone else apart from MK Dons (who netted over 100 of their own). Average home gates were a respectable 3309, but still exceeded only those of Crawley and were dwarfed by those of the likes of Sheffield United (19,805)

Unsurprisingly Ian Henderson was the player of the year and Peter Vincenti was club man of the year. At a Football League awards evening kitman Jack Northover was deservedly recognised as an official 'club legend'. Away from the playing side, chairman Chris Dunphy and chief executive Colin Garlick received long service awards from the FL for 21 years involvement in the game.

Elsewhere, Will Buckley had appeared in the Premier League for Sunderland, making it seven ex-Dale players in the top flight in the last five seasons, following Matt Gilks, Grant Holt, Craig Dawson, Rickie Lambert, Adam Le Fondre and Glenn Murray.

Keith Hill managed to retain all his regulars apart from Stephen Dawson, who opted to join Scunthorpe, and there was correspondingly little in the way of incoming transfers, experienced defender Jim McNulty from Bury and midfield man Donal McDermott from Ramsbottom United, getting a second chance at league level, being the main additions. Nineteen year old Jamie Allen was named as club captain.

Dale opened up the league campaign with victory over Peterborough, Callum Camps becoming their youngest scorer of the season's first goal. They also beat Coventry in a cup yet again when they removed them from the League Cup on penalties after a stunning first goal for McDermott and completed an excellent week by winning at Blackpool. However, the next six games produced only one victory, 3-0 against Barnsley, and saw Dale knocked out of the League Cup by Championship side Hull. Current and ex-Dale 'keepers Josh Lillis and Tommy Lee were the stars in a goalless game at Chesterfield, while Henderson had his stoppage time penalty saved in a draw at Fleetwood.

The reserves figured in the Lancashire Cup Final, delayed from the end of the previous season but were beaten by Bury, while in a perhaps even more extreme version of the then unknown Beckham and company playing against Dale in the Lancashire Cup, Marcus Rashford made his debut from the bench for United's second string against Dale reserves in the same competition, before ending the season scoring for England.

Further home victories over Scunthorpe and Shrewsbury, League 1 player of the month Peter Vincenti scoring in each during a run of seven goals in eight games, kept Dale in the leading pack with 17 points from ten games. They twice pegged back Sheffield United, only to lose 3-2 in front of a 19,000 crowd, and followed this up with four draws, the first three all 0-0 (the first time they had had such a run for 43 years) and the fourth after being two-down at Southend.

In the FA Cup, new signing Nathaniel Mendez-Laing notched a hat-trick as Swindon were easily dispatched and in the league Dale alternated wins and defeats, losing tamely in front of the Sky cameras against eventual champions Wigan, but securing their first away victory since August at Doncaster. A 0-1 defeat to local rivals Bury in the cup (continuing Dale's poor run in televised games, this time by BT) meant that Dale had failed to score in seven of the last eleven games.

Nonetheless, Dale had had an impressive home record over the past year, winning 14 out of 22 home league games and picking up 67% of the available points, the 5th best in the whole Football League.

Seven points from three league games moved Dale back up to ninth in the table after a remarkable 3-0 victory away to leaders Walsall in the first game of 2016, but results continued to bounce from one extreme to another. Barnsley netted five second half goals for the second year in succession to win 6-1, Dale then beat new leaders Burton Albion, Henderson netting for the fifth time in six games, but lost to next to bottom side Crewe.

They also lost the next game and threw way an early two goal lead in the return with Crewe to sink to 16th, after picking up just 21 points from the previous 20 games. The signing of Niall Canavan on loan from Scunthorpe to partner the recalled Ashley Eastham brought about more defensive stability but it was the surprise re-signing on a short contract of ex-Premier League star Grant Holt, a decade after he left Spotland, which rejuvenated both the side and the supporters.

Two goals from the recalled Joe Bunney earned a point at Bradford and he also netted the winner against Fleetwood. Despite defeat by strugglers Shrewsbury, Dale beat two of the 'big' clubs of the division in Sheffield United – Holt netting after a record gap of 10 years between Dale goals - and Coventry, before a brilliant week at the end of March. Dale overran Bury 3-0 on the Saturday and defeated their other closest neighbours Oldham 3-2 the following weekend in Keith Hill's 400th game in charge.

However, the even bigger news came out on the Thursday in between, when it was announced that the deal for the football club to buy all the remaining shares in the stadium company (valued at around £690,000) had finally been completed, giving Dale full control over the ground, with Hornets as guaranteed tenants. The club accounts, released at the end of March, showed that a loss of £65,000 in the year to April 2014 had been turned into a £1.4M profit in 2015, thanks to the transfers of Scott Hogan and Matt Done. Overall turnover had increased from £3M in League 2 to £5M in League 1.

Dale despatched Southend 4-1 to move above them into 8th spot, but a red card for Henderson for retaliation after a crunching challenge left Dale an uphill task at champions-to-be Wigan, the home side hardly deserving their eventual 1-0 win. Niall Canavan rescued a point with a 96th minute goal against Doncaster as the latter slid towards relegation and two further victories kept alive Dale's outside chance of a play-off place with three games to go. A 4-1 defeat at Port Vale all but ended them, though, and Dale had to come from two-down to draw with nine man Swindon after Henderson had his penalty saved by their 17 year old debutant 'keeper.

They did sign off with a victory, Calvin Andrew curling the final goal of the season into the top corner of Colchester's goal to give them a best ever third tier points tally of 69, though in 10th place. Indeed, this was the first season in which they had won more games (19) than they lost (15) at this level. Jim McNulty played in every game, but player of the year Josh Lillis was the only other to figure in 40 league games. By and large, the manager stuck to the same squad of players through the season, though, 18 of them starting at least 10 times including 13 of the 14 players who appeared on the opening day. Top scorer was again Ian Henderson, with 13, while Nathaniel Mendez-Laing's FA Cup treble gave him a total of 10 for the season.

The long serving Rose, Bennett and Kennedy – with some 400 Dale league games between them - were among those released at the end of the season, while Eastham and Lancashire also decided to move on, but Canavan's loan was made permanent as preparations began for a third consecutive season in League 1.

NOTES TO WHO'S WHO

In the following section, players are listed in the order of their first inclusion in Rochdale's senior squad for a competitive match. An alphabetical table of the players, with the seasons played and appearances and goals in the various competitions is appended. Games counted for these purposes are the Football League (and play-offs), the FA Cup, the Football League Cup (under its various sponsors' names) and the Football League Trophy (aka, in the seasons relevant here, the Auto Windscreens Shield, LDV Vans Trophy and Johnstone's Paint Trophy). 'Other' games include the summer Isle of Man tournament in 2002 and the most recent pre-season Charity Rose Bowl games against Oldham Athletic between 2003 and 2007.

In the individual players' career details, FL appearances for any club are given in square brackets. In addition, Scottish League appearances are denoted ScL, those in the top level of the non-league game (currently the National League) by 'Conf' and appearances in Major League Soccer in the USA as MLS. Details related to the 'new' League Divisions 1, 2 and 3 after the renumbering in 1992-93 (and prior to the creation of the Championship, League 1 and League 2) are labelled Division 1+ etc. A £ sign indicates that a fee was paid for the player's transfer but the amount was undisclosed. Under 'Honours', players or managers who were with a club at some point during a season when promotion or a championship was won, but had moved on before the end of the season, have the relevant honour in brackets, as do players who were unused substitutes in a cup final etc. Probable but unconfirmed details are in curly brackets. In a few cases where exact dates of birth are not known, JFM signifies the first quarter of the year (January, February, March) and so on. An asterisk denotes that a player was still with his last named club as of the end of 2015-16 and if relevant may add to the appearances given.

Duncan Wayne Evans 1999-2005

Born: Abermule 25.8.71
5'10" 12st5
Right back
FL Apps/Gls 259/3
Total Apps/Gls 299/4
Career: Welshpool HS,
Welshpool, Walsall
13.8.93 [173+10/1], Dale
7.99 [259/3],
Kidderminster H. cs.05
[13/- Conf], TNS coach
2005-06, (USA coaching
12.05 to 5.06),
Welshpool player-coach
1.07, Valley District Soccer Association (Canada)
technical director 5.07, Alberta Soccer Association
(Canada) player development manager 3.09,
Shrewsbury T. centre of excellence manager 12.09,
academy manager 10.11 to 11.13 (also Newtown
1.11), Harbour City (Nanaimo, Canada) head coach
7.14*
Honours: Division 3+ promotion 1995, Division 2+
promotion 1999

Welsh full back Wayne had spent six years with
Walsall, accumulating around 200 senior
appearances and twice playing in promotion
winning sides, when he became one of Steve
Parkin's first signings for Dale in the summer of
1999. An automatic choice in the defence, in front
of compatriot Neil Edwards, in the sides which
twice came close to the play-offs before finally
claiming fifth place under John Hollins, Wayne is
frequently cited by Dale fans as their best right
back of recent times. He missed only a handful of
games in his six years with the club, ending just
short of 300 games due to two unfortunate red
cards in his final season. A UEFA 'A' licence
holder, he coached in Canada as well as becoming
Academy boss at Shrewsbury.

David John (Dave) Flitcroft

1999-2003, 2006-2011
Born: Bolton 14.1.74
5'11" 13st5
Midfield
FL Apps/Gls 141+20/4
Total Apps/Gls
164+28/4
Career: Preston NE jnr
1988, yts 1990, pro
2.5.92 [4+4/2], Lincoln
C. 17.9.93 [2/-], Chester
9.12.93 [146+21/18],
Dale 5.7.99 [141+19/4], Macclesfield T. 11.7.03
[14+1/-], Bury 30.1.04 [95+5/4], Hyde U. 11.06,
Dale player-assistant manager 1.07 [+1/-],
Barnsley assistant manager 1.6.11, caretaker
manager 12.12, manager 13.1.13 to 30.11.13, Bury
manager 9.12.13*

Honours: Division 3+ promotion 1994. As
coach/manager: League 2 play-off final 2008,
promotion 2010, 2015

Brother of Blackburn's Gary, Dave was a tough
tackling midfielder who later went on to play his
part in the "Hillcroft" revolution which took Dale
into League 1. Having few opportunities at
Preston, despite scoring in his first start in 1992,
he spent nearly six years at Chester, assisting them
to promotion in his first campaign. One of Steve
Parkin's first signings, he announced himself as
something of a 'character' by rugby tackling the
Cheltenham mascot prior to their inaugural game
in the FL! He figured in the sides which just
missed and then made the play-offs, and was one
of the few players to prosper in 2002-03 – Dale
arranging a match when they would be missing
three other players in order that Dave's suspension
would not keep him out of the Wolves cup tie.
Disappointingly allowed to leave that summer,
after being voted player of the year, he
subsequently completed another century of
appearances at Bury but was playing for Hyde
United when former team-mate Keith Hill
recruited him as his number two back at Spotland.
'Flicker' played an important part in turning Dale
from strugglers to one of the best sides in League
2, reaching Wembley and then earning promotion
in 2010. He moved with Hill to Barnsley and took
over as manager when Hill was sacked. Despite
keeping them up, he too was sacked after a year,
immediately taking over at Bury who he took to
promotion in 2015.

Tony Ford MBE 1999-2002

Born: Grimsby 14.5.59
5'10" 13st
Midfield/wing back
FL Apps/Gls 81+8/6
Total Apps/Gls 95+9/7
Career: Wintringham
GS, Grimsby T. app
1975, pro 1.5.77
[321+34/55],
Sunderland loan 27.3.86
[8+1/1], Stoke C. 8.7.86
£35,000 [112/13], West
Bromwich A. 24.3.89
£145,000 [114/14], Grimsby T. 21.11.91 £50,000
[59+9/3], Bradford C. loan 16.9.93 [5/-],
Scunthorpe U. 2.8.94 [73+3/9], Barrow cs.96,
Mansfield T. player-assistant manager 25.10.96
[97+6/7], Dale player-assistant manager 7.99
[81+8/6], Barnsley assistant manager 11.01 to
2002-03, Dale assistant manager 6.03 to 12.06.
Grimsby T. scout
Honours: England 'B' (2 caps) 1989, Division 4
promotion 1979, Division 3 champions 1980, FL
Group Cup winners 1982, PFA Merit Award 1999

While with Dale, Tony became the first outfield player to make 1000 senior appearances, ending on 931 FL games and a grand total of 1072, even without his appearances for Barrow in the NPL. For good measure, he also scored 108 FL goals and was awarded the PFA Merit Award and then an MBE for services to football in 2000. He started out with Grimsby as a 16 year old, assisting the Mariners to rise from the fourth to second divisions in successive seasons, missing only one game and netting 15 goals, including a hat-trick against Bradford City, in their first promotion campaign when still only 19. Twice voted player of the year, he played more than 350 games, primarily as a winger but also in central positions, before moves to fellow second division sides Stoke and West Brom, where he made his two England 'B' appearances at the age of 30. Returning to Grimsby, he appeared to be winding down his career with a spell at Scunthorpe and then joining non-league Barrow, but former Stoke team-mate Steve Parkin recruited him as his number two when he became Mansfield boss. The pair moved on to Spotland in 1999 and Tony continued to play regularly, making over 100 appearances either on the right of midfield or at wing back until finally closing his league career at the age of 42 when he and Parkin took over as the management team at Barnsley. When he played against Kidderminster, it gave him another remarkable record in having played on 100 FL grounds. He reappeared at Spotland as assistant manager during the short reign of his former Grimsby boss Alan Buckley, and stayed on when Steve Parkin returned for his second spell in charge, even playing for the reserves again in 2004. His son Josh played for Crewe and Shropshire Boys and was a junior with Dale reserves from 2000 to 2003. A biography "The Tony Ford Story" was published in 2005.

Clive Linton Platt 1999-2003

Born: Wolverhampton 27.10.77 6'4" 13st
Striker
FL Apps/Gls 151+18/30 Total Apps/Gls 178+18/37
Career: Walsall yts 1995, pro 25.7.96 [18+14/4], Dale loan 5.8.99, signed 8.9.99 £100,000 [151+18/30], Notts Co. 7.8.03 [19/3],
Peterborough U. 7.1.04 [35+2/6], Milton Keynes Dons 13.1.05 [91+11/27], Colchester U. 12.7.07 £300,000 [109+16/25], Coventry C. 29.7.10 [45+22/7], Northampton T. 25.5.12 [32+15/12], Bury 24.1.14 [8+11/2], retired injured 10.14
Honours: Division 2+ promotion 1999, League 2 play-off final 2013, (promotion 2015)

Clive arrived at Spotland on loan from Walsall on the eve of the 1999-2000, the first in which Dale used squad numbers, taking the number 21 shirt, and was soon signed for Dale's first six figure fee. A classic target man, rather than prolific scorer, he was a key figure as the side made successive bids for promotion under Steve Parkin. Unfortunately, when Dale did reach the play-offs for the first time in 2002, he was injured in the first leg and Dale went out on aggregate to Rushden & Diamonds. After almost 200 games he left for Notts County, but really made his mark at MK Dons with 18 goals in 2006-07 (including a hat-trick against Barnet) when they missed promotion by one point. He moved up to the championship for the first time when almost 30 and in his last full season, finally made it to Wembley with Northampton. Notably, he scored for them against Rochdale in 2013, 14 years after scoring for the Dale against the Cobblers. Finishing at Bury under former Dale team-mate Dave Flitcroft, after 110 goals in 617 FL games, Clive subsequently worked as a financial advisor to other players.

Steven Michael (Steve) Lenagh 1999-2000
Born: Durham 21.3.79 5'11" 10st9
Central defender
FL Apps/Gls +0/0 Total Apps/Gls +0/0
Career: Sheffield W. yts 1996, Chesterfield 3.11.97 [6+7/1], Dale 6.7.99, Kettering 8.00 [11+8/2 Conf], Kings Lynn loan 2000-01, Hucknall T. cs.02, Leek T. 3.03, Gresley 9.03 to 3.04

Steve was signed by Dale after a handful of appearances for Chesterfield, where he had figured mostly as a stand-in up front, though he was really a centre back. He played in the friendly victory at Berwick, but due to a long term injury did not progress beyond four games on the bench as Messrs Hill, Monington and Bayliss shared the central defensive duties. Steve later made some appearances at Conference level and was subsequently in the police force.

Julian Whytus Lennox Dowe 1999-2000
Born: Manchester 9.9.75 6'2" 12st5
Striker
FL Apps/Gls 1+6/0 Total Apps/Gls 2+7/1
Career: Everton jnr, Leeds U. jnr, Manchester C. jnr, Wigan A. yts 9.91, pro 17.9.92, Atletico Marbella (Spain) 1.7.94, Ayr U. 25.11.94 [4+3/1 ScL], Tidaholm (Sweden) summer 1995, Woking 8.95 [1+2/- Conf], Hyde U. 1995-96. Colne Dynamoes 1998-99, Dale 27.8.99 [1+6/-], Burton A. loan 2.12.99 to 4.1.00, Cardiff C. trial 8.00, Morecambe 12.00 [7/- Conf], Ventspils (Latvia), Carlisle U. trial, Oldham T., Bacup Borough 10.01, Hyde U. 2002-03, New Mills 2003-04
Honours: Trafford Schoolboys, Ayrshire Cup winners 1995

Julian had a somewhat eccentric playing career after heading off to play in Spain at the age of 18, when he didn't break into the Wigan side despite being a regular scorer for the youth and reserve sides. He then appeared in the Scottish League, in Sweden and at various levels of non-league football as well as having two years out of the game working as a personal trainer. Picked up by Dale early in 1999-2000, he had a run of games on the bench and started twice up front when Dale went seven games without a goal, helping to end the drought when he came on to net Dale's third in the cup replay against Burton, subsequently being loaned to the Brewers. Resuming his travels, he figured in Latvia and Bacup amongst other places, and later ran coaching web sites.

Damon Peter Searle 1999-2000

Born: Cardiff 26.10.71
5'11" 10st4
Left back
FL Apps/Gls 13+1/0
Total Apps/Gls 13+1/0
Career: Cardiff C. yts 1988, pro 20.8.90 [232+2/3], Stockport Co. 28.5.96 [34+7/-], Carlisle U. 6.7.98 [57+9/3], Dale loan 17.9.99 to 19.12.99 [13+1/-], Southend U. 10.7.00 [126+7/3], Colchester U. trial cs.03, York C. trial cs.03, Chesterfield 15.8.03 [4+1/-], Forest Green Rovers 10.03 [31/4 Conf], Hornchurch 2004, Forest Green Rovers 11.04 [63/2 Conf], Newport Co. 2006-07, Carmarthen 7.08, Barry T. 2.09, Haverfordwest County 8.09, (also Cadoxton Imps coach 1.10), Barry T. 1.10, Haverfordwest County 11.10, Barry Town U. player-assistant manager 7.11*
Honours: Wales Schools, Wales youth international, Wales under-21s (6 caps), Wales 'B', Wales semi-pro 2006, Four Nations champions 2006, Welsh Cup winners 1992, 1993, FAW Premier Cup final 2007, winners 2008, Division 3+ champions 1993, Division 2+ promotion 1997, PFA Division 3 team of the year 1993, Welsh League division 3 champions 2014, Welsh League division 2 champions 2015

A Welsh international at various levels up to the under-21s and Wales 'B', Damon was a Cardiff regular for six seasons at the start of his career. He assisted them to two Welsh Cup wins and to the championship of Division 3 in 1993, when he was voted into the PFA team of the year. While with Carlisle he played in the famous 'Jimmy Glass game' when the 'keeper scored a last gasp goal to keep the Cumbrians in the league. He then had a lengthy loan spell at Spotland, figuring regularly at left back, but Dale were unable to arrange his permanent signing and he subsequently joined Southend, appearing well over 100 times. He had a successful spell with Forest Green Rovers, also appearing for the Welsh semi-pro side which won the Four Nations championship in 2006. Later with various Welsh non-league clubs, winning the FAW Premier Cup with Newport, he was still playing in his forties – winning Welsh League divisional titles with the resurrected Barry Town United in 2014 and 2015 - while coaching junior sides and working for Cardiff City's commercial department.

Richard Edward Green 1999-2000, 2001-02

Born: Wolverhampton 22.11.67 6'1" 13st7
Central defender
FL Apps/Gls 6/0
Total Apps/Gls 6/0
Career: Shrewsbury T. yts 1985, pro 19.7.86 [120+5/5], Swindon T. 25.10.90, Gillingham 6.3.92 [206+10/16], Walsall 10.8.98 [22+8/1], Dale loan 24.9.99 to 25.10.99 [6/-], Northampton T. 7.1.00 [55+4/2], Dale 7.01, retired injured 2001-02
Honours: Division 3+ promotion 1996, 2000, Division 2+ promotion 1999

Richard was an experienced lower league defender with well over 300 games to his credit, mostly for Shrewsbury and Gillingham when Dale borrowed him in the injury absence of Dave Bayliss. While with the Gills, he had figured at centre back and right back in a defence so solid – with just 20 goals against - that they finished 2nd despite scoring only 49 goals themselves, and he had also been in the Walsall side promoted in 1999. Dale conceded only three goals in the six games he played, but only scored one and a new striker became more of a priority. He joined Northampton in time to assist their promotion run and a year later, Steve Parkin did sign him, but he never managed a first team appearance due to a pre-season injury. Earlier in his career he had been out for a year with a chronic back problem, but his then Swindon manager Glenn Hoddle sent him to his famous faith healer Ellen Drewery.

Scott Wilson 1997-2000
Born: Farnworth 25.10.80 5'7" 9st8
Midfield
FL Apps/Gls +1/0 Total Apps/Gls +1/0
Career: St James School (Bolton), Dale as 1995, yts 5.97, pro 6.99 [+1/-], Altrincham loan 15.1.00 [3+2/- Conf], Radcliffe Borough cs.00, Rossendale U. 5.03, Radcliffe Borough 7.04 to 12.07
Honours: Bolton Boys, Manchester County under-16s, Northern Premier League division 1 promotion 2003

Scott played for Dale's under-14 side, progressing to be a youth team regular from 1997-98. He played in midfield in the friendly at Berwick after signing pro in 1999, and after recovering from a broken elbow and appearing on loan for Altrincham, made his sole FL appearance as substitute against Barnet in the final game of that season. He subsequently had a very long spell at Radcliffe Borough (playing in the 9-0 friendly defeat by Dale in 2003).

Warren Peyton 1999-2001
Born: Manchester 13.12.79 5'10" 10st9
Midfield
FL Apps/Gls 1/0 Total Apps/Gls 1/0
Career: Bolton W. jnr, Morecambe, Dale trial 25.10.99, pro 8.1.00 [1/-], Bury 18.9.00 [+1/-], Nuneaton Borough 6.7.01 [37+7/9 Conf], Doncaster R. 14.12.02 [4+2/- Conf], Leigh RMI 3.8.03 to 31.5.05 [57+11/3 Conf], Altrincham 11.11.05 [128+25/8 Conf], Stalybridge Celtic cs.09, Guiseley 6.10, Droylsden 8.11 to cs.12
Honours: England semi-pro international 2001-02, Conference promotion 2003, NPL play-off final 2011

After a trial earlier in the season, when he was an unused substitute in the cup tie at Burton, Warren signed a short term contract with Dale and replaced the injured Jason Peake in midfield for the victory against York in January 2000. Subsequently having to have an appendix operation, he did figure in a pre-season game but then signed for Bury, playing an 'international' against Pakistan as well as making one substitute appearance in the league. While at Nuneaton he became a non-league international and he was later a regular at Altrincham for some years, also working as a bricklayer rebuilding Altrincham's ground. He scored in Guiseley's NPL play-off semi-final in 2011.

Anthony Joseph (Tony) Ellis 1999-2001

Born: Salford 20.10.64
5'11" 11st
Striker
FL Apps/Gls 55+4/17
Total Apps/Gls 62+6/18
Career: Horwich RMI 1985-86, Oldham A. 22.8.86 [5+3/-], Preston NE 16.10.87 £23,000 [80+6/26], Stoke C. 20.12.89 £250,000 [66+11/19], Preston NE 14.8.92 £140,000 (including G. Shaw) [70+2/48], Blackpool 25.7.94 £165,000 [140+6/54], Bury 12.12.97 £75,000 [24+14/8], Stockport Co. 3.2.99 £25,000 [17+3/6], Dale 1.11.99 [55+4/17], Burnley 20.7.01 [+11/1], (Australia 2002), Leigh RMI 2002-03, Mossley 2002-03, Hyde U. player-assistant manager 2002-03, (also Burnley under-15s coach), Dale youth team manager 6.07, centre of excellence manager*
Honours: Lancashire Cup final 1988-89, winners 1994-95, 1995-96, Division 3+ play-off final 1994

Starting out with Horwich RMI, playing alongside Dale old boy Brian Hart, Tony was signed by Oldham when he was 21. He soon moved on to Preston for the first of two productive spells which saw him net 74 league goals in only 158 game, with a best of 26 in 1993-94 and four hat-tricks. In between, the striker had had a big money move to Stoke and he later had another to Blackpool, scoring another 50 goals. Working his way around the north west, he arrived at Spotland when he was 35 to boost an attack that had scored only twice in 10 games. A regular for the rest of the season, partnering either Clive Platt or Graham Lancashire, he top scored with 11 goals and a year later had a surprise last run in the first division at Burnley finishing with a tremendous 210 senior goals in 609 games. After a move to Australia was ruined by a knee injury, he became player-assistant manager at Hyde, scoring four times in an FA Cup tie and netting in his last match when he was 40. He also coached Burnley's juniors before joining up with former team-mates Keith Hill and Dave Flitcroft as Dale's highly successful director of youth development.

Christopher John (Chris) Bettney 1999-2000

Born: Chesterfield 27.10.77
5'10" 11st4
Winger
FL Apps/Gls 12+12/0
Total Apps/Gls 15+15/0
Career: Sheffield U. as 1992, yts 1994, pro 15.5.96 [+1/-], Hull C. loan 26.9.97 [28+2/1], Chesterfield 3.7.99 [7+6/3], Dale 5.11.99 [12+12/-], Macclesfield T. trial 7.00 [+2/-], Worksop T. 10.10.00, Staveley Miners Welfare, South Normanton, Ilkeston T. 1.02, Alfreton T. 12.7.02, Harrogate T. 21.7.06, Bradford PA 11.6.08, Retford T. 28.12.08, Worksop T. 5.10, Matlock T. 6.11, Staveley 8.12, Stocksbridge Park Steels 10.12, (also AFC Walton player-manager 10.11, AFC Whitecotes 2.12, player-manager 11.12, FC Britania 8.14; Chesterfield Sunday League), Brigg T. 1.15, Rainworth MW 2.15, Heanor T. 8.15*

Chris came through the junior ranks at Sheffield United but made only a single substitute appearance for the first team, gaining most of his senior experience while on loan at Hull. After a brief spell at Chesterfield he joined Dale, figuring as a skilful winger in most of the remaining games that season, though often starting on the bench. He has subsequently had a very extensive career in the non-league game.

Paul Richard Gibson 1999-2000

Born: Sheffield 1.11.76
6'3" 13st
Goalkeeper
FL Apps 5
Total Apps 5
Career: Manchester U. as 1990, yts 1993, pro 1.7.95, Halifax T. loan 10.96 [3 Conf], Mansfield T. loan 20.10.97 [13], Hull C. loan 6.11.98 [4/-], Notts Co. 25.3.99 [11], Dale loan 4.2.00 to 4.3.00 [5], Northwich Victoria 8.01 [54 Conf], Droylsden 10.02, Witton A. 12.02, New Saints/TNS 7.04, Witton A. 2005 to 2008
Honours: FA Youth Cup 1995

Paul spent almost ten years at Old Trafford, working his way through the youth sides – winning the Youth Cup in 1995 - to figure in one first team game, playing the second half of Brian McClair's testimonial in front of a crowd of 67000. His FL career spanned just 33 games, five of them during a month's loan at Spotland when he stood in for the injured Neil Edwards. The first two games

were won, but his last ended 4-1 to Darlington and Steve Parkin decided to give reserve keeper Phil Priestley a chance instead. After leaving Notts County, Paul moved on to a lengthy non-league career – he was everpresent for Northwich in his first season - and became a PE teacher at Marlborough School.

Sean McAuley 1999-2002

Born: Sheffield 23.6.72 5'11" 11st12
Left back
FL Apps/Gls 34+3/0
Total Apps/Gls 41+4/0
Career: Manchester U. yts 7.88, pro 21.6.90, Sheffield U. trial, St Johnstone £80,000 22.4.92 [59+3/- ScL], Chesterfield loan 4.11.94 [1/1], Hartlepool 21.7.95 [84/1], Scunthorpe U. 26.3.97 [63+6/1], Scarborough loan 25.3.99 [6+1/-], Dale 11.2.00 [34+3/-], Portland Timbers (USA) player-coach 4.02, Halifax T. 8.02 [17+8/-], player-coach, assistant manager cs.04 to 6.05, Sheffield W. academy manager 1.06, caretaker manager 10.06 and 12.09 (also Victoria Highlanders, Canada coach 4.09), Portland Timbers assistant manager 7.12*
Honours: Sheffield City Select, Scotland youth international, Scotland under-21s v Poland 1993, Division 3+ promotion (1995), 1999. As coach: MLS Western Conference winners 2013, MLS Western Conference play-off winners 2015, MLS Cup winners 2015

Another former Manchester United trainee, Sean first played senior football with St. Johnstone, also being selected for the Scottish under-21s. Returning to England he was a regular for Hartlepool, but less so at Scunthorpe before joining Dale. Losing the left back slot to Lee Todd in his second season, he reappeared when Todd was injured in 2001-02, but then missed the latter stages of the season injured himself, and was not retained. At Halifax he moved up from player to assistant manager and later took on the academy manager role at Hillsborough, twice acting as Wednesday's caretaker manager over the next few years. He was suggested as a possible Dale manager before Steve Eyre was appointed. He then returned to Portland Timbers (where he had earlier been a player), as their assistant coach, as they enjoyed a very successful spell in the MLS.

Matthew (Matt) Gilks 1998-2007

Born: Oldham
4.6.82
6'1" 12st7
Goalkeeper
FL Apps 174+2
Total Apps 197+2
Career: Firbank
School, North
Chadderton HS,
Heyside Juniors
1992, Dale as
1996, yts 7.98,
pro 4.7.01
[174+2], Norwich
C. 27.6.07,
Blackpool 21.7.08
[181+1],
Shrewsbury T.
loan 21.11.08 [4], Burnley 7.14, Rangers 6.16*
Honours: Oldham Town under-15s, North West Schools, Championship play-off winners 2010, final 2012, (champions 2016), Scotland (3 caps) 2012 to 2013

Originally a central defender, Matt had only been playing in goal for a year when he was selected for Dale's under-14s and a couple of years later was in the youth cup side. He was substitute goalkeeper for the first time in March 2000 in the FRT game in which Tony Ford made his 1000th appearance. Taking over from Phil Priestley as second string, he made his debut a year later when Neil Edwards was suspended. With Edwards injured, Matt became a regular choice in the first part of 2001-02, before Dale borrowed the more experienced Hahnemann and Banks. Matt remained Edwards' number two until finally taking over in the latter part of 2004-05 and playing in 122 consecutive FL games. Out of contract, he joined Norwich in 2007, but failed to make their first team and moved on to Blackpool. He gained a regular place during 2009-10, appearing in their play-off final success which took them into the Premier League. He was absent from half of their campaign in the top flight due to a knee injury but missed only five games in three years back down in the Championship, being their player of the year in 2013-14. Matt had also made his debut for Scotland in 2012, qualifying via his Scottish grandmother. In 2014 he moved to newly promoted Burnley, becoming understudy to former Dale loanee Tom Heaton, playing in just a couple of cup ties over the next two years.

Sean Patrick McClare 1999-2000, 2003-04

Born: Rotherham
12.1.78 5'10"
11st12
Midfield
FL Apps/Gls
38+9/0
Total Apps/Gls
42+9/0
Career: Barnsley as
1992, yts 1994, pro
3.7.96 [29+21/6],
Dale loan 22.3.00 to
5.00 [5+4/-], Port
Vale loan 20.10.01,
signed 12.01
[28+12/1], Dale
24.7.03 [33+5/-],
Drogheda cs.04, Halifax T. 2.05 [1/- Conf], Bradford PA 3.05, Stirling A. 2005-06 [2+1/- ScL], Scarborough 11.11.05 [6+9/- Conf], Grantham T. 8.06 to 1.07
Honours: Republic of Ireland under-21s (3 caps)

Sean first played for Dale on loan from Barnsley in the latter stages of 1999-2000 when they fell just short of the play-off places, and reappeared three years later when signed by Alan Buckley after a stint at Port Vale. Dale suffered a mid season slump and though Sean continued to play quite regularly in midfield he was released by Steve Parkin and went to play in Ireland. (Though born in Rotherham, he had earlier played for the Republic's under-21 side). He also played in the Scottish League with Stirling Albion and at one time worked at a soccer camp in Denver.

Daniel John (Danny) Taylor 1998-2001
Born: Oldham 28.7.82 6'0" 11st10
Left back
FL Apps/Gls +1/0 Total Apps/Gls +1/0
Career: St Hugh's School, Breezehill, Oldham A. as 1994, Boundary Park Juniors, Dale as 1997-98, yts 1998 to 2001 [+1/-]. Royton T. 2002-03 to 2008-09, Rochdale T. 2009 to 2010, (+ North Star FC 2010-11; Sunday League)
Honours: Oldham Town under-11, under-15

Danny played in Dale's 'A' team as a schoolboy in 1997-98 and figured in the youth team and reserves at left back or on the left wing before appearing as first team substitute in the last game of 1999-2000 against Barnet. He also played in pre-season games the following August on Dale's Scottish tour, but was not selected for the first team again. His brother Carl was also a trainee at Spotland and the pair both later appeared with Rochdale Town in the North West Counties League.

Matthew J. (Matt) Duffy 1999-2003

Born: Oldham c.1983
Defender
FL Apps/Gls +0/0
Total Apps/Gls +0/0
Career: Hopwood
School, Siddal Moor
School, Siddal Moor
Sports College,
Clarence Ath., Dale
jnr 1995, as 1997, yts
1999, Altrincham
2002-03 loan, Hyde
U. 14.2.03, Salford C.
2003-04
Honours: Rochdale
Boys under-14s,
under-15s, Greater
Manchester Schools under-16s

Matt was one of the first players to wear a Dale shirt at Wembley when Siddal Moor School represented them in a 6-a-side final against a school representing Cambridge United before the 1996 Division 3 play-off final. Already with Dale's centre of excellence, he worked his way up through the under-14s into the youth team at full back in 1999 and was the unlucky one amongst the young substitutes on the final day of that season when Scott Wilson and Danny Taylor both got a league bow. Appearing in a pre-season game at Stenhousemuir alongside brother Lee, he subsequently suffered a broken leg and though figuring in pre-season games again in 2002, he never had another chance in the senior team, later playing a few games for Hyde with Tony Ellis and Simon Coleman (q.v.).

Lee Todd 2000-02

Born: Hartlepool 7.3.72
5'6" 11st2
Left back
FL Apps/Gls 48+2/3
Total Apps/Gls 52+2/3
Career: Hartlepool U.
yts 1989, Stockport Co.
23.7.90 [214+11/2],
Southampton 28.7.97
£500,000 [9+1/-],
Bradford C. 6.8.98
£250,000 [14+1/-],
Walsall loan 17.9.99
[1/-], Dale 9.8.00
[48+2/3], retired 2002.
Mossley 8.03,
Stalybridge Celtic 2003-04. (Fingerpost Flyers;
Stockport Sunday League)
Honours: Division 4 promotion 1991, Division 3 play-off final 1992, Division 2+ play-off final 1994, promotion 1997, Division 1+ promotion 1999, Autoglass Trophy final 1992, 1993

Let go by Hartlepool, Lee played well over 200 games for Stockport, assisting them to promotion in his first and last campaigns before a half million pound transfer to Premier League Southampton, managed by his former County boss Dave Jones. After ten games, he moved to Bradford City, who also gained promotion to the top flight, but Lee didn't play at all after their elevation, except in the Inter Toto Cup in the summer of 2000, before being allowed to sign for Dale. A class act at left back, Lee had a tremendous first season, his spectacular free kick equaliser against Brighton reigniting the late Dale bid for the play-offs. However, the following year was almost a complete write-off due to injury and he decided to retire, though he did come back at non-league level a year later.

Paul David Ware 2000-02

Born: Congleton 7.11.70
5'9" 11st8
Midfield
FL Apps/Gls 21+17/2
Total Apps/Gls 25+17/2
Career: Stoke C. yts
1987, pro 15.11.88
[92+23/10], Stockport
Co. 8.9.94 £10,000
[42+12/4], Cardiff C.
loan 29.1.97 [5/-],
Hednesford T. 15.7.97
[68+5/12 Conf],
Macclesfield T. 14.7.99
[9+9/2], Nuneaton
Borough loan 12.99 [2/3
Conf], Dale 10.07.00 [21+17/2], Hednesford T. 7.02
Honours: Division 2+ champions 1993, promotion 1997

Steve Parkin's boot boy when an apprentice at Stoke, Paul himself played well over 100 games in midfield for the Potters. He scored the winning goal in the 1992 Autoglass Southern Section final, but did not appear in the final. He assisted the Potters to the second division title in 1993, before a less productive three seasons at Edgeley Park, though Stockport, too, gained promotion. After spells in the Conference, he was brought back into league football by Parkin and played fairly regularly in his first season, scoring after coming on as substitute when Dale came back from 2-0 down against his previous club Macclesfield. He was later a financial advisor but sadly died of a brain tumour when he was only 42.

Simon Ithel Davies 2000-01

Born: Winsford
23.4.74 6'0"
11st11
Outside left
FL Apps/Gls
7+5/1
Total Apps/Gls
8+8/1
Career:
Manchester U.
yts 1991, pro
6.9.92 [4+7/-],
Exeter C. loan
17.12.93 [5+1/1],
Huddersfield T.
loan 29.10.96
[3/-], Luton T.
5.8.97 £150,000 [10+12/1], Macclesfield T.
17.12.98 [39+9/3], Dale 4.8.00 £2000 [7+5/1],
Bangor C. cs.01, TNS 2003, Bangor C. 2004-05,
Rhyl 2005, Airbus UK, Chester C. youth team
coach 2006, caretaker manager 4.07, youth team
manager, manager 11.3.08 to 10.11.08, youth team
manager 10.12.08, assistant manager to 9.09,
youth team manager, Manchester C. junior coach
2.10, under-21s assistant manager 7.13, under-21s
manager 12.15*
Honours: Wales v Switzerland 1996, FA Youth Cup
winners 1992, Lancashire Cup final 1993-94,
Premier League champions 1996, Welsh Premier
League player of the season 2002-03. As coach:
Premier League International under-21 Cup
winners 2015

Another one from the Old Trafford youth system,
Simon managed a handful of games for United,
including in their 1996 title winning season, after
figuring in the same Youth Cup winning side as
David Beckham, Gary Neville and Ryan Giggs. His
one United goal came in Europe during a 4-0
defeat of Galatasaray and he made his full
international debut for Wales after only nine FL
starts. Playing largely on the left wing, the majority
of his league experience came at Macclesfield and
he then joined Dale, making a promising start by
netting a penalty on his debut, but soon fading out
of the picture. He had a lengthy spell in the Welsh
Premier League, playing in Europe with Bangor,
winning the league's player of the year award in
2003 and playing for TNS against Manchester City
in the UEFA Cup the following year. Later
Chester's youth team manager, he had spells as
caretaker manager and briefly full time manager in
2008, before the club was wound up in 2010. He
then coached in Manchester City's academy,
eventually taking over Patrick Viera's role as the
elite development squad manager.

Michael Oliver 2000-03

Born: Middlesbrough
2.8.75 5'10" 12st4
Midfield
FL Apps/Gls 87+16/9
Total Apps/Gls
105+17/11
Career: Middlesbrough
yts 1991, pro 19.8.92,
Stockport Co. 7.7.94
£15,000 [17+5/1],
Darlington 30.7.96
[135+16/14], Dale
14.7.00 [87+16/9],
Barrow 6.8.03 to cs.04,
Thornaby, Newcastle
Blue Star 28.11.05,
Gateshead cs.06, Durham C. 8.10.06
Honours: Division 3+ play-off final 2000,
Northern League XI 2006

Michael appeared in a number of games in the
same Stockport side as Lee Todd and Paul Ware
before spending four years as a regular at
Darlington, figuring either in midfield or at full
back. He played in their defeat in the play-off final
in 2000 but turned down a new contract and
moved to Spotland. A regular member of the
squad, though often a substitute in his first year,
he missed only one game as a defensive central
midfielder in 2001-02, netting seven goals, as
Dale, too made the play-offs only to fail to gain
promotion. A reported falling out with new boss
Paul Simpson restricted his appearances the
following term and he moved to Barrow where he
played alongside a much earlier Dale old boy Lee
Warren.

Phillip Jonathan (Phil) Hadland 2000-01

Born: Warrington 20.10.80
5'11" 11st8
Winger
FL Apps/Gls 12+20/2
Total Apps/Gls 14+21/2
Career: Reading yts 1997,
pro 22.6.99, Aldershot T.
loan 18.12.99 to 15.1.00,
York C. trial 7.00, Dale
8.8.00 [12+20/2], Orient
9.7.01 [+5/1], Carlisle U.
loan 19.11.01 [4/1], Brighton
& HA 19.3.02 [+2/-], Darlington 16.8.02 [4+2/-],
Chester C. 10.02, Gillingham trial 28.11.02, Leek T.
3.03, Colchester U. n/c 8.8.03 [+1/-], Leek T.
30.9.03, Northwich Victoria 2.7.04 [4+9/- Conf],
Leek T. loan 23.11.04, Stalybridge Celtic 21.12.04,
Leek T. loan 11.3.05, Bradford PA 8.05,
Hednesford T. 6.06, Kidsgrove Ath. 7.07, Colwyn
Bay 6.08, Warrington T. 8.08 to 2009. Fisher FC
11.10. Kidsgrove Ath trial 9.14

Honours: Division 2+ champions 2002, Staffordshire Senior Cup final 2008

Phil played just once, in the League Cup, for Reading before joining Dale. A promising prospect on the wing, he was in the squad for most of the games in 2000-01 but became impatient of a regular starting slot and turned down a new contract to sign for Orient instead. However, he played only eight further full games in spells with seven league clubs (and made a couple of substitute appearances when Brighton won Division 2), before playing for an even longer string of non-league sides.

Gary Hamilton 2000-01

Born: Banbridge, N. Ireland 6.10.80
5'9" 11st11
Forward
FL Apps/Gls +3/0
Total Apps/Gls +3/0
Career: Lisburn Youth, Blackburn R. yts 1996, pro 10.97, Dale loan 11.8.00 to 9.00 [+3/-], Wigan A. trial 2001, Raufoss IL (Norway) summer 2001, Brentford trial 8.01, Portadown 2001-02, NY Metro Stars (USA) summer 2004, Glentoran 3.06, Kilmarnock trial 5.10, Glenavon loan 31.8.10, Glenavon 8.11, player-manager 12.11*
Honours: FA Youth Cup final 1998, N. Ireland schools, N. Ireland youth international, N. Ireland under-21 (12 caps) 2000 to 2001, N. Ireland (5 caps) 2002 to 2004, N. Ireland 'B' 2003, Irish FA Cup final 2002, winners 2005, 2014, 2016, County Antrim Shield winners 2008, 2011, Irish Premier League champions 2002, 2009, Co-operative Insurance (League) Cup winners 2006-07, 2009-10, Mid-Ulster Cup winners 2002, 2003, 2011, Irish Premier League XI 2006, N. Ireland XI v Everton 2006

A scorer in the 1998 Youth Cup Final for Blackburn, Gary actually made an international appearance while with Dale on loan, scoring for the N. Ireland under-21s against Malta the day before his third and last substitute appearance. He played once as substitute for Rovers in the League Cup the same month but left the following summer. He really made his mark on returning home, though, scoring a record number of goals for Portadown, including a double hat-trick against Omagh Town and earning his first full cap in 2002 against Italy. In 2002-03 he netted a total of 40 goals and won the Northern Ireland Footballer of the Year award. Moving to Glentoran after 79 goals in 140 games, he continued to score prolifically –

94 goals in 189 games - appearing in several cup finals and in the Europa League. He then played for and managed Glenavon where he has added further domestic honours.

David Andrew Walsh 2000-02

Born: Rochdale 12.7.83
6'1" 12st8
Forward
FL Apps/Gls + 0/0
Total Apps/Gls +1/0
Career: St Vincent's RC School, St Cuthbert's RC HS, Dale as 1997, sch 2000, Stalybridge Celtic 3.02, Rochdalians 2003, Whitworth Valley 8.05 (+ Dog & Partridge 8.03 to 2005, Copperpot 2005-06; Sunday League)
Honours: Rochdale town boys, North of England Schools under-14s, Greater Manchester Schools under-16s 1998-99, Lancashire and Cheshire League XI 2003-04, Rochdale SL XI 2005, Lancashire Sunday Trophy winners 2006, Chris Shyne Memorial Trophy 2006

A prolific schoolboy striker for St Cuthbert's in the England Schools Cup, also playing for the North of England Schools, David was with Dale from the under-14s upwards and played in the youth cup in 1998 and 1999. In September 2000 he was called up as one of the substitutes for the League Cup tie at Blackburn, making his senior debut. Unused substitute in a league game a week later, David was thereafter restricted to reserve appearances, later figuring in local football and with the successful Sunday League side Copperpot.

Simon Coleman 2000-02

Born: Worksop 13.3.68 6'0" 11st8
Central defender
FL Apps/Gls 13+3/1
Total Apps/Gls 14+4/1
Career: Mansfield T. jnr, pro 29.7.85 [96/7], Middlesbrough 26.9.89 £600,000 [51+4/2], Derby Co. 15.8.91 £300,000 [62+8/2], Sheffield W. 20.1.94 £250,000 [11+5/1], Bolton W. 5.10.94 £350,000 [34/5], Wolverhampton W. loan 2.9.97 [3+1/-], Southend U. 20.2.98 [98+1/9], Dale 10.7.00 [13+3/1], Halifax T. trial

cs.02, Whitby T. trial, Ilkeston T. 8.02, Hyde U. 3.03 to cs.03
Honours: Division 1+ promotion 1995, ZDS Cup final 1990

Attending the same school as Steve Parkin, Simon joined Mansfield as a junior, going on to be almost everpresent for two seasons and earn a big money move to Middlesbrough, replacing Manchester United bound Gary Pallister. He was a fairly regular performer in the second tier over the next few years and played in the Premier League with both Wednesday and Bolton, racking up transfer fees totalling £1.5M but suffering a broken leg at Bolton. After a year in their reserves, Simon added almost 100 FL games for Southend before signing for Dale. However, he was on the injured list for the majority of his stay and is mostly recalled by Dale fans for being brought into the side after several months out only for Dale to lose 7-1 at home to Shrewsbury. Nicknamed 'Homer' on account of his hairline, he scored the winner at Oxford's new stadium on the opening day of 2000-01. Simon later played masters football for Middlesbrough and ran a football academy in Mansfield as well as working at a local college as a PE teacher.

Lee David Buggie 2000-01

Born Bury 11.2.81
5'9" 11st
Forward
FL Apps/Gls +2/0
Total Apps/Gls +2/0
Career: Bolton W. yts 1997, pro 18.2.98, Bury 27.5.99 [+1/-], Dale loan 15.9.00 to 15.10.00 [+2/-], Whitby T. loan 2000-01, South Melbourne (Australia) 2001, Stalybridge Celtic trial 7.01, Accrington St. cs.01, Clitheroe loan 9.02,
Rossendale U. 25.2.03, Salford C. 9.03, Ramsbottom U. 11.03, Bacup Borough 11.04

Lee was borrowed by Dale as cover for their strikers after playing against the reserves early in 2000-01. He added just two brief substitute appearances to the one he had made for his own club Bury, one of them in a 4-0 win at Shrewsbury. He played for Accrington against Dale in a pre-season friendly in 2002 and worked in the sports development department of Bury council.

Christian Earle Lee 2000-01

Born Aylesbury 8.10.76
6'2" 11st7
Forward
FL Apps/Gls 2+3/1
Total Apps/Gls 2+3/1
Career: Doncaster R. yts, Northampton T. 13.7.95 [25+34/8], Gillingham 3.8.99 £35,000 [1+2/-], Dale loan 20.10.00 [2+3/1], Orient loan 6.3.01
[2+1/-], Bristol R. 22.3.01 [8+1/2], Farnborough T. 9.01, Rushden & Diamonds loan 28.9.01 [1/-], Eastwood T. 11.01, Farnborough T. 1.02 [30+10/8 Conf], Halifax T. 5.03 [17+9/6 Conf], retired injured 2005
Honours: Division 3+ play-off winners 1997, Division 2+ promotion 2000

The majority of Christian's FL exposure came in four seasons at Northampton, though he never became a regular, despite playing in their play-off final success in 1997. After a year out with injury at Gillingham he was loaned to Dale early in 2000-01. He and fellow substitute Paul Ware both scored when Dale came back from 2-0 down to Macclesfield and Christian started the next two games up front. While with Farnborough he was sent off in a cup tie against Arsenal, and later retired with a chronic back injury.

Kevin Alistair Kyle 2000-01

Born: Stranraer 7.6.81
6'3" 13st7
Striker
FL Apps/Gls 3+3/0
Total Apps/Gls 3+3/0
Career: Stranraer Academy, Lugar Boswell, Ayr U. jnr, Sunderland 25.9.98 [59+32/11], Huddersfield T. loan 8.9.00 [+4/-],
Darlington loan 1.11.00 [5/1], Dale loan 26.1.01 [3+3/-], Coventry C. 25.8.06 £600,000 [25+19/5], Wolverhampton W. loan 31.1.08 [3+9/1], Hartlepool U. loan 1.10.08 [15/5], Kilmarnock 29.1.09 [40+3/16 ScL], Spartak Nalchik (Russia) trial, Heart of Midlothian 3.6.10 to 3.12 [16+3/7 ScL], Dunfermline trial cs.12, St Johnstone trial cs.12, Rangers 7.8.12 to 3.13 [3+5/2 ScL], Ayr U. trial 8.13, signed 27.9.13 to 1.14 [22+4/5 ScL]
Honours: Dumfries and Galloway, Scotland under-21 (12 caps) 2000 to 2003, Scotland 'B', Scotland (10 full caps) 2002 to 2010, Premier Reserve League (north) champions 2003, FL Championship winners 2005, (2007), (Scottish Division 3 champions 2013)

A tall striker, Kevin still had to make his Sunderland debut when he joined Dale on loan, though he had already played for the Scottish under-21s. He figured in six games but Dale failed to score in four of them and the last was the infamous 7-1 defeat by Shrewsbury. Remarkably he then won two full caps before making a start for Sunderland, eventually gaining a regular place in 2003-04 when he netted 16 goals. A serious hip injury then kept him out of action until 2006. A fairly unsuccessful spell at Coventry was followed by a move to Kilmarnock, where he scored a hat-trick against St. Mirren and helped keep Killie in the SPL. He captained them the following term and gained a recall to the Scotland side after a five year absence, but was again troubled by his hip problem. Off the field he backed an initiative to help young Scottish players with gambling problems. In 2012 he joined Rangers after they had been demoted to Scottish Division 3, later claiming that most of their players were only there for the still huge salaries being paid despite the level Rangers were playing at.

Dean George Howell   2000-01

Born: Burton-on-Trent 29.11.80 6'0" 12st5
Outside left
FL Apps/Gls 2+1/0
Total Apps/Gls 2+1/0
Career: Stoke C. as, Notts Co. yts 1997, pro 1.7.99 [+1/-], Spalding U. loan 1999-00, Crewe A. 26.7.00 [+1/-], Dale loan 1.3.01 [2+1/-], Southport loan, signed 12.01 [54+7/4 Conf], Morecambe 6.03 [24+6/3 Conf], Halifax T. 7.04 [26+8/6 Conf], Colchester U. 5.8.05 [1+3/1], Halifax T. 1.06 [1/- Conf], Weymouth 6.06 [11+6/- Conf], Grays Ath. 31.1.07 [3+6/- Conf], Rushden & Diamonds 8.07 [40+3/1 Conf], Aldershot T. 11.5.08 [14+3/1], Bury loan 27.11.08 [+3/-], Crawley T. 7.10 [35/1 Conf, 36+1/3], Fleetwood 5.12 to 31.1.14 [36+2/1], Bury loan 5.11.13 to 5.1.14 [8/-]
Honours: (League 1 promotion 2006), Conference Setanta Shield final 2008, Conference champions 2011, Conference team of the year 2011, League 2 promotion 2012, (2014)

Dean made one substitute appearance each for Notts County and Crewe before the latter loaned him to Dale for a month, where he played just three times on the wing. He had much more productive spells in the Conference, particularly with Southport, interrupted by another very brief stint in the FL at Colchester in 2005 and a slightly longer one at Aldershot in 2008. In 2011, by now

playing in defence, he assisted Crawley to the Conference title (and was selected at left back in the Conference team of the year) and the following term was in their side promoted to League 1. He repeated this with Fleetwood (his 15th FL or Conference side) two seasons later, though he had left the club before they actually went up.

Kevin Townson   2000-05

Born: Liverpool 19.4.83 5'8" 10st3
Striker
FL Apps/Gls 41+61/25
Total Apps/Gls 50+72/30
Career: Everton as 1996, Mossley Hill, Dale 6.7.00 [41+61/25], Scarborough loan 30.9.04 [4/- Conf], Macclesfield T. loan 24.3.05 [2+4/-], Macclesfield T. 27.6.05 [5+19/2], Northwich Victoria 16.6.06 [22+23/3 Conf], TNS 1.08, Droylsden 7.08, Melbourne Knights (Australia) 2010, AFC Fylde 10.10 to 6.11, Warrington T. trial 3.12, signed 8.12, Bootle 1.13 to cs.13, Dandenong C. (Australia) 2013, Langwarrin (Australia) 3.14 to 5.15, Sacre Coeur FP 2015-16*
Honours: Liverpool County FA, England youth international

Spotted when playing for Liverpool County after his release by Everton, Kevin joined Dale from Sunday League football when he was 17. He played with the first team on their pre-season tour of Scotland, and was handed his FL debut up front the following March. He started the next season as a regular on the bench, netting seven times as a substitute, including two against Premier League Fulham (on 9/11). Eventually gaining a semi-regular starting place, he played an important part, as top scorer with 17 goals, as John Hollins' Dale side made the play-offs for the first time. Apparently watched by Manchester U., Liverpool and Sunderland, the diminutive striker was hailed as a great prospect and was selected to play for England under-19s at the end of the season, the first Rochdale player to be selected at that level. When Paul Simpson became manager, though, he was an almost permanent substitute and scored only one goal in 2002-03. In and out of the side under both Alan Buckley and the returning Steve Parkin the next season, he did hit 12 goals. He played only once the following term and drifted off to Macclesfield and then the non-league game when he was still only 23 (having only ever started 48 FL games). In 2010 he was voted player of the year in the Victorian Premier League while playing in Melbourne and regaining his scoring touch at lower levels of the game, netted 22 times in 35 NPL games for AFC Fylde. Kevin's agent was ex-Dale player Shaun Reid, who was also his manager at Warrington. In 2015-16 Kevin was playing in the Liverpool Old Boys Amateur League, remarkably enough alongside Lee McEvilly.

Paul Connor 2000-04

Born: Bishop Auckland 12.1.79 6'1" 11st5
Striker
FL Apps/Gls 76+18/28
Total Apps/Gls 90+22/33
Career: Middlesbrough yts 1995, pro 4.7.96, Gateshead loan 8.97, Hartlepool U. loan 6.2.98 [4+1/-], Stoke C. loan 25.3.99 [2+1/2], Stoke C. cs.99 [16+17/5], Cambridge U. loan 9.11.00 [12+1/5], Dale 9.3.01 £150,000 [76+18/28], Swansea C. 12.3.04 £35,000 [51+14/16], Leyton O. 31.1.06 £40,000 [20+14/7], Cheltenham T. 15.1.07 £25,000 [53+26/7], Lincoln C. 21.7.09 [8+7/-], Mansfield T. 28.7.10 [38+17/15 Conf], Gainsborough Trinity 12.11, Shildon 3.7.13*
Honours: Bishop Auckland Schools, Durham Schools, League 2 promotion 2005, 2006, FA Trophy final 2011, Conference North play-off final 2012, Northern League champions 2016, Northern League Cup winners 2016

Paul didn't appear in the first team for Middlesbrough but scored twice on his home debut for Stoke on loan, leading to a permanent move to the Potteries. In March 2001, with Dale' play-off hopes fading, Steve Parkin signed him for a club record £150,000. Three of the next four games were drawn, but Paul then reignited the season with a hat-trick in a 6-0 trouncing of Carlisle and netted 10 times in 14 games as Dale agonizingly missed out on the final day of the season. Injured for much of the following term when Dale did make the play-offs – 'Trigger' was thrown on as a substitute in the second leg after several months out – he managed 17 goals in all games in 2002-03. He scored after only 18 seconds against Huddersfield the following term but suspension following a sending off against York and further injuries meant that this was his last Dale goal. Sold to Swansea before his contract ran out, he gained successive promotions with the Swans and then Orient. He later reached the FA Trophy Final at Wembley with Mansfield and almost repeated this with Gainsborough Trinity who were beaten semi-finalists in 2013. Still going

strong in his late thirties, he netted 24 times for Shildon in 2014-15 and played in virtually every game when they won the Northern League and Cup double the following term. Paul's grandfather Bill Hindmarsh was right back in the Portsmouth side which won the league championship in 1949 and 1950.

John Baker 2000-03

Born: Bromley 23.11.82
6'0" 11st3
Goalkeeper
FL Apps +0
Total Apps +0
Career: Siddal Moor School, Siddal Moor Sports College, Boundary Park Juniors, Dale as 1997, yts 2000, pro 2002, Hyde U. 8.03
Honours: Rochdale Schools under-13s, Greater Manchester Schools under-16s

A team-mate of Matt Duffy in the Siddal Moor School side that represented Dale at Wembley, John also worked his way through the Dale's youth system, generally being understudy to Matt Gilks who was just a few months older. In the youth team from 1998, he was first team sub when Gilks made his league debut in March 2001. He was on the bench numerous times over the next two years, but the only times he actually appeared were in pre-season games (though his No. 25 shirt did appear in one league game, Neil Edwards wearing it when his own was lost!).

Andrew Peter (Andy) Turner 2000-01

Born: Woolwich 23.3.75
5'10" 11st12
Outside left
FL Apps/Gls 2+2/0
Total Apps/Gls 2+2/0
Career: Tottenham H. yts, pro 8.4.92 [8+12/3], Wycombe W. loan 26.8.94 [3+1/-], Doncaster R. loan 10.10.94 [4/1], Huddersfield T. loan 28.11.95 [2+3/1], Southend U. loan 28.3.96 [4+2/-], Portsmouth 4.9.96 £250,000 [34+6/3], Crystal Palace 27.10.98 [+2/-], Wolverhampton W. 25.3.99, Rotherham U. 1.7.99 [29+7/1], Boston U. loan 2000-01 [4/- Conf], Dale loan 22.3.01 to 4.01 [2+2/-], Yeovil 6.01 [14+7/1 Conf], Nuneaton Borough loan 2001-02 [2+1/- Conf], Kettering T. loan 2002, Tamworth 6.02, Northampton T. 17.1.03 [+3/-], Northwich Victoria 3.03 [+2/1

Conf], Moor Green 6.03, Chasetown 2005-06, player-coach, Kidsgrove Ath. coach, Alsager T. manager 5.12, Coalville T. manager 1.14, Romulus FC joint manager 2.15 (and academy director 6.15)*

Honours: Republic of Ireland schools, Republic of Ireland youth international, Republic of Ireland under-21s (7 caps), Division 3+ promotion 2000, Division 2+ promotion 2001

The Premier League's youngest goalscorer when he scored for Spurs aged 17 years and 166 days, Andy never quite made the break through at White Hat Lane, but was bought by his former Spurs boss Terry Venables for Portsmouth for £250,000 and Venables also signed him for Palace. Though a Republic of Ireland international at all levels up to the under-21s, his 40 appearances on the wing for Pompey were the most he managed with any of his eleven league clubs, though he did gain promotion with Rotherham, Dale borrowing him from the Millers just before the transfer deadline in 2001. He also played for numerous non-league clubs and was player-coach of the Chasetown side which had a long cup run in 2006.

Gareth John Griffiths 2001-06

Born: Winsford 10.4.70 6'4" 14st
Centre half
FL Apps/Gls
176+8/14 Total
Apps/Gls 199+8/18
Career: Verdin CS (Winsford), Crewe A. jnr 1982 to 1984, White Swan (Sunday League), Winnington Park, Rhyl, Port Vale 8.2.93 £1000 [90+4/4], Shrewsbury T. loan 31.10.97 [6/-], Wigan A. 2.7.98 [44+9/2], Dale 18.7.01 [176+8/14], Northwich Victoria cs.06 to 2007 [25+3/1 Conf]

Honours: Division 2+ promotion 1994, (play-off final 2000), Anglo-Italian Cup final 1996, Lancashire Cup winners 1998-99

Gareth was a late comer to the professional game, after gaining a first class honours degree in business studies. He figured around a hundred times for Port Vale, scoring twice in just his second game when they were promoted in 1994 and appearing in the Anglo-Italian Cup Final against Genoa at Wembley. The best run of his career was undoubtedly at Spotland, though, as a commanding figure at the back for five years, including when they reached the play-offs in 2002 – 'Griff' being voted played of the year - and the

fifth round of the FA Cup in 2003, when he scored in the victory over Coventry. He also became the first Dale central defender to score a hat-trick when he did so in an Auto Windscreens Shield game against Scarborough, and until beaten by Craig Dawson had the most goals of any Dale defender. Briefly assisting Keith Hill at the start of his reign, while he was on the injured list at Northwich, Gareth left the professional game when he was 37 to become a financial consultant, including working for the PFA, and became a partner in ProSport Wealth Management.

Matthew Liam (Matt) Doughty 2001-04

Born: Warrington 2.11.81 5'8" 10st8
Midfield/left back
FL Apps/Gls
96+12/1 Total
Apps/Gls 115+15/2
Career: Chester C. jnr 1995, yts 1998, pro [19+14/1, 35+5/1 Conf], Dale 20.7.01 [96+12/1], Halifax T. cs.04 [119+11/1 Conf], Altrincham cs.08, Witton Albion 2010, Hyde U. 25.3.11, Warrington T. 8.11 to 9.11. Altrincham 7.12,
Warrington T. 6.14, Trafford 1.15

Honours: Conference play-off final 2006, Conference North promotion 2014

Matt made his debut for Chester when he was 17, and soon becoming a regular, he would have had a trial at Southampton but for suffering an untimely injury. Signed by Dale for free when Chester, by now in the Conference, forgot to retain him, 'Buzz' played fairly regularly on the left of midfield or his more normal left back position for three seasons, figuring in the Dale's first ever play-off campaign. His single FL goal for Dale was the first ever scored at Oxford's new Kassam stadium. In a long spell at Halifax he was in the side which was within ten minutes of regaining their FL status, only to lose the Conference play-off final to Hereford in extra time. Though he was hampered by a number of injuries both while at the Shay and later in his career, he also had two productive stints at Altrincham, figuring well over 100 times, and was still playing in the NPL in 2015. Matt is also a useful amateur golfer.

Keiron John Durkan 2001-03

Born: Chester
1.12.73 5'11"
12st10
Winger
FL Apps/Gls
16+14/1 Total
Apps/Gls 23+16/1
Career: Wrexham
jnr 1988, yts 1990,
pro 16.7.92
[43+7/3], Stockport
Co. 16.2.96 £95,000
[52+12/4],
Macclesfield T.
25.3.98 £15,000 [92+11/13], York C. loan 5.10.00
[7/-], Dale 4.7.01 [16+14/1], Swansea C. 10.1.03
[19+8/1], Caernarfon T. 3.04, Runcorn Halton
cs.04, Leek T., NEWI Cefn Druids 6.05
Honours: Runcorn Schoolboys, Cheshire
Schoolboys, Republic of Ireland under-21 (3 caps),
Welsh Cup winners 1995, Division 3+ promotion
1993, 1998, Division 2+ promotion 1997

Keiron was born in England and first played in
Wales, appearing in a Welsh Cup winning side
with Wrexham, but appeared for the Republic of
Ireland under-21s. A sizeable fee took him to
Stockport and he was a regular on the right wing
when they won promotion to the second tier. He
moved to Macclesfield in time to play a few games
in their promotion run in 1998 and appeared
regularly for a couple of years. He made less
impact with Dale, fading out of the picture mid-
season when Paddy McCourt came on to the scene,
though he did net a hat-trick for the reserves. He
figured only in pre-season games in 2002-03, later
joining Swansea. After finishing playing he became
a community police officer.

Lee Alan Duffy 1998-04

Born: Oldham 24.7.82
5'7" 10st7
Right back/midfield
FL Apps/Gls 20+8/0
Total Apps/Gls
29+10/0
Career: St Hugh's,
Breezehill, Heyside
Juniors, Liverpool
trial, Boundary Park
Juniors, Dale as 1996,
yts 6.98, pro 6.9.01
[20+8/-], Rossendale
U. loan 12.03, Halifax
T. 12.3.04, Radcliffe
Borough 4.04, Glenrothes 7.07, Bo'ness U. 7.11,
Dundonald Bluebell 7.12, player-assistant manager
cs.15*

Honours: Oldham Town Boys under-11, under-15,
Dundonald Tournament final 2014, SJFA East
Region south league promotion 2014

Like brother Matt, Lee worked his way through
Dale's junior sides, figuring in pre-season games in
2000. He made his league debut as substitute,
playing left back, at Hull in September 2001 and
made two starting appearances later in the season.
The rest of his senior games were the following
season, either in midfield or at right wing back
when Wayne Evans was moved into the centre, as
he wasn't used at all after Paul Simpson was
succeeded by new boss Alan Buckley. After moving
north of the border, he became a prominent figure
in Junior Football with an excellent goalscoring
record for a midfielder, netting 91 times in 261
games and skippering Dundonald when they were
promoted and reached the Scottish Junior Cup
quarter-final for the first time in 2014.

Stephen Bryan Hill 2000-04

Born: Prescot 12.11.82
5'10" 11st2
Left back
FL Apps/Gls 10+1/0
Total Apps/Gls
13+2/0
Career: St Anne
School, St Cuthberts
(St Helens), Wigan A.
jnr, Penlake Juniors,
Dale jnr 1998, yts
2000, pro 3.7.02
[10+1/-], Morecambe
loan 23.03.04,
Radcliffe Borough
cs.04, Leigh RMI 7.07,
Radcliffe Borough 3.08 to 2009
Honours: St Helens Town boys, Cheshire Schools
Cup winners, Lancashire under-14s Cup winners,
under-16s final, Merseyside county schools under-
16s

A winner of the Cheshire Cup with St Helens town
team and a finalist in Lancashire junior cups with
Penlake, Stephen was a member of Dale's youth
squad and first appeared with the first team during
the pre-season tour of Scotland in 2001. An
unused substitute in FL games soon afterwards, he
was brought into the side by Paul Simpson the
following season, remarkably making his debut in
the cup victory over Coventry and also figuring
against Wolves. However he played only once
under Alan Buckley and like Lee Duffy had a spell
with Radcliffe Borough.

Richard Jobson 2001-03

Born: Holderness
9.5.63 6'1" 13st5
Central defender
FL Apps/Gls 49+2/3
Total Apps/Gls
62+2/3
Career: Burton A.,
Watford 5.11.82
£22,000 [26+2/4],
Hull C. 7.2.85 £40,000
[219+2/17], Oldham A.
30.8.90 £460,000
[188+1/10], Leeds U.
26.10.95 £1,000,000
[22/1], Southend U.
loan 23.1.98 [8/1], Manchester C. 12.3.98
[49+1/4], Watford loan 7.11.00 [2/-], Tranmere R.
28.12.00 [17/-], Dale 28.9.01 [49+2/3], retired
cs.03. PFA vice-chairman, chairman, senior
executive
Honours: England 'B' 1992, Division 3 promotion
1985, Division 2 champions 1991, Division 1+
promotion 2000

A hugely experienced central defender, Richard
was 6 days short of 40 when he played his last Dale
game, his 587th in the FL. He had started a civil
engineering degree at Nottingham University but
was offered a contract by Watford, making his
debut in Division 1 as sub for John Barnes in 1983.
He also played in the Sheriff of London Charity
Shield for Watford when the teams wore 19th
century kit! He had a long spell at Hull after
helping them to promotion immediately on his
arrival, then returned to the Premier League with
Oldham, subsequently representing England 'B'
and being called up for an England squad by his
old Watford boss Graham Taylor. A remarkable
million pound fee took him to Leeds when he was
already 32 and he missed only two games when
Manchester City were promoted to the top flight in
2000. He helped Dale reach the play-offs,
unfortunately having to go off injured in the
second leg. Richard was PFA vice chairman, then
chairman from November 2002 until retiring
when he became senior executive.

Paul Michael Wheatcroft 2001-02

Born: Bolton 22.11.80
5'9" 9st11
Forward
FL Apps/Gls 6/3
Total Apps/Gls 6/3
Career: Bolton School,
Manchester U. jnr 1995, yts
1997, pro 8.7.98, FC Fortune
(SA) loan 1999-2000, Bolton
W. 6.7.00, Dale loan 27.9.01
to 10.01 [6/3], Mansfield T.
loan 26.2.02 [1+1/-],

Scunthorpe U. 9.8.02 [2+2/-], Southport 9.1.03
[6+2/1 Conf], Oldham A. trial 7.03, Stalybridge
Celtic 19.9.03, Radcliffe Borough 1.04, Rossendale
U. loan 3.04. Old Boltonians 2013-14
Honours: England Schools 1996, England youth
international, (Division 3+ promotion 2002)

Paul was one of the many juniors on Manchester
United's books and featured in a television
programme discussing the fate of those who didn't
make the grade and a similar article in the
Observer on former England Schools players (the
one from Paul's year who did make it was Scott
Parker). He didn't figure with Bolton either, but
had a successful short stint at Spotland, scoring in
three of his six games from which Dale took 11
points. He played a handful of other FL games and
figured for Oldham against Dale in the 2003 Rose
Bowl game. He later turned out for his school's old
boys team.

Marcus Stephen Hahnemann 2001-02

Born: Seattle, USA 15.3.72
6'3" 16st2
Goalkeeper
FL Apps 5 Total Apps 7
Career: Kentridge HS
(Seattle), Newport HS (New
York), Seattle Pacific
University Falcons 1991,
Seattle Sounders (USA)
1.5.94, Colorado Rapids
(USA) 1997 [66 MLS],
Fulham 9.7.99 £80,000 [2],
Dale loan 12.10.01 to 11.01 [5], Reading loan
14.12.01 [6], Reading 14.8.02 [276],
Wolverhampton W. 17.6.09 to 5.11 [39], Everton
23.9.11 to 18.5.12, Seattle Sounders (USA) 14.9.12
to 12.14 [4 MLS]
Honours: All-King County (NY), NCAA division 2
national champions 1993, A-League champions
1995, 1996, USA (9 full caps) 1994, 2003 to 2005
and 2011, (CONCACAF Gold Cup winners 2005),
World Cup squad 2006, 2010, Division 1+
champions 2001, (Division 2+ promotion 2002),
FL Championship winners 2006

A cult hero with Dale, despite playing just seven
games on loan, Marcus had a playing career
spanning 24 years. In four years in his university
side he kept 46 clean sheets and they lost just five
of 78 games. He then joined his local A-League
side Seattle Sounders and won his first USA cap
the same year (though in a defeat by Trinidad).
After a stint in the MLS with Colorado Rapids he
moved to Fulham but was unable to gain a place in
their side. The Cottagers' substitute goalkeeper
when Dale played them in the League Cup (on
9/11), he moved to Spotland shortly afterwards
and kept four clean sheets in his five league games.
If Dale could have afforded to keep him longer, it

could well have been the difference between the play-offs and automatic promotion, but as it was he next went on loan to Reading and helped them to promotion instead. Joining up permanently with the Royals, he regained his place in the USA side and was a key figure as Reading went up to the top flight in 2006 with a record 106 points. (Unsurprisingly, he was in the PFA's championship team of the year). He kept 13 clean sheets the following term as they remarkably finished in 8th place, making the most saves of any Premier League goalkeeper. Also figuring for Wolves in the top division, after a year as back up 'keeper at Everton he returned to his roots in Seattle and played for the Sounders in the CONCACAF champions league, retiring when he was 42. Marcus psyched himself up for games by playing heavy metal and while at Reading collaborated with local death metal band Malefice.

Patrick James (Pat, Paddy) McCourt
2000-05

Born: Derry 16.12.83
5'10" 11st
Winger
FL Apps/Gls 31+48/8
Total Apps/Gls 35+61/9
Career: Steelstown School, St Bridget's HS (Derry), Foyle Harps, Trojans Coleraine 1999, Shantallow Celtic, Dale trial 10.00, yts 1.01, pro 11.2.02 [31+48/8], Norwich C. trial 8.9.03, Crewe A. trial 2003-04, Motherwell trial 12.04, Shamrock Rovers 2.05, Derry C. 5.05 £5000, Celtic 18.6.08 £200,000 [15+51/9 ScL], Blackpool trial cs.13, Peterborogh U. trial cs.13, Hibernian trial 6.8.13, Barnsley 22.8.13 [15+8/2], Brighton &HA 19.8.14 [+10/-], Notts Co. loan 20.2.15 [11+1/1], Luton T. 1.7.15 to 5.16 [15+9/1]
Honours: Derry Boys, Merseyside under-16s tournament winners 1999, N. Ireland schools, N. Ireland under-21 (9 caps) 2002 to 2005, N. Ireland under-20s 2002, N. Ireland (18 caps) 2002, 2009 to 2015, N. Ireland 'B' 2009, FAI Cup 2006, League of Ireland Cup 2006, 2007, Wembley international tournament winners 2009, Scottish Reserve League winners 2009, Scottish League Cup final 2010-11, Scottish Cup winners 2011, Scottish League champions 2012, 2013

Spotted by scout Frank Vickers in Derry and given a trial at Spotland when he was 16, Pat broke into the reserves almost immediately and was signed on YTS forms in January 2001. Arguably Dale's most naturally talented player ever, he had a meteoric rise, making his FL debut that November and figuring for the senior Northern Ireland side in April 2002 when he was still only 18. He made 23 appearances, often from the bench, as Dale made the play-offs for the first time, his mazy dribbles setting up numerous chances, particularly for fellow youngster Kevin Townson. However, like Townson, this spell under John Hollins proved to be his peak as a Dale player. He missed large parts of 2002-03 through injury, though becoming a regular for the Irish under-21s, and played relatively little before being released by Steve Parkin due to his lack of fitness early in 2005 – remarkably Paddy only ever started 35 games for Dale. Back in Ireland, he was quickly voted PFAI young player of the year and when back with his hometown club was dubbed "the Derry Pele". Figuring in three cup winning sides, and playing against PSG in Europe, he was expected to sign for West Brom in 2008 until a counter offer from his boyhood heroes Celtic. Although rarely starting games, Paddy did figure in three further cup finals and continued to build his reputation as a fans favourite. Known for scoring amazing goals after beating defender after defender, one such effort won him the SPL goal of the season in 2009-10. He also returned to the Northern Ireland side, scoring two solo goals against the Faroe Islands. Less pleasantly, he, like his manager Neil Lennon, another Northern Irishman from a catholic background, received bullets through the post as a sectarian threat. Though hailed as one of the most gifted footballers he'd ever seen by Scotland boss Gordon Strachan, Paddy was released by Celtic in 2013, having started just 15 SPL games. He returned to England to play for former Dale teammate Dave Flitcroft's Barnsley and other lower league sides in quick succession. Pat's elder brother Harry was an Irish League and League of Ireland player from the late 1980s onwards, including a spell with Derry.

Simon Grand   2000-04

Born: Chorley 23.2.84
6'1" 10st12
Central defender
FL Apps/Gls 33+7/2
Total Apps/Gls 43+7/2
Career: Charnock Richard School, Southlands HS, Blackpool as 1997, Dale yts 7.00, pro 3.7.02 [33+7/2], Carlisle U. 1.7.04 [23+2/Conf, 3+9/2], Grimsby T. 9.1.07 [4+3/-], Morecambe 3.8.07 [4+2/1], Northwich Victoria 8.08 [63/9 Conf], Fleetwood T. cs.10 [4/- Conf], Mansfield T. loan 10.10 [6/1 Conf], Aldershot T. loan 1.11 [6/-], Southport 6.11 [83/11 Conf], AFC Telford U. 10.5.13, Barrow 6.14 to 5.16 [43+3/5 Conf]

Honours: Chorley Schools, Preston Boys, Lancashire County under-16s 1999-2000, England non-league XI v Holland 2004, Conference champions 2005, League 2 champions 2006, FL Trophy final 2006, Conference North champions 2014, 2015, Conference North team of the year 2014, 2015

Simon was unused substitute in a couple of games in 2001 and after turning pro made his debut at centre half in the FA Cup at Bristol Rovers in November 2002, immediately becoming a fixture in the side which reached round five. He was given the captain's armband for the game at Rushden the following March at the age of only 19 and responded with a goal in a 3-3 draw. Largely a stand-in the following year he moved to Carlisle, managed by his former Dale boss Paul Simpson. A regular as the Cumbrians won back their place in the FL, also playing for England at non-league level, he made only a handful of appearances as they went on to gain promotion to League 1. After brief stints at various clubs, he made a few final FL appearances, somewhat oddly, when loaned out by Conference side Fleetwood to League 2 Aldershot in 2011. Simon subsequently skippered AFC Telford and Barrow to promotion to the Conference in successive seasons.

Karl Barrie Rose 2001-02
Born: Barnsley 12.10.78 5'10" 11st 8
Forward
FL Apps/Gls 0/0 Total Apps/Gls 1/0
Career: Barnsley jnr, pro 7.11.95 [2+2/-], Mansfield T. loan 25.3.99 [+1/-], Goole T., Dale trial 8.01, n/c 25.10.01, Scarborough 11.01 [50+16/12 Conf], Leigh RMI cs.04 [20+1/2 Conf], Tamworth 2.05 [5/- Conf], Arnold T. 2005-06, Worksop T. 2.06, Garforth T. 2006, Hednesford T. 10.06, Goole T. 2007, manager 9.09, Frickley A. manager 5.12*
Honours: As manager; Sheffield and Hallamshire Cup winners 2013, 2015

Karl had played very briefly under Steve Parkin at Mansfield and was Parkin's final signing of his first spell in charge at Spotland, playing up front in one LDV Vans Trophy game during a trial at Spotland. He later had more productive spells at Conference level after a mystery illness had been cleared up, but he had moved into non-league management by the age of 30.

Darren Dunning 2001-02

Born: Malton, Yorkshire 8.1.81 5'6" 11st12
Midfield
FL Apps/Gls 4+1/0
Total Apps/Gls 4+1/0
Career: Brooklyn Junior FC, Malton School, Blackburn R. jnr 1995, yts 1997, pro 25.2.99 [1/-], Bristol C. loan 12.8.00 [9/-], Dale loan 29.11.01 to 12.01 [4+1/-], Blackpool loan 28.3.02 [5/-], Torquay U. loan 7.11.02 [4+3/1], Macclesfield T. loan 16.1.03 [17/-], York C. 29.7.03 [42/3, 78+1/4 Conf], Harrogate T. 7.06, Gainsborough Trinity 5.09 to 4.10, Old Malton St Marys player-manager 6.11*
Honours: Division 1+ promotion 2001. As manager: North Riding FA County Cup winners 2014, final 2015, York FA Senior Cup winners 2012, final 2015, York premier league champions 2012, 2014, York league cup winners 2012

Darren joined Dale on loan from Blackburn - where he played just one FL game in their promotion side but three cup ties - taking the midfield spot vacated by Gary Jones leaving for Barnsley. He started four games but Dale didn't win any of them and he was on the bench for the remainder of his stay. He had loan spells at four other clubs, but in terms of games played, his best spell was at York, though they suffered relegation to the Conference. He played at Harrogate with his twin brother Richard and after a serious cruciate injury, like Karl Rose, turned to management when only 30, Old Malton St Marys of the York League winning a treble in his first year in charge.

James Vincent (Vince) O'Keefe 2001-2002
Born: Coleshill 2.4.57 6'0" 11st
Goalkeeper
FL Apps 0 Total Apps +0
Career: Paget Rovers, Birmingham C. 7.75, Peterborough U. loan 1975-76, Walsall 7.76, AP Leamington 1977-78, Exeter C. 6.78 [53], Torquay U. 2.80 [108], Blackburn R. 8.82 [68], Bury loan 10.83 [2], Blackpool loan 12.86 [1], Blackpool loan 2.89 [6], Wrexham 7.89 [83], Exeter C. 8.92 [2], Blackburn R. academy goalkeeping coach 1998 to 6.07, Dale n/c 12.01
Honours: Full Members Cup winners 1987, Lancashire Cup final (1982-83), (1984-85), winners (1985-86), 1987-88, (Isle of Man tournament final 1984-85)

Vince had been a long serving league goalkeeper, starting out with Birmingham in 1975 and while Blackburn's goalkeeping coach was bizarrely recruited by his one time Rovers team-mate David Hamilton to sit on the bench for Dale's FA Cup tie at Blackpool, at the age of 44, nearly nine years after his previous senior involvement. Vince had earlier had useful spells with Exeter, Torquay and Wrexham as well as Blackburn. He played in second division Rovers' Wembley win in the Full Members Cup and in Wrexham's famous FA Cup victory over Arsenal. As well as Rovers goalkeeping coach, he was also coach at Queen Elizabeth Grammar School and an FA coach. He acted as agent for several goalkeepers including England international Ben Foster. Vince's son Josh was a trainee at Blackburn, representing the Republic of Ireland under-21s, and played in the FL for Walsall and Lincoln.

Steven (Steve) Banks 2001-02

Born: Hillingdon 9.7.72
6'0" 13st2
Goalkeeper
FL Apps 15
Total Apps 15
Career: West Ham U. yts 1988, pro 24.3.90, Gillingham 25.3.93 [67], Blackpool 18.8.95 £60,000 [150], Bolton W. 25.3.99 £50,000 [20+1], Dale loan 14.12.01 to 11.3.02 [15], Bradford C. loan 30.8.02 [8+1], Stoke C. loan 6.12.02, signed 2.03 [14], Wimbledon 1.8.03 [24], Gillingham 12.3.04 [39], Heart of Midlothian 8.05 [35+2 ScL], goalkeeping coach 2007-08, Dundee U. 2.6.09 player/goalkeeping coach [1 ScL], St. Johnstone player/goalkeeping coach 8.7.13 [4 ScL], Blackpool goalkeeping coach 6.15*
Honours: Division 1+ play-off final 1999, promotion 2001, (Scottish Cup winners 2006, 2010, 2014)

Steve had played well over 200 games for Gillingham and Blackpool (and one Anglo-Italian cup tie for West Ham) but despite figuring in their play-off final side in 1999 was Bolton's third choice 'keeper when they lent him to Dale two years later. He figured in almost all John Hollins' early games in charge and helped keep Dale in the top flow. After leaving Bolton he had further English clubs, each in the second tier at the time, before joining Scottish Premier League Hearts, continuing to play odd games for them even after becoming their goalkeeping coach. He was sacked by chairman Vladimir Romanov along with captain Steven Presley in 2008-09 and joined Dundee United and then St. Johnstone in the same capacity, retaining his playing registration when past 40. As back-up keeper, he won three Scottish Cup medals without leaving the bench!

Alan Francis McLoughlin 2001-2

Born: Manchester 20.4.67 5'8" 10st10
Midfield
FL Apps/Gls 15+3/1
Total Apps/Gls 17+3/1
Career: Manchester U. app 1983, pro 25.4.85, Swindon T. 15.8.86 [101+5/19], Torquay U. loan 13.3.87 [21+3/4], Southampton £1,000,000 13.12.90 [22+2/1], Aston Villa loan 30.9.91, Portsmouth 17.2.92 £400,000 [297+12/54], Wigan A. 9.12.99 £250,000 [12+10/1], Dale 21.12.01 [15+3/1], Forest Green Rovers player-coach 7.02 [10+2/- Conf], assistant manager cs.03 to cs.05, acting manager 9.04 to 10.04. Portsmouth academy coach 7.11, first team coach 8.7.13 to 4.12.14, Swindon T. academy coach 2.15*
Honours: Republic of Ireland (42 full caps) 1990 to 1999, World Cup squad 1990, 1994, Republic of Ireland 'B' (3 caps), (Division 2 promotion 1987), Division 2 play-off winners 1990 (not promoted)

Alan was a veteran midfielder recruited by John Hollins to keep Dale on track for the play-offs. He had first come to prominence with a century of appearances for Swindon, scoring the winner in the play-off final at Wembley (though Swindon were demoted back down again because of financial irregularities). He also earned a call up to the Republic of Ireland's 1990 World Cup squad, subsequently costing Southampton £1M when they signed him. However, he made little impression before moving to Portsmouth where he racked up over 300 league games and over 50 goals over the next seven years. He also became a regular in the Republic team - his goal against N. Ireland taking them to the 1994 World Cup finals - and eventually winning 42 caps. His single Dale goal came when he scored the winner from the spot in the last game of the regular season as Dale missed automatic promotion by a single point. He subsequently played for and managed Forest Green Rovers and became a radio commentator in Portsmouth before returning to Pompey on their academy staff. After surviving cancer, he became first team coach under successive new managers as Portsmouth struggled in League 2. His autobiography 'A Different Shade of Green' was shortlisted for the Irish sports book of the year in 2014.

Lee Richard McEvilly 2001-04, 2007-08, 2008-09

Born: Liverpool 15.4.82
6'0" 13st
Striker
FL Apps/Gls 62+46/33
Total Apps/Gls
71+51/37
Career: Burscough
1999, Dale 24.12.01
£20,000 [55+30/25],
Accrington St. loan
17.1.04 [3+3/2 Conf],
Accrington St. 22.7.04
[36+3/15 Conf],
Wrexham 11.7.05
[33+18/14], Accrington St. 30.7.07 [3+8/-], Dale loan 21.11.07 to 6.1.08 [3+4/3], Cambridge U. loan 18.1.08 [13+1/3 Conf], Cambridge U. 19.6.08 [17+1/8 Conf], Dale loan 26.11.08, signed 1.1.09 [4+12/5], Barrow loan 3.09 [6/1 Conf], Grays Ath. 28.9.09, Marine 1.10.09, Barrow 5.3.10 [1+5/- Conf], Sligo R. 6.10, Burscough 11.10, Droylsden 2.11, Chorley 10.8.11, Colwyn Bay 27.10.11, AFC Fylde 27.2.12, Warrington T. 8.12, Barrow 31.1.13 [+6/- Conf], Droylsden 8.3.13 to cs.13. Sacre Coeur F.P. 2015-16*
Honours: N. Ireland v Spain 2002, N. Ireland under-23 (1 cap) 2004, N. Ireland under-21 (9 caps) 2002-03, Conference play-off final 2008, FA Trophy winners 2010

Lee had netted 19 goals for Burscough in the first half of 2001-02 when John Hollins acquired him for the Dale (Hollins later becoming the player's agent). A powerful striker, he made a sensational start to his senior career, becoming Rochdale's first ever full international when he went on as substitute for N. Ireland against Spain just three months later (beating Paddy McCourt to the honour by just a few minutes). 'Evil' top scored with 17 in all games the following term, also playing regularly for the Irish under-21s and scoring against Scotland. He also created the unlikely record of becoming the first Rochdale 'goalkeeper' to score a FL goal when, having replaced the injured Matt Gilks between the posts, he scored from a penalty! He gradually fell out of favour in his third season, though, the returning Steve Parkin sending him off on loan at Accrington to improve his fitness. He subsequently had two further spells with Stanley and, oddly, made a loan move the other way, reappearing at Spotland in 2007 and scoring three times in his first four games. He scored twice to take Cambridge to the Conference play-off final at the end of the season and Dale borrowed him again the following term. However after signing him permanently they loaned him out, in turn, to Barrow, who he later assisted in their victory in the FA Trophy Final. He had 12 further spells with non-league outfits before

finishing in 2013, later figuring in the same side as Kevin Townson in Liverpool amateur football.

Stephen Graham (Steve) Jones 2001-02

Born: Derry 25.10.76
5'4" 10st9
Forward
FL Apps/Gls 6+3/1
Total Apps/Gls 6+3/1
Career: Chadderton, Blackpool 30.10.95, Bury 23.8.96, Sligo Rovers cs.97, Bray Wanderers loan 1999, Chorley 1999, Leigh RMI 8.99 [41+1/19 Conf], Crewe A. 4.7.01 £75,000 [122+37/39],
Dale loan 5.2.02 to 3.02 [6+3/1], Burnley 1.8.06 [38+20/6], Crewe A. loan 27.3.08 [2+2/1], Huddersfield T. loan 17.10.08 [2+2/-], Bradford C. loan 27.11.08 [25+2/3], Walsall 10.7.09 [34+9/9], Motherwell loan 20.1.11 [10+2/1 SPL], Newport Co. cs.11, Droylsden 12.8.11, AFC Telford 18.11.11 [35+10/13 Conf], Airbus UK Broughton 22.5.13, Nantwich T. 19.5.14*
Honours: N. Ireland B 2003, N. Ireland (29 caps) 2003 to 2007, England 'C' 2000, Unibond (NPL) champions 2000, Division 2+ promotion 2003, Conference team of the year 2001, League of Ireland Cup winners 1998, Scottish Cup final 2011

Though a product of Chadderton, Steve's first senior football was back in Ireland with Sligo, winning the League of Ireland Cup with them in 1998. He really made his mark at Leigh RMI with 45 goals in 103 games, being voted into the Conference team of the year in 2001 and appearing for the England semi-pro side against Scotland. Signed by Crewe he was allowed to join Dale on loan, netting just the once, but back at Gresty Road he helped them gain promotion in 2003 and netted 15 first division goals the following term, winning the player of the year award. He won the first of his 29 N. Ireland caps the same year and remained a Crewe regular until deciding to join Burnley in 2006. He was not a regular starter at Turf Moor, despite four goals in a pre-season game in Verona, and had several loan spells before signing for Walsall three years later. Oddly, with the Saddlers struggling at the foot of League 1, his final senior goal came when on loan to Scottish Premier League side Motherwell, for whom he played in the Scottish Cup Final just before he moved back to non-league football.

Paul David Simpson 2001-03

Born: Carlisle 26.7.66
5'6" 11st10
Winger
FL Apps/Gls 37+5/15
Total Apps/Gls
46+6/17
Career: Manchester C.
app 1982, pro 4.8.83
[99+22/18], Finn
Harps loan 1984-85,
Oxford U. 31.10.88
£200,000 [138+6/43],
Derby Co.20.2.92
£500,000
[134+52/48], Sheffield U. loan 6.12.96 [2+4/-],
Wolverhampton W. 10.10.97 £75,000 [32+20/6],
Walsall loan 17.9.98 [4/1], Walsall loan 11.12.98
[6/-], Blackpool 11.8.00 [69+7/13], Dale 25.3.02,
player-manager 6.02 to 7.5.03 [37+5/15], Carlisle
U. 7.8.03, player-manager 10.03 [30+5/6, +2/-
Conf], Preston NE manager 6.06 to 11.07,
Shrewsbury T. manager 12.3.08 to 5.10, Stockport
Co. manager 12.7.10 to 4.1.11, Cheadle College
coach 11.11, Northwich Victoria manager 1.2.12,
Rio Maior (Portugal) head coach 3.12 to 6.13,
Derby Co. coach 10.13, Newcastle U. assistant
manager 7.15 to 3.16
Honours: England youth international (3 caps),
England under-21 (5 caps) 1986-87, Full Members
Cup final 1986, LDV Vans Trophy winners 2002,
Anglo-Italian Cup winners 1993, Division 2
promotion 1985, (1989), Division 1+ play-off final
1994, promotion 1996, (Division 2+ promotion
1999), Division 3+ play-off final winners 2001. As
manager; Conference play-off winners 2005,
League 2 champions 2006, FL Trophy final 2006,
League 2 Play-off final 2009, LMA League 2
manager of the season 2006

Paul made his debut for Manchester City when he
was just turned 16, subsequently playing in their
1985 promotion campaign and winning five caps
for England under-21s as a winger with an eye for
goal. Sold to then second division Oxford he added
another century of appearances to those with City
and was then sold to Derby for £500,000 scoring
10 goals when they were promoted to the top flight
in 1996. He moved on to Wolves, who reached the
FA Cup semi-final, and then Blackpool, where he
was a member of the side which pipped Dale to a
play-off place in 2001 (scoring in the final). He
appeared at Wembley in the LDV Vans Trophy just
a few days before being Dale's last signing as they
finally did reach the play-offs for the first time,
scoring five times in seven games. When Johnny
Hollins left in the summer, Paul was given the role
of player manager and the side were 2nd after 11
games, with Paul himself netting a hat-trick in a 5-
2 win at Wrexham. However, despite a sensational
run to the 5th round of the FA Cup, beating first
division sides Preston and Coventry, a steady slide

down the table, with only one win in 14 games at
one stage, saw them only just avoid the relegation
places and Paul left the club. Joining Carlisle as a
player, with them at the foot of the table, he was
soon promoted to player-manager but despite
some improvement was unable to prevent their
relegation. Promoted from the Conference at the
first attempt, Paul led the Cumbrians to promotion
to League 1 the following year, also taking his
overall tallies to 673 games and 150 goals in the
FL. Unable to repeat this success at Preston, he
took Shrewsbury to the play-offs in 2009 but was
sacked when they failed to repeat that the
following year and Paul was boss of Stockport at
the start of the season that saw them lose their FL
place. Holder of a degree in sports science
undertaken while still playing, and a postgraduate
qualification in applied management from
Warwick Business School, he later worked as a
coach with VisionPro Sports Institute in Portugal
before becoming assistant manager back at Derby
and then following boss Steve McLaren to
Newcastle. Paul's son Jake played for Shrewsbury
and Stockport while he was their manager and
another son, Joe, became a referee.

Eduard (Eddie) Loewen 2002-03
Born: Lithuania c.1979 6'2"
Central defender
FL Apps/Gls 0/0 Total Apps/Gls 1+1/0
Career: FC Preussen Espelkamp (Germany) jnr, SC
Herford (Germany) jnr, FC Remscheid (Germany)
pro 1998, Berry College (Georgia, USA) 2000,
University of Akron (USA) 2002, Dale trial 7.02 to
8.02, Cincinatti Riverhawks (USA) 2004, Cocoa
Expos (USA) 2005, Armenia Bielefeld (Germany),
BSV Rehden (Germany) 2006, TUS Dielingen
(Germany) player-coach 2007 to 2008.
CONCACAF coaching instructor 1.14 and St Pete
Strikers (Florida, USA) director of coaching 6.14*
Honours: Germany (at beach football) 2000 to
2009

A trialist central defender with a rather unusual
pedigree, Eddie figured for Dale in the Isle of Man
tournament games in the summer of 2002. Born in
Lithuania but brought up in Germany where he
turned professional with Remscheid, he left for
college in the USA, where he took a masters in
sports science, before resuming his senior career
with Cincinatti Riverhawks in the A-League. He
also played for further clubs in Germany but by
this point he was more prominent in beach
football. First playing for the German national side
in 2000 against Eric Cantona's French side, he
played in the 2001 beach world cup in Brazil and
was player coach of the German side in the 2004
world cup, continuing in the role until 2009. He
also coached the Israeli and Indian beach soccer
sides. As "one of the world's most respected beach
soccer coaches", he co-authored the official FIFA

beach soccer coaching manual, ran the Everton Florida soccer camps and was then recruited by the United Soccer League to promote beach soccer events in the US. In 2012 he became CEO of GFL Soccer Enterprises and also worked for CONCAFAF.

Stephen Roy (Steve) Macauley 2002-03

Born: Lytham 4.3.69 6'1" 12st10
Central defender
FL Apps/Gls 6/0 Total Apps/Gls 7/0
Career: Manchester C. yts 1986, pro 5.11.87 to 1988-89, Fleetwood T., Crewe A. 24.3.92 £25,000 [247+14/26], Macclesfield T. loan 14.12.01 [4/-], Macclesfield T. loan 15.2.02 [8/-], Dale 29.7.02 [6/-], Macclesfield T. loan 22.11.02 [4/1], Macclesfield T. loan 16.1.03, signed 3.03 [32/-], Bamber Bridge cs.04, Fleetwoood T. coach and physio 2005 to 5.08, caretaker manager 9.08, coach 10.08
Honours: FA Youth Cup 1986, Division 3+ promotion 1994, Division 2+ play-off winners 1997

Steve had a very long association with Crewe, appearing 317 times in all games over the course of a decade with the club. He played in two promotion winning sides and scored 30 goals from his central defensive position. One of Paul Simpson's first signings in 2002, he lasted just six games before an injury led to him losing his place back to the even older Richard Jobson and he headed off on loan to Macclesfield (for the third and fourth times) before eventually signing for them. He also had a somewhat delayed joint testimonial at Crewe with long time defensive colleague Shaun Smith (q.v.) in 2003. Towards the end of his career he gained a degree in physiotherapy at Salford University and subsequently worked as Fleetwood Town physio as well as having his own practice.

Christopher Stephen (Chris) Beech 2002-04

Born: Blackpool 16.9.74 5'11" 11st12
Midfield
FL Apps/Gls 25+7/1 Total Apps/Gls 31+8/2
Career: Fleetwood HS, Blackpool jnr, yts 1991, pro 9.7.93 [53+29/4], Hartlepool U. 18.7.96 [92+2/23], Huddersfield T. 27.11.98 £65,000 [63+8/12], Dale 22.7.02 [25+7/1], Barrow cs.04, Lancaster C., Fleetwood T. 10.04, Bury youth team manager 2005, Dale youth team manager 6.07, caretaker manager 12.11 to 1.12, assistant manager 1.13*
Honours: Lancashire Schools, Lancashire Cup winners 1993-94, 1994-95, NWC League promotion 2005. As coach; Youth Alliance winners 2011, League 2 promotion 2014

After three seasons in and out of the Blackpool side, Chris became a regular at Hartlepool, scoring against Dale in three consecutive meetings, but after a contract dispute was sold to Huddersfield. A midfielder with a good scoring record, he lost his place when Huddersfield were relegated from Division 1 and signed for Dale. Unfortunately he suffered a succession of injuries and his biggest contribution to the Dale's cause came after he returned to the club to run a highly successful youth team. (In between he appeared for Fleetwood at the start of their dramatic rise up the leagues, one of seven members of his family to do so over the years). After gaining his UEFA licence, he was caretaker manager for six games after Steve Eyre was sacked, before returning to the youth set-up. When Keith Hill returned, Chris was promoted to assistant manager and was able to see several of his youth team products make it at league level as Dale moved up to League 1.

Lee Leslie Hodges 2002-03

Born: Plaistow 2.3.78 5'5" 10st2
Winger
FL Apps/Gls 3+4/0 Total Apps/Gls 6+5/1
Career: Arsenal jnr, West Ham U. jnr 1992, yts 1994, pro 2.3.95 [+3/-], Exeter C. loan 13.9.96 [16+1/-], Leyton O. loan 28.2.97 [3/-], Plymouth A. loan 6.1.97 [9/-], Ipswich T. 20.11.98 [+4/-], Southend U. loan 25.3.99 [10/1], Scunthorpe U. 8.7.99 £50,000 [97+16/20], Dale trial 7.02, signed 9.8.02 [3+4/-], Colchester U. trial 11.02, Bristol R. loan 21.3.03 [7+1/-], Bristol R. 5.03 [5+8/2], Thurrock T. 8.04, Billericay T. 2.06, AFC Hornchurch cs.08, East Thurrock 12.08, Billericay T. player-assistant manager 3.09, Tilbury player-coach cs.09, Braintree T. 1.10, East Thurrock U. player-coach 8.10, Malden & Tiptree, Thurrock player-coach 1.11, Aveley manager 11.11 to 2.12 (+ Ockendon Motor Spares; Thurrock Sunday League)
Honours: England Schools, England under-16s (9 caps), PFA Division 3 team of the year 2001, 2002

A West Ham youngster, Lee made his mark as an exciting winger in three seasons at Scunthorpe, twice being voted into the third division PFA team of the year. Viewed by Dale fans as a tremendous signing when he arrived, in the event a lack of match fitness and his being primarily an outside left like player-manager Paul Simpson, led to a rapid disappearance from the scene. After a loan spell at Bristol Rovers, he fared little better there when signing permanently and left for non-league football when still only 26, playing and coaching in the Essex area for a number of years.

Scott John Warner 2000-06

Born: Rochdale 3.12.83 5'11" 11st11
Midfield
FL Apps/Gls 57+16/2
Total Apps/Gls 63+21/2
Career: Lowerplace School, Springhill HS, Butterworth Sports Norden, Rochdale Rangers, Rochdale St Clements, Dale as 1999, yts 2000, pro 29.7.03 [57+16/2], Radcliffe Borough 4.8.06, Hyde U. 1.2.07 to 2008, Copperpot (Sunday League) 2009 to 2011, {Sacred Heart 8.13?}
Honours: Rochdale Town boys, Greater Manchester County Schools, North of England Schools v South of England, Ireland 1999, Rochdale Sunday League cup winners 2010, premier division champions 2011

The captain of the North of England Schools team, Scott was in Dale's youth cup team in 1999 along with Matt Gilks, the Duffy brothers, Stephen Hill, Danny Taylor and David Walsh, and apart from Gilks was the one with the most impact in the senior side. After two seasons in the reserves he was given his chance by Paul Simpson in the summer tournament in the Isle of Man and made his first league starts on the right wing or at wing back at the end of 2002. His second game was the giant killing defeat of Preston, and Scott and Stephen Hill both featured in the televised Wolves cup tie. Ignored by Alan Buckley, he reappeared under Steve Parkin and was a fairly regular performer in midfield for the next two seasons, though frequently on the bench. His strike against Torquay in 2005 was voted goal of the season. He later played for top local Sunday League outfit Copperpot.

Ian William Bishop 2002-03

Born: Liverpool 29.5.65
5'9" 10st12
Midfield
FL Apps/Gls 5+3/0 Total Apps/Gls 6+3/0
Career: Everton app 1982, pro 24.5.83 [+1/-], Crewe A. loan 22.3.84 [4/-], Carlisle U. 11.10.84 £15,000 [131+1/14], Bournemouth 14.7.88 £35,000 [44/2], Manchester C. 2.8.89 £465,000 [18+1/2], West Ham U. 28.12.89 £500,000 [240+14/12], Manchester C. 26.3.98 [53+25/2], Miami Fusion [23/- MLS] 26.3.01, Barry T. summer 2002, Dale 30.8.02 [5+3/-], Radcliffe Borough 11.02, New Orleans Shell Shockers (USA), Syracuse Salty Dogs (USA) 2003, Burscough player-assistant manager 2003-04, Radcliffe Borough 2003-04, Burscough coach 2004, West Ham international academy (USA) coach
Honours: England 'B' 1991, Division 2 promotion 1991, Division 1+ promotion 1993, 2000, Division 2+ play-off winners 1999, (NPL Division 1 promotion 2003)

Ian had four seasons at Carlisle, being sent off at Spotland in 1987, but first came to real prominence at Bournemouth who sold him to Manchester City for a huge fee. After only a few months he was transferred to West Ham, missing only two games in midfield in their promotion campaign in 1991 and only one in the top flight the following year, eventually playing over 250 times in total. A return to City saw him figure in two more promotion sides, playing at Wembley for the first time at the age of 34, but a stint in Miami ended when Fusion went out of business. He played for Barry Town in the preliminary rounds of the Champions League and was with Dale briefly early in the 2002-03 season. Alternating between local non-league and US football, Ian played amongst others for 'sixties Dale player Laurie Calloway's Syracuse Salty Dogs in the A-League and moved permanently to Florida to run his own soccer academy, also coaching at the West Ham International Academy in North America.

Rory Christopher Patterson 2001-04

Born: Strabane 16.7.84 5'10"
10st13
Forward
FL Apps/Gls 5+10/0 Total Apps/Gls 6+13/0
Career: St Mary's School (Strabane), Sion Swifts, Moorfield Celtic, Townend U., St Colman's HS (Strabane), Dunganon Swifts,

Foyle Harps, Tranmere R. trial, Dale trial cs.01, sch 2001 [5+10/-], Radcliffe Borough cs.04, Mossley 11.04, Lancashire Lass (Sunday League) 2004-05, FC United of Manchester cs.05, Bradford PA 7.08, Droylsden 2009, Coleraine 29.6.09, Plymouth A. 7.10 [21+14/4], Linfield loan 8.11, Derry C. 1.12, Cockburn C. (Perth, Australia) 2.15, FC United of Manchester 30.10.15, Derry C. 23.12.15*
Honours: County Tyrone, N. Ireland youth international, N. Ireland under-19, N. Ireland (5 caps) 2010, N. Ireland (junior) cup winners (twice), North West Ireland (junior) league and cup, NW Counties League division 2 champions 2006, NWC division 1 champions 2007, President's Cup (NPL) winners 2008, FA of Ireland Cup winners 2012, Setanta Cup final 2012, Ulster footballer of the year 2010

A schoolboy star in Northern Ireland (where he also competed in hurling), Rory first appeared for Dale in pre-season games in 2001 and after joining them as a scholar netted a hattrick in the Youth Cup. His first senior appearance came in a FRT game in October 2002, but despite appearing for the Irish under-19s the same season made only a handfull of starts before dropping into non-league football two years later. A member of the first ever FCUM side, he figured in three successive promotions and his 33 goals in 2007-08 – he netted a total of 107 in 126 games – earned him moves back up the pyramid. A season back in his native country saw him net 41 times for Coleraine, including four against Glentoran. He also won his first full cap the same year and was voted Ulster footballer of the year. He was supposed to have signed for Glentoran in 2010, before Plymouth negotiated his transfer. Recapturing his goalscoring form with Derry, he netted 61 times in 92 games, including an extra time winner in the Setanta Cup final and a hat-trick in a Europa League qualifier. In 2015 he left to play in the Western Australia Premier League but then returned to Derry.

Shane Lewis Cansdell-Sherriff

2002-03, 2012-13
Born: Sydney, Australia 10.11.82 6'0" 11st12
Central defender
FL Apps/Gls 19+1/0
Total Apps/Gls 20+1/0
Career: Westfield Sports High, NSW Institute of Sport, Leeds U. 1.2.00, Dale loan 8.11.02 to 12.02 [3/-], Aarhus GF (Denmark) 2003, Tranmere R. 24.7.06 [83+4/6], Shrewsbury T. 5.8.08 £300,000

[142+8/9], Preston NE cs.12 [14+1/1], Dale loan 30.1.13 to 4.13 [16+1/-], Burton A. loan 9.13 [32/-], Burton A. 28.5.14 to 5.16 [66/2]
Honours: Australian under-17s (16 caps), FIFA under-17 World Cup runners-up 1999, Australia under-23 (Olympic tournament) 2004, League 2 promotion 2012, champions 2015, play-off final (2009), 2014, League 1 promotion 2016

A member of the Australia side which lost on penalties to Brazil in the final of the under-17s World Cup, Shane joined Leeds the following year, being transformed from a midfielder to a central defender. His FL debut came in a brief stint at Spotland before he headed off to Denmark figuring over 80 times in their Superliga. Returning to the UK in 2006, he was subsequently transferred to Shrewsbury for a big fee and earned promotion from League 2 in 2012. Briefly at Preston, he had a second, lengthier, loan spell with Dale in Keith Hill's first season back with the club, but then figured in Burton Albion's remarkable rise, winning successive promotions.

Jesus ('Chus') Fernandez-Mengual 2002-03
Born: Barcelona, Spain 25.12.79 6'2" 13st
Midfield
FL Apps/Gls +0/0 Total Apps/Goals +0/0
Career: Real Zaragoza B (Spain) 1998-99, SD Huesca (Spain) 2001-02, Oldham A. trial 8.02, n/c 9.02, Dale trial, n/c 11.02 to 12.02, CD Binefar (Spain), UD Barbastro (Spain) 2005-06, CD Olimpic de Xativa (Spain) 2007-08, Burjassot CF (Spain) 2008-09

Perhaps unsurprisingly named Jesus as he was born on Christmas Day, 'Chus' had played in the reserves at Real Zaragoza and for Huesca, both in the Spanish Liga 2B, before coming to the UK to study economics at Salford University. He was briefly on non-contract forms at Oldham and was recommended to Dale by Dave Cross. He was on the bench for a couple of league games but was not retained. After his studies he returned to Spain and played for a number of third division sides.

Gavin Mark John Melaugh 2002-03

Born: Derry 9.7.81
5'9" 9st7
Midfield
FL Apps/Gls 17+2/1 Total Apps/Goals 22+2/2
Career: Oxford U. Stars (Derry) jnr, Aston Villa jnr 1996, yts 1997, pro 17.7.98, Dale 7.11.02 [17+2/1], Partick Thistle trial, Glentoran 7.03, Donegal Celtic 7.06, Ballymena U. 1.07, Lisburn Distillery 6.09 to 2010

Honours: N. Ireland under-21 (11 caps) 2002 to 2003, N. Ireland senior squad 2002, Irish League champions 2005, Irish Cup winners 2004, final 2006

A junior with Villa, Gavin's progress had been disrupted by a serious neck injury in an under-19s game. Even so, he had been an unused substitute for a weakened Northern Ireland team the day that Lee McEvilly and Paddy McCourt made their debuts. Paul Simpson recruited him half way through his season in charge just in time for him to figure in the famous cup run and his best remembered moment was when he deflected the manager's shot into the net for the equaliser against Wolves. He played for the Irish under-21s the same season, along with McCourt and McEvilly, and he and McEvilly both scored against Finland. Returning to Ireland, he won both league and cup honours with Glentoran.

Lee David Andrews 2002-03

Born: Carlisle 23.4.83
6'0" 10st12
Defender
FL Apps/Gls 8/0 Total
Apps/Gls 8/0
Career: Carlisle U. yts
1999, pro 27.6.01
[82+10/-, 12+2/- Conf],
Dale loan 25.2.03 to
30.3.03 [8/-], York C. loan
11.05 [9/- Conf], Torquay
U. loan 17.3.06 [6+1/-],
Torquay U. 6.06 [46/-],
Newcastle Blue Star 9.07, Workington 4.08, coach
2014-15, assistant manager 6.15*
Honours: Conference promotion 2005, League 2
champions 2006

Lee spent his early career with his home town club Carlisle, being player of the year in his first season (and one of only two players paid that summer by eccentric chairman Knighton). He suffered relegation to the Conference with them in 2004, but then played in successive promotion sides, albeit only in one game in the second campaign. He had also played for Paul Simpson in 2002-03 when Dale borrowed him as defensive cover, Lee figuring at wing back or centre back in eight games in a month, only two of which were lost. Unusually, he played in every game for Torquay in what turned out to be his last season in the FL, the Gulls also losing their league place. He has since had a very long spell with Workington, playing well over 200 games by 2016.

Michael John Taylor 2002-03

Born: Liverpool 21.11.82
6'1" 12st13
Defender
FL Apps/Gls 2/0 Total
Apps/Gls 2/0
Career: Blackburn R. yts
1998, pro 25.11.99, Carlisle
U. loan 27.9.02 [10/-], Dale
loan 27.3.03 to 4.03 [2/-],
Cheltenham T. 29.7.04
[19+4/-], Forest Green
Rovers loan 3.06 [10/-
Conf], Halifax T. 4.7.06,
Lancaster C. 8.06, Barrow 10.06, Hyde U. 10.06,
TNS 2007, Fleetwood T. 1.09, Hyde U. 9.7.10,
Chester FC 29.12.10, AFC Fylde loan 9.12, signed
11.12, Marine 10.13
Honours: League 2 promotion 2006

Michael had played a number of games on loan to Carlisle when Dale borrowed him along with Darren Hockenhull in March 2003. He played in the next two games at centre back in the absence of Wayne Evan but didn't appear further. After leaving Blackburn he had two years on the fringes of the side at Cheltenham before a lengthy trail around the non-league circuit, ending with Marine in 2013.

Darren Hockenhull 2002-03

Born: St Helens 5.9.82
5'9" 10st10
Defender/midfield
FL Apps/Gls 6+1/1
Total Apps/Gls 6+1/1
Career: Burscough,
Blackburn R. yts 2001,
pro 4.7.02, Darlington
loan 28.2.03, Dale loan
27.3.03 to 5.03 [6+1/1],
Halifax T. 7.03 [32+6/-
Conf], Stalybridge Celtic
10.8.05, Woodley
Sports, Witton Albion,
Bradford PA 5.8.07, Salford C. 8.3.09, caretaker
manager 4.12 to 5.12

Joining Dale along with fellow Blackburn reserve defender Michael Taylor, Darren figured at wing back on his Dale debut but played his other games on the right of midfield, netting the winner against Hull. These proved to be Darren's only FL games, but he played at right back for Halifax in the Conference as well as for other non-league sides. He was Salford City's player of the year in 2010-11 and as captain took over briefly as caretaker manager when Rhodri Giggs resigned in April 2012.

Neil Robert Bennett 2002-03

Born: Dewsbury
29.10.80 6'2" 13st
Goalkeeper
FL Apps 1 Total Apps 1
Career: Sheffield W. yts
1997, pro 20.10.98,
Ossett T. cs.00, Trafford
loan, Airdrieonians
7.8.01 [10+1 ScL],
Barrow 8.02, Drogheda
U. 11.02, Bradford C.
1.03, Dale 27.3.03 [1],
Coventry C. trial cs.03,
Derry C. 8.03, Skelmersdale 8.03, Albion R. 9.03
[26+1 ScL], Partick Thistle cs.04 [1 ScL], Forfar
loan 9.04, Ossett T. 9.05, Ossett Albion 2006,
Guiseley 3.10, Ossett T. 8.10, **Wakefield T. 9.12**,
Ossett Albion cs.14 (also commercial manager
5.15)*
Honours: (Scottish League Challenge Cup winners
2002)

Neil managed the unlikely feat of playing against
Barcelona after being freed by the Dale. Though on
Wednesday's books as a teenager, his only senior
games prior to arriving at Spotland had been for
Airdrie, where he was unused substitute in the
Challenge Cup Final and played in the team which
finished runners up in Division 1 but went
bankrupt. He played one game for Dale, a 1-0
home defeat by Kidderminster in April 2003, when
Matt Gilks was injured, and was on the bench for
the rest of the season. The following year he
figured in the UEFA Cup with Derry City, after
playing in their prestigious friendly with
Barcelona. He spent the rest of the season with
Albion Rovers and was then Kenny Arthur's (q.v.)
deputy at Partick before returning to a long stint in
Yorkshire non-league football, doubling as Ossett
Albion's commercial manager.

Daryl Burgess 2003-05

Born: Birmingham
24.1.71 5'11" 12st4
Central defender
FL Apps/Gls 52+4/0
Total Apps/Gls 61+4/0
Career: West Bromwich
A. yts 1987, pro 1.7.89
[317+15/10],
Northampton T. 5.7.01
[60+1/2], Dale 6.8.03
[52+4/-],
Kidderminster H. cs.05
[34/- Conf], Nuneaton
Borough cs.06,
Bromsgrove Rovers
1.08, assistant manager
cs.08, caretaker manager 9.08
Honours: Division 2+ promotion 1993

An experienced centre back, Daryl was new Dale
manager Alan Buckley's first signing, having
played under him during a long stint at West
Brom, where he also played alongside Tony Ford.
In all Daryl played 377 games for the Baggies,
gaining promotion to the second tier with them in
1993. He played regularly for much of his single
season at Spotland until replaced by Greg Heald.
Returning to the midlands to play non-league
football, he joined Kidderminster Harriers along
with Wayne Evans. He was assistant manager at
Bromsgrove Rovers for a short time and became a
partner in a coaching academy.

Michael James Simpkins 2003-04

Born: Sheffield
28.11.78 6'1" 12st
Left back
FL Apps/Gls 25+2/0
Total Apps/Gls
29+2/0
Career: Sheffield W.
yts 1996, pro 9.7.97,
Chesterfield 26.3.98
[22+4/-], Cardiff C.
29.5.01 [13+4/-],
Exeter C. loan
20.9.02 [4+1/-],
Cheltenham T. loan
23.12.02 [2/-], Dale
6.8.03 [25+2/-],
Burton A. 8.04
[14+6/1 Conf],
Alfreton T. loan 1.05, Leigh RMI 3.05 [6/- Conf],
Worksop T. 27.7.05, Buxton 9.06, Grantham T.
9.10.06, Retford U. 1.08, Worksop T. 10.5.10,
Frickley Ath. 6.11, Belper T. 29.10.11 to cs.13
Honours: Division 3+ promotion 2001, NPL
division 1 south champions 2008, 2009

Michael had played a number of games for
Chesterfield when they were promoted and for
Cardiff in Division 2 and was first choice left back
under Alan Buckley, but never endeared himself to
Dale fans as the side struggled. He was sent off
when Dale won their first game of the season at the
fifth attempt, collected more yellow cards than any
other player in the division and was later
disciplined by the club for arguing with fans during
a game. He played only three games after Steve
Parkin's return but subsequently had a lengthy
non-league career despite being released because
of his poor disciplinary record in his first spell at
Workop and apparently left Frickley after a similar
incident to that at Spotland.

Leonida Christos (Leo) Bertos 2003-05

Born: Wellington, New Zealand 20.12.81 6'0" 12st6
Winger
FL Apps/Gls 73+9/13
Total Apps/Gls 80+10/14
Career: Wellington College 1995, Wellington Oympic 1997, Manchester C. trial cs.00, Barnsley 1.9.00 [4+8/1], Dale 25.7.03 [73+9/13], Swindon T. trial, Bristol R. trial, Chester 22.8.05 [2+3/-], Barrow trial, York C. 11.05 [3+3/- Conf], Scarborough 2006 [1/- Conf], Worksop T., Perth Glory cs.06, Skoda Xanthi (Greece) loan 2007, Wellington Phoenix 24.1.08, East Bengal (India) 19.7.14, NorthEast United loan 10.14, Northern New South Wales Football Federation youth coach 10.15, Hamilton Olympic 2016*
Honours: New Zealand schools, New Zealand youth international, New Zealand under-19, New Zealand under-21, New Zealand under-23s (5 caps) 2003-04 (Olympic tournament), New Zealand 2003 – 2013 (52 full caps), A-League preliminary final 2010, New Zealand futsal 2014 (2 caps)

Undoubtedly the most successful of the new signings in 2003, Leo had left New Zealand to join Barnsley whose youth team manager was a New Zealand international. He scored a spectacular goal in a pre-season friendly and was quickly signed up by the Dale. He was their usual right winger over the next two years, netting ten goals in his first season including the winner against Kidderminster that guaranteed Dale's survival. He made his debut for the New Zealand international team just a couple of months after arriving at Spotland and also played for the New Zealand under-23s in the Olympic football qualifiers. Following unsuccessful trials at other clubs, he returned home and became a fixture in the 'All Whites' side, playing against Brazil in 2006 and in the Confederations Cup in South Africa in 2009, before figuring – at wing back - in the greatest result in their history when they drew with Italy in the 2010 World Cup finals. Leo is easily the most capped ex-Dale player, with 52 appearances. At club level he was Wellington Phoenix's player of the year in 2009 and they reached the finals series in 2010 and 2012. He was recruited to play for the New Zealand futsal team in 2014, then left to play in the I-League, also figuring for the NorthEast franchise in the new Indian Super League. Leo is also a trustee of the Aotearoa football charity providing opportunities for Maoris and Pacific islanders through football.

Christopher Alan (Chris) Shuker 2003-04

Born: Liverpool 9.5.82
5'5" 10st1
Forward
FL Apps/Gls 14/1 Total Apps/Gls 15/1
Career: Everton jnr, (Sunday League), Manchester C. yts 1998, pro 21.8.99 [1+4/-], Macclesfield T. loan 27.3.00 [6+3/1], Walsall loan 26.2.03 [3+2/-], Dale loan 7.8.03 to 10.03 [14/1], Hartlepool U. loan 13.12.03 [14/1], Barnsley 17.3.04 [93+7/17], Tranmere R. 17.7.06 [106+17/14], Motherwell trial cs.10, Wellington Phoenix trial cs.10, Morecambe 8.10 to cs.11 [12+15/2]. Port Vale trial 12.11, n/c 2.12, signed 5.12 [27+28/1], retired 5.14. Tranmere R. coach 10.14, player-coach 23.12.14 [1+2/-], Trafford 9.15, assistant manager 11.15*
Honours: Division 1+ champions 2002, League 1 play-off winners 2006, League 2 promotion 2013, PFA League 1 team of the year 2007

Chris scored on his Manchester City debut in the League Cup and made two substitute appearances when City were promoted to the Premier League. One of his several loan spells took him to Dale after scoring against them in a pre-season friendly. Initially used up front in place of Kevin Townson, his size meant he was better suited to the wide role he subsequently undertook. He made centuries of appearances for both Barnsley and Tranmere, where he was used mainly in midfield. He scored one of the penalties in Barnsley's shoot-out victory over Swansea in the 2006 play-off final and missed only one league game between 2004 and 2007, when he was included in the League 1 team of the year. In 2010 he had a trial with Leo Bertos's Wellington Phoenix in a friendly against Boca Juniors before joining Morecambe and later winning another promotion with Port Vale. Retiring with a chronic knee injury in 2014, he followed his former Port Vale boss Micky Adams to Tranmere as coach and subsequently made a brief playing comeback but could not prevent Rovers' relegation to the Conference.

Robert Betts 2003-04

Born: Doncaster
21.12.81 5'10" 11st
Midfield
FL Apps/Gls 4+1/2
Total Apps/Gls
4+2/2
Career: Doncaster R.
yts 1997 [2+1/-],
Coventry C. yts 1998,
pro 23.12.98 [5+8/-],
Plymouth A. loan
16.2.01 [3+1/-],
Lincoln C. loan
11.10.01 [1+2/-], AIK
Solnia, Dale n/c 5.8.03 [4+1/2], Kidderminster H.
12.9.03 [8+1/-], Hereford U. 24.3.04 [3+2/- Conf],
Racing Club Warrick n/c cs.04, **Forest Green
Rovers** 9.04, Racing Club Warwick 10.04, Quorn
2006, (Australia 2008)
Honours: Youth cup final 1999, 2000

The nephew of former Manchester United player
Maurice Setters, Robert played for Doncaster when
he was 16, figuring in their last three games before
they dropped out of the league. Taken on by
Premier League Coventry, he appeared in two
Youth Cup Finals but in only a handful of senior
games, though he did score in an 8-0 League Cup
demolition of Rushden & Diamonds. He joined
Dale on non-contract terms and his two goals at
Torquay earned their first victory of the season. He
turned down the offer of a contract for the rest of
the season, preferring to sign for Kidderminster.
He was voted Midland Alliance player of the year
in 2007 while with Quorn.

Gerard Daniel (Ged) Brannan 2003-04

Born: Prescot
15.1.72 6'0" 12st3
Midfield
FL Apps/Gls 11/1
Total Apps/Gls
13/1
Career: Tranmere
R. yts 1987, pro
3.7.90
[227+11/20],
Manchester C.
12.3.97 £750,000
[38+5/4], Norwich
C. loan 21.8.98
[10+1/1],
Motherwell
28.10.98 £375,000
[81/16 ScL], Wigan A. 16.2.01 £175,000 [49+3/-],
Dunfermline loan 31.1.03 [8/- ScL], Dale loan
11.9.03 [11/1], Accrington St. 11.03 [45+4/7 Conf],
Radcliffe Borough 10.05, Morecambe 11.05 to
cs.07 [40+16/1 Conf], Vauxhall Motors 11.07,
Burscough 2008

Honours: Division 3 play-off winners 1991,
Division 2+ champions 2003, Conference play-off
winners 2007, Leyland Daf Trophy final 1991,
Cayman Islands XI v D.C. United

Ged made his name in a long spell at Tranmere,
playing left back in their play-off final victory and
in the Leyland Daf Trophy final at the end of his
first season, though he also appeared in midfield.
He was signed by Manchester City for a big fee, but
City dropped into the third tier for the first time
and Ged was released. While with Motherwell, he
was one of a number of British players (none with
any connections to the place) invited to play for the
Cayman Islands in the World Cup, before FIFA
intervened. He spent two months on loan with
Dale, playing 13 games in midfield and scoring
from the spot in one of only two victories in that
time. He later netted a Conference hat-trick for
Accrington (including two penalties) and helped
Morecambe gain a place in the league, becoming
the first player to win play-offs at both the old and
new Wembley.

Mickael Antoine-Curier 2003-04

Born: Orsay, France
5.3.83 6'0" 12st4
Striker
FL Apps/Gls 5+3/1
Total Apps/Gals 5+5/1
Career: Paris Saint-
Germain (France) jnr,
OG Nice (France) jnr
1999, Nancy (France),
Preston NE 29.11.00,
Nottingham F. 22.6.01,
Brenford loan 10.3.03
[11/3], Oldham A.
8.8.03 [5+3/2],
Kidderminster H.
19.9.03 [+1/-], Dale
23.9.03 n/c [5+3/1], Sheffield W. 21.11.03 [+1/-],
Burnley n/c, Lillestrom (Norway) trial c.1.04,
Notts Co. 19.2.04 [4/1], Grimsby T. 19.3.04
[3+2/-], Vard Haugesund (Norway) cs.04, FK
Haugesund (Norway), Hibernian trial 7.07, signed
31.8.07 [8+5/3 ScL], Dundee loan 1.08, signed
7.5.08 to 15.10.10 [40+3/22 ScL], Hamilton Ac.
loan 8.09 [25+1/7 ScL], Hamilton Ac. 11.1.11
[10+3/4 ScL], Ermis Aradippou (Cyprus) 14.7.11,
Ethniko Achnas (Cyprus) 8.11, Felda U. (Malaysia)
4.12, Etyrau (Kazakhstan) 2.13, Hamilton Ac. 8.13
[37+14/20 ScL], Burton A. 18.2.15 [1+4/-],
Dunfermline A. trial 8.15, signed 9.15 [1+8/2 ScL],
Royal Union Saint-Gilloise (Belgium) 1.16*
Honours: Guadaloupe international 2008-2012
(16 caps), Scottish Championship play-off winners
2014, League 2 champions 2015

Mickael started out in beach football in Guadeloupe, then signed for Paris Saint-Germain as a junior before moving to the UK. Despite being top scorer with 22 goals and player of the year in Forest's academy side he did not make the first team and at the start of 2003-04 signed for Oldham. He then spent 10 days at Kidderminster before two months as a non-contract player with Dale, netting on his debut. By November he was at Sheffield Wednesday and by the end of the season had also played in the league for Notts County and Grimsby, stints with Lillestrom and Burnley giving him a remarkable eight clubs in one season. Next moving to Norway, he became more settled, winning the golden boot, with 27 goals in 21 games, and the division 2 player of the year in 2005. He netted four goals in a pre-season friendly for Hibs, unsurprisingly signing for them shortly afterward, but had more success when joining Dundee, with 14 goals in 2008-09, later extending his globe-trotting career to other countries including, somewhat bizarrely, Kazakhstan. Back at Hamilton, he scored four in a 10-2 thrashing of Morton as the Accies won promotion to the Scottish Premier and headed the table in October 2014. In 2016, he added Belgium to his repertoire. Mickael played for Guadeloupe in the Caribbean Cup in 2008 and the CONCACAF Gold Cup the following year, netting nine goals in 16 internationals.

Craig Scott Strachan 2003-04

Born: Aberdeen 19.5.82 5'8" 10st6
Midfield
FL Apps/Gls +1/0 Total Apps/Gls +1/0
Career: Coventry C. yts 1998, pro 20.12.99, Dale n/c 5.8.03 to 10.03 [+1/-], Halesowen T. 2003-04 to 2006

Son of then Coventry boss Gordon, the former Scottish international, and brother of Gavin, who was also with Coventry, Craig's progress was hampered by injuries and in a last attempt to resurrect his career signed non-contract forms for Dale in 2003. He managed a single substitute appearance, in a defeat at Macclesfield, before giving up with shin splints. He later changed sports and became a PGA golf pro, though also helping to run the Strachan soccer schools.

Andrew Jamie (Andy) Bishop 2003-04

Born: Stone 19.10.82
6'0" 11st2
Striker
FL Apps/Gls 8+2/1
Total Apps/Gls 9+2/1
Career: Walsall jnr 2000, yts 2001, pro 5.8.02, Kidderminster H. loan 18.11.02 [22+7/5], Kidderminster H. loan 5.8.03 [8+3/2], Dale loan 20.11.03 to 26.1.04 [8+2/1], Yeovil T. loan 5.2.04 [4+1/2], York C. 7.04 [72+6/34 Conf], Bury 1.7.06 [198+40/69], Wrexham loan 9.12 [4/2 Conf], Wrexham 9.7.13 [57+20/14 Conf], FC Halifax T. 23.6.15 [1+2/- Conf], Southport 28.8.15 [13+10/3 Conf], caretaker manager 3.16*
Honours: England 'C' (4 caps), League 2 promotion 2011

Andy did not make the first team at Walsall but had useful loan spells at Kidderminster before joining Dale on similar terms and being used up front in succession to Antoine-Curier. He was the Conference's top scorer with 23 goals while at York, gaining four caps for England 'C'. This led to a move to Bury, where he netted 21 times in his first season and grabbed 19 league goals in 2007-08. Hit by injuries later in his spell at Gigg Lane, he nevertheless accumulated well over 250 appearances and 83 goals in all games, assisting Bury to promotion in 2011 before leaving for Wrexham two years later. He became Southport manager in 2016, being assisted by Dale legend Gary Jones.

Kevin Donovan 2003-04

Born: Halifax 17.12.71
5'8" 11st2
Winger
FL Apps/Gls 4+3/0
Total Apps/Gls 4+3/0
Career: Elland Ath., Huddersfield T. jnr, yts 1988, pro 11.10.89 [11+9/1], Halifax T. loan 13.2.92 [6/-], West Bromwich A. 1.10.92 £70,000 [139+29/19], Grimsby T. 29.7.97 £300,000 [150+6/24], Barnsley 2.7.01 [48+6/1], Dale 23.12.03 [4+3/-], Doncaster R. n/c 2.04, York C. n/c 3.04, signed cs.04 [30+1/2 Conf], Alfreton T. 7.05 to 2007. Brighouse T. youth coach

Honours: Division 2+ play-off winners 1993, 1998, Auto Windscreens Shield winners 1998

Kevin was Alan Buckley's final signing for Dale, having earlier played for Buckley at West Brom and Grimsby. He had played over 150 games on the wing for both clubs, scoring at Wembley in Albion's play-off final victory and repeating that after moving to the Mariners for £300,000. He scored a total of 21 goals in the 1997-98 season and also appeared at Wembley in the AWS final. More recently he had been released by Barnsley, but it was under his former Tykes manager Steve Parkin that Kevin started his four games on the right flank for Dale while Leo Bertos was away with New Zealand. After retiring he ran his own soccer school in Brighouse.

Martin Calvin Pemberton 2003-04

Born: Bradford 1.2.76
5'11" 12st6
Left back
FL Apps/Gls 1/0 Total Apps/Gls 1/0
Career: Hanson Upper School, Oldham A. jnr 1991, yts 1992, pro 22.7.94 [+5/-], Ards loan, Doncaster R. 21.3.97 [33+2/2], Scunthorpe U. 26.3.98 [3+3/-], Hartlepool U. 3.7.98 [+4/-],
Harrogate T. 30.9.98, Bradford PA. 8.99 £1000, Mansfield T. 3.8.00 £10,000 [49+7/5], Stockport Co. 30.4.02 [20+6/-], Dale loan 9.1.04 [1/-], Farsley Celtic 2005 to 2007
Honours: Bradford Boys, Division 3+ promotion 2003

Martin had the misfortune to be a regular for Doncaster the year they crashed out of the league, but was rescued before they did so by a move to Scunthorpe. He did not play a substantial number of games in the league again until joining Mansfield, with whom he gained promotion, and his loan move to Dale was particularly brief. Replacing the suspended Michael Simpkins, he was taken off injured after an hour.

Grant Holt 2003-06, 2015-16

Born: Carlisle 12.4.81
6'1" 12st7
Striker
FL Apps/Gls 78+11/37 Total Apps/Gls 87+11/45
Career: Harraby Sec. School, Carlisle U. jnr, Workington 1998, Halifax T. £10,000 16.9.99 [+6/-], Barrow loan 2.01, Senkang Marine (Singapore), Workington 2000-01, Barrow 8.01, Sheffield W. 27.3.03 [12+12/3], Dale £25,000 30.1.04 [75/35], Nottingham F. 12.1.06 £300,000 [74+22/21], Blackpool loan 20.3.08 [+4/-], Shrewsbury T. 14.7.08 £170,000 [43/20], Norwich C. 24.7.09 £400,000 [135+19/68], Wigan A. 8.7.13 £2M to 29.1.16 [9+11/2], Aston Villa loan 14.1.14 [3+7/1], Huddersfield T. loan 27.9.14 [14+1/2], Wolverhampton W. loan 30.10.15 [+4/-], Dale 19.2.16 [3+11/2], Hibernian 6.16*
Honours: League 1 promotion 2008, League 2 play-off final 2009, PFA League 2 team of the year 2009, League 2 player of the year 2009, League 1 champions 2010, (2016), PFA League 1 team of the year 2010, Championship promotion 2011, PFA Championship team of the year 2011

Steve Parkin saw something in the raw 22 year old striker, who had earlier scored 35 goals in 69 games for Barrow but made little impact at league level, and the £25,000 he paid Wednesday proved a shrewd investment. Grant netted 24 times in 2004-05, including a spell of 11 in 11 games and all five of Dale's goals in a run to the third round of the FA Cup, despite his robust style earning him three suspensions. His partnership with Rickie Lambert was key as Dale challenged at the top of the table in the first half of the following campaign, Grant scoring in seven successive league games. His last two Dale goals came in a victory over Shrewsbury when the side came from 3-1 down to win 4-3. He was then sold to Championship side Notts Forest for £300,000 becoming their player of the year the following term when he scored 17 times. He dropped back down to League 2 with big spending Shrewsbury but was soon back in the big time, winning successive promotions with Norwich and being voted into PFA teams of the year three times in succession in different divisions. Figuring in the Premier League for the first time when he was 30, he was the second highest English goalscorer after Wayne Rooney – being suggested for an England call-up - and won Norwich's player of the year award for the third time. A £2 million pound move to Wigan in 2013 proved unsuccessful though, as Grant was plagued by injuries and he canceled his contract in January 2016. Making a surprising move back to Spotland on a short contract, he helped inspire the late season run which put Dale in contention for the play-offs.

Daniel Richard (Danny) Livesey 2003-04

Born: Salford 31.12.84 6'2" 13st Central defender FL Apps/Gls 11+2/0 Total Apps/Gls 11+2/0 Career: Bolton W. yts 2001, pro 17.8.02 [+2/-], Notts Co. loan 5.9.03 [9+2/-], Dale loan 6.2.04 to 4.04 [11+2/-], Blackpool loan 4.8.04 [1/-], Carlisle U. 24.12.04 [20/2 Conf, 247+16/17], Wrexham loan 31.1.14 [16/- Conf], Barrow cs.14 [43/4 Conf]*
Honours: Conference play-off winners 2005, League 2 champions 2006, FL Trophy final 2006, (Johnstone's Paint Trophy winners 2011), PFA League 1 team of the year 2008, Conference North champions 2015

Danny made his debut for Bolton against Liverpool when he was 17, but only played three more games for Wanderers. A tall central defender, he had a spell at Spotland soon after Steve Parkin's return, as Dale just managed to stay out of relegation trouble. Moving to Carlisle, he helped them regain their FL place and immediately win promotion to League 1. He also appeared in the FL Trophy Final and was selected in the PFA team of the year for 2007-08. Eventually staying with the Cumbrians for ten seasons, he accumulated well over 300 appearances before joining their neighbours Barrow, the Conference North champions in 2015.

Kangana Lord N'diwa 2003-04

Born: Maquela do Zombo, Angola 28.2.84 6'3" 13st3 Defender FL Apps/Gls +1/0 Total Apps/Gls +1/0 Career: Djurgaardens (Sweden) 2001, Vartans IK (Sweden) loan 2002, Celtic trial, Rennes (France) trial, Bolton W. 2.03, pro 15.7.03, Oldham A. loan 8.8.03

[3+1/-], Dale loan 6.2.04 to 3.04 [+1/-], Macclesfield T. trial 11.04, Queens Park R. trial, Stalybridge Celtic 12.04, NK Drava Ptuj (Slovenia) 2005, Scarborough trial 1.06, Reading trial, Worthing 8.06, Montrose am 11.06 [1/- ScL], MVV Maastricht (Holland) 2.07, Wealdstone 3.07, Stoke C. trial 4.07 to 7.07, Hednesford T. 2.08, Ferencvaros (Hungary) trial 3.08, Radcliffe Borough cs.08, AFC Liverpool 9.08, Lincoln C. trial 11.09
Honours: Swedish youth international, DR Congo (2 full caps) 2004

A somewhat multi-national career saw the Angolan born Kangana play for Sweden at youth level but become a full international for the Democratic Republic of Congo, for whom he appeared in the 2004 African Nations Cup. His club career also saw him play in Sweden before signing for Bolton and being loaned out to Oldham and then to Dale with Danny Livesey. His career at Spotland was even shorter than Martin Pemberton's, as he came on for just the last four minutes of a 3-0 victory over Mansfield. He later added Slovenia, Scotland, Holland and Hungary to his world tour - though with virtually no senior appearances anywhere - before reappearing in Lancashire with Radcliffe Borough.

Jeffrey (Jeff) Smith 2003-04

Born: Middlesbrough 28.6.80 5'10" 11st8 Winger FL Apps/Gls 1/0 Total Apps/Gls 1/0 Career: Hartlepool U. yts 1997, pro 3.7.98 [2+1/-], Barrow 10.99, Bishop Auckland 3.00, Bolton W. 21.3.01 [1+1/-], Macclesfield T. loan 23.11.01 [7+1/2], Scunthorpe U. loan 16.1.04 [1/-], Dale loan 20.2.04 to 3.04 [1/-], Preston NE 4.3.04 [+5/-], Port Vale 5.7.04 [65+23/5], Carlisle U. 26.1.07 £60,000 [41+14/2], Darlington 6.09 [22+2/-], Aberdeen trial 7.10, ROC de Charleroi-Marchienne (Belgium) 8.10, Rotherham U. trial 7.11, Whitby T. 11.11, Celtic Nation (Carlisle) 7.12, Bishop Auckland 2.7.13 to 12.13
Honours: Durham Senior Cup 2000-01, Division 1+ promotion 2001

Jeff started out at Hartlepool but dropped out of the league, working as a postman, before being recruited by Bolton from Bishop Auckland and playing one game as they were promoted to the Premier League. Dale borrowed him in February 2004 but after just one game on the wing he was recalled and transferred to Preston. The majority of his league games came at Port Vale and Carlisle prior to appearing for Darlington the year they were relegated out of the league. He then played in Belgium before finishing his career back at Bishop Auckland.

Gareth Shaun Smith   2003-04

Born: Lees 9.4.71
5'10" 11st
Left back
FL Apps/Gls 13/0 Total Apps/Gls 13/0
Career: Halifax T. yts 1987, pro 1.7.89 [6+1/-], Emley 5.91, Crewe A. 31.12.91 [380+22/41], Hull C. 12.7.02 [17+5/1], Stockport Co. loan 5.9.03 [3+3/-], Carlisle U. loan 21.10.03 [4/-], Dale 5.3.04 [13/-], York C. 27.7.04 [16+3/- Conf]
Honours: Division 3+ play-off final 1993, promotion 1994, Division 2+ play-off winners 1997

Despite playing only a handful of games at Halifax, Shaun went on to be a tremendous servant of Crewe, making over 400 league appearances and playing 469 games in all, mostly at left back, though he could also play in central defence. A dead ball specialist he also netted over 50 goals, many of them from the penalty spot. He played in two promotion campaigns, Crewe remarkably making at least the play-offs six years in succession, and scored both the decisive goal in the second leg of the semi-final and the only goal in the final when Crewe won the Division 2 play-offs in 1997. He was Crewe's player of the year in 2001 and later had a joint testimonial game with Steve Macauley (q.v.). After over 10 years at Gresty Road he moved to Hull and then spent the back end of 2003-04 at Spotland as Steve Parkin recruited a number of experienced players to save Dale from the drop.

William Robert (Willo) Flood   2003-04

Born: Dublin 10.4.85
5'6" 9st11
Midfield
FL Apps/Gls 6/0 Total Apps/Gls 6/0
Career: Cherry Orchard (Dublin), Manchester C. yts, pro 13.4.02 [5+9/1], Dale loan 15.3.04 to 4.04 [6/-], Coventry C. loan 19.8.05 [7+1/1], Cardiff C. 2.8.06 £200,000 [5+20/1], Dundee U. loan 8.07 [33+3/1 ScL], Dundee U. loan 8.08 [20/- ScL], Celtic 30.1.09 [2+4/- ScL], Middlesbrough 1.10 [12+4/1], Dundee U. 24.5.11 [67+2/3 ScL], Aberdeen cs.13 [71+9/3 ScL]*
Honours: Republic of Ireland youth international, Republic of Ireland under-20s (4 caps) and under-21s (11 caps), All-Ireland cup winners 1999, Scottish League Cup final 2008, winners 2014

Willo was recruited by Manchester City as a youngster and made a handful of senior appearances while appearing regularly for the Republic at youth, under-20 and under-21 levels. He played a number of games on loan at Spotland but Steve Parkin subsequently decided that the talented but frail looking midfielder was not best suited to a Division 3 relegation battle. Although Cardiff bought him for a sizeable fee, it was after moving to Scotland that Willo came into his own in three spells with Dundee United (despite being sent off on his debut for them). His strike against St. Mirren in December 2007 was voted the SPL goal of season. He joined Aberdeen in 2013, winning the League Cup with them the following year, also figuring in European games as he had previously with City, Dundee United and Celtic.

Gregory James (Greg) Heald   2003-05

Born: Enfield 26.9.71 6'1" 12st8
Central defender
FL Apps/Gls 39/3 Total Apps/Gls 43/3
Career: Orient jnr 1982, Norwich C. app 1988, Enfield 1990, Peterborough U. 8.7.94 £35,000 [101+4/6], Barnet 8.8.97 £130,000 [141+13, 61/7 Conf], Leyton O. 27.3.03 £9000 [9/1], Dale 15.3.04 [39/3], Burton A. trial cs.05, Ashton U. 8.05, Aldershot 9.05 [28/- Conf], Thurrock 16.6.06, Wycombe W. youth team coach 18.7.07, Enfield 1.08
Honours: England Schools, England semi-pro international 2002

Greg was another experienced defender recruited during Dale's fight against relegation in 2004. He had previous experience of the same battle having been a member of the Barnet team that slipped back into the Conference in 2001, (though this did enable him to play for England at semi-pro level). Barnet's most expensive signing, he played just over 200 games for them over six seasons. A tough central defender, Greg also appeared fairly regularly in Dale's much more successful following campaign, scoring in a 5-1 victory over Oxford in his final game before moving into non-league football and training as a firefighter. He subsequently became a teacher and also coached Wycombe's youth team.

Neil Redfearn 2003-04

Born: Dewsbury 20.6.65 5'9" 13st Midfield
FL Apps/Gls 9/0
Total Apps/Gls 9/0
Career: Nottingham F. jnr 1981, Bolton W. 23.6.82 [35/1], Lincoln C. 23.3.84 £8250 [96+4/13], Doncaster R. 22.8.86 £17,500 [46/14], Crystal Palace 31.7.87 £100,000 [57/10], Watford 21.11.88 £150,000 [22+2/3], Oldham A. 12.1.90 £150,000 [56+6/16], Barnsley 5.9.91 £150,000 [289+3/71], Charlton A. 1.7.98 £1,000,000 [29+1/3], Bradford C. 3.8.99 £250,000 [14+3/1], Wigan A. 17.3.00 £112,500 [18+4/7], Halifax T. 16.3.01 [39+3/6], acting manager 30.8.01 to 12.10.01 and 4.3.02 to 25.4.02, Boston U. player-coach 3.8.02 [46+8/12], Dale 19.3.04 [9/-], Scarborough player-coach cs.04, player-manager 1.11.05 [53+7/17 Conf], Bradford PA 7.06, Stocksbridge Park Steels 3.07, Northwich Victoria manager 19.6.07, Frickley Ath 9.07, Bridlington T. 5.11.07, York C. youth team coach 2.08, Emley 7.08, Salford C. 10.08, York C. caretaker manager 21.11.08, assistant manager 28.11.08, Leeds U. academy coach 2008, under-18s coach 1.09, reserve team coach 12.10, acting manager 2.12 and 3.13, first team coach 4.13, academy director 5.14, caretaker manager 28.8.14, head coach 27.10.14 to 20.5.15, academy manager 6.15 to 7.15, Rotherham U. manager 9.10.15 to 2.16
Honours: Division 2 (promotion 1989), champions 1991, Division 1+ promotion 1997, Division 2+ play-off final 2000

Neil's father Brian played 130 times in the FL for Bradford Park Avenue in the 1950s and Neil remarkably played his 1000th first team game for Park Avenue in the FA Trophy in 2006 at the age of 41. He had made his league debut with Bolton in 1983 and missed only a couple of games in three seasons at Lincoln and Doncaster, playing for Lincoln at Valley Parade on the day of the tragic fire disaster. Gradually working his way up the league, he was virtually everpresent in midfield for Oldham in 1990-91, coming on as substitute to score the penalty that secured the second division championship for the Latics. However, he was sold before the new season started and had to wait another six years before his 17 goals helped Barnsley into the top flight for the first time. After

338 games for the Tykes, scoring 84 goals, he was sold to Charlton for the remarkable fee for a 33 year old of £1M, playing in the Premier League both for them and for Bradford City, another of his father's old clubs. He was later Halifax's caretaker manager on two occasions and was player-coach at Burton when recruited by Dale for the run-in to the 2003-04 season, being given squad number 38 to match his age. His appearance in the draw at Southend was the 790th of his FL career, giving him the fifth highest total up to that time. He continued to play, coach and manage at non-league level (though his managerial record at this point did not match that as a player, with just 10 wins in 58 games in charge of various clubs), before becoming an academy coach at Leeds. He was acting manager briefly both before and after Neil Warnock's spell as boss in 2012-13, but this was nothing compared to 2014-15 when under their new Italian owner Leeds got through six managers in 12 months including Neil having two separate (successful) spells in charge. He was then reinstated but almost immediately sacked again as academy manager. He was boss at Rotherham for a time before being replaced, coincidentally, by Warnock. His autobiography "There's Only One Neil Redfearn" appeared in 2006.

Kevin Paul Gibbins 2002-06

Born: Manchester 3.9.85 6'1" 11st7
Defender
FL Apps/Gls +0/0 Total Apps/Gls +0/0
Career: Dale sch 2002, pro cs.05, Witton A., Ashton U. 11.06 to 3.07. Dale academy coach c.2013*

Kevin figured in Dale's reserves in central defence in 2002-03, and the pre-season friendlies the following summer. He was an unused substitute for the final game of 2003-04 and again for a number of games in each of the next two seasons but without ever getting on to the field. In 2004 he did, though, score in a 7-2 friendly defeat of Stenhousemuir. His non-league career was curtailed by a bad back injury but he then gained a degree in applied sports science and a masters in sports psychology at Liverpool John Moores and Salford universities. He worked for the International Lacrosse Federation before taking up the position of head of sports science for Dale's academy.

Alan Jeffrey Goodall 2004-07, 2010-11

Born: Birkenhead 2.12.81 5'9" 11st6
Left back/midfield
FL Apps/Gls 113+12/8
Total Apps/Gls 126+13/8
Career: Rock Ferry HS, Birkenhead Young Lions, Tranmere R. jnr, as 1996, Cammel Laird c.1998, Bangor C. cs.01, Wrexham trial c.4.04, Dale 30.7.04 [110+10/8], Luton T. 27.6.07 [25+4/1], Chesterfield 7.8.08 [38+7/3], Dale 1.7.10 [3+2/-], Newport Co. loan 4.11.10 [8/- Conf], Stockport Co. 31.1.11 [13/-], Mansfield T. trial 7.11, Fleetwood T. 7.11 [29+2/- Conf, 46+2/4], Grimsby T. loan 2.9.13 [7/- Conf], Morecambe 15.7.14 to 5.16 [54+11/4]
Honours: Welsh Cup final 2002, Conference champions 2012, League 2 play-off winners 2014

Alan was at Cammel Laird and Bangor with Peter Davenport, the former England striker, figuring in the UEFA and Intertoto Cups for Bangor. Davenport then recommended him to Steve Parkin and he was a regular at Spotland for three seasons, playing mostly at left back, though he also figured on the left of midfield. He left for Luton on a 'Bosman' in 2007 but moved to Chesterfield after financial irregularities saw Luton docked points and relegated to the Conference. He returned to Spotland on a short term contract as defensive cover at the start of 2010-11, but with Dale fielding a settled line-up Alan had few opportunities and went on loan to Newport. Joining Stockport, Alan was unable to save them, too, from dropping out of the FL but the following year he helped Fleetwood move into the League and gain promotion again via the play-offs in 2014.

Neil Anthony Brisco 2004-06

Born: Wigan 26.1.78
6'0" 11st5
Midfield
FL Apps/Gls 20+7/0
Total Apps/Gls 22+8/0
Career: Manchester C. jnr, yts 1996, pro 4.3.97, Port Vale 7.8.98 [105+13/2], Dale 29.7.04 [20+7/-], Northwich Victoria loan 11.04 [5/1 Conf], Northwich Victoria loan 1.05 [5/- Conf], Scarborough 7.06, Barrow 10.06, Mossley 11.06, Leigh RMI 1.07, Chorley 11.09
Honours: Auto Windscreens Shield winners 2001

One of only two debutants in the first game of 2004-05 with previous league experience, Neil had turned down a one year contract to stay at Vale Park in favour of a longer deal at Spotland. He had figured well over 100 times in midfield for Vale after making his debut in an FA Cup tie against Liverpool and figured in their AWS success in 2001. He was in and out of the Dale side, spending time on loan at Northwich, even before a lengthy absence with a dislocated shoulder. He later played for several other non-league sides and entered the prison service.

Paul Tait 2004-06

Born: Newcastle 24.10.74
6'1" 11st10
Striker
FL Apps/Gls 31+16/3
Total Apps/Gls 39+17/6
Career: Wallsend BC, Everton jnr 1989, yts 1991, pro 8.7.93, Wigan A. 22.7.94 [1+4/-], Runcorn 16.2.96 [4/- Conf], Northwich Victoria cs.96 [95+18/37 Conf], Crewe A. 9.6.99 [31+32/6], Hull C. loan 5.11.01 [+2/-], Bristol R. 12.7.02 [61+13/19], Dale 30.7.04 [31+16/3], Chester C. 10.3.06 [3+6/-], Boston U. 11.7.06 [9+5/2], Southport loan 10.06, signed 23.1.07 [6+9/2 Conf], Northwich Victoria 7.07 [13+3/3 Conf], (also Everton junior coach from 2007), Barrow 1.08 to 5.09 [6+19/2 Conf], Everton under-19s coach*
Honours: Lancashire Cup final 1995-96, Conference North play-off winners 2008

The second experienced newcomer in the summer of 2004, Paul had been Bristol Rovers leading scorer with 12 goals the previous term. His league debut had been with Wigan in 1994, but his longest spell had been with Northwich Victoria in the Conference where he scored 65 times in 157 games in all competitions. Although Paul's partnership with Grant Holt produced goals for the latter, Paul himself didn't manage a league goal until December, though he did score with a bullet header against Wolves in the League Cup, and he managed only a handful of starts after the arrival of Rickie Lambert. In 2008 he scored twice for Barrow in the play-off semi finals on the way to promotion from the Conference North. He had already started coaching back at Everton and carried this on after retiring from playing.

Ashley Probets 2004-05

Born: Bexleyheath 13.12.84 5'9" 10st11
Winger
FL Apps/Gls 4+5/0
Total Apps/Gls 6+8/0
Career: Arsenal yts 2001, pro 7.7.03, Colchester trial cs.04, Dale 22.7.04 [4+5/-], Welling U. 12.04, VCD Athletic 8.05, Chatham T. 7.08, Dartford T. trial 7.10, Thamesmead T. 8.10, Canvey Island cs.15*

Honours: Isthmian League division 1 north play-off winners 2013

An Arsenal trainee, Ashley was recommended to Steve Parkin by his one-time team mate and then Gunners coach Steve Bould. Either a left back or left winger, Ashley figured in the latter role for Dale, but was released after only a few months and returned to play in his native Kent. He was player of the year for Ryman Isthmian league Chatham Town in 2010 and then had a long stint at Thamesmead Town.

Leighton Terence McGivern [-Henshaw] 2004-05

Born: Liverpool 2.6.84 5'8" 11st1
Forward
FL Apps/Gls 2+23/1
Total Apps/Gls 2+29/1
Career: Everton jnr, Waterloo Dock c.2001, Aberystwyth T. 2002-03, Kidsgrove Ath. 7.03, Waterloo Dock 9.03, (+Britannia; Liverpool SL), Vauxhall Motors 3.04, Dale 30.7.04 [2+23/1], Vauxhall Motors 8.05, Waterloo Dock 8.06, Chester C. trial 10.06, Accrington St. 9.11.06 [5+14/2], Waterloo Dock cs.08, Vauxhall Motors 1.11, Stockport Co. trial cs.11, Vauxhall Motors 8.11, Altrincham 2.12 to 7.12, Red Rum FC by 1.15, Waterloo Dock cs.15* (+ Oysters Martyrs by 2011*; Liverpool Sunday League)

Honours: Liverpool Combination champions 2004, Liverpool County FA Cup winners 2004, Liverpool County Premier League champions 2009, 2010, Liverpool Senior Cup final 2009, FA Sunday Cup winners 2011, 2013, final 2014

Leighton probably created some kind of record at Spotland in 2004-05 when he was named as substitute 42 times. A striker in a similar mould to Kevin Townson, with whom he initially shared the bench, he had netted 37 times for Waterloo Dock the previous season in the Liverpool Combination. After playing for Vauxhall Motors, he reappeared in the league with Accrington but started only five games in a season and a half. He then had further stints, scoring regularly, with both Waterloo Dock – playing against Liverpool Reserves in the Liverpool Senior Cup Final - and Vauxhall Motors. He also turned out in Sunday football for Oysters Martyrs, scoring the winner in the 2011 FA Sunday Cup Final and a hat-trick when Oysters won for a second time two years later. In 2015 he scored a remarkable 11 goals in a 14-1 win for them in a local cup tie. [NB. Leighton changed his surname to McGivern-Henshaw subsequent to playing for Dale.]

James William (Jamie) Clarke 2004-06

Born: Sunderland 18.9.82 6'2" 12st9
Defender/midfield
FL Apps/Gls 53+10/1 Total Apps/Gls 61+13/1
Career: St Aidan's RC School, Mansfield T. jnr 2000, yts 2001, pro 5.7.02 [29+5/1], Dale 5.7.04 [53+10/1], Boston U. 20.1.06 [42+10/3], Grimsby T. 5.7.07 [67+7/3], York C. 1.10 [7/- Conf], Darlington trial 7.10, Gateshead trial 8.10, St. Johnstone trial 8.10, Gainsborough Trinity 8.10, Guiseley 7.11, Thailand Football Academy head coach 12.12, Broughty Ath. 27.2.15, Arbroath 10.7.15 [9+5/- ScL], Montrose 25.1.16 [11+1/- ScL]*

Honours: Division 3+ promotion 2002, Johnstone's Paint Trophy final 2008

The son of former Newcastle and Sunderland defender Jeff, Jamie was a full back at Mansfield – playing once while still on YTS forms during their 2001-02 promotion campaign - and was signed by Dale as a reserve defender. However, after coming on for his debut as substitute and having to play in midfield he found himself a regular in that position. His single league goal again came from the bench, when he was thrown on up front for the last few minutes of a game at Lincoln and grabbed the equaliser. Jamie later returned to right back but was released in January 2006 and played for Boston until their relegation from the league. At Grimsby he was again moved into midfield, but was released half way through the season that saw the Mariners lose their FL place. He later emigrated to Thailand to coach at an academy in

Chiang Mai, but made a playing comeback in Scotland in 2015.

Anthony Mark (Tony) Gallimore 2004-06

Born: Nantwich 21.2.72 5'11" 12st6
Left back/centre back
FL Apps/Gls 64+4/0 Total Apps/Gls 72+4/0
Career: Port Vale jnr 1984, Stoke C. yts 1989, pro 11.7.90 [6+5/-], Carlisle U. loan 3.10.91 [8/-], Carlisle U. loan 26.2.92 [8/-], Carlisle U. 3.93 £15,000 [124/9], Grimsby T. £125,000 28.3.96 [263+10/4], Barnsley 8.8.03 [20/-], Dale 19.8.04 [64+4/1], Northwich Victoria 8.6.06 [12+1/1 Conf], Hucknall T. loan 10.1.07, retired 5.07. (Grimsby SL)
Honours: Staffordshire Schools, Division 3+ champions 1995, Division 2+ play-off winners 1998, Auto Windscreens Shield final 1995, winners 1998

Tony was coached as a youngster at Stoke by former Dale left back Tony Lacey, and went on to play over a hundred games, as a left back himself, at Carlisle. He won promotion with them in 1995 and did so again after a sizeable fee took him to Grimsby, being a winner at Wembley in both the Auto Windscreens Shield final and the Division 2 play-off final in 1998. He played over 300 times for the Mariners but had been troubled with injuries before signing for Dale in 2004 and missed the start of the season. Nevertheless, he was a regular for two years, alternating between his usual left back position and centre back. After retiring he played for a Sunday League side back in Grimsby.

Brian Dominic Cash 2004-05

Born: Dublin 24.11.82 5'9" 12st
Winger
FL Apps/Gls 6/0 Total Apps/Gls 7/0
Career: Nottingham F. yts 1998, pro 15.12.99 [+7/-], Swansea C. loan 19.10.02 [5/-], Dale loan 20.8.04 to 20.9.04 [6/-], Bristol R. n/c 17.12.04 [+1/-], Heart of Midlothian

trial, St Johnstone trial, Derry C. 2005, Sligo R. 2007, St Patricks Ath. 2010, Galway U. 3.11 to 7.11
Honours: Republic of Ireland youth international, Republic of Ireland under-21s

Brian joined Dale on loan soon after the start of the 2004-05 season and was played on the right wing in place of the suspended Leo Bertos. Returning to Forest, he could have caused their disqualification from the League Cup when they selected him on the bench though he had already played for Dale against Wolves in the first round. An international at various levels for the Republic, he returned to Ireland the following year, playing fairly regularly for six seasons.

Ernest George (Ernie) Cooksey 2004-07

Born: Bishops Stortford 11.6.80 5'9" 11st4
Midfield
FL Apps/Gls 64+23/8 Total Apps/Gls 76+25/8
Career: Addey Stanhope School, Villa Court Rovers, Charlton A. jnr, Colchester U. yts 1996, Heybridge Swifts 1998, Bishops Stortford 1998, Bromley 2000, Chesham U. 2002, Crawley T. 7.02, Oldham A. 8.8.03 [23+14/4], Dale 17.9.04 [64+23/8], Boston U. 31.1.07 [11+5/-], Barnet trial, Grays Ath. cs.07 [18+1/- Conf] (d. 7.08)
Honours: Blackheath District Boys, Inner London Counties

Ernie spent several years in non-league football around London and the south east, working as a builder, before joining Oldham and playing against Dale in the 2003 Rose Bowl game. He played a part in the majority of their games that season, figuring in midfield, on the wing, or even left back. Early the following term, he was allowed to join Dale and took over on the left flank from the out of favour Paddy McCourt and the inexperienced Ashley Probets. Something of a cult figure, with his prematurely balding pate and old fashioned sounding name, he played fairly regularly, sometimes in a more central role, over the next eighteen months, but faded out of contention just before Keith Hill took over and left for Burton soon afterwards. Sadly Ernie was diagnosed with malignant melanoma, possibly as a result of summers working in soccer camps in the USA, and died in July 2008, not long after his final appearances for Grays Athletic. Coincidentally Oldham met Dale in the league cup shortly afterwards and both sets of players came out wearing shirts labelled "4 Ernie".

Paul Anthony Weller 2004-05

Born: Brighton 6.3.75 5'8" 11st2
Midfield
FL Apps/Gls 5/0
Total Apps/Gls 5/0
Career: Durrington HS, Worthing Dynamos jnr, pro 1991, Burnley yts 11.91, pro 30.11.93 [199+53/11], Chester trial 8.04, Dale n/c 30.9.04 to 11.04 [5/-], Port Vale trial, Leek T., Stalybridge Celtic, Carlisle U. trial 7.05, Workington 8.05, Burnley community sports trust 11.05, Bury community trust 8.09 to 2.14
Honours: Division 2+ promotion 2000

Originally a winger and later a central midfielder, Paul was with Burnley for more than a decade, accumulating over 250 league appearances, despite problems with injury and illness. Although he played only once when they were promoted in 2000, he became a regular in Division 1, winning the Claret's player of the year award in 2001. Released in 2004 he trained with Dale to try and regain fitness and figured in five games as a non-contract player. He retired early the following term, still aged only 30, and returned to Turf Moor to work in their leisure and community department, then taking charge of Bury's Community Trust when they also took responsibility for running the club's centre of excellence.

Taiwo Lee Awuonda (Tai) Atieno 2004-05

Born: Brixton 6.8.85 6'2" 12st13
Forward
FL Apps/Gls 6+7/2
Total Apps/Gls 8+8/2
Career: Walsall jnr 2000, yts 2003, pro 2.7.04 [1+4/-], Nuneaton Borough loan 2004, Dale loan 22.10.04 [6+7/2], Chester C. loan 1.2.05 [3+1/1], Kidderminster H. loan 8.8.05 [13+9/5 Conf], Darlington loan 23.3.06 [+3/-], Dagenham & Redbridge cs.06 [+2/- Conf], Tamworth 8.06 [37+2/12 Conf], Puerto Rico Islanders (USA) 7.07, Charleston Battery (USA) 2009, Rochester Rhinos (USA) 3.09, Luton T. 3.10, Supersport United (South Africa) trial cs.10, Luton T. 2.9.10 [6+7/3 Conf], Stevenage B. 11.2.11 [1/-], Torquay U. 25.7.11 [17+26/6], Southend U. trial 8.12, Barnet 26.12.12 to 1.13 [1+3/1], Rotherham U. trial 3.13, (Kenyan Premier League)
Honours: Kenyan international 2009 and 2012 to 2013 (5 caps), USL 1st division Commissioner's Cup 2008, (Conference champions 2007), League 1 promotion 2011

Tai was borrowed by Dale to boost an attack that had only Grant Holt as a regular scorer and did manage a couple of goals when played alongside Holt or as a third striker. Back at Walsall he netted a pre-season hat-trick but started only one league game and after further loan spells moved into the Conference for a season. A move to Puerto Rico Islanders of the US Soccer Leagues saw him win club honours – scoring when the Islanders reached the CONCACAF champions league group stage – and being selected by Kenya for their World Cup qualifiers. Returning to the UK he figured in virtually every game in a season at Torquay, often as substitute, as when scoring in the Gulls' defeat in the play-off semi-final, but was then freed and actually played his final game for Kenya when without a club. His move to the US scene had been inspired by his identical twin brother Kehinde Roberts starring at basketball for West Chester University in Pennsylvania. (Tai, born Opiyo Taiwo Lee Awounda, took his grandfather's African name, his brother their mother's name).

Daniel (Danny) Woodhall 2004-06

Born: West Bromwich 10.12.87 6'1" 12st7
Goalkeeper
FL Apps +0
Total Apps +0
Career: Alexandra HS (Tipton), Walsall jnr, Manchester U. jnr 2002 to 2003, West Bromwich A. as, Dale sch 6.04, pro 2005, Halesowen T. 1.7.06, Bromsgrove R. 18.1.07, Team Bath 1.7.07, Willenhall loan 12.07, Hednesford T. loan 22.9.08, Yate T. 1.12.08, Hednesford T. 7.2.09, Halesowen T. cs.10
Honours: Birmingham County FA, Lancashire Senior Cup winners 2005

Danny moved from West Brom to Dale as a scholar and as youth team 'keeper was third in line behind Edwards and Gilks, hence appearing on the first team bench when Edwards was unavailable in January and February 2005. He was also Gilks' deputy the following term but without getting a game. He did, though, play in Dale's Lancashire Senior Cup success, and while at university figured for Team Bath alongside another ex-Dale youth player Matt Williams (working with the world's oldest coach, the former Wales international Ivor Powell who was over 90 at the time). Continuing playing non-league football, Danny worked as a coach for a goalkeeping development school run by his father Dave, Walsall's goalkeeping coach. He also attended Loughborough University.

Rickie Lee Lambert 2004-07

Born: Liverpool 16.2.82 5'10" 11st2 Forward FL Apps/Gls 61+3/28 Total Apps/Gls 66+3/28 Career: Ruffwood School (Kirkby), Liverpool jnr 1992 to 1997, Marine trial, Blackpool yts 8.98, pro 17.7.00 to 11.00 [+3/-], Macclesfield T. 2.3.01 [36+8/8], Stockport Co. 30.4.03 £300,000 [88+10/18], Dale 17.2.05 £25,000 [61+3/28], Bristol R. 31.8.06 £200,000 [113+15/51], Southampton 10.8.09 £1M [197+10/106], Liverpool 2.6.14 £4M [7+18/2], West Bromwich A. 31.7.15 [5+14/1]*

Honours: Kirby Boys, League 2 play-off winners 2007, League 1 promotion 2011, Championship promotion 2012, Johnstone's Paint Trophy final 2007, winners 2010, PFA League 2 team of the year 2009, League 1 team of the year 2010, Championship team of the year 2012, PFA League 1 player of the year 2012, Championship player of the year 2012, England (11 caps) 2013 to 2014

Discovered by former Dale player Peter Farrell, he managed only three substitute appearances for Blackpool. After some months without a club (famously working in a beetroot bottling plant), he had a useful spell at Macclesfield. This earned him a big money move to Stockport, but he was in their reserves when recruited by Steve Parkin as an attacking midfielder. Soon joining Grant Holt up front, the pair spearheaded Dale's challenge at the top of the division in 2005-06 and netted 27 times between them by January. After Holt was sold, Dale slowly slid down the table and it was largely Rickie's goals – he finished with 22 in the league – which prevented them slipping into relegation trouble. Sold to Bristol Rovers for £200,000 just before the end of the transfer window to ease Dale's financial position, he helped the Gas to promotion in his first season. In 2008-09 he shared the League 1 golden boot, with 29 goals, netting four against Southend, before a £1 million move to Southampton. Again top scoring in the division, with 37 goals in all, he was voted PFA League 1 player of the year. Successive promotions – he was player of the year and top scorer (with 31 goals) in the Championship in 2012 – took Rickie into the top flight at the age of 30, exactly mirroring the progress of his old Dale partner Grant Holt with Norwich the previous year. In all he scored well over a century of goals for the Saints including 34 penalties from 34 attempts – drawing comparisons with club legend Matt Le Tissier. In 2013 he was called up for England, sensationally scoring with his first touch after coming on as substitute against Scotland. The following year he was in England's World Cup squad (though only figuring for a few minutes) and obtained what should have been a dream move to his boyhood club Liverpool for £4M. The move never worked out though, with the arrival of Mario Balotelli a confusing factor, and in 2015 he joined West Brom, but again with little impact.

Marcus Glenroy Richardson 2004-05

Born; Reading 31.8.77 6'2" 13st2 Forward FL Apps/Gls 1+1/0 Total Apps/Gls 1+1/0 Career: Burnham, Slough T. 12.99, Cambridge U. trial 7.00, Harrow Borough 8.00, (Reading trial 8.00, Wycombe W. trial 11.00), Cambridge U. 16.3.01 [7+9/2], Torquay U. loan 18.9.01, signed 10.01 £5000 [21+18/8], Hartlepool U. 1.10.02 [23+4/5], Lincoln C. loan 22.8.03 [9+3/4], Lincoln C. loan 8.12.03, signed 1.04 [32+8/10], Dale loan 17.2.05 to 3.05 [1+1/-], Yeovil 23.3.05 £ [2+2/-], Chester 6.7.05 [22+12/4], Macclesfield T. loan 23.3.06 [8/3], Weymouth 7.06, Cambridge U. 21.8.06 [17+3/3 Conf], Crawley T. 3.07 [11+7/2 Conf], Bury 10.8.07 [1/-], Farnborough 10.07, Hanley T. 8.09, Windsor & Eton 2009-10, Reading T. 7.10, Marlow player-assistant manager 6.12, Highmoor Ibis coach 1.14, player-manager cs.14*

Honours: Division 3+ promotion 2003, League 2 champions 2005, Southern League league 1 south & west champions 2008, Hellenic Premier Division champions 2013

After several years on the non-league circuit, playing as a big target-man, Marcus gained his first FL experience towards the end of 2000-01 at Cambridge and subsequently moved clubs on a regular basis, appearing in the Hartlepool side which gained promotion in 2003. He was brought in by Dale in February 2005 after being suspended by Lincoln for a training ground incident (involving another future Dale man Ciaran Toner), but started just one game up front in place of Paul Tait. Bought by Yeovil, he played a few games as they finished top of League 2, but continuing his travels, by the time he reached Southern League Farnborough, where he had the most productive spell of his career with 32 goals in 88 games, he had figured for 11 FL or Conference clubs in the previous six years. He later moved into non-league management, making a playing comeback in the Hellenic League in 2014-15.

Marc John Richards 2004-05

Born: Wolverhampton 8.7.82 6'0" 12st7
Forward
FL Apps/Gls 4+1/2
Total Apps/Gls 4+1/2
Career: Hednesford T., Blackburn R. yts 1998, pro 12.7.99, Crewe A. loan 10.8.01 [1+3/1], Oldham A. loan 12.10.01 [3+2/-], Halifax T. loan 12.2.02 [5/-], Swansea C. loan 22.11.02 [14+3/7], Northampton T. 7.7.03 [35+18/10], Dale loan 24.3.05 to 4.05 [4+1/2], Barnsley 31.8.05 [51+18/18], Port Vale 8.8.07 [162+19/68], Chesterfield 31.5.12 [51+21/20], Northampton T. 14.5.14 [54+8/33]*
Honours: England under-18s (3 caps), England under-20s 2002, League 1 play-off winners 2006, Johnstone's Paint Trophy final 2014, League 2 champions 2014, 2016

A youth international, scoring for England under-20s against Finland, Marc's early experience came in a series of loan moves away from Ewood Park, though he did figure in a couple of League Cup ties for Blackburn. He once scored four goals for Northampton against Macclesfield but his original spell with the Cobblers was affected by illness and injuries and in 2005 he was loaned to Dale to regain match fitness, netting a brace when coming on as substitute against Orient. Promoted with Barnsley the following year, and later with Chesterfield, his most productive spell was actually at Port Vale where he was leading scorer four

times in five years, twice reaching 20 goals. Northampton's player of the year in 2015, during their League 2 championship winning campaign the following year, he passed the 150 league goals mark.

Gary Brown 2002-2008

Born: Darwen 29.10.85
5'6" 10st2
Right back/midfield
FL Apps/Gls 21+17/0
Total Apps/Gls 25+19/0
Career: St Peters School (Darwen), Moorland HS (Darwen), Oggy Hotspurs, Preston NE jnr 1997, Blackburn R. jnr 1999, Dale jnr 2002, pro 4.7.05 [21+17/-], retired injured 2007-08.
Runcorn Linnets 1.09, AFC Darwen 27.8.10 to 2014 (+Darwen Victoria: SL)
Honours: Blackburn & Darwen Schools, Lancashire Schools under-16s 2001-02

Gary trained with Preston from the age of 8 and played at Wembley for his primary school in the English Schools Trophy. He played in Dale's reserves from 2002-03 and was an unused substitute a few times before his debut at right back at Boston in May 2005. The next season, the diminutive Gary got a number of games at right back or the right of midfield, winning the young player of the year in 2006. He suffered a serious cruciate ligament injury in pre season in 2007 and did not play again until a comeback with Runcorn Linnets subsequently playing minor football back in his home town Darwen.

Benjamin (Ben) Kitchen 2004-06

Born: Bolton 19.8.86
5'9" 11st7
Winger
FL Apps/Gls 3+6/0
Total Apps/Gls 3+7/0
Career: Turton HS, Bromley Cross, Bolton W. jnr 1999, Preston NE yts 2002, Chorley cs.04, Dale sch 2004, pro 4.7.05 [3+6/-], Altrincham trial 6.06, Rossendale U. 7.06, Bangor C. 12.06, Chorley 1.07, Woodley Sports, Turton, Ramsbottom U. 10.07,

Rossendale U. 7.08,Turton 2010, Eagley 2012
Honours: Bolton town boys, Lancashire Senior
Cup winners 2005

Ben joined Dale as a scholar in 2004 and was
unused substitute a couple of times before making
his debut when coming off the bench in the last
game of the season, at Boston. He also figured in
Dale's Lancashire Cup winning side two days later.
The following term he was around the squad from
the start of the season and eventually made three
starts on the wing in April 2006, Dale picking up
five points to edge away from the lower reaches of
the table. He was released that summer, later
playing mostly in the North West Counties League.

Matthew (Matt) Williams 2004-06

Born: Bury 21.6.88
5'11" 12st
Defender
FL Apps/Gls +1/0
Total Apps/Gls +1/0
Career: Woodley HS
(Ramsbottom), Dale
sch 2004 [+1/-],
Team Bath 10.05,
Cirencester T. 2008
Honours: (Lancashire
Senior Cup winners
2005), Southern
League promotion
2008

Matt played in Dale's youth and reserve teams in
2003-04 and was selected as substitute for the
final game of the following term, coming on for the
last couple of minutes at Boston. He was also
unused substitute in the youth side which captured
the Lancashire Senior Cup the following week.
While at university he represented Team Bath
when they won the Southern League title, and
subsequently worked for a sports coaching
company.

Clive Zwelibanzi Moyo-Modise 2004-07

Born: London 20.9.87
5'10" 11st5
Forward
FL Apps/Gls 2+26/1
Total Apps/Gls 4+28/1
Career: King Ethelbert's
School, Dale sch 2004,
pro 29.6.05 [2+26/1],
Mossley loan 9.2.07,
Bidvest Wits (South
Africa) cs.07, Stockport
Co. trial 3.09, Mossley
3.09, Bradford C. trial
2009, Altrincham
11.2.10, Ashton U. loan

1.3.10, Ashton U. 9.10 to 1.11
Honours: Lancashire Senior Cup winners 2005,
South Africa under-23s in Sasol Eight Nations
tournament 2007

Clive scored the only goal for Dale's reserves in the
Lancashire Cup final and subsequently appeared
in the first team in the 2005 pre-season friendlies.
He soon made his debut as substitute in the league
and made his first start, on the wing - though
usually playing as a striker at youth level - later in
the season. However, he added only one more
league start, despite numerous appearances from
the bench. In November 2006 he was selected for
the South African under-21 side the 'Amaglug-glug'
but missed out through injury. After leaving
Spotland and figuring in the South African League,
he did feature in the under-23s and attended a
training camp with the senior South Africa squad
in 2008. Back in England, though, he managed
just a couple of dozen non-league games before
disappearing from the scene.

Antony John (Tommy) Jaszczun 2005-06

Born: Kettering 16.9.77 5'10" 10st10
Left back/midfield
FL Apps/Gls 12+5/0 Total Apps/Gls 14+5/0
Career: Sir Charles Hatton School
(Wellingborough), Wellingborough Colts 1988,
Aston Villa jnr 1993, yts 1994, pro 5.7.96 [+1/-],
Blackpool 20.1.00 £30,000 [107+15/-],
Northampton T. 8.7.04 [24+8/-], Dale 7.7.05
[12+5/-], Cambridge U. loan 1.06 [16/- Conf],
Cambridge U. 7.06 [10+1/- Conf], retired injured
3.07. Kettering T. 5.07 [22/- Conf], Corby T. 3.09,
Kettering T. player-coach 5.10 [1/- Conf], Corby T.
1.11, Daventry U., Brackley T. 2012
Honours: Wellingborough & Rushden District
Schools, LDV Vans Trophy winners 2002, 2004,
Division 3+ promotion 2001, Conference North
champions 2008

Tommy made his Aston Villa debut against
Chelsea in the League Cup, but established himself
after a move to Blackpool, figuring regularly when
they were promoted in 2001 though missing the
play-off final. He completed a century of FL
appearances for them and was twice a winner of
the LDV Vans Trophy. Known as a left back, he
actually spent much of his time at Spotland playing
on the left of midfield as extra defensive insurance,
but moved on after only half a season. Although
retiring injured in 2007, he soon made a comeback and won the Conference North title with
Kettering.

Jonathan George (Jon) Boardman 2005-07

Born; Reading 27.1.81 6'2" 13st11
Central defender
FL Apps/Gls 20+5/1 Total Apps/Gls 26+6/1
Career: Theale Tigers, Thatcham Tornadoes, Crystal Palace jnr 1992, yts 6.97, pro 7.7.00, Woking loan 22.3.01 [9/- Conf], Torquay U. trial 23.8.01, Margate loan 10.01 [3/1 Conf], Woking loan 12.01, signed 3.02 [136+1/4 Conf], Dale 17.5.05 [20+5/1], Dagenham & Redbridge 25.1.07 [9/3 Conf, 22+5/-], Woking 7.09 [20/- Conf], Kingstonian 6.10, Hungerford T. 8.10*
Honours: England semi-pro international (8 caps) 2002, Conference champions 2007, Conference South play-off final 2010

Arriving at Spotland with the reputation as one of the best central defenders in the Conference – he was England captain and scored against Italy at semi-pro level while at Woking – Jon never managed to establish himself in Dale's league side, playing only three league games in his second season (and being sent off in the last). He did win the Conference title with Dagenham, though, and played a number of further FL games after their elevation in status, before heading back to Woking. In his first stint with them he had written a regular column on the non-league game for Shoot Monthly. He has had a long stint at Hungerford Town, winning their player of the year three times.

Lee Cartwright 2005-06

Born: Rawtenstall 19.9.72 5'8" 11st
Outside right
FL Apps/Gls 21+6/1
Total Apps/Gls 23+6/1
Career: Fearns HS, Haslingden Juniors, Preston NE jnr, yts 1989, pro 30.7.91 [312+85/22], Stockport Co. 29.11.04 [32+2/1], Dale 4.7.05 [21+6/1], Scarborough cs.06, Hyde U. 5.07 to 12.08
Honours: Rossendale Schools, Division 3+ play-off final 1994, champions 1996, Division 2+ champions 2000, Division 1+ play-off final 2001, Lancashire Cup final 1991-92

A legend at Preston – indeed, he was inducted into North End's Modern Legends Hall of Fame – Lee played 469 times for them in all competions. Playing wide on the right, he helped them to the Division 3 and Division 2 titles during 13 years as a pro, having been given his debut by Les Chapman (q.v.). Player of the year in 1992, he was awarded a testimonial in 2001, when Preston were denied a place in the Premier League by neighbours Bolton in the play-off final, and eventually left for Stockport in 2004. Lee had a single season with Dale without ever cementing a place in the side but was Scarborough's player of the year in the Conference North the following term.

Blair David Sturrock 2005-06

Born: Dundee 25.8.81 6'0" 11st1
Forward
FL Apps/Gls 15+16/6
Total Apps/Gls 16+19/6
Career: Dundee Social, Fairmuir, Dundee U. app 23.7.98, pro 5.9.99, Brechin C. loan 8.8.00 [20+7/6 ScL], Plymouth A. 26.10.01 [9+54/2], Kidderminster H. 24.12.04 [17+5/5], Dale 5.8.05 [15+16/6], Wrexham trial 7.06, Swindon T. 8.12.06 [22+28/6], Bournemouth loan 26.9.08 [1+3/-], Torquay U. loan 27.3.09 [6+1/2 Conf], Mansfield T. 6.09 [10+14/3 Conf], Truro C., Southend U. 5.8.10 to 5.12 [39+13/6], Bishop's Stortford 16.10.12, Basildon U. assistant manager 2013, Victoria Highlanders (Canada) player-coach 4.13, Cowichan FC (Canada) 10.13, Victoria Highlanders 4.14 to 7.14, coach to 4.15, Vancouver Whitecaps (Canada) academy coach 9.15*
Honours: Division 3+ champions 2002, Division 2+ champions 2004, League 2 promotion 2007, (Conference promotion 2009)

The son of Plymouth manager Paul, Blair was certainly not showed any favouritism as he started just 9 games for Argyle but appeared from the bench more than 50 times in two promotion winning seasons. He had also played for his father at Dundee United and did so again at Swindon – again winning promotion - and Southend. In between, he had a season with Dale, netting six times as a useful stand-in for Holt and Lambert, and while on loan at Torquay helped them regain their FL place. He emigrated to Canada in 2013 and figured in the United Soccer League Premier

Development League and the Vancouver Island Soccer League, and has worked for a number of coaching schools.

Rory Alexander McArdle 2005-06, 2006-10

Born: Sheffield 1.5.87
6'1"   11st5
Central defender
FL Apps/Gls 141+7/5 Total Apps/Gls 160+7/6
Career: Brimsworth CS, Whitehill Rovers, Barnsley jnr 1998, Sheffield W. jnr 1999, sch 2003, pro 15.7.05 [+1/-], Dale loan 26.7.05 to 3.4.06 [16+3/1], Dale loan 7.11.06, signed 1.07 [125+4/4], Aberdeen 6.10 [47+6/2 ScL], Bradford C. 6.6.12 [157+2/11]*
Honours: N. Ireland youth international, N. Ireland under-19s 2005-06, N. Ireland under-21s (19 caps), N. Ireland (7 full caps) 2010-2015, League 2 play-off final 2008, League 2 promotion 2010, League 2 play-off winners 2013, League Cup final 2013

Rory was twice loaned to Dale after signing pro for Wednesday, the second time turning his loan into a permanent contract just after Keith Hill took over as manager. A regular in central defence as Dale made successive challenges for promotion, Rory had the honour of scoring the opening goal of the 2008 play-off final at Wembley. He also became a regular for N. Ireland under-21s. However, when Dale finally went up two years later he had been injured in pre-season and lost his place to newboy Craig Dawson, playing just a few games mostly as a stand-in full back. He then signed for Scottish Premier League Aberdeen (a loop-hole in transfer regulations between leagues losing Dale any fee or compensation), though technically he was still a Rochdale player when he made his full debut for N. Ireland in May 2010. Playing primarily as a right back with the Dons, he had the misfortune to be in the side hammered 9-0 by Celtic. In 2012 he joined Bradford City and, reverting to central defence, shared in their remarkable run to the League Cup Final, defeating Arsenal and Aston Villa (when Rory netted to give them a first leg lead) on route. He also repeated his Wembley goal, scoring when Bradford won in the play-off final and was a regular up in League 1.

Warren Ernest Goodhind 2005-07

Born Johannesburg 16.8.77 5'11" 11st6
Right back
FL Apps/Gls 10/0
Total Apps/Gls 12/0
Career: Bishopsholt School, Southampton jnr 1987, Brentford jnr 1993, Barnet yts 1995, pro 3.7.96 [73+20/3], Cambridge U. 21.9.01 £80,000 to cs.05 [95+8/-], Dale 26.9.05 to 1.07 [10/-], Oxford U. loan 10.2.06 [4+2/-], Ebbsfleet 24.8.07 [7+1/- Conf], Eastleigh 11.07, Harrow Borough cs.08, Eastleigh 9.08, Hemel Hempstead T. 7.11, Thurrock 29.12.11, Hendon 4.3.13, Cheshunt assistant manager 2.14, Harlow T. 12.14 to 4.15
Honours: AutoWindscreens Shield final 2002

Making nearly 100 appearances with Barnet, despite being out 15 months with a broken leg, Warren was also a favourite with the Cambridge supporters before joining Dale in another attempt to replace the long serving Wayne Evans. Unfortunately, despite the first four games he played in being victories, he also played in the depressing string of defeats over the New Year – being sent off for pulling Wycombe's Torres back by his pony-tail – and was then loaned to Oxford, who followed his previous clubs Barnet and Cambridge in being relegated out of the league. He did not play at all in 2006-07 following a hernia operation, before heading for the uniquely fan owned and run Ebbsfleet United and a continuing non-league career. In Harlow's 2015 Ryman Division 1 North play-off semi-final defeat by his former side Thurrock, he scored at both ends and was then sent off. He also worked as a PE teacher.

Christopher (Chris) Dagnall 2005-10

Born; Liverpool 15.4.86 5'8" 11st9
Striker
FL Apps/Gls 124+33/57 Total Apps/Gls 144+35/64
Career: Alsop Senior School, Plannexcel, Tranmere R. jnr 1999, sch 2002, pro 11.7.03 [18+21/7], Dale 12.1.06 £25,000 [124+33/57], Scunthorpe U. 2.6.10 [50+10/9], Barnsley 5.1.12 £ [34+19/6], Bradford C. loan

16.3.12 [5+2/1], Coventry C. loan 28.11.13 [4+2/1], Leyton Orient 16.1.14 [45+13/17], Kerala Blasters (India) 6.15, Hibernian 23.12.15 [3+8/- ScL]*
Honours: Liverpool Boys, League 2 play-off final 2008, League 2 promotion 2010, League 1 play-off final 2014, (Scottish League Cup final 2016), (Scottish FA Cup winners 2016)

Chris netted six goals when Tranmere finished third in League 1 in 2004-05 (having started the season by being sent off for over celebrating his winning goal). He was back in the reserves the following term (scoring against Dale's second string) when Steve Parkin signed him after the departure of Grant Holt. With Dale having slipped into the relegation battle, Chris' first major intervention came when he scored a late leveler against Rushden & Diamonds, the deflated home side failing to beat the drop. The following term, with Lambert also gone, he teamed up with Glen Murray to grab the goals that elevated Dale to ninth place by the end of the season, Chris netting a hat-trick against Macclesfield and 18 goals in all. A serious injury ruled him out for much of 2007-08 but he came back in astounding fashion with a nine minute hat-trick when coming on as substitute against Rotherham. He also netted crucially in both legs of the play-off semi-finals against Darlington as Dale won through to Wembley for the first time. Less prolific the following term, when Adam Le Fondre was the main goalscorer, he again scored in the play-offs but Dale were beaten by Gillingham. In 2009-10 he was teamed up with Chris O'Grady and the classic 'big man, little man' strike partnership saw them both hit 20 goals and fire Dale to promotion for the first time for 41 years. Chris also netted his fourth Dale hat-trick. Choosing to move on, Chris signed for Scunthorpe, then in the Championship, but after their relegation joined Keith Hill again at Barnsley. He was never able to rediscover his Dale goalscoring form, though, and despite a useful return in eighteen months with Orient, again scoring in a play-off semi-final, he had the misfortune to miss a penalty in the final which would have taken them into the Championship. In the summer of 2015 he joined cricket legend Sachin Tendulkar's Kerala Blasters franchise in the Indian Super League before returning to the UK to play for Hibs, where he was an unused substitute in their two cup final appearances.

John Doolan 2005-08

Born: Liverpool 7.5.74
6'1" 13st
Midfield
FL Apps/Gls 75+8/3
Total Apps/Gls 82+10/5
Career: Campion HS (Liverpool), Stansfield & Mawdsley, Everton yts 1990, pro 1.6.92, Mansfield T. 2.9.94 [128+3/10], Barnet 13.1.98 £60,000 [132+2/7, 47+3/5 Conf], Doncaster R. 20.3.03 £10,000 [8/- Conf, 68+9/2], Blackpool 1.7.05 [15+4/-], Dale 20.1.06 [75+8/3], Southport player-assistant manager cs.08 to 2.09, Everton academy coach 2007, under-18s coach*
Honours: Liverpool Boys, Conference play-off winners 2003, Division 3+ champions 2004, (League 2 play-off final 2008), Lancashire Senior Cup final 1995-96

John played under Steve Parkin at Mansfield and was a Dale target on more than one occasion while with the Stags, and later Barnet. He played over 150 games for each club, despite Barnet's relegation to the Conference, and after successive promotions with Doncaster from the Conference to League 1 the solidly built midfielder did eventually arrive at Spotland in 2006. An important member of the side in his first full season, alongside Gary Jones or David Perkins, he was little used in the latter part of 2007-08, though he did come on as substitute in the play-off semi-final second leg against Darlington after Perkins was sent off, and was an unused sub at Wembley. As well as working for Everton's academy, John became an after dinner speaker, teaming up with another former Dale man and comedian John Stiles as double act 'the two Johnnies'.

Simon Paul Ramsden 2005-09

Born: Bishop Auckland 17.12.81
6'1" 12st4
Right back/central defender
FL Apps/Gls 107+5/6
Total Apps/Gls 121+5/6
Career: Woodham CS, Newton Aycliffe YC, Sunderland yts 1998, pro 7.8.00, Notts Co. loan 16.8.02 [21+11/-], Grimsby T. 2.8.04 [31+6/-], Dale 30.1.06 [107+5/6], Bradford C.

7.09 [48+2/1], Motherwell cs.12 [66+5/1 ScL], Gateshead 10.7.15 to 5.16 [24/- Conf]
Honours: Bishop Auckland Schools, Durham Schools, League 2 play-off final 2008, Scottish Premier play-off winners 2015

A dedicated Makem, Simon made one substitute appearance for his boyhood club, but then played for the only other FL teams to share deadly rivals Newcastle's black and white stripes, even Dale switching to them in their Centenary season! Arriving in January 2006 he was generally Dale's first choice right back as they twice made the play-offs, but was switched to midfield in the Wembley final to cover for the suspended David Perkins. The scorer of only eight senior goals, oddly, his first three for Dale were all against his previous club Grimsby, with a brace in 2006-07. Leaving when his contract expired in 2009 he was appointed Bradford skipper but had a bad time with injuries before following manager Stuart McCall to Scottish Premier League Motherwell. 'Well twice finished runners-up to Celtic and figured in Europe, but Simon's last two appearances were as substitute in the 2015 play-offs when Motherwell beat Rangers to preserve their place in the top division.

Mark Graham Jackson 2005-07
Born: Barnsley 30.9.77 5'10" 11st12
Central defender
FL Apps/Gls 20+4/0 Total Apps/Gls 21+5/0
Career: Crawshaw HS (Pudsey), Leeds U. jnr, Farsley Celtic 1990, Leeds U. as 1991, yts 1993, pro 1.7.95 [11+8/-], Huddersfield T. loan 29.10.98 [5/-], Barnsley loan 14.12.00 [1/-], Scunthorpe U. 9.3.00 [127+9/4], Kidderminster H. 18.2.05 [13/-, 26/3 Conf], Dale 31.1.06 £35,000 (with I. Christie) [20+4/-], Farsley Celtic 6.07 [26+5/1 Conf], Football in the Community, under-19s manager 7.08, assistant manager 2009, Farsley AFC 7.10, under-19s manager 2011, assistant manager 2013 (also Bradford C. academy coach), Leeds U. academy coach 10.10.15*
Honours: Leeds City Boys, England under-20 1997 (4 caps), (League 2 promotion 2005)

Mark played at centre half for England in the under-20 World Cup in Malaysia (in the same side as Michael Owen) but made only a few appearances for Leeds in the Premier League. The majority of his FL appearances came at Scunthorpe before a move to Kidderminster just before they lost their league place. Injured in his first game for Dale after signing for a sizeable fee, along with Iyesden Christie, Mark's Dale career never really took off and he later served Farsley Celtic in a variety of roles until they were wound up and he moved to the reformed Farsley AFC. He also became head of football at Leeds City College and took a position with Leeds United's academy.

Iyesden Christie 2005-07

Born: Coventry 14.11.76 6'0" 12st6
Striker
FL Apps/Gls 14+5/2
Total Apps/Gls 16+5/2
Career: Coventry C. jnr 1991, yts 1993, pro 22.5.95 [+1/-], Bournemouth loan 18.11.96 [3+1/-], Mansfield T. loan 7.2.97 [8/-], Mansfield T. 16.6.97 [44+37/18], Leyton O. 2.7.99 £40,000 [32+26/12], Mansfield T. 9.8.02 [53+11/26], Kidderminster H. 6.8.04 [1+7/-, 23+1/10 Conf], Dale 31.1.06 £35,000 (with M. Jackson) [14+5/2], Kidderminster H. loan 8.06, signed 1.07 [56+16/26 Conf], Stevenage Borough 7.08 [2+1/- Conf], Kettering T. loan 2.9.08 [11+2/5 Conf], Torquay U. 2.2.09 [2+4/1 Conf], Hibs (Malta) trial cs.09, Kings Lynn 8.09, AFC Telford U. 11.9.09, Coventry Sphinx, Farnborough T. 10.09, Tamworth n/c 11.09 [20+4/6 Conf], Kettering T. cs.10 [12+7/6 Conf], Nuneaton T. 30.3.11, Tamworth 7.11, Alfreton T. 8.8.12 [1/- Conf], Halesowen T. 2013, Barwell cs.15, Sutton Coldfield T. 12.15, Bedworth U. 1.16*
Honours: Conference promotion 2009, (Southern League premier division champions 2010), NPL division 1 (South) champions 2014

A well travelled striker, like John Doolan Iyesden had played under Steve Parkin at Mansfield in the late 'nineties – scoring a hat-trick in the League Cup against Stockport in a record four minutes - but like Mark Jackson had most recently been with Kidderminster when they lost their league place. Unfortunately, the significant sum that Parkin spent to recruit the pair gave little return as Iyesden managed to find the net just twice – albeit in two of only three Dale victories in their last 18 games - and was back at Kidderminster almost as soon as the following season got under way. Rediscovering his goal scoring touch, he netted 17 times in 2007-08 before spells with other Conference sides, helping Torquay regain FL status in 2009. In 2014, when almost 38, he scored a double hat-trick for Halesowen in a 7-1 FA Cup victory.

Theodore Aaron Anthony (Theo) Coleman
2005-07, 2008-9

Born: Manchester
5.5.89 5'11" 10st7
Forward
FL Apps/Gls 1/0
Total Apps/Gls 1/0
Career: Parrs Wood
HS, Manchester U.
jnr, Blackburn R.
jnr, Dale sch 2005,
released 1.07 [1/-],
Bury trial c.3.07, FC
United of
Manchester 10.07,
Salford C. c.1.08,
Dale n/c 24.11.08, Salford C. 2009, Mossley 9.11
Honours: Greater Manchester County Schools
2005, Greater Manchester Schools Cup winners
2005, ESFA Under-16 Inter County Trophy final
2005

A star in schools football, Theo made his mark
during 2005-06 with a pre-season hat-trick for the
second string and another treble in a 7-1 defeat of
Burnley Reserves. He made his senior debut on the
left wing, in what turned out to be his only league
appearance, three days before his 17th birthday,
against champions Carlisle. He was given another
trial as a non-contract player in 2008 after a spell
at Salford.

Joseph (Joe) Thompson 2005-12, 2012-13

Born: Rochdale 5.3.89
6'0" 9st7
Forward
FL Apps/Gls 89+58/15
Total Apps/Gls
99+64/17
Career: St Cuthberts
RCHS, Manchester U.
as 2003, Dale sch
2005, pro 5.7.07
[84+56/15], Tranmere
R. cs.12 £ [13+12/3],
Dale loan 2.13 [5+2/-],
Bury 2.8.14 [+1/-],
Wrexham loan
27.11.14, Southport
loan 14.2.15 [3+1/- Conf], St Johnstone trial
21.4.15, Carlisle U. 31.7.15 to 5.16 [4+11/1]
Honours: Lancashire Senior Cup winners 2005,
League 2 promotion 2010, 2015

Joe was a junior at Old Trafford with Tom
Cleverley, but returned to his home town to figure
in Dale reserves before his 16th birthday, playing in
the Lancashire Cup winning side. He made his
senior debut as substitute in the penultimate game
of 2005-06. He was chosen for his first start when
his youth team coach Keith Hill became caretaker
manager and won the League 2 trainee of the year
award. Largely on the bench in 2007-08, he was
unfortunate not to be included in the squad for the
play-off final. Eventually becoming more of a
regular the following term, usually on the right
wing, though he could play further forward, he
netted a hat-trick against Aldershot. He scored the
first goal of the promotion season against Port
Vale, hitting eight in all, and produced another
memorable strike when Dale completed the double
over Southampton in League 1. Out of the picture
under Steve Eyre and John Coleman he moved to
Tranmere but was briefly borrowed back when
Keith Hill returned to Spotland. He was diagnosed
with Hodgkin's lymphoma in November 2013, but
fought back after chemotherapy and remarkably
was able to resume his career in less than a year.
Signing for Dave Flitcroft's Bury, he was
unsurprisingly short of match fitness and figured
only once. He spent 2015-16 at Carlisle.

Lloyd Joseph Rigby 2005-08

Born: Preston
27.2.89 6'2"
12st5
Goalkeeper
FL Apps +0
Total Apps +0
Career: Deanery
HS (Wigan),
Wigan A. jnr, Dale
sch 2005, pro
2007, Rossendale
U. loan 12.07,
Vauxhall Motors
loan 1.08,
Rossendale U.
3.08, Vauxhall
Motors 5.08,
Stockport Co. 8.08
[2], Radcliffe
Borough loan
2009-10, Barrow
trial 7.10, Royal Racing Montignee (Belgium)
c.8.10, Chorley 12.10, Leigh Genesis cs.11, Salford
C. 1.12 to 7.12

Lloyd's first association with Dale's first team
squad was in pre-season 2005, just after joining as
a 16 year old scholar, and he was a substitute
'keeper for a number of league games a year later.
He eventually made a couple of appearance in the
FL after joining Stockport from Vauxhall Motors,
before further spells at non-league level.

Anthony John (Tony) Vaughan 2006-07
Born: Manchester 11.10.75 6'1" 11st2
Left back
FL Apps/Gls 0/0 Total Apps/Gls 1/0
Career: Manchester C. jnr, Ipswich T. jnr 1989, yts 1992, pro 1.7.94 [56+11/3], Manchester C. 9.7.97 £1,350,000 [54+4/2], Cardiff C. loan 15.9.99 [14/-], Norwich C. trial 1.00, Nottingham F. loan 8.2.00, signed 23.3.00 £350,000 [38+5/1], Scunthorpe U. loan 26.3.02 [5/-], Mansfield T. loan 25.10.02   [4/-], Motherwell loan 31.1.03 [12/1 ScL], Mansfield T. 4.8.03 [32/2], Barnsley 5.7.04 [25+2/4], Stockport Co. loan 26.8.05 [10/1], Dale trial 7.06 to 8.06. Hucknall T. 1.07
Honours: England Schools, England youth international, Division 2+ play-off winners 1999, (Division 1+ promotion 2000), League 1 promotion 2006

Tony first made a mark at Ipswich, figuring for the England youth team, and after just three seasons in the league was transferred to Manchester City – where he had been a junior - for a huge fee. Although he played just over 50 games in their back four, figuring alongside Lee Crooks (q.v.) in the 1998-99 promotion campaign, City made a loss of £1M when they traded him to Notts Forest. Coincidentally, he played just once during both City's 1999-2000 promotion campaign and Barnsley's in 2005-06. A transfer target of Alan Buckley in 2003 before joining Mansfield, he eventually arrived on trial at Spotland in pre-season three years later, figuring in the Rose Bowl match against Oldham, before deciding to retire.

Craig Dove 2006-07
Born: Hartlepool 16.8.83 5'8" 11st6
Forward
FL Apps/Gls 0/0 Total Apps/Gls +1/0
Career: Middlesbrough yts 1999, pro 7.7.00, Scunthorpe U. trial 9.02, York C. loan 10.10.03 [1/-], Carlisle U. trial 1.04, Rushden & Diamonds 22.7.04 [31+5/6], Chester C. 6.7.05 [2+3/-], Forest Green Rovers loan 3.06 [1+4/- Conf], Northwich Victoria trial 7.06, Dale trial 15.7.06, Buxton 8.06 to 10.06. Kidsgrove Ath. 7.08, Alsager T. player-assistant manager 1.14, joint manager 7.14 to c.3.15
Honours: England youth international 1999

Craig was a youth international winger, appearing for England alongside Jermaine Jenas and Jermaine Pennant when they beat Argentina (including Carlos Tevez) at under-16 level. He also appeared as substitute in a couple of cup ties for Middlesbrough but the majority of Craig's league appearances came in a season at Rushden. He had a trial at Spotland in July 2006 and came on as substitute in the Rose Bowl game against Oldham. He later had a lengthy stint at Kidsgrove, skippering the side from left back.

Bryan James Gilfillan 2006-07
Born: Cardenden 14.9.84 6'0"
Midfield
FL Apps/Gls 0/0 Total Apps/Gls +1/0
Career: Craigmount HS, Inverness Caledonian Thistle 10.00 [+3/- ScL], Brora Rangers loan 10.01, Cowdenbeath 7.03 [33+1/7 ScL], Gretna 16.08.04 £10,000 [21+5/6 ScL], Stranraer 01.06 [14+1/- ScL], Dale trial 7.06, Peterhead 1.8.06 [31+4/1 ScL], Cowdenbeath 8.07 [22+1/2 ScL], Sunshine Coast (Australia) 2008, Annan Ath. 12.08 [77+14/12 ScL], Clyde 7.12 [16+1/3 ScL], Peterhead loan 31.1.13 [7+5/1 ScL], Peterhead 7.13 [34+13/6 ScL], Airdrieonians 14.1.15 [11+1/1 ScL], Annan Ath 9.15 [10+1/1 ScL], Threave Rovers manager 4.16*
Honours: N. Ireland under-21s 2004, Scottish Division 3 champions 2005, play-off final 2011, Scottish League 2 play-off final 2013, champions 2014

A regular in the lower leagues in Scotland, helping Gretna to promotion, and a N. Ireland under-21 international, Bryan had a trial with Dale just before the 2006-07 season and like Craig Dove came on as a substitute against Oldham in the Rose Bowl. He then resumed his Scottish career and also had a spell playing in Queensland. He scored twice to pull the aggregate score back to 3-4, but was then sent off, in Annan Athletic's defeat by Albion Rovers in the third division play-off final in 2011. After another play-off disappointment, he then won the League 2 title with Peterhead and moved into management at the end of 2015-16.

Lee Robert Crooks 2006-08

Born: Wakefield 14.1.78 6'0" 12st1
Midfield/central defender
FL Apps/Gls 31+9/0
Total Apps/Gls 37+9/0
Career: Manchester C. as 1991, yts 1993, pro 14.1.95 [52+24/2], Northampton T. loan 26.12.00 [3/-], Barnsley 2.3.01 £190,000 [50+17/-], Bradford C. 6.8.04 [44+3/1], Notts Co. loan 9.1.06 [18/1], Dale 3.8.06 [31+9/-], Guiseley 3.08, Ossett T. 1.1.09
Honours: England youth international, Division 2+ play-off winners 1999, Division 1+ promotion 2000

Working his way up through Manchester City's junior sides, Lee eventually played over 50 games for them mostly at right back or in midfield. His best season came in 1998-99 when he figured in the famous play-off final against Gillingham and he also appeared in City's second consecutive promotion campaign. Arriving at Spotland in 2006, having previously played for Steve Parkin at Barnsley, he alternated between midfield and central defence. He faded out of the picture early in his second term and left for Guiseley, also making preparations for a charity climb up Mount Kilamanjaro that summer. He subsequently joined the RAF Regiment as an infantryman with the rank of Leading Aircraftsman.

Darrell James Clarke 2006-07

Born: Mansfield 16.12.77 5'10" 11st6
Midfield
FL Apps/Gls 5+7/1
Total Apps/Gls 6+7/1
Career: Mansfield T. yts, pro 3.7.96 [137+24/24], Hartlepool U. 17.7.01 £80,000 [98+25/19], Stockport Co. loan 12.1.05 [1/-], Port Vale loan 27.9.05 [+1/-], Dale loan 27.7.06 to 1.07 [5+7/1], Salisbury C. 3.7.07 [101+14/11 Conf], player-coach 2008, (also Football in the Community 2008), player-manager 8.10, Bristol R. assistant manager 6.13, manager 3.14*
Honours: Division 3+ promotion 2003. As manager; Southern League play-off winners 2011, Conference South play-off winners 2013, Conference play-off winners 2015, League 2 promotion 2016

Another player who had been at Mansfield at the same time as Steve Parkin, Darrell accumulated over 150 games for the Stags and also had a productive spell at Hartlepool. He netted a hat-trick in a 7-1 defeat of Swansea and assisted their promotion run in 2003, but suffered a fractured bone in his knee in 2004. With Dale short on numbers at the start of 2006-07, Parkin recruited Darrell on loan and he figured in a few games on the right flank though he was more often on the bench. Moving to Salisbury City, he served as player, coach and manager over the next few seasons and doubled as their Football in the Community officer. He was linked with the manager's job at his old club Hartlepool in 2012 but stayed with Salisbury steering them back up from the Southern League to promotion to the Conference before taking the assistant manager's post at Bristol Rovers. He was promoted to manager, with John Ward moving 'upstairs', late

in the disastrous season which saw Rovers lose their league place, but oversaw their immediate return via the play-offs and then their final day promotion to League 1 in 2016.

Adam Rundle 2006-10

Born: Durham 8.7.84 5'10" 11st2
Winger
FL Apps/Gls 95+32/17 Total Apps/Gls 114+35/19
Career: Newcastle U. jnr, Darlington sch 12.01 [8+9/-], Carlisle U. 31.12.02 £40,000 [25+19/1], Dublin C. 19.8.04, Mansfield T. 14.1.05 [45+8/9], Dale 5.7.06 [95+32/17], Rotherham U. loan 23.11.09 [4/-], Chesterfield 1.2.10 [12+4/-], Morecambe 26.5.10 [8+9/-], Gateshead loan 28.2.11 [7/- Conf], Darlington 7.11 [36+2/5 Conf], Accrington St. trial cs.12, West Auckland T. 7.12, Cork C. 28.1.13, Whitby T. 8.13, Shildon 6.14, Norton and Stockton Ancients manager 15.5.15 to 15.8.15, Jarrow Roofing 8.15*
Honours: South Tyneside Schools, Durham Schools, LDV Vans Trophy final 2003, League 2 play-off final 2008, (League 2 promotion 2010), Durham Challenge Cup winners 2015, (Northern League cup winners 2015)

Adam was a skilful winger with a decent goal tally who was bought by Carlisle when only 18 and played for them in the LDV Vans Trophy final at the Millennium Stadium a few months later. He became a league regular at Mansfield, being signed by their new manager Carlton Palmer, with whom he had played in Ireland. His most productive spell was at Spotland, though, especially after Keith Hill became manager, Adam netting a spectacular volley at Wembley in the play-off final. After missing only a handful of games in two years, he was only on the fringes of the side early in 2009-10 and joined Chesterfield in the January transfer window, thus not being there to be part of Dale's final successful promotion push. A year later he went full circle by signing for original club Darlington, just before they hit terminal financial problems and found themselves demoted to the Northern League, Adam generally figuring at this level for the rest of his career. Adam was also a talented guitarist (and former Pop Idol contestant, particularly popular with Dale's female fans) who often provided the backing for team-mates' karaoke sessions during Dave Flitcroft inspired team-building exercises! He became manager of the wonderfully named Norton and Stockton

Ancients when still only 30 but was bizarrely sacked a week into the season, after just three games.

Lewis John Spencer Edge 2006-07

Born: Lancaster 12.1.87
6'2" 12st10
Goalkeeper
FL Apps +0 Total Apps +0
Career: Dolphinholme, Blackpool sch 2003, pro 26.7.06 [2+1], Worksop T. loan 17.2.06, Dale loan 7.06 to 8.06, Bury loan 14.10.06 [1], Dale loan 31.1.07 to 3.07, Northwich Victoria loan 25.1.08 [4 Conf], Morecambe 21.10.08, AFC Fylde 10.09 to 2012
Cricket for Morecambe and Cumberland
Honours: League 1 promotion 2007, Evo-Stick 1st Division North play-off final 2011

Even before turning pro at football, Lewis was a well known cricketer, a wicket keeper/batsman following in the footsteps of his father David who was also a wicket keeper and goalkeeper. Lewis was man of the match on his Blackpool debut in May 2004 but had few other opportunities, though he did keep a clean sheet in his one game in Blackpool's promotion run-in in 2007. He spent much of 2006-07 on loan at Spotland as deputy to Matt Gilks without getting a game. He then had a year in Morecambe's reserves while resuming his cricket career with the town's Northern League side.

Nathan Stanton 2006-10

Born: Nottingham 6.5.81 5'9" 11st3
Central defender
FL Apps/Gls 138+1/0
Total Apps/Gls 153+1/0
Career: Notts Co. jnr, Lincoln C. trial, Scunthorpe U. yts 1997, pro 19.3.99 [215+22/-], Dale 25.7.06 [138+1/-], Burton A. cs.10 [60+3/1], Grantham T. 8.13, Corby T. 1.14, Scunthorpe U. Centre of Excellence and Football in the Community coach, kit manager 16.6.15*
Honours: England under-17s 1997, Division 3+ promotion 1999, League 2 play-off final 2008, League 2 promotion 2005, 2010, PFA League 2 team of the year 2004

Nathan's father was on Notts Forest's books, but Nathan was a junior with County. He played for England at youth level, made his FL debut at 16 and captained Scunthorpe in a cup tie against Bolton when he was only 17. He went on to figure 276 times at right back in all competitions for the Iron, twice playing in a promoted side. Moving to Spotland in 2006 he was switched to central defence and was a key player as Dale won through to Wembley two years later, being unfortunate enough to deflect Stockport's first goal past Tommy Lee. He remained a regular as Dale finally won promotion in 2010, partnering the inexperienced Craig Dawson. Deciding to accept a longer term contract at Burton, he played in the league for three further seasons passing 400 league games and even scoring his first ever league goal (his only other senior goal had been in a play-off semi-final for Scunthorpe 10 years earlier). He returned to Scunthorpe to join their backroom staff after retiring from playing.

Callum Warburton 2005-08

Born: Stockport 25.2.89 5'9" 11st
Midfield
FL Apps/Gls 4/0
Total Apps/Gls 4+2/0
Career: Reddish Vale Tech., Dale sch 2005, pro cs.07 [4/-], Northwich Victoria loan 3.07 [+2/- Conf], Kendall T. loan 8.07, signed 1.08, Stalybridge Celtic 13.8.10 to 5.14. New Mills 9.15, Mossley 12.12.15*
Honours: Stockport Schools, Greater Manchester Schools 2005, ESFA under-16 trophy 2005, Lancashire Youth Cup final 2007

Callum played in the Manchester Schools side that shared the 2005 ESFA under-16 Trophy, along with several other players with Dale connections, Theo Coleman, Scott Spencer, subsequent loanee Lewis Montrose and Mario Bryan who figured in the reserves. He played for a Dale XI in pre-season 2005-06 and was on the bench for the third league game of the following term. He made his senior bow as substitute in a televised cup tie against Hartlepool and played in midfield in Steve Parkin's last two, and Keith Hill's first two games in charge. He later had lengthy spells with Kendall Town and Stalybridge Celtic, leaving the latter after 139 games when he snapped his Achilles tendon. In

2015 he was briefly in the New Mills side subsequently dubbed "the worst in the country" during a 26 match losing streak.

Morike Sako 2006-07

Born: Paris 17.11.81 6'7" 13st11 Forward FL Apps/Gls 14+3/3 Total Apps/Gls 15+5/3 Career: US D'Ivry (France) jnr, pro c.2000, SR Delemont (Switzerland) 7.04, Torquay U. 25.7.05 [10+15/3], Bristol C. trial cs.06, Blackpool trial cs.06, Dale 25.8.06 [14+3/3], Bournemouth trial 12.06, St Pauli (Germany) 1.07, (Hereford U. trial cs.08), Arminia Bielefeld (Germany) 9.10, FC Sylt (Germany) 11.11 to 6.12, AFC Telford U. trial 2.13, Hessen Kassell (Germany) 19.9.13 to cs.14, Eintracht Norderstedt (Germany) 27.1.15 to cs.15
Honours: Regionalliga Nord promotion 2007, Bundesliga second division promotion 2010

The lofty French striker of Malian descent, almost certainly Dale's tallest ever player, first came to England to play for Torquay. He joined Dale on a short contract a year later and with the departures of Rickie Lambert and Iyesden Christie formed part of a three man attack for much of the first half of the season, his best moment undoubtedly the 5-0 away success at Darlington when he scored twice. He subsequently played for 'kult' left wing Hamburg side St. Pauli, assisting them to promotion to the top flight in 2010 before joining another Bundesliga side, Arminia Bielefeld. He later played for regional league sides in Germany. His brother Bakary played for Saint-Etienne before a successful stint in the UK with Wolves and Crystal Palace. Morike's firm friend at Spotland was diminutive kit man Jack Northover, about two feet shorter than him!

Keith Hubert Douglas Barker 2006-07

Born: Accrington 21.10.86 6'2" 12st12 Striker FL Apps/Gls 11+1/0 Total Apps/Gls 13+3/1 Career: Blackburn R. sch 2003, pro 9.3.05, Cercle Bruges (Belgium) loan 1.06, Dale loan 31.8.06 to 1.07 [11+1/-], Shrewsbury T. trial, St Patrick's Ath. 7.07, Northwich Victoria 3.1.08 to cs.08 [+4/- Conf] Cricket for Enfield, Warwickshire (72 first class games) 2008 to 2015*
Honours: England under-18s, England under-19 v Belgium 2005, National Academy play-off winners 2005

Son of Keith snr, himself a well known cricketer, Keith is the godson of his father's British Guiana (now Guyana) teammate Clive Lloyd, the former West Indies and Lancashire captain (with whom Keith jnr shares his second name). A schoolboy cricketer and footballer, he was top scorer for Blackburn's academy side with 17 goals in 2004-05 and was farmed out to Cercle Bruges. However, his only senior appearances came during a three month loan at Spotland when he played up front with Chris Dagnall, Dale being beaten only once in his first ten games for them, even though he didn't find the net himself. He scored in the Lancashire Cup semi-final for Blackburn towards the end of that season but had been released before the final was played. Having also turned out for his father's old club Enfield in the Lancashire League, Keith was recommended to Warwickshire by David Lloyd. Giving up on his football career, Keith became a county regular as a fast bowling allrounder from 2009, Warwickshire winning the County Championship in 2012.

James Sharp 2006-07

Born: Reading 2.1.76 6'1" 14st6 Central defender FL Apps/Gls 12/1 Total Apps/Gls 14/1 Career: Wimbledon jnr, Reading yts 1992-93, Florida Tech (USA) 8.94, Aldershot T. 11.95, Marlow 1.96, Kintbury Rangers 2.96, Wokingham T. 9.97, Andover 1.8.99, Hartlepool U. 10.8.00 [44+5/2], Falkirk 1.7.03 [33+1/1 ScL], Brechin C. 18.2.05 [13/1 ScL],

Torquay U. 26.7.05 [30+2/-], Wycombe W. trial 7.06, Shrewsbury T. 7.8.06, Dale 31.8.06 to 12.06 [12/1], Airdrie U. cs.07 to 1.08 [8/- ScL]
Honours: Scottish Division 1 champions 2005, Scottish Division 2 champions 2005

James, a left sided defender, was on YTS forms at his local club Reading, but after a year in Florida spent a number of years with lower level clubs before making his FL bow with Hartlepool and then heading even further north to Falkirk. In 2005 he managed the remarkable feat of winning two titles, his parent club winning the first division and Brechin, where he was on loan, the second. However, he then spent a year as Torquay skipper before arriving at Spotland. Partnering Nathan Stanton in central defence, only one of his first ten games was lost, but after the 7-1 humiliation at Lincoln he was soon left out of the side and was released at the end of December. His one goal came against Shrewsbury, for whom he had played a league cup tie earlier in the season.

Glenn Murray 2006-08

Born: Maryport 25.9.83 6'2" 12st7
Striker
FL Apps/Gls 50+4/25 Total Apps/Gls 56+4/26
Career: Workington Reds jnr 2000, pro cs.02, Wilmington Hammerheads (USA) 2.04, Barrow 10.04, Carlisle U. 17.12.04 [5+15/2 Conf, 3+24/3], Stockport Co. loan 2.8.06 [11/3], Dale loan 20.10.06, signed 1.07 [50+4/25], Brighton & HA 25.1.08 £300,000 [101+17/53], Crystal Palace 5.11 [81+31/44], Reading loan 1.9.14 [18/8], Bournemouth 1.9.15 £4M [6+13/3]*
Honours: Conference play-off winners 2005, League 2 champions 2006, League 1 champions 2011, Championship promotion 2013, FL Trophy final 2006

Glenn started out with Workington, netting 36 times in 57 games and also had a stint in the USL with Wilmington Hammerheads. Working his way across Cumbria, he arrived at Carlisle in 2004-05 as they headed for promotion back into the FL and then up to League 1. Loaned to and then signed by Dale in 2006-07, despite a debut in the 7-1 thrashing at Lincoln, he enjoyed a spectacular end of season, hitting 12 goals in the last 15 games (for a season's tally of 19) and winning the player of the year award. Sold to Brighton for £300,000 as Dale headed for a play-off spot the following term – manager Hill always maintaining that they would have made automatic promotion if he had stayed – he scored 22 goals for the Albion side which won League 1 in 2011, before a move to Palace. In 2013 he completed a (presumably very rare) quadruple of promotions from each division from Conference to Championship, his 30 goals making him second highest scorer in the whole FL and seeing his side into the play-offs, which Palace won despite Glenn himself being injured. He figured in his first Premier League games as a late season revival saw Palace move from the foot of the table up to 11th and after a loan at Reading returned to Selhurst Park to net memorable goals in victories over both Manchester City (the reigning champions) and Liverpool (in Steven Gerard's last match at Anfield). Indeed, he ended the season as top scorer for both clubs. (He was also voted into the 'Football Manager' FL team of the decade, along with Dale predecessor Rickie Lambert). In September 2015 he moved to PL newboys Bournemouth for £4 million, scoring their winner at Chelsea.

William Mocquet 2006-07

Born: Valognes, France 23.1.83 5'10" 10st7
Winger
FL Apps/Gls 6+1/1
Total Apps/Gls 6+1/1
Career: Cherbourg (France) jnr, Le Havre (France) jnr 1998, pro 2000, Louhans-Cuiseaux (France) loan 2005, Sunderland 29.8.06, Dale loan 23.11.06 to 1.07 [6+1/1], Bury loan 22.3.07 [9/-], St. Pauli (Germany) trial cs.07, FC Brussels (Belgium) trial cs.07, Pau (France) am 20.9.07, AS Moulins (France) am 7.08, USON Mondeville (France) am 8.11, ES Uzes Pont du Gard (France) 2012-13
Honours: France under-21, Ligue 2 promotion 2002

A French under-21 international, William had played a number of games in the French League with Le Havre, who won promotion in 2002, before joining Sunderland. However, he never appeared for the Black Cats and was loaned to Dale. An exciting winger, nicknamed 'Billy Rocket' by Dale fans, his time with the club overlapped the transition from Steve Parkin to Keith Hill and his goal came in the 4-0 victory over Boston at the end of December 2006. He also had a stint at Bury before returning to play in the lower leagues in France.

Kelvin Peter Etuhu 2006-07

Born: Kilanas, Brunei 30.5.88 6'0" 11st2
Forward
FL Apps/Gls 3+1/2
Total Apps/Gls 3+1/2
Career: St Thomas School (Peckham), Manchester C. sch, pro 9.11.05 to 3.11 [4+6/1], Dale loan 5.1.07 [3+1/2], Leicester C. loan 5.3.08 [2+2/-], Cardiff C. loan 22.8.09 [7+9/-]. Portsmouth 19.1.12 [9+4/1], Barnsley 8.6.12 [33+13/-], Bury 27.6.14 [59+2/2]*
Honours: England youth international, Youth Cup final 2006, Championship play-off final 2010, League 2 promotion 2015

Of Nigerian descent, Kelvin and his brother Dickson were brought up in London and then Manchester. Both were on the books at City, Kelvin scoring in the FA Youth Cup semi-final against United. (Dickson also played for Preston, Norwich, Sunderland, Fulham and Nigeria). A striker or wide player, Kelvin had a promising spell on loan at Spotland ended by injury, but did manage a few PL games and later reached Wembley when loaned to Cardiff. After City released him he returned to football with Portsmouth, then signed for Keith Hill again at Barnsley. In 2014-15 he was almost everpresent in midfield for Dave Flitcroft's promoted Bury, but appeared less in League 1.

Glenville Adam James Le Fondre 2006-07, 2007-10

Born: Stockport 2.12.86 5'10" 11st4
Striker
FL Apps/Gls 65+33/37
Total Apps/Gls 73+40/42
Career: Crewe A. jnr, Stockport Co. sch 2003, pro 18.2.05 [29+34/17], Dale loan 19.1.07 [7/4], Dale 3.7.07 £25,000 [58+33/33], Rotherham U. £145,000 11.8.09 [87+1/52], Reading 27.8.11 £350,000 [53+51/39], Cardiff C. 28.5.14 £ [19+4/3]*, Bolton W. loan 26.1.15 [16+1/8], Wolverhampton W. loan 3.8.15 [10+16/3]

Honours: League 2 play-off final 2008, 2010, (League 2 promotion 2010), Championship winners 2012, PFA League 2 team of the year 2010

Adam, actually more often referred to as Alf or Alfie, from his initials, made his Stockport debut in 2004. In 2006-07 he scored four goals in a game against Wrexham but was then allowed to join Dale on loan, scoring twice on his debut in a 5-0 victory over MK Dons. Bought during the summer, he was a key member of the side which reached Wembly in the play-offs, only to lose to his former club. A similarity in style to Chris Dagnall meant that each often had to settle for a place on the bench, but Adam still netted 20 goals in 2008-09 making him top scorer for the second time and the club's player of the year. One game into the following season he was sold to Rotherham for a modest fee to cover the club's debt to the Inland Revenue. Nevertheless, despite Alf scoring 30 goals for the Millers, it was Dale who were celebrating automatic promotion the following summer while Rotherham were beaten in the play-off final. He repeated his four goal haul, against Cheltenham, before a move to Reading, scoring 16 times as the Royals won the Championship title. Though they struggled in the top flight, Adam netted doubles against Everton, Newcastle and Chelsea, was voted PL player of the month in January 2013 and was easily top scorer despite starting only 11 games. He signed for his boyhood hero Ole Gunnar Solskjaer during the latter's brief tenure at Cardiff, but had few opportunities and spent long spells out on loan, actually top scoring for Bolton.

Rory Prendergast 2006-08

Born: Pontefract 6.4.78 5'8" 11st13
Winger
FL Apps/Gls 6+13/2
Total Apps/Gls 8+16/4
Career: {Frickley Ath. jnr?}, Dale jnr 1994, Barnsley yts 1995, pro 8.4.97, York C. 6.8.98 [1+2/-], Oldham A. n/c 25.1.99, Gainsborough Trinity 1998-99, Northwich Victoria 1.8.99 [8+2/- Conf], Nuneaton Borough 4.2.00 [3+3/- Conf], Wakefield & Emley 2000, Frickley Ath. 2001-02, Bradford PA 1.8.02, Accrington St. 20.12.02 £7500 [56+14/11 Conf], Blackpool {£100,000?} 22.7.05 [22+7/-], Halifax T. loan 24.11.05 [6/- Conf], Dale 22.1.07 [6+13/2], Darlington loan 22.3.07 [5+3/-], Farsley Celtic 8.2.08 [16+1/- Conf], Eastwood T. 8.09, Bradford PA 10.09, Goole 11.09, Ilkeston T. 11.09, Goole

12.09, (USA 2.10), Yeovil T. youth coach, Tiverton T. 2011-12, Clevedon T. 10.12, Bristol C. academy coach 2013, Aylesbury T. academy coach 10.14
Honours: (League 1 promotion 2007), Unibond League (NPL) champions 2003

Rory spent most of his career at non-league level, but moved up to the FL on occasions, most prominently with Blackpool after helping Accrington Stanley establish themselves in the Conference. He joined Dale as Keith Hill's first permanent signing and scored on his debut in the remarkable 5-0 victory over Milton Keynes. When Adam Rundle reclaimed the left wing slot, Rory went on loan to Darlington, but reappeared at Spotland for the remainder of his year's contract, most notably scoring an injury time goal against Stoke in the League Cup. Rory worked as a fitness instructor when in non-league football, latterly playing and coaching in the south west, working with a number of club academies and coaching agencies.

David Philip Perkins 2006-08

Born: Heysham 21.6.82
5'6" 11st06
Midfield/left back
FL Apps/Gls 54+4/4
Total Apps/Gls 59+4/6
Career: Blackburn R. as 1997, Morecambe jnr 1999, pro 8.00 [168+8/1 Conf], Dale 22.1.07 [54+4/4], Colchester U. 15.7.08 £150,000 [71+8/7],
Chesterfield loan 2.10.09 [11+2/1], Stockport Co. loan 18.1.10 [22/-], Barnsley 7.6.11 [85+6/2], Blackpool 17.1.14 [65/-], Wigan A. 20.5.15 [44+1/-]*
Honours: England semi-pro international (9 caps), (Conference promotion 2007)

David had a lengthy non-league career at Morecambe (where he played alongside Keith Hill), figuring mainly as a left back, and progressed to captain the England semi-professional side. Signed by Hill for Dale when he was 24, he was a key player in midfield in Dale's run to the play-offs in 2008 but was victim of a controversial decision in the semi-final second leg when, having scored the crucial goal that took the game to penalties, he was sent-off. An appeal failed and David was forced to sit out the final. Earlier in the season, with only two career goals previously, he hit a hat-trick in a 4-3 win at Chesterfield. Deciding to move on, he was transferred to Colchester, eventually making his mark there in his third season when he was voted player of the year. He signed for Keith Hill again at Barnsley and was their player of the year, too. He moved to Blackpool as they slid down

the Championship table in 2013-14 – he was signed in the middle of a 17 match winless run - and were catastrophically relegated with just 26 points a year later, David being the only remotely regular performer, missing just one game. Results went completely the other way the following year as, again missing only one game, he was voted player of the season when Wigan ran away with the League 1 title. During the campaign he passed 600 senior games.

Reuben James Reid 2006-07

Born: Bristol 26.7.88
6'0" 12st2
Striker
FL Apps/Gls +2/0
Total Apps/Gls +2/0
Career: Fairfield GS, Millfield School, Plymouth A. jnr 9.05, pro 18.1.06 [1+6/-], Kidderminster H. loan 5.10.06 [6/2 Conf] Dale loan 26.1.07 to 2.07 [+2/-], Torquay U. loan 22.3.07
[4+3/2], Wycombe W. loan 31.8.07 [1+10/1], Brentford loan 31.1.08 [1+9/1], Oxford U. trial 6.08, Rotherham U. 5.8.08 [38+3/18], West Bromwich A. cs.09 £ [+4/-], Peterborough U. loan 1.10 [5+8/-], Walsall loan 19.8.10 [13+5/3], Oldham A. 28.1.11 [28+11/7], Yeovil T. 1.7.12 [7+12/4], Plymouth A. loan 1.13 [18/2], Plymouth A. loan 6.13 [44+2/17], Plymouth A. 7.14 [64+7/25]*
Cricket for Millfield, Gloucestershire 2nd XI
Honours: Championship promotion 2010, League 1 promotion 2013, League 2 play-off final 2016

Signed on loan from Plymouth as an 18 year old, Reuben was substitute just twice for Dale before being sent back to the Devon club and subsequently suspended by his manager Ian Holloway. He also had several other loan spells before making the grade at Rotherham with 18 goals in 2008-09. An expensive transfer to West Brom was unproductive, but he regained form when re-signed on a season long loan by Argyle in 2013, becoming their first scorer of a hat-trick for seven years and the first to net 20 goals since 1984. Unsurprisingly player of the year, he then signed a permanent deal and was in the Plymouth side which lost in the 2016 play-off final.

Benjamin Robinson (Ben) Muirhead 2006-

07, 2007-08
Born: Doncaster
5.1.83 5'9" 10st5
Outside right
FL Apps/Gls
30+13/3 Total
Apps/Gls 33+16/3
Career: Leeds U. jnr,
Manchester U. jnr
1997, sch 1998, pro
7.1.00, Doncaster R.
loan 2002-03
[3+3/- Conf],
Bradford C. 6.3.03
[70+42/4], Dale
loan 8.2.07 to 4.07
[12/3], Dale 5.7.07
[18+13/-], Darlington trial 7.08, Alfreton T. 8.08,
Retford T. trial cs.09, Farsley Celtic 8.09, Kings
Lynn 9.09, Harrogate T. 12.09, Buxton 8.3.10,
Armthorpe Welfare 8.10, Retford U. 9.13,
Eastwood T. 12.13, Retford U. 7.14, Armthorpe
Welfare 3.15, player-assistant manager cs.15*
Honours: England youth international 1999,
(Conference promotion 2003), League 2 play-off
final 2008

Ben was a member of the England under-16 squad
that beat their Argentinian counterparts (playing
with Jermaine Jenas and Jermaine Pennant and
against Carlos Tevez) in 1999. Although he had
trained with Leeds from the age of 8, he was on
Manchester United's books by that point and
turned pro the following year. He then played well
over 100 games for Bradford City before a loan
spell at Spotland late in 2006-07. Ben's form on
the wing made him a target that summer, and
Keith Hill was able to tie up a permanent deal. He
only started a further 18 league games but was
responsible for possibly the greatest individual
moment in the club's history when his penalty in
the play-off semi-final shoot-out took Dale to
Wembley. There, he played his last senior match
before heading for the non-league game when he
was still only 25, spending several seasons with
Armthorpe Welfare and becoming assistant
manager.

Stephen Turnbull 2006-07

Born: South Shields 7.1.87
5'10" 11st
Midfield
FL Apps/Gls 2+2/0
Total Apps/Gls 2+2/0
Career: Hartlepool U. sch
2003, pro 4.7.06 [16+8/-],
Gateshead loan 12.05,
Bury loan 22.11.06
[4+1/-], Dale loan 1.3.07
to 4.08 [2+2/-],

Gateshead 2.6.08, Blyth Spartans cs.09, Harrogate
T. 5.11, Bayswater City (Australia) 18.2.12, Blyth
Spartans 2.13, Shildon 3.7.13, Blyth Spartans 9.14*
Honours: Durham Schools, Pontins League
Division 1 East champions 2008, Northumberland
Senior Cup winners 2015

A product of Hartlepool's youth team, making a
couple of appearances when still 17, Stephen was
taken on loan by Dale in March 2007, helping to
fill in for injured skipper Gary Jones in midfeld.
He later played for Gateshead with his twin
brother Phil, also a former Hartlepool player. He
was Blyth Spartans' player of the year in 2011,
figuring with the Spartans in three separate spells
and helping them reach the 3rd round of the FA
Cup in 2015.

Louis Bartholomew Dodds 2006-07

Born: Leicester 8.10.86
5'11" 11st11
Forward
FL Apps/Gls 6+6/2
Total Apps/Gls 6+6/2
Career: Ratby & Groby
FC, Leicester C. sch
2003, pro 15.7.05,
Northwich Victoria
loan 9.10.06 [6/3
Conf], Dale loan
20.2.07 to 5.07
[6+6/2], Lincoln C.
loan 31.7.07 [38+3/9],
Port Vale 4.8.08
[201+88/51], Shrewsbury T. 5.16*
Honours: England under-18s, Westerby Challenge
Trophy 2006, League 2 promotion 2013

Though Leicester's academy player of the year in
2006 and scorer of 65 goals in three seasons, Louis
never made the first team. He spent a couple of
months at Spotland in 2007, gaining a starting
position when Adam Le Fondre's loan ended. He
also had a successful season long loan at Lincoln
before signing for Port Vale. Though not always an
automatic choice, he played both in his favoured
striking role and in midfield, helping Vale to
promotion in 2013 and accruing over 300
appearances and 50 goals before joining
Shrewsbury in 2016.

Kyle Buckley 2004-08

Born: Droylsden 9.6.89
5'11" 9st12
Forward
FL Apps/Gls +0/0
Total Apps/Gls +0/0
Career: St. Matthews
RCHS, Dale jnr, sch
2005, pro 2.07,
Woodley Sports loan
11.07, signed 1.08, FC
Halifax T. trial 7.08
Honours: Lancashire
Senior Cup winners
2005, Lancashire
Youth Cup final 2007

Kyle was a substitute for the Lancashire Cup Final
in 2005 and appeared for a Dale reserve side
which beat Radcliffe Borough 9-2 in the following
pre-season. He also played in the Lancashire
Youth Cup final but the nearest he came to a senior
appearance was when he was on the bench at
Hereford in February 2007.

Charlie Comyn-Platt 2006-07
Born: Manchester 2.10.85 6'2" 12st
Defender
FL Apps/Gls +0/0 Total Apps/Gls +0/0
Career: Parrs Wood Technology College, Bolton W.
sch 2002, pro 17.9.04, Wycombe W. loan 18.9.04
[3+1/-], Swindon T. 8.8.05 [15+9/1], Grays Ath.
loan 11.06 [4/- Conf], Dale 31.1.07, Weston-super-
Mare, ECU Joondalup (Australia) 2009, Perth
Glory (Australia) trial 6.11, Forest Green R. trial
cs.11, Cirencester T. 10.11 to 12.11. ECU Joondalup
by 7.13 (also junior coach) to 9.15
Cricket for Cheadlehulme

Charlie played in four cup ties for Bolton but his
only FL outings came on loan at Wycombe and
then after he joined Swindon. He spent the second
half of 2006-07 at Spotland but got no further
than being an unused substitute on two occasions.
Coincidentally he was at college with Lewis
Montrose who similarly remained on the bench
throughout his stay the following year. Charlie
later went to play in Australia, doubling as player
and junior coach for Joondalup.

Daniel Steven (Danny) Reet 2006-07

Born: Sheffield 31.1.87
6'0" 13st9
Forward
FL Apps/Gls +6/0
Total Apps/Gls +6/0
Career: Sheffield U.
jnr 2003, Sheffield W.
jnr 2004, pro 8.7.05,
Bury loan 4.11.05
[6/4], Mansfield T.
13.1.06 £25,000
[24+17/11], Dale loan
22.3.07 to 5.07 [+6/-],
Alfreton T. 14. 9.07
loan, Dinnington T.,
Glapwell, Dinnington
T. 9.08, Buxton 10.08, Thackley 8.09. Dinnington
T. 8.11 to 2.12 (+ Chapeltown 1.09, Arbourthome
EA 2012, Norton Oakes 6.13*; Sheffield Sunday
League)

Danny played most of his league football at
Mansfield – having scored two against them while
on loan at Bury - and he was recruited by Dale as
cover for their strikers for the last few weeks of
2006-07. Although not scoring, or even starting,
for the first team, he did score from the half-way
line directly from the second half kick-off for the
reserves against Accrington. He subsequently
played non-league football back in the Yorkshire
and Derbyshire area for several years.

Glenn Stephen Poole 2006-07

Born: Barking 3.2.81
5'7" 11st4
Winger
FL Apps/Gls 1+5/0
Total Apps/Gls 1+5/0
Career: Tottenham H.
jnr 1997, Ford U.,
Yeovil cs.99 [11+8/-
Conf], Bath C. loan 1.01
[1/- Conf], Redbridge
cs.02, Thurrock 7.04,
Grays Ath. 7.05
[63+12/19 Conf], Dale
loan 22.3.07 to 5.07
[1+5/-], Brentford
29.5.07 [60+11/19],
Dagenham & Redbridge trial cs.09, Grays Ath.
26.08.09 [13+1/2 Conf], AFC Wimbledon 12.1.10
[12+5/3 Conf], Barnet 14.6.10 [6+4/1], Braintree
T. 3.2.11, Thurrock cs.11, Billericay T. 21.12.11,
(also Redbridge under-14s manager 2012), Canvey
Island 6.15, Billericay T. 1.16, Thurrock player-
coach 6.16*
Honours: FA Trophy final 2006, League 2
champions 2009, Conference South promotion
2011, Isthmian League champions 2012, Essex
Senior Cup final 2015

Glenn spent several years in non-league football, scoring 33 times in 80 games for Redbridge. Latterly with Grays Athletic, for whom he scored in the FA Trophy Final, Dale then offered him a chance at a higher level, taking him on loan for the last couple of months of 2006-07. A goal scoring winger, he made his FL debut in a goalless draw with Hereford and started for the first time in a victory at Mansfield. In the summer he decided to sign for Brentford, where he was top scorer from midfield in his first season and won promotion in his second. After another stint in the Conference he reappeared briefly in the FL with Barnet before further success at non-league level, especially in a long run at Billericay Town. He also ran his own coaching school.

Tom Bates 2006-07
Born: Coventry 31.10.85 5'10" 12st
Midfield
FL Apps/Gls +2/0 Total Apps/Gls +2/0
Career: Woodlands School, Mount Ned Highway Youth 2001, City College (Coventry) 2002, Bedworth U. jnr 2002, Coventry C. 24.1.03 [+1/-], Stratford T. cs.04, Ards 11.05, Bedworth U. 1.06, Brooklands Jaguar, Massey Ferguson 10.06, AP Leamington 10.06, Dale trial 22.3.07 to 5.07 [+2/-], AP Leamington 7.07, Coventry Sphinx c.1.08, Atherstone T. 7.08, Halesowen T. cs.09, Alvis, Bedworth U. 12.09, Nuneaton T. 8.10, Barwell 12.10, Daventry T. 1.11, Bedworth U. 9.11, Barwell 6.12, Bedworth U. 2.13, Barwell 17.8.13, Hinckley U. loan 9.13, Nuneaton Griff 5.14 (acting manager 8.14), Hinckley 19.1.16*

Tom had made one substitute appearance for Coventry in 2003, just a week after his reserve debut, but then played mostly in minor football until being offered a trial at Spotland. He came on as substitute in a victory at Mansfield in mid-April 2007 and also in the last game of the season before re-signing for AP Leamington. He subsequently did the rounds of midlands non-league teams, making around 15 moves in the next seven years.

James Matthew Spencer 2007-09

Born: Stockport 11.4.85 6'5" 15st2
Goalkeeper
FL Apps 20 Total Apps 23
Career: Stockport Co. yts 2001, pro 19.4.02 [90+1], Dale 5.6.07 [20], Chester C. 9.4.09 [5], Oldham A. trial 7.09, Northwich Victoria 8.09, FC United of Manchester cs.11 to 2015

A physically imposing goalkeeper, James made his FL debut in 2002, just before his 17th birthday. He had a couple of spells as Stockport's first choice, unfortunately when County finished bottom of Division 2 and then were almost relegated from the FL, James's clean sheets in the last two games of the latter campaign helping them to safety. He was signed by Dale in 2007 and played regularly until suffering a couple of injuries, the second leading to the arrival of Tommy Lee, but did not subsequently regain his place. He played in Chester's last few FL games as an emergency signing when they had no fit goalkeeper. A regular for a couple of years at Northwich, he later had a lengthy stint with FC United but missed the whole of 2014 with a cruciate injury.

Thomas Gordon (Tom) Kennedy 2007-10,

2010-11, 2014-16
Born: Bury 24.6.85
5'10" 11st1
Left back
FL Apps/Gls 177+2/9
Total Apps/Gls 200+3/9
Career: Woodhey HS (Ramsbottom), Bury yts 2001, pro 2.11.02 [131+12/5], Dale 5.7.07 [132/9], Leicester C. 1.7.10 [5+1/-], Dale loan 1.11.10 to 13.1.11 [6/-], Peterborough U. loan 20.1.11 [14/-], Peterborough U. loan 30.9.11 [8+2/-], Barnsley n/c 21.9.12, signed 1.13 [67+1/1], Dale 13.8.14 to 1.15 [4+1/-], Bury loan 13.10.14 [1+1/-], Blackpool loan 22.11.14 [5/-], Dale 1.15 to 5.16 [35+1/-]
Honours: League 2 play-off final 2008, League 2 promotion 2010, (2015), (League 1 promotion 2011), PFA League 2 team of the season 2009, 2010

The son of Bury stalwart Keith and nephew of Liverpool's England international Alan, Tom joined his father's old club, turning pro when he was 17. He compiled around 150 appearances over the course of four years, as a left wing-back or conventional left back, being everpresent in 2004-05. Moving to Spotland at the start of the Centenary season, he was an integral part of the side which went all the way to Wembley in the play-offs. He was voted into the 2009 PFA League 2 team of the season when Dale again made the play-offs, and subsequently starred in the Dale side which finally won promotion the following year. A highlight for Dale fans was his length of the pitch celebration after scoring a late penalty against his old side. Deciding to move on, Tom signed for Championship Leicester, but played only half a dozen games in two years and had a loan spell back at Spotland. Joining Keith Hill at Barnsley he made his debut in a 5-0 victory over Birmingham and was a fairly regular performer, sometimes in central defence, until the Tykes were relegated in 2014. Re-joining Dale (and Hill) on a short term contract he actually had a couple of loans away from Spotland when not figuring in the side, but after continuing to train with Dale he signed another deal in January 2015, technically making him the first player to sign for the club on four occasions, albeit with two of them in the same season. He figured regularly for the next twelve months but was out of the picture in the second half of 2015-16.

Samuel Ian (Sam) Russell 2007-09

Born: Middlesbrough 4.10.82 6'0" 10st13 Goalkeeper FL Apps 38 Total Apps 46 Career: Middlesbrough yts, pro 7.7.00, Gateshead loan c.3.02, Darlington loan 28.12.02 [1], Scunthorpe U. loan 22.8.03 [10], Darlington 5.8.04 [107], Dale n/c 10.8.07, signed 12.07 [38], Wrexham 8.09 [18 Conf], Darlington 5.10 [65 Conf], Forest Green Rovers 1.12 [110 Conf], Gateshead 6.15 [44 Conf] (also Middlesbrough academy goalkeeping coach)*
Honours: FA Trophy winners 2011

Sam saved a penalty against Dale when on loan at Scunthorpe, but his main FL experience came with a century of appearances for Darlington, where he was everpresent in 2004-05. At Spotland, he came into the side when James Spencer was injured, but then broke a finger. He played all the games in the first half of 2008-09 but was then replaced by loan 'keeper, Frank Fielding. In 2011 he was a member of the Darlington side which won the FA Trophy at Wembley but after they went broke he moved to Forest Green. He saved four penalties in his first eight games and went on to make 144 consecutive apearances before returning to the north east.

Nathan Amarkine D'Laryea 2007-09

Born: Manchester 3.9.85 5'10" 10st Defender FL Apps/Goals 2+4/0 Total Apps/Gls 6+5/0 Career: Manchester C. yts 2002, pro 17.7.03, Macclesfield T. loan 19.1.07 [1], Dale 17.7.07 [2+4/-], Farsley Celtic loan, Hyde U. 7.09, retired injured 2010
Honours: League 2 play-off final 2008

A product of Manchester City's academy like his twin brother Jonathan, who later played for Mansfield, Nathan had a short but eventful senior career. He made his Dale debut as substitute in the first game of 2007-08 and played in both the League Cup and FA Cup. After figuring at centre back as cover for the suspended Stanton in the play-off semi-final first leg against Darlington, the last of his six Dale starts was at right back at Wembley in the final, when Simon Ramsden was moved into midfield in place of the suspended David Perkins. IIe was unable to break into the side again the following term and gave up the professional game to go to university. Attending Sheffield Hallam, he then worked as a maths teacher. The club's PFA rep while at Spotland, after his non-league career was ended by a knee injury he also took up refereeing and was a match summariser for BBC Radio Manchester.

Jerome Anthony Watt 2007-08

Born: Preston 20.10.84
5'10" 11st11
Winger
FL Apps/Gls   +0/0
Total Apps/Gls +0/0
Career: Fulwood HS, Blackburn R. yts 2000, pro 26.10.01, Cercle Bruges (Belgium) loan 2003-04, Northampton T. 10.8.06 [2+8/-], Morecambe loan 26.1.07 [1+2/- Conf], Salisbury C. loan 22.3.07, Dale trial 8.07, Southport 14.9.07, Fleetwood 10.07, Leigh Genesis cs.08, Fylde 12.08, Lancaster C. 2009, retired 1.11. Plungington Celtic (Lancashire Sunday League) 2013, Bamber Bridge 12.13, Longridge T. 7.14 to 2015
Honours: England schoolboys and youth international (30 caps), (Conference promotion 2007)

Like Keith Barker, who had figured for Dale the previous year, Jerome was loaned out to Blackburn's Belgian feeder club Cercle Bruges, but after a cruciate knee ligament injury his only FL appearances came in a spell at Northampton. Earlier he had represented England at all levels from schools up to the under-20s, figuring in two European championship campaigns alongside the likes of Darren Bent and Stewart Downing. He had a trial at Spotland in the summer of 2007, figuring on the wing in three friendlies, and was unused substitute for the first league game of the season. He gave up his non-league career for two years when his full time job included working on Saturdays, but reappeared at Bamber Bridge in 2013.

Guy Peter Bromley Branston 2007-08

Born: Leicester 9.1.79
6'0" 13st12
Centre half
FL Apps/Gls 4/0
Total Apps/Gls 6/0
Career: Bosworth College, Narborough & Littlethorpe, Leicester C. jnr 1993, yts 1995, pro 3.7.97, Rushden & Diamonds loan 10.10.97 [10+1/- Conf], Colchester U. loan 9.2.98 [12/1], Colchester U. loan 7.8.98 [+1/-], Plymouth A. loan 20.11.98 [7/2], Rushden & Diamonds loan 19.3.99 [10/- Conf], Lincoln C. loan 10.8.99 [4/-], Rotherham U. loan 15.10.99, signed £50,000

18.11.99 [101+3/13], Wycombe W. loan 19.9.03 [9/-], Peterborough U. loan 25.2.04 [14/-], Sheffield W. 21.7.04 [10+1/-], Peterborough U. loan 31.12.04 [4/1], Oldham A. 18.2.05 [44+1/2], Peterborough U. 24.7.06 [24+2/-], Dale loan 24.8.07 to 10.07 [4/-], Northampton T. loan 15.11.07 [3/-], Notts Co. 1.1.08 [1/-], Kettering T. 30.1.08 [39/- Conf], Burton A. 15.7.09 [18+1/-], Torquay U. loan 29.1.10 [16/-], Torquay U. 21.7.10 [45/2], Bradford C. cs.11 [15+1/1], Rotherham U. loan 14.10.11 [2/-], Aldershot T. 25.6.12 [3/-], Bristol R. loan 11.12 [4/1], Plymouth A. 1.13 [30+1/-], retired 7.14. Notts Co. head of recruitment 1.15 to 5.16
Honours: Division 3+ promotion (1998), 2000, Division 2+ promotion 2001, (League 1 promotion 2005), (League 2 promotion 2008), Conference North champions 2008, League 2 play-off final 2011, PFA League 2 team of the year 2011

A man of many clubs – 19, in fact, in the FL or Conference, with return trips to several of them – Guy was an uncompromising old fashioned centre half who collected even more red cards, a total of 20 during his career. He never made the first team at Leicester but was loaned out seven times (helping Colchester gain promotion) before finally signing for Rotherham where he was promoted twice. He had several spells with Peterborough, and it was from there that he joined Dale on loan while Nathan Stanton was injured. Continuing his tour of the country, he finally got to play at Wembley, for Torquay in the 2011 play-off final, but an accumulation of injuries ended his career at Plymouth in 2014. He also developed a website company 'All About Ballerz', designed for players to promote themselves to find new clubs (something he could definitely claim expertise in!), authored 'The Footballer's Journey", wrote for the Western Morning News and had a regular spot on Sky Sports radio. Unsurprisingly, on retiring, he stated that 'football has got softer'.

Kallum Michael Higginbotham 2007-2010

Born: Salford 15.6.89
5'11" 10st10
Forward
FL Apps/Gls 31+38/7
Total Apps/Gls 37+43/7
Career: Salford Lads' Club, Salford C. jnr, Oldham A. 1.8.06, Dale 19.6.07 [31+38/7], Accrington St. loan 17.10.08 [1+4/-], Accrington St. loan 23.1.09 [4+3/-], Falkirk 7.10 [39+11/7 ScL], Huddersfield T. 31.1.12 [3+1/-], Barnsley loan 23.3.12 [2+3/-], Carlisle U. loan 20.9.12 [7+3/-], Motherwell loan 9.1.13

[3+7/1 ScL], Partick Thistle 8.8.13 [57+9/10 ScL], Kilmarnock 25.6.15 [23+4/5 ScL]*
Honours: NWC League Cup winners 2006, Lancashire Youth Cup winners 2007, Youth League winners 2007, League 2 play-off final 2008, League 2 promotion 2010, League 1 play-off winners 2012, (SPL/Scottish Championship play-off winners 2016)

Kallum had trials at Manchester United as a junior, but came to notice when Salford won the North West Counties cup final, the 16 year old Kallum scoring from the halfway line, a taste of things to come. Released by Oldham after scoring against Dale in the Lancashire Youth Cup Final (though not netting a hat-trick as claimed elsewhere), he signed for Dale and gradually established himself in the side during 2007-08, ending the campaign playing at Wembley. Primarily played on the right wing, the following campaign saw him supplanted by another talented youngster in Will Buckley and spend time on loan at Accrington. He spent virtually all of the promotion season on the bench, but scored one of the all time great Rochdale goals with a volley from the touchline virtually on half way to seal the 4-2 success at Accrington. Moving to Scottish Division 1 Falkirk, he was their man of the match against Celtic in the League Cup semi-final immediately before signing for Huddersfield. Though he made only a handful of appearances and was loaned to Barnsley, he did appear at Wembley again in the League 1 play-off final. Returning to Scotland, he helped Motherwell finish 2nd in the SPL and hit the crossbar straight from the kick off in a match for Partick in 2013. After two years with Thistle, he moved to SPL rivals Kilmarnock.

Kelvin Lomax [aka Trippier] 2007-08

Born: Bury 12.11.86
5'11" 12st3
Right back
FL Apps/Gls 10/0
Total Apps/Gls 10/0
Career: Woodhey HS (Ramsbottom), Oldham A. yts 2003, pro 12.7.05 [65+18/-], Dale loan 13.9.07 to 11.07 [10/-], Chesterfield loan 11.10 [3+1/-], Shrewsbury T. 31.1.11 [+1/-], Barrow 8.11 [22+4/- Conf], Hyde 10.8.12 [26+3/- Conf], Shepparton U. SC (Australia) 3.13, Ramsbottom U. 10.13, Hyde 1.1.14 [10+3/- Conf], Shepparton U. SC (Australia) 26.3.14, Hyde 10.14 to 1.15. Bacup Borough 26.7.15*
Honours: (League 2 champions 2011), Goulburn North East All Stars XI 2013

Kelvin attended the same school as Tom Kennedy, but joined Oldham rather than Bury. He made his FL debut in the last game of 2003-04 but was unable to claim a fairly regular place in the Latics' side until after a two month stint at Spotland when he partnered Kennedy at full back early in the campaign that ended with Dale at Wembley. He was also on loan briefly at Chesterfield the year they won League 2, but when released by Oldham after seven seasons managed just one game for Shrewsbury, later alternating between the non-league game and stints in Australia. During 2015-16 he netted a hat-trick when Bacup Borough beat Rochdale Town 9-2. The older brother of Oldham and Burnley full back Kieran Trippier, Kelvin also adopted the name Trippier late in his career.

Marcus Lewis Holness 2007-12

Born: Swinton 8.12.88
6'0" 12st2
Defender
FL Apps/Gls 93+15/4
Total Apps/Gls 110+17/4
Career: Oldham A. yts 2005, pro 3.7.07, Ossett T. loan 8.07, Dale loan 2.10.07, signed 1.08 [93+15/4], Barrow loan 1.09 to 2.09 [11+1/- Conf], Burton A. 16.7.12 [32+7/1], Tranmere R. 27.6.14 to 5.16 [15+2/-, 1+3/- Conf], Altrincham loan 26.1.16 [14/1]
Honours: Lancashire Youth Cup winners 2007, League 2 play-off final (2008), 2014, League 2 promotion 2010

Another loanee from Oldham in 2007-08, before signing permanently, Marcus played a number of games in place of first choice pairing McArdle and Stanton and was an unused substitute at Wembley. Little used over the next two seasons, starting only seven games in the promotion campaign, 'Bob' became first choice centre back after Stanton's departure, being everpresent in the first season in League 1. Unsurprisingly unable to maintain his form in the following catastrophic campaign, he moved to Burton Albion where he was in two further losing play-off squads. He missed the second half of the season which saw Tranmere drop into the Conference in 2015 with knee ligament damage.

Raphale Mondale Evans 2006-09

Born: Manchester
7.5.90 6'0" 14st7
Defender
FL Apps/Gls 1/0
Total Apps/Gls 1/0
Career: Dale jnr, sch
2006, pro 5.08 to 4.09
[1/-], Bradford PA
loan 10.08, Leigh
Genesis loan 3.09.
Northwich Victoria
1.11, Salford C. 10.11,
Woodley Sports/
Stockport Sports 2.12,
Alsager T. 3.13,
Northwich Flixton Villa 8.13 to cs.14

Raphale figured in Dale's youth sides from 2006 and was an unused sub for a Freight Rover game the following year. He then made his one senior appearance, at left back though he was usually a central defender, in the last league game of 2007-08 when most of the senior players were rested ahead of the play-offs. Also an unused sub a couple of times the following term, his contract was cancelled in 2009. He returned to minor non-league football a couple of years later.

Scott James Taylor 2007-08

Born: Chertsey 5.5.76
5'10" 11st4
Forward
FL Apps/Gls 2+2/0
Total Apps/Gls 2+2/0
Career: Staines T.,
Millwall 8.2.95
£15,000 [13+15/-],
Bolton W. 29.3.96
£150,000 [2+10/1],
Rotherham U. loan
12.12.97 [10/3],
Blackpool loan 26.3.98
[3+2/1], Tranmere R.
9.10.98 £350,000
[78+30/17], Stockport
Co. 10.8.01 [19+9/4],
Blackpool 25.1.02
[97+19/43], Plymouth A. 30.12.04 £100,000
[17+17/4], Milton Keynes Dons 16.1.06 £100,000
[16+29/5], Brentford loan 8.3.07 [3+3/-], Dale
loan 19.10.07 to 11.07 [2+2/-], Grays Ath. 1.08
[11+7/3 Conf], Lewes 7.08 [19/5 Conf], Staines T.
28.11.08, assistant manager 2012 to 6.14,
Shrewsbury T. scout*
Honours: Division 1+ champions 1997, Football
League Cup final 2000, LDV Vans Trophy winners
2002, Isthmian League play-off final winners
2009, PFA Division 2 team of the year 2004

Scott was a well travelled winger turned striker who cost several clubs sizeable fees. His best returns were at Tranmere and Blackpool, figuring over 100 times for each He appeared in Tranmere's unlikely visit to Wembley for the 2000 League Cup Final and hit a purple patch in front of goal at Bloomfield Road with 41 goals coming in his last two and a half seasons, including one in the LDV Vans Trophy final. He was included in the 2004 PFA second division team of the year. Largely used as a substitute by Milton Keynes, he spent a month on loan at Spotland as back-up striker after Chris Dagnall was injured. In 2008 he re-signed for Staines Town with whom he had first appeared in the early 'nineties and scored the goal that gave them promotion to the Conference South. He later became their assistant manager.

Robert Guy (Rob) Atkinson 2007-08

Born: North Ferriby
29.4.87 6'1" 12st
Central defender
FL Apps/Gls +2/0 Total
Apps/Gls +2/0
Career; Barnsley as, yts
2003, pro 5.7.06 [6+2/-],
Scarborough loan
24.11.05 [20+2/- Conf],
Halifax T. loan 14.11.06
[4/2 Conf], Dale loan
19.10.07 to 11.07 [+2/-],
Grimsby T. loan 22.11.07
[24/1], Grimsby T. loan
31.10.08, signed 1.1.09 [91+1/5, 24+1/- Conf],
Fleetwood T. 10.6.11 [15+2/1 Conf, 18/-],
Accrington St. loan 9.12 [12/-], Accrington St.
16.7.13 [55+4/3], Guiseley 3.8.15 [38/5 Conf]*
Honours: Johnstone's Paint Trophy final 2008,
England 'C' 2011 (2 caps), Conference champions
2012

Rob, who had made his debut as a substitute for Barnsley when still only 16, joined Dale on loan as defensive cover early in 2007-08. He had more opportunities in spells at Grimsby, eventually signing permanently for them in January 2009. Having played at Wembley for them in the JP Trophy final, he remained at Blundell Park after their relegation to the Conference and won two caps for the England semi-pro side. When he switched to Fleetwood, they could field a complete back four of former Dale players as they also had on their books Matt Flynn, Alan Goodall and former youth team player (and Celtic reserve) Matty Hughes. Rob was a member of their side which was promoted to the FL, subsequently moving to Accrington. He left Stanley after his most productive FL season ever, having made 44 appearances, and signed for Conference newcomers Guiseley.

Benjamin Francis (Ben) Wharton 2006-08

Born: Stockport 17.6.90
6'1" 13st
Forward
FL Apps/Gls +1/0
Total Apps/Gls +1/0
Career: Stockport Co.
jnr, Dale sch 2006
[+1/-], Mossley 8.08,
Padiham, Atherton
Collieries, Northwich
Victoria 10.08, Buxton
11.08, Radcliffe Borough
3.09, Warrington T.
5.13, Ashton U. 1.16,
Colne 3.16*

Ben trained with home town club **Stockport** from the age of 7, but became a scholar at Spotland. Top scorer in the reserve and youth sides in 2007-08 with a total of 24 goals, he was given just one chance in the first team, coming on as a substitute in the 2-1 win at Accrington when the on loan Lee McEvilly was ineligible to play. He netted 19 times for Radcliffe Borough in 2009-10, hitting his 50th goal for them in February 2013, and was in the Warrington side which beat Exeter in the FA Cup in 2014. He also worked for League Football Education, advising young players on alternative careers.

Jermaine Renee (Rene) Howe 2007-08

Born: Bedford 22.10.86
6'0" 14st3
Striker
FL Apps/Gls 19+1/9
Total Apps/Gls 21+2/9
Career: Mark
Rutherford School
(Bedford), Bedford T.
2003, (Aston Villa
trial), Kettering T.
cs.06, Peterborough U.
19.7.07 [2+13/1], Dale
loan 8.1.08 to 27.5.08
[19+1/9], Morecambe
loan 23.7.08 [35+2/10],
Lincoln C. loan 3.8.09 [14+3/5], Gillingham loan 20.1.10 [18/2], Rushden & Diamonds 13.8.10 [18+1/6 Conf], Bristol R. loan 28.1.11 [8+4/1], Torquay U. 14.7.11 [78+3/28], Burton A. 13.7.13 [7+8/1], Newport Co. 9.1.14 to 24.3.15 [17+12/3]. Gateshead trial cs.15, Notts Co. trial cs.15, Kettering T. 11.15*
Honours: Southern League Premier division promotion 2006, League 2 play-off final 2008, League 2 promotion 2008

A qualified electrician, Rene made his mark as a powerful front man in non-league football when he scored 23 goals for Bedford Town in 2005-06 and

then 25 for Kettering the following term, including five in a 10-1 FA Cup defeat of Clitheroe. Signing for Peterborough, he was unable to gain a regular place in the team and joined Dale on loan. Replacing the transferred Glenn Murray, his most remarkable performance came against Grimsby when he netted a hat-trick after coming on as substitute. His nine goals in the second half of the season helped Dale reach Wembley, while his parent club simultaneously gained automatic promotion. Still unable to make the Posh side he had further lengthy loan spells before eventually signing for Torquay in 2011, scoring seven times in his first seven games, including two against the Dale. An injury hampered spell at Newport ended when he gave up the game to look after his ill wife but he later reappeared in the Southern League.

Lee Anthony Thorpe 2007-09

Born: Wolverhampton
14.12.75 6'1" 12st4
Striker
FL Apps/Gls 23+13/6
Total Apps/Gls
28+16/7
Career: Walsall jnr,
Wolverhampton W.
jnr, Blackpool yts 1992,
pro 18.7.94 [2+10/-],
Bangor C. loan 19.9.95,
Lincoln C. 4.8.97
[183+9/58], Leyton O.
3.5.02 [42+13/12],
Grimsby T. loan 6.2.04
[5+1/-], Bristol R.
12.3.04 [25+10/4],
Swansea C. 8.2.05 [9+9/3], Peterborough U. loan 30.9.05 [6/-], Torquay U. loan 13.2.06, signed 19.5.06 [49+2/11], Brentford 4.7.07 [17+2/4], Dale 31.1.08 [23+13/6], Darlington 7.09 [7+1/-], Fleetwood T. 3.10 [4+14/- Conf], AFC Fylde 7.11 to 12.11, Blackpool junior coach*
Honours: Division 3+ promotion 1998, League 2 promotion 2005, Conference North play-off winners 2010, Lancashire Senior Cup winners 1996-97, FAW Premier Cup winners 2005

A long serving striker in the lower divisions, Lee played nearly 200 league games and scored well over 50 goals in five years at Lincoln, assisting them to promotion in his first term. Shorter spells at several other clubs, most productively Orient and Torquay, brought him to Spotland at the end of the January transfer window in 2008 as Dale looked to boost their challenge for the play-offs. Unfortunately he suffered a series of injuries and was already out for the season when he bizarrely broke his arm on the coach trip to Darlington when arm wrestling Rene Howe. He got more game time the following term when, as a big target man, he proved a useful partner for the smaller

Dagnall or Le Fondre and played in both legs of the play-off semi-final. In 2010 he scored the winning goal in Fleetwood's Conference North play-off final.

Christopher Paul (Chris) Basham 2007-08

Born: Hebburn
20.7.88 5'11" 12st8
Midfield
FL Apps/Gls 5+8/0
Total Apps/Gls
5+8/0
Career: Newcastle U.
jnr 2003-04, Chester-
le-Street, Gateshead
College, Bolton W. yts
cs.06, pro 20.10.07
[6+13/1], Stafford R.
loan 23.11.06
[3/- Conf], Dale loan
8.2.08 to 5.08
[5+8/-], Blackpool 13.8.10 £1.2M [70+15/5],
Sheffield U. 5.6.14 [78+3/3]*
Honours: Lancashire Senior Cup final 2007

Another Dale loanee in the latter part of 2007-08, Chris was a regular squad member, though making only five starts. An unused sub in the first leg of the play-off semi-final, unfortunately his loan ended before the final when he would have been the obvious replacement for the suspended Perkins. He only managed about 20 games for Bolton but still commanded a fee of over a million pounds when he was transferred to Blackpool. He made his debut in their first ever PL game but only established himself in the side after they returned to the championship, missing only a handful of games in 2013-14. He then joined Sheffield United, scoring in the remarkable 5-5 play-off semi-final draw at Swindon, the only goal of his first season.

William Edward (Will) Buckley 2007-10

Born: Oldham 21.11.89
6'0" 12st9
Winger
FL Apps/Gls 41+18/14
Total Apps/Gls
48+21/14
Career: Boundary Park
Juniors, Oldham A. jnr,
Hopwood Hall College,
Curzon Ashton, Dale
trial 7.07, pro 18.8.07
[41+18/14], Watford
26.1.10 £200,000
[31+8/5], Brighton &
HA 6.6.11 £1M
[64+32/19], Sunderland 14.8.14 £2.5M [9+13/-]*,
Leeds U. loan 2.10.15 [1+3/-], Birmingham C. loan
15.1.16 [5+5/1]

Honours: League 2 play-off final 2008, (League 2 promotion 2010)

Hopwood Hall student Will joined Dale after a successful trial when he was 17. He was introduced into the squad in February 2008 when Lee Thorpe was injured but had made only one start when he came on as substitute at Wembley in the play-off final. Playing mostly on the right flank, he quickly established himself the following term, netting six times in ten games and by the following January he was included in the Times list of 50 rising stars. He ended the season with 11 league goals as Dale again made the play-offs and despite being injured for much of the first half of 2009-10 was then transferred to Watford for a sizeable fee. His next move took him to fellow Championship side Brighton for £1M and he scored their first goals at their new AMEX stadium, coming on as substitute to net twice against Doncaster. After over 100 appearances in three years, he signed for his former Brighton boss Gus Poyet at Sunderland for an even larger fee, making 22 appearances in his first season in the top flight but was subsequently loaned out.

Thomas Edward (Tommy) Lee 2007-08

Born: Keighley 3.1.86
6'2" 12st
Goalkeeper
FL Apps 11 Total
Apps 14
Career: Oakworth
Juniors, Manchester U.
jnr 2002, yts 2004, pro
6.7.05, Macclesfield T.
loan 18.1.06 [11],
Macclesfield T. 26.7.06
[51+1], Dale loan
21.3.08 to 5.08 [11],
Chesterfield 1.8.08 [321]*
Honours: Premier Reserve league northern champions 2006, League 2 play-off final 2008, League 2 champions 2011, 2014, JPT winners 2012, final 2014, PFA League 2 team of the year 2011, 2014

Tommy played a few games for United's reserves when they won their league in 2006, but was not close to first team selection so joined Macclesfield. Against Chelsea in the FA Cup he was injured in one challenge and later sent off after another. Out of the side early in 2008, Dale took him on loan when both Spencer and Russell were injured and the pony-tailed 'keeper made his own spot of Rochdale history when his penalty save from Jason Kennedy paved the way for Ben Muirhead's spot-kick to take Dale to Wembley. Signing for Chesterfied, he became an immediate fixture in their side and played in two League 2 winning sides – being voted in to the PFA select XI each time - as well as in two Johnstone's Paint Trophy finals. He was also Chesterfield's player of the year in 2010 and 2011 and by 2016 had accumulated 366 appearances for the Spireites.

David Robert Edmund Button 2007-08

Born: Stevenage 27.2.89
6'3" 13st1
Goalkeeper
FL Apps +0
Total Apps +0
Career: Stevenage B. jnr, Tottenham H. jnr 2003, sch 2005, pro 3.3.06, Grays Ath. loan 1.08 [1 Conf], Dale loan 3.08, Grays Ath. loan 9.08 [13 Conf], Bournemouth loan 1.09 [4], Luton T. loan 6.3.09, Dagenham & Redbridge loan 16.4.09 [3], Crewe A. loan 8.09 [3], Crewe A. loan 1.9.09 [7], Shrewsbury T. loan 20.11.09 [26], Plymouth A. loan 3.8.10 [30], Leyton Orient loan 8.11 [1], Doncaster R. loan 1.12 [7], Barnsley loan 19.3.12 [9], Charlton A. 28.8.12 [5], Brentford 30.7.13 £ [134]*
Honours: England under-16s (3 caps), under-17s (17 caps), under-19s (10 caps), under-21s v Italy 2009, (Johnstone's Paint Trophy winners 2009), League 1 promotion 2014

A regular for England at various age levels, playing in the European under-17s championships in 2005 and the under-19s in 2008, David spent six years as a pro with Spurs without a FL appearance, though he did appear as a substitute in a League Cup game. In that time he went out on loan no fewer than 13 times, including a stint at Spotland as understudy to Tommy Lee, though his loan ended before Dale reached Wembley. (He was later substitute goalkeeper for Luton when they reached Wembley in the JPT). He spent a year at Charlton but finally became a league regular on signing for Brentford who were promoted in his first season.

Lewis Robert Egerton Montose 2007-08

Born: Manchester 17.11.88
6'0" 12st
Midfield
FL Apps/Gls +0/0
Total Apps/Gls +0/0
Career: Manchester C. jnr, Wigan A. yts 2006, pro 5.7.07, Dale loan 27.3.08 to 27.4.08, Cheltenham T. loan 24.9.08 [4/-], Cheltenham T. loan 6.1.09 [1/-], Chesterfield loan 26.2.09 [11+1/-], Wycombe W. 6.09 [38+12/4], Gillingham 7.11 [40+12/5], Oxford U. loan 4.1.13 [5/-], York C. 28.6.13 [36+11/1], Stockport Co. 23.7.15*

Honours: Greater Manchester Schools, ESFA under-16 trophy winners 2005, League 2 promotion 2011, champions 2013

A member of the Greater Manchester Schools side that shared the ESFA under-16s trophy, playing alongside the likes of Scott Spencer (q.v.), Lewis moved from Manchester City to Wigan as a scholar and progressed to make a couple of appearances in the League Cup. He spent a month on loan at Spotland but spent most of the time injured and was an unused substitute just twice. He had further loan spells before joining Wycombe and played around 50 FL games for them and then for Gillingham, figuring in promoted sides for each. He also had a couple of seasons at York but was sent off twice for Stockport in the Conference North in 2015-16.

George Bowyer 2007-09

Born: Stockport 11.11.90 6'0" 10st2
Defender
FL Apps/Gls +1/0
Total Apps/Gls +1/0
Career: Dale jnr 2006, sch 2007 [+1/-], Ramsbottom U. 10.09, Woodley Sports 8.10, Bamber Bridge 11.10, Curzon Ashton cs.12, Bamber Bridge 7.13, Ramsbottom U. 1.15, Droylsden 1.8.15,

Bamber Bridge 10.15*

George skippered Dale's youth team and was shortlisted for the League 2 apprentice of the year in 2008-09. His one moment of league action had actually come the year before when he came off the bench to replace Marcus Holness in the final game of the regular season, a draw against Shrewsbury. His progress was later hampered by a series of injuries and he subsequently coached on Stockport's community football programme and joined the staff of the PFA as an administrator in 2011 while playing North West Counties football.

Andrew (Andy) Brown 2007-09
Born: Wythenshaw 2.10.90
Midfield
FL Apps/Gls +0/0 Total Apps/Gls +0/0
Career: Manchester GS, Dale jnr 2006, sch 6.07 to 2008-09
Honours: Manchester Schools Cup winners 2007

Andy became a scholar at Spotland in 2007 and after appearing in the youth team was an unused substitute in the final league game of the season when Dale rested most of their regulars before the play-off games. Generally playing on the right wing, he figured in the reserves the following term but was then released.

Reece Derek Kelly 2006-08
Born: Salford 29.9.89
Midfield
FL Apps/Gls +0/0 Total Apps/Gls +0/0
Career: Manchester C. jnr, Wigan A. jnr, Dale sch 2006, Leigh Genesis 7.08, Salford C. loan 9.08, Mossley 10.08, Chorley 9.09, Radcliffe Borough 7.10 to 2012-13

Like Andy Brown, Reece was an unused substitute in the Shrewsbury game in May 2008. He moved into the north west non-league circuit, playing at Radcliffe Borough with former Dale youth team colleague Ben Wharton and subsequently ran the Coach Right UK football academy.

Clark Stuart Keltie 2008-10

Born: Newcastle 31.8.83 6'0" 12st7
Midfield
FL Apps/Gls 26+5/1
Total Apps/Gls 30+6/1
Career: Walker Central 2000, Sunderland trial 2001, Darlington 19.9.01 [129+32/9], Dale 4.8.08 [26+5/1], Chester C. loan 9.09 [11/- Conf], Darlington trial, Gateshead loan 11.09 [3/- Conf], Lincoln C. 1.10 [25+4/-], Cork C. trial, Akureyri (Iceland) 21.7.11, Stalybridge Celtic, Cork C. 9.1.12, Darlington n/c 31.1.12 [14+1/- Conf], Vikingur Olafsvik (Iceland) 15.5.12, Darlington 10.12, Perth SC (Australia) 1.13*
Honours: Icelandic Cup final 2011

Clark figured with Darlington for seven seasons without ever quite becoming an automatic choice in the side. After playing in the side beaten by Dale in the 2008 play-offs, he moved to Spotland and helped Dale secure another top seven finish, though by the time of the play-off matches he was out of favour and didn't appear in either leg. The following term he did not figure at all and went out on loan before being transferred to Lincoln. After they slipped into the Conference he twice played in Iceland and had two more spells with Darlington, who had by this point reformed down in the Northern League. Heading to Australia in 2013, by now a central defender, he won the Western

Australia soccer player of the year award when Perth finished runners up in the league.

Scott Nigel Kenneth Wiseman 2008-11

Born: Hull 9.10.85
6'0" 11st6
Right back
FL Apps/Gls 100+5/1 Total Apps/Gls 107+7/1
Career: Hull C. yts 2002, pro 8.4.04 [10+6/-], Boston U. loan 18.2.05 [1+1/-], Rotherham U. loan 4.8.06 [9+9/1], Darlington loan 8.3.07, signed 5.07 [12+5/-], Dale 3.7.08 [100+5/1], Barnsley 6.11 [91+11/1], Preston NE 10.1.14 [30+7/2], Scunthorpe U. 28.5.15 [21+3/-]*
Honours: England under-20s 2005 (3 caps), Division 3+ promotion 2004, League 1 promotion 2005, 2015, League 2 promotion 2010, Gibraltar international (7 caps) 2013 to 2015

Though an England under-20s international, Scott was unable to break into Hull's team on a regular basis, though figuring in two promotions, and he joined Darlington in 2007. After Darlo lost to Dale in the play-offs, Scott switched his allegiance to Spotland and shared the right back berth with Simon Ramsden in his first seson. Initially released in 2009, when Ramsden moved to Scotland Scott was quickly re-signed and became one of the stars of Dale's promotion run. After Dale established themselves in League 1 the following term, he followed manager Hill to Barnsley. He again played over 100 games, often at centre back, before moving on to Preston where he figured in a fourth promoted side, though he was not in the squad that triumphed in the play-off final. In 2013 he remarkably became a full international, qualifying to play for Gibralter via his mother's birthplace and starring in a 0-0 draw against Slovakia in Gib's first game after becoming a full member of UEFA. However, he also played in five European championships qualifiers, the outgunned Gibralterians going down by an aggregate 27-1.

Ciaran Toner 2008-10

Born: Craigavon
30.6.81 6'1" 12st4
Midfield
FL Apps/Gls 39+11/1
Total Apps/Gls
45+12/1
Career: St. Colman's
College, Tottenham H.
yts, pro 14.7.99,
Peterborough U. loan
21.12.01 [6/-], Bristol
R. 28.3.02 [6/-],
Leyton O. 7.5.02
[41+11/2], Lincoln C.
4.8.04 [10+5/2],
Cambridge U. loan
19.3.05 [6+2/-],
Grimsby T. 18.7.05 [80+14/14], Dale 4.8.08
[39+11/1], Harrogate T. 8.10, Guiseley 7.11 to 5.12,
York C. junior coach 10.12 to 5.13, (also
Rotherham U. p/t coach and Dearne Valley College
head coach 8.13), Gainsborough Trinity player-
coach 13.9.13 to 4.15, Rotherham U. academy
coach 9.15*
Honours: N. Ireland schools, N.Ireland youth
international, N.Ireland under-21s (17 caps),
N.Ireland (2 caps) 2003 v Spain, Italy, (League 2
play-off final 2006), League 2 promotion 2010,
Johnstone's Paint Trophy final 2008

Ciaran never made the first team at Spurs but
gathered a large collection of N. Ireland youth caps
at various levels, with no less than 17 appearances
for the under-21s. While with Orient in Division 3
he won two full caps in impressive company,
playing against Spain and Italy, but did not play
regularly in the league again until a spell at
Grimsby, for whom he was twice a substitute at
Wembley. Signing for Dale in the summer of 2008,
he played in most of their games, partnering Gary
Jones in central midfield, as they reached the play-
offs. He missed most of the following season, but
nevertheless made a number of appearances in the
run-in to promotion and came on as substitute in
the final victory over Northampton. He later
combined playing at non-league level with
coaching.

Kyle Mathew Lambert 2006-09

Born: Wigan 26.3.90 5'10"
11st8
Midfield
FL Apps/Gls +1/0 Total
Apps/Gls +1/0
Career: Hindley Tigers, Bolton
W. jnr, Dale sch 2006, pro
4.8.08 [+1/-], Bradford PA
loan 10.08, Leigh Genesis
20.1.09 to cs.09

A former Dale scholar and regular in the reserves,
Kyle was handed a short term professional
contract at the start of 2008-09. A member of the
party taken on the pre-season training exercise he
was unused substitute for the first two senior
games of the term and made his FL debut when he
came on against Wycombe soon afterwards. He
then went on loan to Bradford Park Avenue, along
with Raphale Evans, before signing for Leigh
Genesis.

Jon Steven Shaw 2008-10

Born: Sheffield 10.11.83
6'1" 12st9
Striker
FL Apps/Gls 5+2/1
Total Apps/Gls 7+6/1
Career: Abbey Lane
Juniors, Sheffield W. yts
2001, pro 2.7.03
[8+10/2], York C. loan
14.11.03 [5+3/-], Burton
A. 8.11.04 [78+23/26
Conf], Halifax T. 30.8.07
[36+1/20 Conf], Dale
8.7.08 £ [5+2/1],
Crawley T. loan 1.09 [12+5/5 Conf], Barrow loan
28.8.09 [13+1/5 Conf], Gateshead loan 26.11.09
[1/- Conf], Mansfield T. 1.10 [6+8/3 Conf],
Gateshead 29.5.10 [79+1/45 Conf], Luton T.
21.6.12 [30+12/8 Conf], Gateshead 12.6.14 to 5.16
[44+21/11 Conf]
Honours: England semi-pro international (6 caps)
2006 to 2008, (League 1 promotion 2005),
(League 2 promotion 2010), Conference
champions 2014

A lanky striker, Jon played a number of league
games for Sheffield Wednesday, but came to
prominence at Conference level, playing for Burton
against Manchester United and then scoring 20
goals for Halifax in 2007-08, despite their ultimate
demise. He also won half a dozen caps for England
'C' before joining Dale for an undisclosed fee (often
quoted as £60,000). He netted on his league debut
for Dale but was injured shortly afterwards and
never subsequently gained a place in the side other
than for the odd game and went out on several
loan deals before he joined Mansfield. The
following term he hit hat-tricks for Gateshead in
6-0 and 7-2 victories and netted 29 times in 2011-
12 before a move to Luton. He was in their squad
which won the Conference title in 2014 before
returning to Gateshead for two years.

Jordan Luke Rhodes 2008-09

Born: Oldham 5.2.90
6'1" 11st3
Striker
FL Apps/Gls 5/2 Total
Apps/Gls 5/2
Career: Barnsley jnr,
Kesgrave HS (Ipswich),
Ipswich T. jnr 3.05, sch
2006, pro 22.8.07
[+10/1], Oxford U. loan
10.07 [3+1/- Conf], Dale
loan 11.9.08 to 11.10.08
[5/2], Brentford loan
23.1.09 [14/7],
Huddersfield T. 31.7.09
£350,000 [108+16/72], Blackburn R. 8.12 £8M
[152+7/83], Middlesbrough 1.2.16 £9M [13+5/6]*
Honours: Scotland under-21s 2011 to 2012 (8
caps), Scotland (13 caps) 2011-2015*, (League 2
champions 2009), League 1 play-off final 2011,
winners 2012, Championship winners 2016

Jason's father Andy played in goal for Oldham and
was Ipswich's goalkeeping coach when Jason
joined the club as a junior. He scored 40 goals in
the youth team and reserves in 2007-08 when he
also made his FL debut. A short but quite succesful
loan at Spotland was followed by one at Brenford
where he won the League 2 fans player of the year
award. Surprisingly allowed to join Huddersfield
for a modest fee, he scored a hat-trick of headers in
eight minutes in October 2009. Two season's later
he netted back-to-back hat-tricks and then scored
all the goals in a 4-4 draw with Sheffield
Wednesday, exceeding even that with five against
Wycombe. He finished with 40 goals in all games
and was unsurprisingly voted League 1 player of
the year before being sold to Blackburn for £8M,
making him the most expensive player outside the
Premier League. Eight goals in eight games for
Scotland under-21s had already led to his full
international debut while still playing in League 1.
(He qualified through growing up north of the
border when his father played there). After 83
league goals in three and a half seasons he was
sold to Middlesbrough, and though still only 26
took his tally of goals to 188 by the end of the
season which saw Boro promoted to the Premier
League.

Mark Alan Jones 2008-09

Born: Wrexham 15.8.84
5'11" 10st10
Midfield
FL Apps/Gls 7+2/0
Total Apps/Gls 9+4/0
Career: Rhos Aelwyd,
Wrexham yts 1.8.02,
pro 9.7.03 [102+26/22],
Dale 15.8.08 [7+2/-],
Wrexham 1.7.09
[28+6/4], Bala T. 8.10*
Honours: Wales under-
21s (5 caps) 2003 to
2006, Wales (2 caps)
2006, LDV Vans Trophy
winners 2005, Division 3+ promotion 2003, Welsh
League European play-off final 2012, winners
2013, Welsh League Cup final 2014, 2015, PFA
League 2 team of the year 2006 , Welsh Premier
League player of the year 2012, Welsh Premier
team of the year 2012, 2015, 2016

Mark made his FL debut just a couple of weeks
after signing for Wrexham but only became a
regular in 2005-06, when he netted 13 times from
midfield. By this time he had already played for the
Welsh under 21s and he won two full caps in 2006,
when he was also selected for the PFA League 2
team of the year. Leaving Wrexham after they lost
their league place, he was called up to the Wales
senior squad for matches that summer, despite not
having a club. He was signed by Dale in August
2008 but a combination of injuries and the form of
other players meant that he did not make a league
start for them until the following March, when he
stood-in for his injured namesake Gary. He
subsequently returned to Wrexham and then
played in the Welsh Premier League with Bala
Town, winning the WPL player of the year in 2012
and figuring in the Europa League in 2013 and
2015. By 2016 he had figured in well over 200
Welsh League games for Bala who ended as
runners up.

Francis David (Frank) Fielding 2008-09,

2009-10
Born: Blackburn 4.4.88
6'1" 11st11
Goalkeeper
FL Apps 41
Total Apps 43
Career: Queen Elizabeth
GS (Blackburn),
Blackburn R. sch 2005,
pro 10.7.06, Wycombe
W. loan 28.9.07 [36],
Northampton T. loan
12.9.08 [12], Dale loan
6.1.09 to 11.5.09 [23],
Leeds U. loan 29.9.09,

Dale loan 1.2.10 to 5.10 [18], Derby Co. loan 15.10.10 [10], Derby Co. loan 2.11, signed 9.5.11 £400,000 [76], Bristol C. 26.6.13 £200,000 [83]*
Honours: Independent Schools FA cup winners 2004, England under-19s (2 caps) 2007, England under-21s (12 caps) 2008-2011, European under-21s championships squad 2011, England senior squad 2010, Lancashire Senior Cup winners 2007, League 2 promotion 2010, FA Premier Reserve League Group B winners 2011, League 1 champions 2015, Johnstone's Paint Trophy winners 2015

Frank only played for Blackburn in continental tour games against the likes of Benfica, but spent a year on loan at Wycome as their regular 'keeper when he was 19, also figuring for England under-21s. Borrowed by Dale for the second half of 2008-09, taking over from Sam Russell, he helped them reach the play-offs. He had a second loan spell the following year and this time Frankie assisted Dale to automatic promotion. Remarkably his next selection for a senior squad, three months later, was for England in a goalkeeping injury crisis, his elevation from Dale to England generating some adverse comment in the press about the state of the English game. He played regularly in the Championship for Derby despite being sent off after just 67 seconds against Notts Forest. In 2013 he was transferred to Bristol City and helped them run away with the League 1 title two years later.

Nicholas William (Nicky) Adams

2008-09, 2010-12
Born: Bolton 16.10.86
5'10" 11st
Winger
FL Apps/Gls 67+18/5 Total Apps/Gls 72+20/5
Career: Bury jnr, sch 2003, pro 6.10.05 [61+16/14], Leicester C. 17.7.08 £175,000 [5+25/-], Dale loan 22.1.09 to 22.3.09 [12+2/1], Leyton O. loan 15.1.10 [6/-], Brentford 19.8.10 [3+4/-], Dale loan 14.10.10, signed 1.1.11 [55+16/4], Crawley T. 8.6.12 [69+1/9], Rotherham U. 31.1.14 £150,000 [7+8/1], Bury 16.5.14 £ [29+9/1], Northampton T. 22.5.15 [34+5/3], Carlisle U. 5.16*
Honours: Wales under-21s 2007 (4 caps), League 1 champions 2009, League 1 promotion 2014, League 2 promotion 2015, champions 2016

Nicky made his mark at Bury, making a scoring debut the day before his 19th birthday and netting 12 times from the wing in 2007-08. A move to Leicester led to only a handful of starts in their promotion side and Nicky spent some time on loan at Spotland. He signed for Brentford in 2010 but again soon went on loan to the Dale, subsequently signing a permanent deal. Despite a notable goal against his old club Bury in a rare 4-2 victory (later being sent off), as the disastrous 2011-12 unfolded he asked for a move and signed for FL newboys Crawley. He was transferred to Rotherham for £150,000, reportedly signing a two and a half year contract, but despite the Millers' promotion lasted only three months before returning to his original side Bury who also won promotion. He completed a treble when Northampton ran away with the League 2 title in 2016.

Gary Lee Madine 2008-09

Born: Gateshead 24.8.90
6'2" 11st10
Striker
FL Apps/Gls 1+2/0
Total Apps/Gls 1+2/0
Career: Lord Lawson CS, Middlesbrough jnr, Carlisle U. jnr 2004, sch 2006, pro 13.12.07 [28+38/13], Dale loan 20.3.09 [1+2/-], Coventry C. loan 19.10.09 [+9/-], Chesterfield loan 2.10 [2+2/-], Sheffield W. 15.1.11 £800,000 [67+34/26], Carlisle U. loan 27.3.14 [5/2], Coventry C. loan 30.10.14 [11/3], Blackpool loan 10.2.15 [14+1/3], Bolton W. 7.15 [22+10/5]*
Honours: Johnstone's Paint Trophy final 2010, League 1 promoted 2012

After scoring against the Dale in the JPT, Gary spent a month at Spotland but made only one start, though setting up a last minute winner for Le Fondre against Wycombe. Back at Carlisle he scored in the following season's JPT final and despite having started only 31 league games, he was bought by Sheffield Wednesday for a very big fee in 2011. He netted 18 times when assisting them to promotion the following year, but later had to rebuild his career via a series of loans before joining Bolton in 2015 as they crashed out of the Championship.

Thomas William (Tom) Newey 2008-09

Born: Huddersfield 31.10.82 5'10" 10st6
Left back
FL Apps/Gls 1+1/0
Total Apps/Gls 1+1/0
Career: Aston CS, Leeds U. yts 1999, pro 4.8.00, Dale trial 1.03, Cambridge U. loan 14.2.03 [6/-], Darlington loan 27.3.03 [7/1], Leyton O. 8.8.03 [34+20/3], Cambridge U. loan 21.1.05, signed 3.05 [15+1/-], Grimsby T. 28.7.05 [142+5/3], Dale loan 24.3.09 to 12.5.09 [1+1/-], Bury 28.8.09 [29+3/-], Rotherham U. 15.7.10 [53+5/-], Scunthorpe U. 8.12 [45/-], Oxford U. 4.7.13 [52/-], Northampton T. loan 30.10.14 [2/-] Northampton T. 27.1.15 to cs.15 [3+4/-], Northampton T. trial 7.15. Rotherham U. junior coach 11.15
Honours: Johnstone's Paint Trophy final 2008, League 2 play-off final 2006

A Dale trialist back in 2003 when he was at Leeds, he returned to Spotland on loan towards the end of 2008-09, but his only start was in the final league game when Dale rested most of their regulars ahead of the play-offs. In the interim he had had a decent spell at Orient, netting a winner against the Dale in 2004, and then played over 150 games for Grimsby, including JPT and play-off finals, before losing the left back spot to Joe Widdowson (q.v.). He had a decent run with several further clubs - winning Scunthorpe's player of the year award when he missed only one game in his single season at Glanford Par - until retiring through injury.

Craig Dawson 2008-2011

Born: Rochdale 6.5.90 6'0" 12st4
Central defender
FL Apps/Gls 84+3/19 Total Apps/Gls 91+3/22
Career: St. Clements 2006, Radcliffe Borough 2007, Oldham A. trial 2009, Dale 3.09 £10k [84+3/19], West Bromwich A. 8.10 £ (loaned back to Dale to 5.11) [84+4/6]*, Bolton W. loan 23.1.13 [16/4]
Cricket for Rochdale CC 2006 to 2007
Honours: League 2 promotion 2010, England under-21s (15 caps) 2011 to 2013, Great Britain 2012, PFA League 2 team of the year 2010

Craig was famously working washing glasses when given the chance to turn out for Radcliffe Borough when he was 17. After two seasons he was picked up by the Dale despite competition from Oldham and Crewe, and after being an unused substitute would probably have made his debut near the end of 2008-09 but for an injury. As it was, it was an injury to Rory McArdle in the following pre-season that thrust him into the first team and he never looked back. Already voted into the Dale fans' team of the decade after just half a season, his defensive prowess alongside his senior partner Nathan Stanton was a key factor in Dale's promotion in the bottom division. Perhaps even more remarkable was his 11 goals, the best ever return by a Rochdale centre back, taking John Bramhall's record. Included in the PFA League 2 team of the year, he continued his excellent form in League 1 and was sold to West Brom for a big fee but immediately loaned back to Dale for the season. Dale finished in their joint highest ever position in the third tier and 'Our Craig' took his goals tally to 22, another record for a Dale defender. He had to bide his time at the Hawthorns, but made a big impression when selected for the England under-21 side, netting twice on his debut and scoring six times in all in 15 appearances including in the European championships. He was also selected for the Great Britain squad for the London Olympics. He then spent the second half of 2012-13 at Bolton who moved from relegation candidates to playoff contenders while he was with them. After several changes of manager, Craig eventually began to get significant runs in the Baggies PL side in 2014 and became a regular – at right back – under Tony Pulis. He played every game in 2015-16 and notably scored the equaliser (to his own own-goal!) against Spurs which almost guaranteed Leicester the Premier League title. Craig's brother Andy was captain of Rochdale cricket club, for whom Craig also played a few games as a youngster, and figured for Ramsbottom United and Salford City.

Callum Byrne 2008-11

Born: Liverpool 5.2.92 5'7" 10st1
Midfield
FL Apps/Gls +0/0
Total Apps/Gls +0/0
Career: Dale jnr, sch 7.08, pro 5.10, Trafford loan 9.10, Mossley loan 11.10, Hyde loan 31.3.11, Hyde 6.11 [9+3/- Conf], Colwyn Bay loan 1.13, FC United of Manchester 9.13 to 11.15
Honours: (League 2 promotion 2010), Conference North champions 2012, Northern Premier League champions 2014

Callum came through Dale's Centre of Excellence and was named as substitute for the pre-play-off league game against Gillingham in May 2009. He also played in the following pre-season games and was again an unused substitute in the last game of the following term. However, after being handed a short term professional contract he was loaned out several times before joining Hyde permanently and helping them gain promotion to the Conference. He was later a regular for FCUM when they were promoted to the National League North and figured in their prestige friendly against Benfica for the opening of their new ground.

Christopher Robert (Chris) Brown 2008-11

Born: Hazel Grove 21.2.92 6'3" 12st4
Defender
FL Apps/Gls +0/0
Total Apps/Gls +1/0
Career: Hazel Grove HS, Bury College, Dale jnr, sch 7.08, pro 2.10, Bamber Bridge loan 5.2.10, Droylsden loan 14.3.10, Ashton U. loan 8.10, Hyde loan 31.3.11, Droylsden 6.11, Mossley 10.12, Dale youth development coach 7.13*
Honours: (League 2 promotion 2010), Manchester Premier Cup winners 2013

Chris was a member of Dale's Centre of Excellence, signing on scholarship terms when he was 16. Like Callum Byrne, he was an unused substitute in the end of season game with Gillingham in 2009 while still at Bury College. After figuring in the following pre-season games he made his one senior

appearance as a substitute for Dave Flitcroft in the Johnson's Paint Trophy game with Bradford City. He was on the bench for a number of other games and was also nominated for League 2 apprentice of the year for 2009. Again like Byrne, after signing pro he had several loan spells before, in his case, signing permanently for Droylsden. By the time he reached Mossley, when he was 20, he was recorded as being 6'5" tall. Involved in coaching from an early age, he returned to Spotland as a youth development coach when Keith Hill rebuilt his backroom staff on his own return to the club in 2013.

Kenneth James (Kenny) Arthur 2009-10

Born: Bellshill 7.12.78 6'3" 13st8
Goalkeeper
FL Apps 15 Total Apps 18
Career: Possil YMCA, Partick Thistle jnr 1994, pro 1.6.97 [242+1 ScL], Accrington St. 1.6.07 [66], Dale 6.09 [15], Grimsby T. 8.6.10 [28 Conf], Gainsborough Trinity loan 3.11.11, Airdrie U. 20.6.12 [16+2 ScL], Annan Ath. 7.13 [33 ScL], Queen of the South goalkeeping coach cs.14*
Honours: Scottish Division 2 champions 2001, Scottish Division 1 champions 2002, Scotland 'B', Scotland under-21 squad, Scotland squad 2002, League 2 promotion 2010

One of Scotland's top 'keepers just after the turn of the millenium, Kenny had ten seasons with Thistle, assisting them to promotion from the second division to the Scottish Premier League in successive seasons and accumulating over 240 league appearances. He was included in the Scottish under-21 squad on six occasions and was twice unused substitute for the senior side, but won his only cap at 'B' international level. He had a testimonial against Celtic in 2006 but the following year moved to Accrington Stanley, appearing regularly for two years despite spending some time in hospital with kidney damage sustained during a match. He joined Rochdale in 2009 and though sharing in Dale's promotion success, hardly played in the second half of the season, following a back injury, subsequently moving to Grimsby and then back to Scotland. Kenny has his own goalkeeping glove business, KA Goalkeeping, and a degree (suitably for a goalkeeper) in risk management, from Glasgow Caledonian University.

Jason Brian Kennedy 2009-2013, 2013-14

Born: Stockton
11.9.86 6'1" 11st10
Midfield
FL Apps/Gls
170+14/11 Total
Apps/Gls 186+14/14
Career:
Middlesbrough yts
2003, pro 3.2.05
[1+3/-], Boston U.
loan 3.11.06 [13/1],
Bury loan 2.3.07
[12/-], Livingstone
loan 1.8.07 [18/2
ScL], Darlington
29.2.08 [57+2/7],
Dale 20.5.09
[166+11/11], Bradford C. 2.7.13 [22+6/3], Dale
loan 24.1.14 [4+3/-], Carlisle U. loan 12.3.15 [11/3],
Carlisle U. 19.5.15 [44/2]*
Honours: FA Youth Cup winners 2004, League 2
promotion 2010, (2014)

A member of their surprise Youth Cup winning
side, Jason appeared in a few senior games for
Middlesborough including one on their run to the
UEFA cup final in 2006. With Darlington, he was
unwittingly involved in a great moment in
Rochdale history when – having scored in the first
leg - his penalty was saved by Tommy Lee in the
play-off semi-final shootout. He signed for Dale a
year later and missed only a handful of games
partnering Gary Jones in central midfield as they
finally won automatic promotion. He remained a
regular as Dale challenged the play-off places in
League 1 in 2011, but were then calamitously
relegated in 2012 before reviving when Keith Hill
returned in 2013. Turning down a further contract,
he joined Bradford City but failed to gain a regular
spot and was loaned back to Dale for a couple of
months, thus participating in a second promotion
campaign. After a loan spell, he moved to Carlisle
in 2015.

Matthew Philip (Matty) Edwards 2009-13

Born: Liverpool 22.8.90
6'2" 12st11
Goalkeeper
FL Apps 5+3 Total Apps
6+3
Career: Manchester U. jnr,
Leeds U. sch, pro 2008,
Salford C. loan 1.09, Dale
cs.09 to cs.13 [5+3]
Honours: (League 2
promotion 2010), Scotland
under-21s v Italy 2012

Matty joined Dale on being released by Leeds, on
the recommendation of Ian Wilcox who doubled as

goalkeeping coach for both clubs. Despite four
years at Spotland, Matty was hampered by a
number of injuries and nearly all his appearances
were during 2011-12 under John Coleman. The
same year he made an appearance (as substitute
for the injured substitute!) for Scotland under-21s.
He didn't figure at all the following term and was
then released, subsequently working as a
goalkeeping coach for youngsters on the Wirral.

Joshua Daniel (Josh) Brizell 2008-10

Born: Liverpool
15.12.91
5'10" 12st
Full back
FL Apps/Gls 0/0
Total Apps/Gls +1/0
Career: Dale sch
7.08, Cammell Laird
8.10, Hyde 14.10.11
[73+3/3 Conf], Osset
T. loan 11.11, AFC
Telford U. 3.6.15,
Glossop North End
loan 24.10.15, signed 3.16*
Honours: Conference North champions 2012

A scholar at Dale, Josh captained both the youth
team and reserves, playing primarily as a right
back. He made his senior debut as substitute
against Sheffield Wednesday in the League Cup in
August 2009 and was also unused substitute in the
two FA Cup ties with Luton. He was later with
Hyde with several other former Dale juniors,
including Scott Hogan and Callum Byrne and the
on loan Reece Gray, as they progressed from the
Conference North to the Conference itself. They
crashed back down in 2014, however, Josh being
sent off in an opening day 8-0 mauling that set the
tone for a season in which they picked up just one
win and 10 points.

Dennis Sherriff 2008-10
Born: Stockport 22.1.92 5'9" 11st
Striker
FL Apps/Gls 0/0 Total Apps/Gls +0/0
Career: Manchester C. jnr, Dale jnr 2.08, sch 7.08,
Woodley Sports loan 2.10, Woodley Sports 6.10,
Stalybridge Celtic 4.9.10, Worksop T. 2.9.11,
Radcliffe Borough loan 11.11, Nantwich T. loan,
Ashton U. 10.1.13, Radcliffe Borough 8.13,
Winsford U. c.11.13, Stockport T. 8.15*

A regular scorer for Dale youth team and reserves,
totalling 41 goals in two seasons, like Josh Brizell,
Dennis was also named as substitute at Sheffield
Wednesday but didn't appear. He spent time at
Woodley Sports on loan and then signed for them
(along with other former Dale juniors George
Bowyer and Scott Hogan), netting over 40 goals.

Later he joined Callum Warburton and another ex-Dale reserve Tom Buckley at Stalybridge and then figured for Radcliffe Borough, netting a hat-trick when they beat Harrogate Railway 10-3.

Matthew (Matt) Flynn 2009-11

Born: Preston 10.5.89
6'0" 11st8
Right back
FL Apps/Gls 7+4/0
Total Apps/Goals 8+4/0
Career: Myerscough College, Macclesfield T. sch 2006, pro 4.7.07 [23+5/-], Warrington T. loan 10.07, Ashton U. loan 2.08, Dale 13.8.09 [7+4/-], Falkirk trial 7.11, Fleetwood 8.11 [3/- Conf], Altrincham loan 1.12.11, Barrow 3.6.12 [19+3/3 Conf], FC Halifax T. trial 7.13, Southport 9.8.13 [17+1/- Conf], Hyde 21.11.14, Chorley 23.1.15, Curzon Ashton 10.9.15*
Honours: League 2 promotion 2010, Conference champions 2012

Matt came through the ranks at Macclesfield and was going to join Dale on loan as defensive cover early in 2009-10, but in the event signed a two year contract. With Scott Wiseman and Rory McArdle sidelined, Matt appeared at right back in several games immediately after signing, but spent the rest of the term on the bench. In his second season he made just one appearance, as substitute for Alan Goodall, and then signed for Fleetwood, as coincidentally did Goodall, at the start of a round of non-league sides.

Scott Kernaghan Spencer 2009-10

Born: Manchester 1.1.89 5'11" 12st8
Forward
FL Apps/Gls +4/0
Total Apps/Gls +5/0
Career: Oldham A. jnr, sch 2005, Everton sch 8.6.06 £225,000, Yeovil T. loan 1.08, Macclesfield T. loan 7.3.08 [+3/-], Dale n/c 8.09 to 26.11.09 [+4/-], Southend U. trial, signed 1.10 [6+11/4], Lincoln C. loan 31.1.11 [2+8/-], Barrow trial 7.11, Southport trial 7.11, FC Halifax T. trial 8.11, Hyde 12.8.11

[51+11/18 Conf], FC Halifax T. loan 26.3.14 [4+3/2 Conf], Stockport Co. 1.7.14, Hyde U. 8.7.15*
Honours: (League 2 promotion 2010), Liverpool Senior Cup winners 2011, Conference North champions 2012, England 'C' (2 caps) 2012

Scott was a highly promising junior at Oldham and Everton reportedly paid £225,000 compensation to the Latics when he moved his scholarship to Goodison, but he only ever started eight FL games. His first senior appearances came while on loan at Macclesfield and he added four more substitute appearances for Dale after he was released by Everton. He next joined Southend and followed manager Steve Tilson to Lincoln a year later but could not help the Imps avoid relegation to the Conference. During a trial at Southport he played in the Liverpool Senior Cup Final against an Everton XI and he then spearheaded Hyde's promotion to the Conference with 31 goals, earning a call-up to the England semi-pro squad.

Dale Christopher Stephens 2009-10

Born: Bolton 12.6.89
5'7" 11st3
Midfield
FL Apps/Gls 3+3/1
Total Apps/Gls 3+3/1
Career: Bury sch 2006, pro 5.7.07 [6+3/1], Droylsden loan 8.07, Hyde U. loan 2007-08, Oldham A. 7.08 [58+2/11], Dale loan 8.09 to 16.11.09 [3+3/1], Southampton loan 24.3.11 [5+1/-], Charlton A. 29.6.11 £350,000 [78+6/10], Brighton &HA 30.1.14 £ [67+8/11]*
Honours: (League 2 promotion 2010), (League 1 promotion 2011), League 1 champions 2012

Dale made his mark after moving from Bury to Oldham, though still spending time out on loan, including a three month stint at Spotland where he scored a debut goal when Rochdale came back from 3-0 down to draw with Morecambe. The Latics sold him to Charlton for a significant fee which soon proved well spent as he assisted their League 1 title winning effort in his first campaign (the third season in a row in which he had been with a promoted team, albeit while on loan in the first two). In January 2014 he was sold to Championship rivals Brighton. In the final game of 2015-16 against Middlesbrough he scored the equalising goal but was then contentiously red carded, Brighton missing promotion on goal difference.

Christopher James (Chris) O'Grady 2009-12

Born: Nottingham 25.1.86 6'1" 12st8
Striker
FL Apps/Gls 88+2/31 Total
Apps/Gls 93+2/31
Career: Leicester C. yts 2002, pro 3.8.04 [6+18/1], Notts Co. loan 24.9.04 [3+6/-], Rushden & Diamonds loan 12.8.05 [20+2/4], Rotherham U. 19.1.07 £65,000 [46+5/13], Oldham A. 4.6.08 [3+10/-], Bury loan 17.10.08 [3+3/-], Bradford C. loan 2.1.09 [+2/-], Stockport Co. loan 2.2.09 [17+1/2], Dale loan 21.8.09, signed 13.1.10 £65,000 [88+2/31], Sheffield W. 9.8.11 £350,000 [39+14/9], Barnsley loan 31.1.13 [13+3/5], Barnsley 20.6.13 [39+1/15], Brighton & HA 19.7.14 £2M [15+16/1]*, Sheffield U. loan 27.11.14 [4/1], Nottingham F. loan 1.9.15 [15+6/2]
Honours: Division 1+ promotion 2003, League 2 promotion 2010, League 1 promotion 2012

Before signing for Dale, Chris had had a modest return of 20 career goals, shared between eight clubs. Nine of these were for Rotherham in 2007-08 after they signed him from Leicester, but he had no success at Oldham who lent him, and then sold him, to Dale in 2009. His partnership with Chris Dagnall proved to be the catalyst for Dale's long awaited promotion run, as the front two both reached 20 goals, the first time two Dale forwards had ever achieved this. In mid-season 'COG' hit 17 goals in 21 games, including a hat-trck against Cheltenham, and fittingly he netted the winning goal against Northampton which guaranteed promotion. His 22 goals also earned him the vote as the Dale supporters' player of the year. Not as prolific the following year, with Dale adopting a different playing style, he was still key to Dale equalling their best ever finish in the third tier. Transferred to Wednesday for a sizeable fee just as the 2011-12 season got underway, he played in another promotion campagn. He later had an excellent personal season at Barnsley, netting 15 times despite their relegation from the Championship, to earn a £2 million move to Brighton. However he scored only once and was loaned to Forest for most of 2015-16.

Simon Paul Whaley 2009-10

Born: Bolton 7.6.85 5'11" 11st7
Winger
FL Apps/Gls 8+1/2
Total Apps/Gls 8+1/2
Career: Bury yts 2001, pro 30.10.02 [48+25/11], Preston NE 9.1.06 £250,000 [74+46/14], Barnsley loan 7.11.08 [4/1], Norwich C. 24.7.09 £250,000 [3/-], Dale loan 18.9.09 to 18.11.09 [8+1/2], Bradford C. loan 20.11.09 [5+1/1], Oldham A. trial 2.10, Chesterfield 19.2.10 to cs.10 [5+1/1], Doncaster R. n/c 11.10 to 1.11, Oldham A. trial 9.2.11, Burton A. 4.3.11 [1+2/-], Bury trial 7.11, Chorley 8.11 to 12.11. Eagley FC assistant manager 7.14, player-manager 10.14*
Honours: (League 1 champions 2010), (League 2 promotion 2010)

Simon came to the fore as a youngster at Bury and cost Preston £250,000 when they signed him in 2006. Appearing regularly in the Championship for the next two years, he moved to Norwich for a similar fee but was almost immediately loaned to Dale after a change in management. A speedy goalscoring winger, he netted in his first start, a 4-1 victory over Hereford, but left after two months and subsequently had short stays with several other clubs before retiring through injury at the end of 2011. He later moved into non-league management.

Marc Andre <u>Manga</u> Elpresse Priso 2009-10

Born: Cameroon 16.1.88 5'9" 11st5
Forward
FL Apps/Gls +2/0
Total Apps/Gls +3/0
Career: Bordeaux (France) jnr 2004, Stade Lavallois (France) 2005 to 2007, {Dinamo Bucharest (Rumania) trial?}, Hereford U. trial cs.09, Dale n/c 9.09 to 26.11.09 [+2/-], Stade Reims 'B' (France), Accrington St. trial 7.10, Tranmere R. trial 8.10. Corby T. 9.12, St. Ives T. loan 11.12, Cowdenbeath trial 7.13. AFC Compiegne (France) 2.10.14 to 2015
Honours: (League 2 promotion 2010)

A youth player at Bordeaux, Marc played in French football with Stade Lavallois before trying his luck in England. After a trial at Hereford, he had a brief spell at Spotland as a non-contract player, coming on three times over the course of six games on the bench. He subsequently had trials at a variety of clubs and had a season with Corby Town before returning to France.

Joshua Mark (Josh) Lillis 2009-10, 2010-11, 2012-2016*

Born: Derby 24.6.87
6'0" 12st8
Goalkeeper
FL Apps 169+2*
Total Apps 187+2*
Career: Huntcliff CS (Gainsborough), Scunthorpe U. sch 2005, pro 2.8.06 [33+5], Notts Co. loan 20.1.09 [5], Grimsby T. loan 1.9.09 [4], Dale loan 29.10.09 to 2.11.09 [1], Dale loan 15.7.10 to 20.1.11 [23], Dale 12.6.12 [145+2]*
Honours: League 1 champions 2007, promotion 2009, League 2 promotion (2010), 2014, (Johnstone's Paint Trophy final 2009)

The son of Mark Lillis, the former Huddersfield, Manchester City and Scunthorpe player (more recently coach back at Huddersfield), Josh also joined the Iron as a youngster. He worked his way into the first team squad in 2006-07 but had to settle for an understudy role as Scunthorpe twice gained promotion to the Championship, going out on loan several times. He had one game for Dale in October 2009, a 4-0 victory over leaders Bournemouth that convinced Dale fans that they really were serious promotion contenders. He returned for the first half of their first League 1 campaign and was signed permanently by John Coleman when Dale found themselves back in League 2 in 2012. He missed only one game as Dale were again promoted in 2014, keeping 22 clean sheets in all games, but missed much of the following term after being carried off at Chesterfield. He bounced back in 2015-16 as Dale were again on the edge of the play-offs and won the player of the year award, signing a contract for two further seasons.

Daniel (Danny) Taberner 2009-12

Born: Bolton 17.6.93
6'2" 12st
Goalkeeper
FL Apps +0 Total Apps 1
Career: Dale as 2008, sch 2009, Stockport Sports 2012, Salford C. 8.12, Droylsden 27.9.13, Atherton Collieries cs.14*
Honours: (League 2 promotion 2010), {Alliance League (North West) champions 2011}, NWC League division 1 champions 2015

When Kenny Arthur compounded a back injury in the FA Cup tie against Luton in November 2009 and reserve Matty Edwards was also out of action, first year scholar Danny was drafted in to play in the televised replay a few days later. Aged just 16 years and 147 days he became their youngest ever goalkeeper (and second youngest player), beating Stephen Bywater's old record. He was on the bench for a number of league matches on either side of this game, but a double knee operation in February 2010 kept him out of action until the following season and he only figured in the senior squad once more, in December 2011. He had the misfortune to be with Droylsden in 2014 when they obtained only nine points all season and had a goal difference of a staggering -142. The following year, though, he starred for Atherton Collieries as they won the North West Counties division one title, winning the goalkeeper of the season award. Danny is the nephew of Wigan 'keeper Mike Pollitt.

Jordan Andrews 2009-2012
Born: Salford 23.11.93
Goalkeeper
FL Apps 0 Total Apps +0
Career: Dale as 2009, sch 2010 to 2012, Northwich Flixton Villa 8.13 to 2014
Honours: Youth Alliance champions 2011

Jordan was still 15, and had to have the afternoon off school to prepare, when he was selected on the bench as cover for Danny Taberner in the Luton cup tie just a couple of weeks after making his youth team debut. He figured in the reserves the following season, but was still eligible for the youth team when again on the first team bench in October 2011 for the League Cup tie at Aldershot. Earlier that season he had ended a youth team game playing up front when Dale had only three substitutes, including under-14s 'keeper Johny Diba. Jordan later appeared in the NWCL.

Thomas David (Tom) Heaton   2009-10

Born: Chester 15.4.86
6'1"   13st6
Goalkeeper
FL Apps 12   Total
Apps 12
Career: Wrexham jnr,
Manchester U. as
2000, yts 8.7.02, pro
3.7.03, Swindon T.
loan 18.8.05 [14],
Royal Antwerp loan
2005-06, Cardiff C.
loan 3.7.08 [21],
Queens Park R. loan 15.8.09, Dale loan 12.11.09 to
11.2.10 [12], Wycombe W. loan 12.2.10 [16], Cardiff
C. 16.6.10 [28+1], Bristol C. 27.7.12 [43], Burnley
6.13 [130]*
Honours: Chester Schoolboys, England under-16s
(4 caps) 2001, under-17s (9 caps) 2002-03, under-
18s (2 caps) 2004, under-19s 2004, England
under-21s (3 caps) 2008-09, England (1 cap) 2016,
(FA Youth Cup winners 2003), (Manchester Senior
Cup winners 2004), Premier Reserve League
North champions 2005, Premier Reserve League
play-off winners 2005, Pontins League champions
2005, (League 2 promotion 2010), Championship
promotion 2014, champions 2016, League Cup
final 2012

An England youth international at various age
levels, Tom came through the junior ranks at
United and was sub 'keeper in two cup finals
before figuring in the play-off between the
northern and southern Reserve League champions.
Although becoming an under-21 international, his
only tastes of first team action at Old Trafford
came in friendlies, including the UEFA celebration
match against a European XI in 2007. Arriving at
Spotland on loan in 2009 to replace the injured
Kenny Arthur, apart from his debut Tom went
unbeaten throughout his spell at the club as Dale
stormed to the top of the league, winning six
games in a row conceding only three goals, and
Tom was considered by fans as perhaps the best
'keeper ever to turn out for them. He finally left
United for Cardiff at the end of that campaign but
was relatively little used though he saved two
penalties in the League Cup semi-final shoot-out
and one from Steven Gerrard when the final also
went to spot-kicks. In his first season with Burnley
they unexpectedly won promotion to the top flight
and though immediately relegated again, they won
the Championship title in 2016. Tom – everpresent
in all three seasons - won further recognition when
he made his full England debut in a warm-up game
for the European Championships.

William (Will) Atkinson   2009-10, 2010-11

Born: Driffield
14.10.88 5'10" 10st7
Winger
FL Apps/Gls 30+6/5
Total Apps/Gls
30+6/5
Career: Hull C. sch
2005, pro 14.12.06
[5+1/1], Port Vale
loan 12.10.07 [3+1/-],
Mansfield T. loan
29.1.08 [10+2/-],
Dale loan 19.11.09 to
19.1.10 and 1.2.10 to
3.10 [15/3],
Rotherham U. loan 25.11.10 [3/1], Dale loan 14.1.11
to 5.11 [15+6/2], Plymouth A. loan 12.8.11
[20+2/4], Bradford C. loan 26.1.12 [6+6/1],
Bradford C. 3.7.12 [26+16/1], Southend U. 4.7.13
[97+19/6]*
Honours: (League 2 promotion 2010), League 2
play-off winners 2013, 2015, Football League Cup
final 2013

Will had had a couple of other loan spells, but had
not yet played for Hull's first team when spending
three months with the Dale, generally figuring on
the left wing after the departure of Will Buckley.
His first spell perhaps rates as the most successful
ever by any loan player as Dale won seven and
drew one of the eight games, Will netting twice in
the 4-1 win against Morecambe. After a handful of
games for Hull and another loan spell with Dale as
they consolidated in League 1, he was signed by
Bradford City. He was in their side which
remarkably reached the 2013 League Cup final,
beating Villa and Arsenal along the way, and then
won the League 2 play-off final. He repeated the
latter with Southend two years later.

Jason James Francis Taylor   2009-10

Born: Droylsden
28.1.87 6'1" 11st3
Midfield
FL Apps/Gls 23/1
Total Apps/Gls 23/1
Career: Oldham A. sch
2004, pro 18.2.06,
Stockport Co. loan
17.3.06 [9/-],
Stockport Co. 8.06
[89+6/6], Rotherham
U. 15.1.09
[103+15/10], Dale loan
19.11.09 to 5.10 [23/1],
Cheltenham T. 28.1.13
[55+10/2],
Northampton T. loan 1.1.15, signed 7.1.15
[29+22/1]*

Honours: League 2 promotion 2008, (2010, 2013), champions 2016

Jason played in Stockport's promotion side in 2008, though he was an unused substitute in the play-off final against Dale. He appeared over 100 times for County before a move to Rotherham in preference to the Dale, the Millers offering a better deal though they were only just out of administration, to the annoyance of Keith Hill. Nevertheless, when he became available a few months later, Hill signed him on loan, and like Will Atkinson Jason had an amazing start with six straight wins and 11 wins and three draws in a run of 16 games, mostly replacing the injured Gary Jones in midfield. Despite a sending off at Accrington which disrupted his appearances towards the end of the campaign he was in the side – partnering Jones – for the victory over Northampton which guaranteed promotion. Later appearing regularly for Rotherham, he had moved on to Cheltenham before the Millers completed their promotion in 2013, his new club losing out in the play-offs. However, he was in the Northampton squad which won League 2 by a large margin in 2016 (though on the down side, he was sent off twice).

Daniel (Danny) Glover 2009-10

Born: Crewe 24.10.89 6'0" 11st3
Forward
FL Apps/Gls +2/0
Total Apps/Gls +2/0
Career: Madeley HS, Port Vale sch 2006, pro 27.7.07 [20+21/4], Salisbury C. loan 14.8.09 [2+5/- Conf], Dale loan 26.11.09 to 1.10 [+2/-], Stafford R. loan 3.10, Worcester C. cs.10, Nuneaton Borough 6.11, Worcester C. 7.12, FC Halifax T. loan 3.13, Bradford PA 1.14, Hednesford T. 3.14, Stockport Co. 23.12.14, AFC Telford U. 7.15, (+ Butcher's Arms 8.15; Stoke Sunday League), Hednesford T. 29.1.16*
Honours: (League 2 promotion 2010), (Conference North promotion 2013)

Son of Port Vale stalwart Dean, Danny joined the club as a trainee and made a promising start to his senior career. However after his father became manager in 2008, his presence in the struggling side was questioned by supporters. He had a month on loan at Spotland but managed only a few minutes action as the side was at the top of its form, winning one and drawing the other game in which he came off the bench. A year earlier he had scored then been sent off for two yellow cards (for over celebrating, then a foul) when Vale beat Dale 2-1. He subsequently figured for a succession of teams in the Conference North, netting 18 times for Nuneaton Borough in 2011-12. His contract at Telford was terminated after he was fined by the FA for also playing for a Sunday League side.

Reece Anthony Gray 2009-14

Born: Oldham 1.9.92
5'7" 8st8
Forward
FL Apps/Gls 2+11/2
Total Apps/Gls 2+11/2
Career: Dale sch 4.09, pro cs.11 to 5.14 [2+11/2], Hyde loan 16.12.11 and 23.2.12, Hyde loan 3.10.13 [9/2 Conf], FC Halifax T. loan 28.11.13 [2+5/1 Conf], Hyde U. 29.8.14, Ashton U. 3.16*
Honours: League 2 promotion 2010, Youth Alliance champions 2011, Conference North champions 2012

Reece was the first Dale junior to come all the way through from the Centre of Excellence under 10s, coming on as substitute in the last two games of 2009-10. He was on the bench for a number of games the following term, scoring the winner against Bournemouth on the final day, and after turning pro was seen as the club's most promising product. Loaned to Hyde for most of the following term, to gain experience, he was handed the No. 10 shirt by John Coleman at the start of 2012-13 but suffered a bad injury in a behind closed doors friendly against Liverpool and missed almost all the season. Unable to rediscover his form, he was eventually released by Keith Hill in 2014 having still started only two games, and re-signed for Hyde.

Scott Andrew Hogan 2009-10, 2013-14

Born: Salford 13.4.92
5'10 10st1
Midfield/striker
FL Apps/Gls 29+4/17
Total Apps/Gls 35+5/19
Career: Cadishead HS, Salford College, Dale sch 2009, Woodley Sports cs.10, FC Halifax T. 11.11.10, Mossley loan 8.11, Stocksbridge Park

Steels 1.12.11, (Barnsley trial 7.12), Ashton U. 5.10.12, Hyde U. n/c 8.3.13 [10+1/3 Conf], Birmingham trial, Dale 9.5.13 [29+4/17], Brentford 21.7.14 £750,000 [2+6/7]*
Honours: League 2 promotion (2010), 2014, NPL premier division champions 2011, PFA League 2 team of the year 2014

Scott had two contrasing spells with Dale, the first as a youth team winger who didn't progress beyond sitting on the bench for three mid-season games in 2009-10, the second as one of the most exiting strikers in League 2 when Dale again won promotion. In the interim he figured with several non-league sides, including a spell at Halifax with his brother Liam, and had trials with Barnsley and Birmingham. Re-signed by Keith Hill in 2013, he scored on his debut on the opening day and netted five times in his first nine FL games. He gained further notice when scoring against Leeds in the FA Cup and then scored two hat-tricks in the space of five games, the first Dale player to hit two trebles in a season since Reg Jenkins and the first since Jim Dailey in 1957 to get two in the FL in the same season. Before he was injured in the televised game against Bury, his 19 goals in 32 starts had set Dale well on their way to promotion, and Scott was subsequently included in the PFA team of the year and short listed for the League 2 player of the season. Having turned down a move to Peterborough in the previous transfer window, as the following pre-season got under way, he was signed by Brentford for a reported £750,000. Unfortunately, in just his second substitute appearance for the Bees he suffered an anterior cruciate ligament injury which ruled him out for the season and the following April had to have surgery for a second time after injuring the same knee in training. However, when he returned to the side a year later, he remarkably netted seven times in four games.

Andrew Alan David (Andy) Haworth
2009-10, 2012-13

Born: Lancaster 28.11.88 5'11" 11st10
Winger
FL Apps/Gls 6+8/0
Total Apps/Gls 6+8/0
Career: Blackburn R. sch 2006, pro 4.7.07, Gateshead loan 13.11.09 [5+1/- Conf], Dale loan 21.1.10 to 5.10 [3+4/-], Bury 6.7.10 [20+25/3], Oxford U. 9.11 [2+2/-], Bradford C. loan 12.1.12 [2+1/-], Falkirk 31.5.12 to 30.11.12 [7+5/- ScL], Dale n/c 24.1.13 [3+4/-], Notts Co. 1.7.13 [+2/-], Tamworth loan 28.11.13, signed 7.1.14 [6+5/- Conf], Cheltenham T. 24.6.14

[+5/-], Barrow loan 23.1.15, Barrow 8.6.15 [32+5/3]
Honours: (Lancashire Senior Cup winners 2007), League 2 promotion (2010), 2011, Conference North champions 2015

Andy has his own unique record as a Dale player, having made two debuts both against the same team, Cheltenham (who he later played for). He had figured in both the League Cup and FA Cup for Blackburn before his league debut while at Spotland on loan. A successful season at Bury, missing only a handful of games when they were promoted in 2011, was followed by brief interludes elsewhere before he became Keith Hill's first signing on his return to the club in 2013. Coincidentaly repeating the three starts and four substitute appearances from his first spell, he then continued his travels, figuring with nine sides in four seasons. He was in the Barrow side promoted to the Conference National in 2015.

Temitope Ayoluwa (Tope) Obadeyi 2009-10, 2011-12

Born: Birmingham 29.10.89 5'10" 11st10
Forward
FL Apps/Gls 8+9/2
Total Apps/Gls 8+9/2
Career: Four Dwellings HS, Coventry C. jnr, Bolton W. sch 2005, pro 3.11.06 [+3/-], Swindon T. loan 14.8.09 [9+3/2], Dale loan 1.2.10 to 5.10 [5+6/1], Shrewsbury T. loan 22.10.10 [7+2/-], Chesterfield loan 8.11.11 [3+2/-], Dale loan 14.3.12 to 4.12 [3+3/1], Rio Ave (Portugal) 6.12, Bury 16.8.13 [+7/-], Plymouth A. loan 7.11.13 and 20.2.14 [5+9/1], Kilmarnock 16.7.14 [43+16/12 ScL]*
Honours: England under 19-s (4 caps) 2007-08, England under-19s European championships squad 2008, England under-20s 2009 (2 caps), Lancashire Senior Cup final 2007, (League 2 promotion 2010), SPL/Scottish Championship play-off winners 2016

Like Andy Haworth, Tope had two brief spells with Dale, in his case on loan from Bolton. One towards the end of the promotion campaign saw him in the squad for all the last 19 games of the season, though only starting five times as a wideman, the other came two years later as Dale headed back to the bottom division. He had earlier appeared for England under-19s with the likes of Daniel Sturridge (with whom he went to school) and Victor Moses, netting a hat-trick against Romania. He subsequently played for Rio Ave in Portugal's Primeira Liga, figuring in their side which knocked

Sporting Lisbon out of the cup, but back in England had still made only 32 FL starts in the lower divisions when he joined Kilmarnock for a much more productive spell in the SPL.

Michael Robert Lea 2009-10

Born: Salford 4.11.87
5'8" 10st9
Defender
FL Apps/Gls +0/0
Total Apps/Gls +0/0
Career: Manchester U. sch 2005-06, pro 6.7.07, Royal Antwerp loan 2007-08, Scunthorpe U. 6.8.08, Chester C. 9.7.09 [18+1/- Conf-exp], Hyde U. 3.10, Dale n/c 3.10 to 5.10, Hyde U. 9.7.10, Colwyn Bay U. 27.8.10, Witton Albion 6.14, Marine 25.10.14, Colwyn Bay U. 2.1.15*
Honours: (League 2 promotion 2010), NPL premier division promotion 2011

A regular for Manchester United reserves in 2006-07, Michael also spent half a season on loan in Belgium, but played in just a couple of cup ties for Scunthorpe, one of them against the Dale. He figured regularly for Chester in 2009-10 until they folded, but did not progress beyond being an unused substitute for two games while at Spotland. He figured at Colwyn Bay with another ex-Dale reserve Matty Hughes and was their player of the year when they were promoted to the Conference North.

Joseph (Joe) Widdowson 2010-12

Born: Forest Green 29.3.89 6'0" 12st
Left back
FL Apps/Gls 60+6/0
Total Apps/Gls 66+7/0
Career: West Ham U. sch, pro 6.7.07, Rotherham U. loan 12.2.08 [3/-], Grimsby T. 2.1.09 [55+3/1], Dale 22.6.10 [60+6/-], Northampton T. 5.7.12 [63+1/-], Bury 6.8.14 [+1/-], Morecambe loan 29.8.14 [8/-], Dagenham & Redbridge loan 27.11.14, signed 9.1.15 [51+1/-]*
Honours: League 2 play-off final 2013, (promotion 2015)

Joe made his West Ham debut on a pre-season tour, marking LA Galaxy's David Beckham. He made his mark in the FL at Grimsby, but following their relegation to the Conference signed for the Dale. He was a regular at left back for most of his two seasons with the club, helping them challenge for the League 1 play-offs in 2011, but being unable to help resist the slide back into League 2 after Keith Hill left. He figured in the play-off final for Northampton but then had a bizarely brief connection with Bury, being loaned out three weeks after arriving. In 2016 he had the misfortune to be relegated out of the FL for a second time, with Dagenham.

Brian Barry-Murphy 2010-16*

Born: Cork 27.7.78
6'0" 12st4
Midfield
FL Apps/Gls 57+9/1*
Total Apps/Gls 65+11/1*
Career: Spioraid Naoim, Cork C. 1995, (Arsenal trial, Celtic trial, Middlesbrough trial), Preston NE 3.8.99 [6+15/-], Southend U. loan 11.2.02 [8/1], Hartlepool U. loan 30.10.02 [7/-], Sheffield W. 31.1.03 [55+3/-], Bury 3.8.04 [200+18/13], Dale 7.11, player-coach 4.13 [57+9/1]*
Honours: Republic of Ireland youth international, Republic of Ireland under-21s (6 caps) 1998-99, Division 2+ promotion 2000, (Division 1+ play-off final 2001), (Division 3+ promotion 2003), League 1 promotion 2014, Lancashire Senior Cup final 2015

The son of famous Gaelic footballer and hurler Jimmy, who also played soccer for Cork Celtic, Barry competed in Gaelic games as a junior before following his father into the Cork side. (Both of Brian's grandfathers and his great grandfather had also been Gaelic footballers). Already an under-21 international for the Republic, after approaching a hundred games for Cork he crossed to England to play for Preston in 1999, appearing just once in their side promoted from (the new) Division 2. He was unused substitute when North End lost their play-off for a place in the top flight and only started to have more game time when he signed for Sheffield Wednesday when he was 24. He then had a long stint at Gigg Lane, playing well over 200 games over seven seasons, before heading for Spotland. Most of his Dale appearances came in his first season, forming an experienced midfield trio with Jones and Kennedy as Dale unexpectedly challenged for a League 1 play-off place. Surviving the Eyre and Coleman eras – he was on the bench for nearly every game in 2012-13 - when Keith Hill returned and promoted Chris Beech to assistant manager, 'BBM' became player-coach. He played three games in the 2014 promotion campaign but largely concentrated on his coaching. Barry was a schoolmate of legendary rugby union international Ronan O'Gara.

Jean-Louis Akpa Akpro   2010-12

Born: Toulouse, France 4.1.85 6'0" 10st12
Forward
FL Apps/Gls 38+35/11
Total Apps/Gls 45+38/12
Career: Toulouse (France) jnr 2000, pro 2003, Stade Brestois (France) loan 2007, FCM Brussels (Belgium) cs.07, Milton Keynes Dons trial cs.08, Colchester U. trial cs.08, Grimsby T. 8.12.08 [45+11/8], Dale 7.7.10 [38+35/11], Tranmere R. 19.6.12 [48+5/10], Bury loan 31.1.14 [5+5/-], Shrewsbury T. 2.7.14 to 5.16 [41+41/15]
Honours: League 2 promotion 2015

Jean-Louis and his brothers Jean-Jacques and Jean-Daniel all played in the French League, the latter being included in the Ivory Coast's 2014 World Cup squad. Jean-Louis himself played around 40 games for Toulouse in Ligue 1 and was selected for France under-18s but missed out through injury. He moved to England in 2008, eventually winning a contract at Grimsby. However, when they dropped out of the league he joined Joe Widdowson in signing for Dale. Largely used from the bench, 'JLAA' proved a useful alternative up front or on the wing in his first season, and was one of the few players to keep going throughout the dire 2011-12 campaign and enhance his standing with the fans, finishing as second top scorer. Moving to Tranmere he briefly topped the League 1 scoring charts with seven goals in his first ten games before being injured. Next with Shrewsbury, he scored his first career hat-trick in a 5-0 defeat of Bury and his winner at Cheltenham guaranteed the Shrews promotion in his first season.

Anthony Lee Elding   2010-11

Born: Boston 16.4.82
6'1" 13st10
Striker
FL Apps/Gls 9+8/3
Total Apps/Gls 12+9/5
Career: Nottingham F. jnr, Lincoln C. jnr, Grimsby T. jnr, Boston U. c.4.99, pro 6.7.01 [13+16/6 Conf, 3+5/-], Bedford T. loan 9.01, (Tottenham H. trial 1.02, Bolton W. trial 1.02), Gainsborough Trinity loan 2.03, Stevenage B. 12.2.03 [106/50 Conf], Kettering T. 16.1.06 £40,000 [15/4 Conf], Boston U. 16.8.06 [18+1/5], Stockport Co. 4.1.07 £ [38+7/24], Leeds U. 31.1.08 £ [4+5/1], Crewe A. 25.7.08 £175,000 [14+12/1], Lincoln C. loan 1.09 [15/3], Kettering T. loan 3.11.09 [6/3 Conf], Ferencvaros 1.10, Dale 27.7.10 £20,000 [9+8/3], Stockport Co. loan 7.1.11 [18+3/3], Plymouth A. trial 7.11, Grimsby T. 25.7.11 £ [35+24/14 Conf], Preston NE loan 15.11.12 [2+3/-], Sligo Rovers 2.13, Cork C. 16.11.13, Ballinamallard U. 23.5.14, Derry C. 2.2.15, Sligo R. 11.6.15*
Honours: England 'C' (6 caps) 2003 to 2005, Four Nations Tournament winners 2005, (Southern League champions 2000), Conference champions 2002, Conference play-off final 2005, (League 2 promotion 2008), FA of Ireland Cup winners 2013

A remarkably well travelled striker Anthony, made his debut for his home town club Boston in 2000 and played in their first ever FL game two years later. He made more of a mark back in the Conference, with a half century of goals for Stevenage, also playing for the England semi-pro side. Arriving at Stockport in 2007, he scored 24 goals in a year. A big money transfer then took him to Leeds but only six months later he was on the move again to Crewe. Later moving to Ferencvaros and netting eight times in 15 games, he signed for Dale on his return from Hungary, but made relatively little impact. Sold to Grimsby, oddly he was then loaned by the Conference side to Preston in League 1. He subsequently had a string of clubs in Ireland, winning the FAI Cup with Sligo for whom he scored 19 times in 26 games. Even ignoring trials, he was in a 24th spell with his 18th different club by 2015.

Matthew (Matty) Done   2010-11, 2013-15

Born: Oswestry
22.6.88   5'8"   10st7
Forward/left back
FL Apps/Gls
64+30/15   Total
Apps/Gls 77+33/20
Career: Marches
School, Wrexham sch
2004, pro 3.8.06
[41+25/1], Hereford
U. 4.8.08 [31+25/-],
Dale 31.7.10
[16+17/5], Barnsley
21.6.11 £ [28+16/4],
Hibernian loan
31.1.13 [6+1/- ScL],
Dale 8.7.13
[48+13/10], Sheffield
U. 2.2.15 £ [37+9/11]*
Honours: League 2 promotion 2014

Matty made his debut for Wrexham while still a scholar, but left the Racecourse after they were relegated to the Conference. After a couple of seasons at Hereford, he joined Dale on a short term contract, but this was just the start of a complex story. He became one of three wingers in the side (with Atkinson and Adams), actually playing just behind lone striker O'Grady. Sold to Barnsley when Keith Hill became their manager, he returned to Spotland after his boss did and this time was transformed into a left back in the 2014 promotion side. Dale were struggling for goals at the start of the next campaign and Matty was given the main striker's role, remarkably hitting a hat-trick against Crewe in his first game in his new role. He had 13 goals to his credit by January, including another hat-trick in the FA Cup, and was then sold for a second time, for a much larger fee, to Sheffield United. He added eight more goals, the last in the incredible 5-5 draw in the play-off game against Swindon (the Blades going out 7-6 on aggregate after being 5-1 down), but scored only four in the league the following term when his new side finished below the Dale.

Helio Andre   2009-11

Born: Angola 3.12.92
5'7"
Striker
FL Apps/Gls +1/0 Total
Apps/Gls +2/0
Career: Childwall Sports
College, Dale sch 2009 to
2011 [+1/-], Cammell Laird
9.11, Burscough 8.12, Ashton
Ath. 10.12, AFC Liverpool
11.12, Bootle 4.13 to 11.13
Honours: Liverpool Boys,
English Schools Trophy

winners 2008, Merseyside under-15s cup winners 2008, North West Schools under-15s cup final 2008, Alliance League (North West) champions 2011

Brought up on Merseyside, Helio was a star striker for the all-conquering Liverpool Boys side which won the ESFA Trophy in 2008, scoring twice in a 7-0 demolition of Tameside, a hat-trick against Bishop Auckland and two in the final v Brighton. Joining Dale as a scholar, he scored in a pre-season game against Rossendale in 2010 and was selected on the bench for the first league game of the season, coming on for the last few minutes against Hartlepool. He was also substitute for the next six games, coming on in a Johnstone's Paint Trophy tie, but then returned to the youth side. Not offered a senior contract, he played in minor football back on Merseyside.

Jack Redshaw   2010-11

Born: Salford 20.11.90
5'5"   10st3
Striker
FL Apps/Gls +2/0
Total Apps/Gls 1+2/0
Career: Manchester C.
jnr, pro 2008, Dale
1.7.10 to 10.1.11 [+2/-
], Salford C. 3.11,
Altrincham 13.10.11,
Morecambe 24.1.12
[74+46/36],
Altrincham loan
31.1.12, Blackpool
10.7.15 [27+9/7]*

The son of non-league stalwart Ray, Jack progressed through the various age levels at City's academy to sign pro in 2008, netting four times in a reserve game in February 2009. His one appearance in the senior side came in a friendly against the UAE national side in Abu Dhabi later that year. Released in 2010, he signed for Dale but managed only two early season substitute appearances and a start in the JPT before having his contract cancelled. He broke back into the FL a year later with Morecambe and netted 16 times in his first full season, particularly relishing notching twice against Dale. He moved up a division in 2015, joining neighbours Blackpool, only for the Tangerines to be relegated. Jack's brother Mark is also a semi-professional player and has turned out in Iceland and Holland, while his cousin Charlene Thomas is a well-known middle distance runner.

Andrew William Tutte 2010-11, 2011-14

Born: Liverpool 21.9.90
5'7" 11st8
Midfield
FL Apps/Gls 77+18/10
Total Apps/Gls
90+20/11
Career: Manchester C.
jnr, pro 1.1.10, Dale loan
9.8.10 to 13.11.10 [5+2/-],
Shrewsbury T. loan
25.11.10 [2/-], Yeovil T.
loan 31.1.11 [10+1/-], Dale
24.6.11 [72+16/10], Bury
24.1.14 [77+6/8]*
Honours: England under-
19s (2 caps) 2009, European under-19s
championship final 2009, England under-20s
2009, England under-20s World Cup squad 2009,
FA Youth Cup winners 2008, Manchester Senior
Cup winners 2010, League 2 promotion (2014),
2015

A Youth Cup winner with City's academy side,
Andrew never progessed beyond being an unused
substitute in a cup tie for the first team despite
being in the England squads for the under-19s
European championships -where England lost in
the final to Ukraine -, and the under-20s World
Cup. He was loaned out three times in 2010-11,
spending a couple of months at Spotland. He
signed permanently the following summer after his
old junior coach Steve Eyre took over as Dale
manager. Unable to help prevent the disastrous
slide back towards League 2, which soon saw Eyre
dismissed, he regained his place under John
Coleman and kept it after the return of Keith Hill.
He was everpresent in 2012-13 until injured and
netted eight goals from midfield. Left out the
following year, he joined Bury, figuring in their
side promoted in 2015 and netted a hat-trick from
midfield the following term.

Joshua William C. (Josh) Thompson 2010-11

Born: Bolton
25.2.91 6'4" 12st
Defender
FL Apps/Gls
11+1/1 Total
Apps/Gls 12+2/1
Career: Stockport
Co. sch 2007, pro
28.5.09 [6+3/-],
(Manchester U.
trial 2008-09, West
Bromwich A. trial
2008-09), Celtic
8.8.09 £500,000
[16+2/3 ScL], Dale
loan 20.8.10 to 5.11
[11+1/1],

Peterborough U. loan 8.8.11, Chesterfield loan
17.1.12 [20/1], Portsmouth 31.8.12 [2/-],
Colchester loan 9.11.12, signed 1.1.13 [16+6/1],
Tranmere R. loan 23.10.14, signed 28.1.15 [15/-],
Southport 31.7.15 [36+1/2 Conf]*
Honours: England under-19s (3 caps) 2010,
England squad for European under-19s
championships 2010, Johnstone's Paint Trophy
winners 2012

As a teenager, Josh had a spectacular rise, when
sold to Scotish giants Celtic for £500,000 less than
three months after signing pro for Stockport. After
figuring in the European under-19s
championships, he made 21 appearances in all
competitions in his first season – including the cup
semi-final defeat by minnows Ross County - and
scored twice from centre back against Motherwell.
Despite being voted young player of the year, he
fell out of favour and was loaned to Dale for the
2010-11 season, figuring primarily as back-up to
Scott Wiseman at right back. During a further
loan, he won the Johnstone's Paint Trophy with
Chesterfield. When freed by Celtic he signed for
crisis club Portsmouth – he was one of 45 players
used during the season – but soon escaped to
Colchester. Injured for virtually all of 2013-14, he
then moved on to Tranmere but signed for
Southport after Rovers dropped into the
Conference.

Ryan Jones 2010-11
Born: Liverpool 2.4.92 6'6"
Goalkeeper
FL Apps +0 Total Apps +0
Career: Liverpool jnr, Wigan A. jnr, Leeds U. sch
2008, Aberdeen trial 7.10, Stockport Co. trial 7.10,
Telford trial 8.10, Dale n/c 17.9.10, Northwich
Victoria, Richmond Kickers (USA) 24.3.11, Bacup
Borough loan 12.1.12, Bacup Borough 9.12,
Stockport Co. n/c 28.8.13, AFC Liverpool 2.14*
(+Campfield; Sunday League)
Honours: Lancashire FA Trophy final 2013,
Liverpool Senior Cup final 2015

Ryan trained with several senior clubs as a junior
but was not retained by Leeds at the end of his
scholarship. In October 2010 Dale were without
cover for Josh Lillis when Matty Edwards was
injured and Ryan figured on the bench for five
games. He then made his first senior appearances
with Northwich Victoria before joining Richmond
Kickers in the USA and subsequently figuring in
non-league football with AFC Liverpool, the
Liverpool Senior Cup winners in 2015.

Deane Alfie Michael Smalley 2010-11

Born: Oldham 7.9.88
6'0" 11st10
Forward
FL Apps/Gls +3/0
Total Apps/Gls +3/0
Career: Oldham A. sch 2005, pro 3.7.07 [64+41/10], Dale loan 23.9.10 [+3/-], Chesterfield loan 1.11.10 [22+6/12], Oxford U. 5.11 £ [46+35/13], Bradford C. loan 1.12 [7+6/-], Plymouth A. 20.5.14 to 5.16 [3+14/1], Newport Co. loan 21.1.16 [3/-]
Honours: Youth League winners 2007, Lancashire Youth Cup winners 2007, League 2 champions 2011

A member of the Latics' side which beat Dale in the Lancashire Youth Cup final, along with Marcus Holness, Kallum Higginbottom and Lewis Alessandra (q.v.), Deane had already appeared over 100 times for Oldham's first team before a brief loan at Spotland. A much more productive stint at Chesterfield produced 12 goals in only 22 starts as the Spireites won League 2. Sold to Oxford he figured in about half of their games over the next three seasons, often from the bench, before a further move to Plymouth where he suffered a serious cruciate injury.

Christopher (Chris) Oldfield 2010-11

Born: Liverpool 14.1.91 6'4" 11st
Goalkeeper
FL Apps +0   Total Apps +0
Career: Liverpool jnr, sch 2007-08, pro 7.09, Chester cs.10, Darlington n/c 22.10.10, Dale n/c 12.11.10, Bangor C. 4.1.11, Aberdeen trial 6.11, Warrington T. 9.11, Hume C. (Australia) 3.12* (Melbourne Victory trial 1.13), (Central Coast Mariners trial 9.15)
Honours: Republic of Ireland under-16s 2007, Ballymena international tournament final 2007, (Welsh Cup final 2011)

An Irish youth international, Chris played for Liverpool's under-18s from 2007 and went on tour to Holland with the reserves in the summer of 2009. After being released he figured with Chester and Darlington before a very brief stint as Dale's back-up 'keeper, being on the bench for the game at Sheffield Wednesday. He later figured for several seasons with the largely Turkish-Australian club Hume City in the Victorian Premier League, being voted top goalkeeper in Victoria in 2014 and saving four penalties in a play-off shootout the following year. He became an Australian resident in 2016 to improve his chances of a move to an A-League club.

Robert (Bobby) Grant 2010-11, 2012-13

Born: Liverpool 1.7.90 5'11" 12st
Striker
FL Apps/Gls 40+2/17 Total Apps/Gls 42+3/18
Career: Accrington St. jnr, sch 1.7.06, pro 8.2.08 [53+12/15], Scunthorpe U. 24.6.10 £260,000 [29+30/7], Dale loan 19.11.10 to 4.1.11 [5+1/2], Accrington St. loan 15.3.12 [8/3], Dale 31.8.12 £ [35+1/15], Blackpool 18.7.13 £ [5+1/-], Fleetwood T. loan 28.2.14 [1/-], Shrewsbury T. loan 9.10.14 [28+5/6], Fleetwood T. 22.7.15 [25+13/10]*
Honours: League 2 promotion (2014), 2015

Bobby made his Stanley debut aged 16 years 309 days, their youngest player since 1959 and figured regularly up front for two seasons. Sold to Scunthorpe for a decent fee when still only 19, he made a number of appearances but was still loaned out to Dale – scoring twice in six games in place of Anthony Elding – and original club Accrington. He was bought by his old Stanley boss John Coleman just after the start of Dale's first season back in League 2 and scored five times in his first six starts before being sent off and suspended. He had another burst of six goals in eight games despite Dale sliding down the table after a good start, but after his second red card and third suspension of the season his form tailed off under Keith Hill, though he still finished with 16 goals. Sold to Blackpool in the summer, he appeared infrequently until a loan spell at Shrewsbury, when they gained promotion. He signed for Fleetwood in 2015, top scoring as they retained their League 1 place at Blackpool's expense.

Luke Matthew Daniels 2010-11

Born: Bolton 5.1.88
6'4" 12st10
Goalkeeper
FL Apps 1
Total Apps 1
Career: Manchester U. jnr, West Bromwich A. sch 2004, pro 18.7.06 [+1], Motherwell loan 25.1.08 to 5.08 [2 ScL], Shrewsbury T. loan 1.8.08 to 5.09 [38], Tranmere R. loan 21.7.09 to 5.10 [37], Bristol R. loan

14.7.10, Charlton A. loan 17.9.10, Dale loan 2.12.10 [1], Bristol R. loan 5.1.11 [9], Southend U. loan 25.10.11 [9], Scunthorpe U. 22.1.15 [62]*
Honours: England under-18s 2006, under-19s 2007, (Championship play-off final 2007), League 2 play-off final 2009

With Manchester United from an early age, Luke then took up a scholarship with West Brom. Another England youth player, after turning pro, he went out on a couple of season long loans, being man of the match in Shrewsbury's 2009 play-off final defeat by Dale's conquerers Gillingham. His stint at Spotland must have proved frustrating, though, as he managed just one game in place of the injured Lillis, all the other games during the month being postponed. He finally made his sole Baggies appearance after nine years at the club, as a substitute for the injured Ben Foster in August 2013 (his 100th FL game). In January 2015, bizarrely both Scunthorpe goalkeepers broke an arm in the same game and the Iron signed Luke as their replacement. Despite being sent off on the opening day of 2015-16, he was a regular for the rest of the season.

Liam Michael Dickinson 2010-11

Born: Salford 4.10.85
6'4" 11st7
Striker
FL Apps/Gls 7+7/0
Total Apps/Gls 7+7/0
Career: Blackpool jnr, Bolton W. jnr, Blackburn R. jnr, Irlam T. 2002, Swinton T. 2002-03, Trafford 12.03, Woodley Sports 2004, Stockport Co. 22.12.05 £2000 [57+37/33], Derby Co. 3.7.08 £750,000, Huddersfield T. loan 21.8.08 [13/6], Blackpool loan 27.11.08 [5+2/4], Leeds U. loan 13.3.09 [4+4/-], Brighton &HA 15.7.09 £300,000 [17+10/4], Peterborough U. loan 15.2.10 [9/3], Barnsley 30.6.10 £150,000 [+3/-], Walsall loan 11.10 [2+2/-], Dale loan 6.1.11 to 4.11 [7+7/-], Plymouth A. 4.7.11, Southend U. 27.7.11 to [28+2/10], Port Vale trial 7.12 and cs.13, Stockport Co. 8.11.13, Stalybridge Celtic 3.3.14, Guiseley 6.2.15 [12+19/6 Conf], Bradford PA loan 3.16
Honours: League 2 play-off winners 2008, Conference North play-off winners 2015

A relatively late arrival on the league scene, Liam was a graphic designer playing in the local Sunday League and in the Manchester League for Irlam. After around 100 games for Stockport - including their Wembley play-off victory when he scored the winning goal against the Dale - like his former County strike partner Anthony Elding he gained a big money move. However, he was soon loaned out, scoring twice on his debut as substitute for Blackpool, and never made a single appearance for Derby. Further moves saw him arrive at Barnsley, but he again struggled to gain a place in the side and spent the second half of the campign at Spotland as a potential replacement for Elding (who had been loaned back to Stockport), unfortunately without hitting the net. His senior career was effectively terminated by an ankle injury after a year at Southend when he netted 12 goals. He later rejoined Stockport, now down in the Conference North, before gaining promotion from that level with Guiseley. While on loan at Bradford Park Avenue he had to play a whole game in goal as both their keepers were injured.

Owain fon Williams 2010-11

Born: Penygroes 17.3.87
6'4" 12st2
Goalkeeper
FL Apps 22
Total Apps 22
Career: Crewe A. sch 2003, pro 3.7.06, Stockport Co. 8.7.08 [82], Bury loan 28.10.10 [6], Dale 20.1.11 [22], Tranmere R. 6.11 [161], Inverness Caledonian Thistle 16.7.15 [38 ScL]*
Honours: Wales under-17s 2003, under-19s 2004 to 2006 (4 caps), under-21s (11 caps) 2007 to 2008, Wales senior squad 2009 to 2016, Wales 2015 v Holland, (League 2 promotion 2011)

Another ex-Stockport player and a Wales under-21 international (and rare Welsh speaker among FL professionals), Owain spent the second half of 2010-11 at Spotland, figuring in goal after the end of Josh Lillis' loan. A run of four clean sheets in succession enabled Dale to keep in contention just outside the play-off spots, but at the end of the season Owain was released. He spent the next four years at Tranmere, being called up as Wales' reserve goalkeeper on several occasions. He made his debut for the Welsh senior side in 2015. When Rovers lost their league place he signed for Inverness Caley Thistle in the SPL, actually making his debut in the Europa League before going on to be everpresent. Owain has also had an exhibition of his oil paintings at a gallery in North Wales.

Robert Ian (Robbie) Williams   2010-11

Born: Pontefract
2.10.84
5'10" 11st13
Left back
FL Apps/Gls 9/0 Total Apps/Gls 9/0
Career: Barnsley yts, pro 2.7.04 [44+22/4], Blackpool loan 21.3.07 [9/4], Huddersfield T. 24.8.07 [68+9/4], Stockport Co. 6.8.10 [19+3/1], Dale 31.1.11 [9/-], Plymouth A. 7.11 [40+2/4], Limerick 2.13*

Honours: League 1 promotion 2006, League 1 play-off winners 2007, Munster Senior Cup winners 2015

Making his Barnsley debut in the week of his 18th birthday, Robbie played a number of games, mainly as a left back, over the next five seasons. He spent the last month of 2007-08 at Blackpool, remarkably netting four league goals plus a 30 yard screamer in their play-off final success, while playing in defence. Keith Hill's final signing of his first Dale tenure, Robbie was brought in from Stockport as defensive cover and subsequently had a run of games in place of Joe Widdowson at left back. He was then a regular performer for Plymouth before heading off to play for Limerick where he was a winner in the Munster Cup Final in 2015.

Jacob Kendall (Jake) Kean   2011-12

Born: Derby 4.2.91
6'4" 14st11
Goalkeeper
FL Apps 14
Total Apps 15
Career: Derby Co. jnr 2006, Blackburn R. 5.09 [37], Hartlepool U. loan 6.9.10 [19], Dale loan 2.8.11 to 10.11 [14], Yeovil T. loan 15.9.14 [5], Oldham A. loan 30.1.15 [11], Norwich C. 1.8.15*, Colchester U. loan 7.1.16 [3], Swindon T. loan 14.4.16 [3]

Honours: England under-20 v France 2011, FA Premier Reserve League Group B winners and play-off final 2011

Signed by Blackburn when he was 18, Jake's first senior involvement was in a successful loan spell at Hartlepool a year later. He also had success at reserve level at Blackburn and played with England under-20s. At the start of 2011-12 he was the second goalkeeper signed by new Dale boss Steve Eyre in a matter of days, David Lucas quickly being moved over to a player-coach role. Unfortunately, playing behind a suspect defence, and alternating with Lucas as he wasn't allowed by Blackburn to play in cup ties, Jake's confidence and form suffered and only two months into his proposed season long deal he returned to Ewood Park (reputedly at his own request). He recovered to have lengthy spells as Rovers' first choice in 2013 before the veteran Paul Robinson reclaimed his place. He joined Premier League Norwich but was restricted to the odd game on the bench.

Stephen Mark Darby   2011-12

Born: Liverpool 6.10.88
6'0" 12st6
Right back
FL Apps/Gls 34+1/0
Total Apps/Gls 39+1/0
Career: Maricourt RCHS, Liverpool sch 2005, pro 18.7.06 [+1/-], Swindon T. loan 1.3.10 [12/-], Notts Co. loan 1.11.10 and 21.1.11 [23/-], Dale loan 7.7.11 to 5.12 [34+1/-], Bradford C. 4.7.12 [170+2/-]*

Honours: England under-19s (2 caps) 2007-08, FA Youth Cup winners 2006, 2007, Reserve League champions 2008, League 1 play-off final 2010, League 2 play-off winners 2013, League Cup final 2013

A youth international, double Youth Cup winner and captain of the reserves in 2007-08, Stephen still only made one (last minute) substitute appearance for Liverpool in the FL. He did, though, appear in cup ties and in Europe against PSV Eindhoven and Fiorentina. He played in the League 1 play-off final with Swindon before a season long loan at Spotland. Easily the most productive of Steve Eyre's signings, Stephen made more league starts under Eyre and his successor John Coleman than anyone except old hands Gary Jones and Jason Kennedy. Transferred to Bradford City, he figured in the same side as Jones as the Bantams amazingly reached the League Cup Final, beating Arsenal and Villa along the way, and then won promotion via the play-offs. He remarkably missed only one game in the next three seasons, succeeding Jones as skipper and leading his side to 5th place in 2016.

Neal Anthony Trotman 2011-12

Born: Levenshulme
11.3.87 6'2" 13st7
Centre half
FL Apps/Gls 12/0
Total Apps/Gls 14/0
Career: Burnley sch
2004, Oldham A.
15.9.06 [16+2/1],
Halifax T. loan 1.07
[11/2 Conf], Preston NE
30.1.08 £500,000
[2+1/-], Colchester U.
loan 19.3.09 [5+1/-],
Southampton loan
20.8.09 [17+1/2],
Huddersfield T. loan 1.10 [21/2], Oldham A. loan
25.11.10 [15+3/-], Dale 24.7.11 [12/-], Chesterfield
loan 3.11.11, signed 3.1.12 [54/1], Partick Thistle
trial 7.13, Dundee U. trial 7.13, Plymouth A. 5.8.13
[41/2], Bristol R. 7.8.14 to 5.15 [17+2/1 Conf]
Honours: Conference promotion 2015

Neal impressed sufficiently in a dozen or so games
for Oldham as a big, athletic centre back for
Preston to buy him for £500,000 in 2008.
However, he managed only a couple of games for
them, missing most of the following season though
injury and spending 2009-10 out on loan (making
a total of 39 league appearances). In the summer
of 2012, he was one of Steve Eyre's key signings,
but things quickly went downhill, Neal suffering a
disastrous game against his former side Oldham
when he gave away a penalty and was sent off
before half-time in a 3-0 defeat. In the November
he went on loan to Chesterfield, with Dean Holden
moving the other way, and their respective moves
were made permanent when the transfer window
opened. He subsequently had a productive season
at Plymouth under his old Latics and Chesterfield
boss John Sheridan. He figured for Bristol Rovers
when they regained their league place but his stint
there was ended by injury.

Ashley James Grimes 2011-13

Born: Swinton 9.12.86
6'0" 11st2
Forward
FL Apps/Gls 54+20/18
Total Apps/Gls
60+23/22
Career: Barr Hill Lads'
Club, Manchester U.
jnr, Bolton W. jnr,
Manchester C. jnr 2003,
pro 3.7.06, Swindon T.
loan 22.3.07 [+4/-],
Millwall 1.7.08
[6+15/2], Lincoln C.
loan 29.10.10
[24+3/15], Dale 21.6.11

[54+20/18], Bury 27.6.13 [6+9/-], Walsall 25.7.14
[11+16/2], Barrow 7.15 [8+9/1 Conf], Southport
6.16
Honours: (League 2 promotion 2007), League 1
promotion 2010, Johnstone's Paint Trophy final
2015

The first of a string of ex-City juniors to arrive at
Spotland during their former academy coach Steve
Eyre's time in charge, Ashley was the only one
apart from Andrew Tutte to survive until the
following season. He scored eight times in his first
14 games, but Dale were already in the bottom four
with just eight points by this juncture and he only
managed three more as Dale surrendered their
League 1 place. He still finished as top scorer,
though, as he had the previous season for Lincoln,
who had been relegated out of the league. Indeed,
another burst of six goals in five games towards
the end of John Coleman's reign meant Ashley
reached 11 goals again the following term when he
was in the squad for all except the final game. After
an unsuccessful stint at Bury, he played in some
further League 1 games at Walsall and played at
Wembley for them in the JPT final before joining
Barrow.

David Anthony Lucas 2011-12

Born: Preston 23.11.77
6'2" 13st10
Goalkeeper
FL Apps 16 Total Apps 20
Career: Preston NE sch
1993, pro 12.12.94 [119+5],
Darlington loan 14.12.95 [6],
Darlington loan 3.10.96 [7],
Scunthorpe U. loan 23.12.96
[6], Sheffield W. loan
1.10.03 [17], Sheffield W.
£100,000 14.6.04 to cs.06
[52], Barnsley 4.1.07 [2+1],
Leeds U. 11.9.07 [16], Swindon T. 2.7.09 [61+1],
Dale trial 7.11, Preston NE trial 7.11, Dale
player/goalkeeping coach 3.8.11 [16], Birmingham
player/goalkeeping coach 10.7.12, Fleetwood T.
player/goalkeeping coach 1.13 [1+1]*
Honours: Preston Schools, Lancashire Schools
under-15s 1992-93, England under-18s (5 caps)
1995-96, under-20s (4 caps) 1997, Division 3+
promotion 1996, Division 2+ champions 2000,
Division 1+ play-off final 2001, League 1 play-off
winners 2005, final (2008), 2010, (League 2 play-
off winners 2014)

David started out with Preston (then in the fourth
tier) and first had a lengthy run in the side in
1998-99, sharing the 'keeper's jersey over the next
few years as North End came within one game of
promotion to the top flight in 2001. After 10 years
on Preston's books, he was loaned to Sheffield
Wednesday in 2003. He signed for them for

£100,000 the following summer and again played in around half of their games, including their successful League 1 play-off final and added another play-off final appearance with Swindon. He signed for Dale at the same time as Jake Kean was taken on loan, David being given the role of goalkeeping coach. As it turned out, Kean's parent club Blackburn didn't allow him to play in cup ties, so David figured in Dale's victory over Premier League QPR, the only high spot in a dismal season, and took over when Kean returned to Blackburn and again when the next loanee Peter Kurucz was injured. David had a few months in the same role with Birmingam, playing in one League Cup tie, before signing for Fleetwood, managed by old North End team-mate Graham Alexander. He was on the bench when they too won a play-off final in 2014.

Marc Ian Twaddle 2011-12

Born: Glasgow 27.8.86 6'1" 10st10
Defender
FL Apps/Gls 1+1/0
Total Apps/Gls 2+1/0
Career: Turnbull HS, Rangers 7.02, Falkirk 8.03 [15+10/2 ScL], Partick Thistle 7.07 [60+3/1 ScL], Falkirk 10.7.09 [61+3/3 ScL], Dale 4.7.11 [1+1/-], Ayr U. 24.8.12 [16+1/1 ScL], Irvine Meadow 10.8.13*

Marc made his senior bow with Falkirk at the end of 2003-04, when he was still 17. Although not becoming a regular, he did score against Rangers, who had earlier released him, in Falkirk's first victory over them in more than 30 years. He became a first choice at Partick and then for two years back at Falkirk, generally at left back, though he could play in midfield. For some reason signed by Steve Eyre to play centre back, this idea was abandoned after the pre-season games and Mark was hardly seen again, until given one last game by John Coleman. His contract was then cancelled so he could return to Scotland

Paul Anthony Marshall 2011-12

Born: Gorton 9.7.89 6'1" 12st4
Midfield
FL Apps/Gls +1/0 Total Apps/Gls +1/0
Career: Manchester C. sch 2006, pro cs.07, Blackpool loan 29.1.09 [1+1/-], Port Vale loan 12.2.09 [13/1], Aberdeen loan 2.1.10 [6+3/- ScL], Walsall 16.6.10 [12+6/1], Dale trial 7.11, n/c 2.8.11 [+1/-], Droylsden n/c 9.11, Port Vale n/c 14.2.12

[10+5/-], FC Halifax T. 7.12, Stockport Co. n/c 25.2.13 [4+7/- Conf], FC Halifax T. cs.13 [61+11/5 Conf], Bradford PA 5.15*, Ashton U. loan 13.10.15
Honours: Republic of Ireland under-19s, England under-20s (3 caps) 2009, Manchester Senior Cup winners 2007, (Conference North promotion 2013)

Another City product, Paul was a youth international for two different countries, the Republic at under 19s and England at under 20s, figuring in the latter's 2009 World Cup squad. He scored for City's reserves when they beat United in the Manchester Cup final, but was another never to get near a Premier League appearance. His league debut on loan at Blackpool was brief, as he was replaced by Matt Gilks when the 'keeper was sent off after five minutes. He did figure in the SPL with Aberdeen but was without a club when given a trial by Dale, and managed just eight minutes for them against Carlisle. A year at Port Vale was somewhat more productive, but he then settled into Conference football.

Jordan Olawale A. Fagbola 2010-12

Born: Manchester 1.12.93 6'3" 13st7
Defender
FL Apps/Gls +0/0 Total Apps/Gls +0/0
Career: Trinity HS (Manchester), Fletcher Moss, Dale jnr, sch 6.10, pro cs.11, Stockport Co. 31.7.12 [35+3/1 Conf], Colwyn Bay U. 29.5.15*
Honours: Greater Manchester Schools, ESFA under-16 Trophy winners 2010, Alliance League champions 2011

In the same trophy winning GM Schools side as Godwin Abadaki (q.v.), Jordan (then known as Wale) was man of the match in the final. He broke his arm in a youth team game in March 2011 but made a quick recovery and was included in the first team squad, being unused substitute twice early in 2011-12. Not progressing further, he opted to take a degree in sports science at Manchester Metropolitan University and was one of the few successes at Stockport when they were relegated to the Conference North.

Pim Balkestein 2011-12

Born: Gouda, Holland 29.4.87
6'3" 13st3
Centre back/left back
FL Apps/Gls 12+1/0 Total Apps/Gls 14+1/0
Career: Heerenveen (Holland) jnr 2005, pro cs.06, Ipswich T. trial, signed 16.06.08 £180,000 [23+6/-], Brentford loan 20.11.09 [8/-], Brentford loan 25.3.10 [6/1], Brentford 6.8.10 £ [19+6/1], Dale loan

19.8.11 to 12.11 [12+1/-], AFC Wimbledon loan 9.3.12 [6/-], AFC Wimbledon 17.7.12 [22+2/2], VVV Venlo (Holland) 12.6.13, SV Elversberg (Germany) cs.15, De Treffers (Holland) 1.16*

Bought by Ipswich from his Dutch club Heerenveen before he had made a senior appearance, Pim had been on standby for Holland under-21s. He had a decent run in the side in his first season, generally playing centre back, though sometimes at left back. After two loan spells he was signed by Brentford, but just after the start of 2011-12 Steve Eyre borrowed him to try and remedy the Dale's defensive deficiencies. Unfortunately it was to no avail, both his and defensive partner Neal Trotman's Dale careers ending after a defeat at home to struggling Orient. He later played for Wimbledon before returning to Holland to play 60 games for Eerste Divisie (second tier) side VVV Venlo. Pim's father Luuk was a Dutch international who played for Sparta Rotterham and Feyenoord.

Matthew Brian Barnes-Homer 2011-12
Born: Dudley 25.1.86 5'11" 12st5
Forward
FL Apps/Gls 1+4/0 Total Apps/Gls 2+5/0
Career: Wolverhampton W. jnr 2001, Rochester Raging Rhinos (USA) 2004, Syracuse Salty Dogs (USA) 2004, Virginia Beach Mariners (USA) 2004, Aldershot T. 9.04 [+2/- Conf], Hednesford T. 2005, Bromsgrove R. 4.05, Tividale 2006, Willenhall T. 8.06, Wycombe W. 10.3.07 [+1/-], Kidderminster H. 27.7.07 [79+22/35 Conf], Luton T. loan 26.11.09, signed 13.1.10 £75,000 [48+22/20 Conf], Dale loan 25.8.11 to 1.1.12 [1+4/-], Cheltenham T. trial 1.12, Nuneaton T. 24.2.12, Ostersunds FK (Sweden) 20.3.12, Macclesfield T. 27.6.12 [34+3/18 Conf], Notts Co. trial cs.13, Alfreton T. trial 7.13, Forest Green Rovers 5.8.13 [10+8/5 Conf], Cambridge U. 10.1.14 [9+5/1 Conf], Tamworth loan 28.2.14 [7/1 Conf], Macclesfield T. trial 7.14, Whitehawk 7.8.14, Macclesfield T. loan 10.14 [23+7/9 Conf], Aldershot T. 11.6.15 [7+8/- Conf], Kidderminster H. loan 29.10.15 [6+2/- Conf], Wilmington Hammerheads (USA) 2.16
Honours: England C (5 caps) 2009-11, Conference play-off final 2011, Conference promotion 2014

Despite a decent goal-scoring return with some of his clubs, Matthew had the misfortune to become synonymous with Steve Eyre's doomed reign as Rochdale boss. Somewhat optimistically recruited to boost Dale's fortunes in League 1 when unable to make Luton's side in the Conference, he started just once in the league. Unusually, he had started his senior career in the USA with the likes of Syracuse Salty Dogs (coached by Laurie Calloway, q.v.) in the USL. He had short spells with a string of non-league sides and made one substitute

appearance in the FL with Wycombe. At Conference level he scored regularly for Kidderminster and in his first year at Luton after a £75,000 transfer, later doing so again at Macclesfield (netting twice in an FA Cup tie against Cardiff), during a nomadic tour of the non-league scene, playing for over 20 clubs by the time he was 30.

David Michael Ball 2011-12

Born: Whitefield 14.12.89 6'0" 11st8
Striker
FL Apps/Gls 12+2/3 Total Apps/Gls 13+2/4
Career: Castlebrook HS, Manchester C. jnr, pro 2007, Swindon T. loan 7.10 [7+11/2], Peterborough U. 31.1.11 £50,000 [13+28/9], Dale loan 31.8.11 to 10.10.11 [7/3], Dale loan 24.11.11 to 15.1.12 [5+2/-], Fleetwood T. 23.7.12 [97+35/27]*
Honours: Youth Cup winners 2008, League 1 play-off winers 2011, League 2 play-off winners 2014

Another ex-City youngster, David had scored in their Youth Cup final victory in 2008. He was also second highest scorer in the Premier Reserve League in 2009-10, but like many of his colleagues was unable to break into City's multi-million pound first team and was with Peterborough when borrowed by Dale. His initial stint was successful, Dale winning three of his seven games, but Posh then recalled him and when he returned a month or so later Dale were back in trouble and David did not recapture his earlier form. In a long stint at Fleetwood he scored 13 goals when they reached League 1 via the play-offs in 2014. He was short listed by FIFA for the best goal of 2015 alongside the likes of Lionel Messi.

Ahmad Benali 2011-12

Born: Manchester 7.2.92 5'8" 10st5
Midfield
FL Apps/Gls +2/0
Total Apps/Gls 1+2/0
Career: Stretford GS, Manchester C. jnr, sch 2.09, pro 5.10, Dale loan 31.8.11 to 12.11 [+2/-], Brescia (Italy) 11.7.12, Palermo (Italy) 6.15*, Delferno Pescara (Italy) loan 29.8.15

Honours: England under-17s (5 caps) 2008-09, Libya (2 caps) 2012

The son of a Libyan businessman based in Manchester, Ahmad had been one of Steve Eyre's City juniors. Bizarrely, given Dale's position and need for serious reinforcements, Eyre signed him on loan as a favour to City, to give him the chance to regain fitness. He started just one JPT game and returned to City when Eyre was sacked. The following summer he made his debut for the Libyan national side (having been a youth international for England) and subsequently played regularly as an attacking midfielder for Serie B Brescia before joing Palermo in Serie A, though they immediately loaned him out to Pescara.

Nathan Geoffrey Junior Eccleston 2011-12

Born: Manchester 30.12.90 5'10" 10st6
Striker
FL Apps/Gls 3+2/1
Total Apps/Gls 4+3/1
Career: Failsworth HS, Bury jnr 2005, Liverpool sch 2006, pro 7.09 [+2/-], Huddersfield T. loan 28.1.10 [4+7/1], Charlton A. loan 13.1.11 [8+13/3], Dale loan 20.10.11 to 22.11.11 [3+2/1], Blackpool 31.8.12 £ [2+8/1], Tranmere R. 26.10.12 loan [1/-], Carlisle U. loan 4.10.13 [+2/-], Coventry C. loan 26.3.14 [4+4/-], Partick Thistle 1.9.14 [+9/1 ScL], Kilmarnock 14.2.15 to cs.15 [6+4/1 ScL], Bekescsaba (Hungary) 3.16*
Honours: England under-17 2006

Nathan made his Liverpool debut against Arsenal in the League Cup just a couple of months after turning pro and in all figured nine times for the Reds. Unfortunately this included an extra time substitute appearance in the League Cup against Northampton, when he missed the shoot-out penalty that resulted in an embarrassing defeat by their League 2 visitors. His only start was against Utrecht in the Europa League, but he had a useful loan spell with Charlton. Known to Steve Eyre as an opponent of City's academy teams, Nathan's stint at Spotland was brief, the striker scoring on his debut but otherwise having little impact. Bought by Blackpool, he again spent most of his time out on loan. He moved to Scotland in 2014, but was without a club and running his own sports wear company until trying his luck in Hungary.

Stephen Robert Jordan 2011-12

Born: Warrington 6.3.82
6'0" 11st13
Defender
FL Apps/Gls 17+2/0
Total Apps/Gls 19+2/0
Career: Manchester C. jnr, yts 1998, pro 11.3.99 [49+4/-], Cambridge U. loan 4.10.02 [11/-], Burnley 23.7.07 [69+4/-], Portsmouth trial cs.10, Sheffield U. 22.9.10 to 4.11 [14+1/-], Huddersfield T. loan 2.11 [6/-], Rotherham U. trial, Dale n/c 28.10.11, signed 22.12.11 [17+2/-], Dunfermline Ath. 27.7.12 [20/1 ScL], Fleetwood T. 12.7.13 [70+3/1], Chorley 6.16*
Honours: Championship promotion 2009, League 2 promotion 2014

Stephen was also a former Manchester City player but of a different vintage to the others signed by Dale in 2011. Not making his City debut until he was 21, he first played fairly regularly in 2004-05 and accumulated around 50 appearances, often partnering Sylvain Distin in central defence. He also had three seasons at Burnley, winning promotion to the Premier League in 2009. After a less successful time at Bramall Lane, he was without a club until given a trial at Spotland. He immediately went into the side at left back before taking over at centre back, and after being given a contract by caretaker manager Chris Beech, he played fairly regularly over the next few months though Dale won only three of his 21 games. After a spell in Scotland, he had a lengthier spell at Fleetwood under his former Burnley team-mate Graham Alexander, winning promotion with them in 2014.

Dean Thomas John Holden 2011-12

Born: Salford 15.9.79
6'1" 11st
Defender
FL Apps/Gls 20+1/0
Total Apps/Gls 21+1/0
Career: Bolton W. yts, pro 23.12.97 [7+6/1], Valur (Iceland) loan 2001, Oldham A. loan 12.10.01, signed cs.02 [98+10/10], Peterborough U. 7.7.05 [54+2/4], Falkirk 1.1.07 £ [44+4/2 ScL], Shrewsbury T. 26.6.09 [48+2/-], Rotherham U. loan 5.8.10 [4+2/-], Chesterfield 3.2.11 [26+5/3], Dale loan 3.11.11, signed 2.1.12 [20+1/-], Walsall 16.7.12, player-coach 5.13 [26+3/2], Oldham A.

coach 14.11.14, caretaker manager 25.2.15, manager 17.3.15, assistant manager 6.5.15 to 11.1.16, Walsall coach 3.16*
Honours: England youth international, N. Ireland squad 2007, Championship promotion 2001, League 2 champions 2011

After a number of games at full back for Bolton in 1999-2000 and a spell on loan in Iceland, Dean made his mark with over a century of appearances for Oldham, generally at centre back. A regular in eighteen months at Peterborough, they sold him to Falkirk in 2007, where he unfortunately suffered a broken leg. He was also called up to the N. Ireland squad, despite previously playing for England at youth level. In November 2011, Steve Eyre opted to bring some experience into his defence, and just a few days after signing Stephen Jordan he took Dean on loan from Chesterfield with Neil Trotman moving the other way. One of the few new signings to gain support from the fans, he still left at the end of the season for two years at Walsall, latterly as player-coach. He was coach then manager at Oldham, but was given only a few months in the latter role as the Latics got through four managers in less than a year.

Harry Charles Bunn 2011-12

Born: Oldham 21.11.92 5'9" 11st10
Striker
FL Apps/Gls 5+1/0
Total Apps/Gls 7+1/1
Career: Manchester C. jnr, sch 2010, pro 7.11, Dale loan 3.11.11 to 1.1.12 [5+1/-], Preston NE loan 2.1.12 [1/1], Oldham A. loan 16.3.12 [8+3/-], Crewe A. loan 21.8.12 [2+2/-], Sheffield U. loan 9.13 [+2/-], Huddersfield T. loan 28.11.13, signed 22.1.14 [58+17/15]*

Another loan signing from City by Steve Eyre, Harry was the son of assistant manager Frankie Bunn, the former Oldham striker. He made his FL debut at MK Dons and scored on his first start, in the JPT against Preston (Dale going out on penalties), but returned to City the week after his father was sacked along with Eyre. After further loans he was signed by Huddersfield where Eyre and Bunn senior were now on the coaching staff and established himself in the first team in 2014-15 with nine goals in 24 starts, mainly playing on the left flank.

Roland Adrianus Martinus Bergkamp
2011-12
Born: Amstelveen, Holland 3.4.91 6'3" 13st2
Striker
FL Apps/Gls 2+1/0 Total Apps/Gls 2+1/0
Career: Excelsior Rotterdam (Holland) 2008, pro cs.09, Brighton & HA 1.7.11, Dale loan 17.11.11 to 17.12.11 [2+1/-], VVV Venlo (Holland) loan 31.8.12, FC Emmen (Holland) 26.7.13, Sparta Rotterdam (Holland) 7.15*
Honours: Eerste divisie play-off winners 2010, Holland under-21s v Germany 2011

The nephew of Arsenal and Holland great Dennis Bergkamp and son of Adrian, a member of Excelsior's medical staff, Roland started out at his father's club, assisting them to promotion back to the top flight of Dutch football in 2010. He also appeared for Holland under-21s, but decided to move to Brighton in 2011. Unable to break into their first team, he was Steve Eyre's final loan signng for Dale – they had so many that they were not all allowed in the match day squad at the same time, let alone figure in the starting line-up. He made his debut in a rare victory, at Preston, but appeared only twice more in his month with Dale, his only games in England. He was much more successful on his return to Holland, netting 26 times in 72 games for Emmen before joining Sparta Rotterdam, where he was a regular in the Dutch second tier.

Peter Kurucz 2011-12

Born: Budapest, Hungary 30.5.88 6'1" 12st
Goalkeeper
FL Apps 11 Total Apps 11
Career: Lang SK (Hungary) jnr, Ujpest (Hungary) jnr 2005, pro 6.07, Tatabanya (Hungary) loan 1.2.08, West Ham U. loan 9.2.09, signed 3.6.09 [+1], Dale loan 2.1.12 to 4.12 [11], Crystal Palace trial cs.12, BFC Siofok (Hungary) 28.8.12, Ferencvaros (Hungary) 1.7.13*, Soroksar SC loan 25.7.14, Keflavik (Iceland) loan 2014
Honours: Hungary under-21s (11 caps) 2007 to 2010

When Chris Beech took over as caretaker manager, his first move was to recruit a replacement goalkeeper, as David Lucas had had to go off during Beech's first game in charge. A Hungarian under-21 international, Peter had arrived in England in 2009, making his only appearance as substitute against Manchester United when West

Ham were 4-0 down, not conceding in the remaining 20 minutes. A cruciate injury ruled him out for over a year and his next first team football was at Spotland. When John Coleman took over, Dale briefly looked as if they could stage a recovery, conceding only two goals in five games, but Peter was injured by a late challenge by Dale's nemesis, Notts County's Lee Hughes, and was unable to play any further games. In the summer he returned to Hungary.

Daniel Bogdanovic 2011-12

Born: Misrata, Libya 26.3.80 6'1" 12st2
Striker
FL Apps/Gls 5/1
Total Apps/Gls 5/1
Career: Sliema Wanderers (Malta) 2000, Budapesti Vasas SC (Hungary) 2001, Naxxar Lions (Malta) 2001, Valetta (Malta) 1.8.02, Cherno More Varna (Bulgaria) 2003, Sliema Wanderers (Malta) 1.7.03, Marsaxlokk (Malta) 2004, Sliema Wanderers (Malta) cs.05, Marsaxlokk (Malta) cs.06, Cisco Roma (Italy) 1.7.07, Locomotiv Sofia (Bulgaria) 8.08, Barnsley 26.1.09 £ [33+12/16], Sheffield U. 2.6.10 [12+22/5], Blackpool 31.8.11 £250,000 [1+7/2], Dale loan 2.1.12 to 2.12 [5/1], Notts Co. loan 3.12 [8/2], Mosta (Malta) 5.8.12, Valletta (Malta) loan 21.1.13, Floriana (Malta) 18.8.13, Victoria Wanderers (Gozo) 23.1.14, Xewkija Tigers (Gozo) 9.14*
Honours: Malta (40 caps) 2002-12, Maltese golden boot and footballer of the year 2006-07, Maltese league champions (2004), 2007, (2013), AME Cup winners 2013, Gozo League champions 2015

In a season of players of many nationalities appearing at Spotland, Daniel contributed several countries on his own, being of Yugoslavian Serb descent, born in Libya and playing numerous games for Malta. He figured for most of the top Maltese sides such as Sliema Wanderers and Floriana – several of them on multiple occasions – and in 2007 was the Maltese player of the year and golden boot winner (with 31 goals in 28 games) as minnows Marsaxlokk won their Premier League title for the first time. He also played in Hungary, Bulgaria and Italy (where he partnered Paulo di Canio at fourth tier Cisco Roma) before, perhaps surprisingly, moving to Barnsley. He had a decent goals return in his 18 months there and after a year at Sheffield United joined Blackpool for a sizeable fee. Chris Beech (and assistant Ryan Kidd, who had worked with him at Barnsley) borrowed him

in January 2012 and he scored on his debut, also having an assist for what would have been the winning goal, only for it to be controversially ruled out. Dale remained unable to get a win though and Daniel left after his month. Back in Malta, he still continued to add to his collection of full caps and was with Gozo league champions Xewkija in 2015.

Brett Ryan Ormerod 2011-12

Born: Blackburn 18.10.76 5'11" 11st4
Striker
FL Apps/Gls 4+1/1
Total Apps/Gls 4+1/1
Career: Norden HS (Rishton), Blackburn R. jnr, Accrington St. 1995, Blackpool 3.97 £50,000 [105+23/45], Southampton 7.12.01 £M1.75 [62+37/12], Leeds U. loan 23.9.04 [6/-], Wigan A. loan 18.3.05 [3+3/2], Preston NE 30.1.06 [37+25/13], Nottingham F. loan 7.3.08 [13/2], Oldham A. loan 14.10.08 [2+3/-], Blackpool 30.1.09 [50+37/15], Dale loan 4.1.12 to 23.2.12 [4+1/1], Wrexham 2.7.12 to 4.14 [55+19/12 Conf], Accrington St. trial 7.14, Padiham 9.14, Bamber Bridge 7.15 to 21.1.16
Honours: FA Cup final 2003, Division 3+ play-off winners 2001, (Championship promotion 2005), (League 1 promotion 2008), Championship play-off winners 2010, FA Trophy winners 2013, Conference Play-off final 2013

Another experienced striker from Chris Beech's former club Blackpool, Brett had a special place in Tangerines' folk law. He scored for them in all four divisions and figured in the play-off finals in 2001 (which took them out of the bottom division) and 2010 (which took them into the top flight). Indeed, in 2001 he scored twice in each leg of the semi-final and once in the final, while he netted the winner in the 2010 final. Blackpool had bought him for £50,000 after he netted 28 goals in 1996-97 for non-league Accrington, and, despite Brett missing a year due to a broken leg, sold him to Southampton for £1.75 million. He was never a regular for the Saints, but he did play in the 2003 FA Cup final when they lost to Arsenal. After several other moves, and another broken leg while with Preston, he reappeared at Blackpool in 2009, and took his overall tally to 81 goals in 249 games. After his brief loan at Spotland he played a few further games for Blackpool, then joined Wrexham who reached two finals in his first year, winning the FA Trophy but losing out in the Conference play-offs. In 2016, when playing for Bamber Bridge, he finally announced his retirement at the age of 39.

Kevin Kwaku Osei-Kuffour Amankwaah

2011-12
Born: Harrow 19.5.82
6'1" 11st9
Defender
FL Apps/Gls 15+1/0
Total Apps/Gls
15+1/0
Career: Bristol C. yts
1998, pro 16.6.00
[35+19/1], Torquay U.
loan 25.1.03 [6/-],
Cheltenham T. loan
16.8.03 [11+1/-],
Yeovil T. loan 3.2.05,
signed 24.3.05
[48+5/1], Swansea C. 4.8.06 £200,000 [23+6/-],
Swindon T. 17.7.08 [78+11/5], Dale trial 9.11,
Burton A. 30.9.11 [8/-], Dale 13.1.12 [15+1/-],
Exeter C. 2.7.12 [27+7/-], Northampton T. 29.7.13
[21/-], Salisbury C. 17.2.14 [14/- Conf], Sutton U.
9.14*
Honours: England youth international, Auto
Windscreens Shield final 2000, League 2
champions 2005, League 1 play-off final 2010,
National League South champions 2016

Kevin must have wondered what he had walked into when he came on as substitute for his Dale debut in a 5-1 home defeat by Stevenage. He did subsequently help steady the defence for a while, five games resulting in only two goals against before Kevin was injured (as was goalkeeper Kurucz in the next game), and by the time he came back Dale were on the brink of the drop. He had made his debut for Bristol City when he was 17, but his progress was interrupted by injuries in a car crash in 2002. It was only with Yeovil three years later that he re-established himself, helping them clinch the League 2 title. Sold to Swansea, he was a regular for one season, but did not play at all in the league when they were promoted in 2008. He appeared in nearly every game when Swindon reached the play-off final two years later, playing over 100 games for them in total. After his short term contract at Spotland ended, he had two further seasons in the FL then continued his career at Conference level, winning promotion with Sutton in 2016. His mother Rose represented Ghana in the Commonwealth Games, winning bronze in the relay.

Godwin Olorunfemi Ebenmosi Abadaki

2010-14
Born: Kwara,
Nigeria 12.10.93
5'11" 12st4
Striker
FL Apps/Goals
+2/0 Total
Apps/Gls +2/0
Career: Newall
Green HS
(Wythenshawe),
Dale jnr 2008, sch
7.10, pro 8.11 to
5.14 [+2/-], Hyde
U. loan 2.12,
Huddersfield T.
loan 19.9.12 to 5.13,
Southport loan
22.11.13 [2+1/- Conf], Stalybridge Celtic loan 1.14,
Workington loan 24.3.14, Northwich Victoria
cs.14, Ashton U. cs.15, Mossley 1.16*
Honours: Manchester Schoolboys, Greater
Manchester Schools, ESFA under-16 Trophy
winners 2010, Youth Alliance champions 2011,
(Conference North champions 2012)

Godwin joined Dale's Centre of Excellence in 2008 and scored his first goal for the youth team when still only 14. He scored the winner for GM Schools in the ESFA trophy final against Suffolk and in 2010-11 was Dale's leading scorer when they won the Youth Alliance. He made two substitute appearances for the first team while his youth team boss Chris Beech was in caretaker charge but was subsequently loaned out to Conference North winners Hyde. He spent most of the following term on a youth loan to Huddersfield, where Steve Eyre was coach, and had several further loan spells before his Dale contract ended in 2014. Godwin's brother Osebi was a member of Blackburn's academy and played non-league football.

Kevin Finbarr Long 2011-12

Born: Cork,
Ireland 18.8.90
6'3" 13st1
Central
defender
FL Apps/Gls
16/0 Total
Apps/Gls 16/0
Career: Cork C.
jnr 2007, pro
1.08, Burnley
25.1.10
£100,000
[18+4/-]*,
Accrington St.
loan 15.10.10
and 31.1.11

[11+4/-], Accrington St. loan 5.8.11 [24/4], Dale loan 27.1.12 to 4.12 [16/-], Portsmouth loan 18.8.12 [5/-], Barnsley loan 11.15 [11/2], Milton Keynes Dons loan 3.16 [2/-]
Honours: Republic of Ireland under-21s squad 2009-2012, Championship promotion 2014, (champions 2016)

John Coleman's first signing for Rochdale as he attempted to rescue their dire season, Kevin had previously played for him at Accrington – and been sent off on his debut for a foul on Adam Le Fondre (then at Rotherham). With him partnering Kevin Amankwaah in the back four, Dale conceded only twice in five games before Amankwaah was injured, and though Kevin continued to figure regularly, Dale subsequently failed to build on this. He finally made his debut for Burnley the following term and played a few games when they were promoted but had an exceptionally short Premier League career, coming on as an early substitute against Newcastle, but then being injured himself 20 minutes later. While on loan at Barnsley in 2016, he scored the final goal in Dale's 6-1 defeat at Oakwell.

Michael Symes 2011-12

Born: Great Yarmouth 31.10.83 6'3" 12st4
Striker
FL Apps/Gls 14+1/4
Total Apps/Gls 14+1/4
Career: Maricourt HS (Liverpool), Everton jnr yts 1999, pro 13.2.02, Crewe A. loan 24.3.04 [1+3/1], Bradford C. 6.8.04 [6+9/3], Macclesfield T. loan 1.7.05, Stockport Co. loan 31.1.06 [+1/-], Shrewsbury T. loan 4.8.06, signed 30.8.06
[33+29/14], Macclesfield T. loan 11.1.08 [10+4/1], Bournemouth loan 13.11.08 [3+2/-], Accrington St. loan 20.3.09 [7/1], Accrington St. 1.7.09 [39+2/13], Bournemouth 4.6.10 [23+14/11], Dale loan 31.1.12 to 6.5.12 [14+1/4], Leyton Orient 28.6.12 [5+8/1], Burton A. loan 31.1.13 [14+1/4], Burton A. 29.6.13 to 5.14 [7+6/2]. Southport 1.4.15 to cs.15 [+2/- Conf]
Honours: Youth Cup final 2002, League 2 play-off final 2007

Despite his birthplace, Michael was brought up in Liverpool and remarkably went to the same school as Stephen Darby and Joe Rafferty (q.v.). He was in Everton's Youth Cup final team with Wayne Rooney but a succession of operations restricted his progress. He first made an impression at Shrewsbury, scoring 13 times as they made it to the play-off final in his initial season, but was little used in the next two campaigns. Having been on loan at Accrington, he signed for them in 2009 and bagged a personal best 19 goals. He was in and out of the Bournemouth side for two years before John Coleman made him the second of a steadily increasing roster of ex-Stanley players at Spotland. By far his best game in a Dale shirt saw him grab a hat-trick against Oldham, but he was otherwise unable to affect their inexorable slide back into League 2. He was with Burton when they reached the play-offs in successive seasons but again suffered badly with injuries.

Philip Lee (Phil) Edwards 2011-12, 2012-13

Born: Bootle 8.11.85
5'10" 11st9
Defender
FL Apps/Gls 44+3/0
Total Apps/Gls 49+3/0
Career: Wigan A. yts 2002, pro 9.04, Morecambe loan 9.9.04 [+1/- Conf], Accrington St. loan 18.10.05, signed 12.1.06 [27/- Conf, 193+7/23], Stevenage B. 27.6.11 [11+11/-], Dale loan 3.12 to 4.12
[1+2/-], Dale 8.12 [43+1/-], Burton A. 29.6.13 [130+2/8]*
Honours: Conference champions 2006, League 2 play-off final 2014, League 2 champions 2015, League 1 promotion 2016

A stalwart for Accrington as they gained promotion to the league and consolidated in League 2, Phil played 257 games for them in all, and was twice an everpresent. Playing all across the back four, he also became the side's penalty taker, netting 22 goals in his last two seasons, top scoring when Stanley made the play-offs. After a brief stint at Stevenage he was borrowed by his old Accrington boss John Coleman in a last effort to shore up Dale's defence as they struggled against relegation. Relacing the injured Stephen Derby at right back, he lasted only one game before a knee injury ruled him out for the season. Returning to Spotland for the following campaign, he was almost everpresent this time, mostly playing in central defence, before joining Burton who won the League 2 title in 2015. Phil was then an everpresent as the Brewers remarkably gained promotion to the Championship the following year.

Neill Byrne   2011-13

Born: Portmarnock, Ireland 2.2.93 6'4" 13st3
Central defender
FL Apps/Gls 2+1/0
Total Apps/Gls 2+2/0
Career: Portmarnock, Belverdere, Nottingham F. jnr 2007, sch 2009, Leyton Orient trial 11.11, Dale trial 12.11, signed 1.1.12 [2+1/-], Barrow loan 11.12, [1/- Conf], Southport loan 2.13 [10/2 Conf], AFC Telford U. 21.6.13 [38/4 Conf], Macclesfield T. 6.8.15 [25+2/2 Conf]*
Honours: Republic of Ireland under-19s (3 caps) 2011, Conference North champions 2014

Although captaining the Irish at under-19 level while on Forest's books, Neill's only FL appearances came with Dale, starting one game at right back and one in central defence just before Dale's relegation was confirmed (they conceded eight times in the two games). Loaned out twice the following term, he eventually joined AFC Telford who were promoted to the Conference in his first season. When they were relegated again, he signed for Macclesfield.

Sean Joseph McConville   2011-12

Born: Liverpool 6.3.89 5'11" 11st7
Midfield
FL Apps/Gls 2+2/0
Total Apps/Gls 2+2/0
Career: Burscough, Skelmersdale U. 2008, Stockport Co. trial 2008, Accrington St. 2.2.09 [53+23/14], Stockport Co. 7.11 [21+2/4 Conf], Dale loan 3.12 to 4.12 [2+2/-], Dale trial 7.12, Barrow 14.9.12 [14+11/- Conf], Stalybridge Celtic 9.7.13, Chester 12.5.14 [35+7/9 Conf], Accrington St. 24.6.15 £ [40+2/5]*

Sean was a regular goalscorer for Skelmersdale (playing alongside George Donnelly, q.v.) before starting his FL career at John Coleman's Accrington, generally playing on the left flank. After netting 13 goals in 43 games in 2010-11 when Stanley reached the play-offs (where he was sent off), he decided to move to Stockport in the Conference. After a change in manager at Edgeley Park, he was then recruited by Coleman and assistant Jimmy Bell (Sean's uncle) for a month at the tail end of Dale's relegation from League 1. He also trialled at Spotland over the summer, figuring in several friendlies, but then spent three years back in the Conference, latterly with Chester, before John Coleman bought him for Accrington again and he was a regular in the side that missed promotion on the final day in 2016.

Samuel Joseph (Sam) Minihan   2010-13

Born: Rochdale 16.2.94 6'1" 11st9
Right back
FL Apps/Gls 1/0
Total Apps/Gls 1/0
Career: Bacup & Rawtenstall GS, Dale sch 7.10, pro 1.5.12 to 10.5.13 [1/-], Droylsden 10.12 loan, Loughborough University FC 10.13, Worcester C. 7.15, Stockport Co. 6.16*
Honours: Alliance League (North West) champions 2011

Sam joined Dale as a scholar in 2010 and made his FL debut at right back in April 2012, winning the man of the match award as Dale came from behind to beat Exeter 3-2 and keep their hopes of League 1 survival alive for another week. Also winner of the young player of the season award, he turned pro in the summer but was included in the first team squad only once more before leaving to go to university, captaining Loughborough's Midland League side which played Manchester United's youth team in a friendly. In 2015, along with another ex-Dale man Wayne Thomas, he was in the Worcester City side which met Sheffield United in the FA Cup.

Simon John Hackney   2011-12

Born: Manchester 5.2.84 5'8" 10st3
Winger
FL Apps/Gls 1+1/0 Total Apps/Gls 1+1/0
Career: Nantwich T. 2002, Woodley Sports 6.03, Carlisle U. 16.2.05 [+2/- Conf, 78+35/17], Colchester U. 26.1.09 £110,000 [20+15/1], Morecambe loan 8.3.10 [8/1], Oxford U. loan 1.11 [2+11/-], Dale 24.6.11 [1+1/-], Wrexham trial 5.7.12, FC Halifax T.

14.9.12, Hereford U. 7.12.12 [1/- Conf], Stockport Co. n/c 2.13 [2+8/- Conf], Ashton U. 4.9.13, Northwich Victoria 21.9.13, Trafford 1.12.13 to c.12.14
Honours: Conference promotion 2005, League 2 champions 2006, FL Trophy final 2006, (Conference North promotion 2013)

Simon made a mark with Carlisle when they won successive promotions and had a useful scoring rate for a winger, netting eight times in 45 games in 2007-08. Sold to Colchester for a sizeable fee, despite a promising start he started only 15 league games in two and a half seasons. Signed by Steve Eyre in the summer of 2011, he spent almost the entire season out injured, figuring in just the last two games – remarkably the 44th player used during the season (considerably more than the number of points collected).

Matthew Joe (Matty) Pearson   2012-13

Born: Keighley 3.8.93
6'3" 11st5
Right back
FL Apps/Gls 8+1/0
Total Apps/Gls 11+2/0
Career: Blackburn R. jnr, sch 2010, pro 8.11, Lincoln C. loan 1.12, Dale 2.7.12 [8+1/-], FC Halifax T. loan 1.3.13, FC Halifax T. 30.6.13 [79+5/5 Conf], Accrington St. 28.5.15 [46/3]*
Honours: England under-18s 2010, England 'C' (10 caps) 2014, Conference North play-off winners 2013

Despite training with Blackburn from the age of nine, and becoming an England youth international, Matty never made the first team and played his first senior game in the FA Trophy while on loan at Lincoln. Signed by John Coleman as he planned for Dale's campaign back in League 2, Matty played only a few games at right back before losing out to Joe Rafferty. After Keith Hill took over, Matty went on loan to Halifax and appeared in their Conference North play-off final victory before signing permanently. A regular for two seasons, often figuring in midfield rather than defence, he played ten times for England 'C', captaining them in his last game, against the Irish under-21s. Coleman gave him a second chance in the FL in 2015, signing him for Accrington, and he was everpresent as Stanley missed out on promotion on the final day.

Kevin McIntyre   2012-13

Born: Liverpool
23.12.77 5'11" 11st2
Left back
FL Apps/Gls 37+1/1
Total Apps/Gls 42+1/1
Career: Tranmere R. yts 1995, pro 6.11.96 [+2/-], Doncaster R. loan 14.8.98 [10/- Conf], Barrow loan 27.11.98 [5/- Conf], Doncaster R. 19.1.99 [85+2/6 Conf], Chester C. 15.5.02 [79+1/2 Conf, 9+1/-], Macclesfield T. 24.12.04 [130+4/16], Shrewsbury T. 4.1.08 £50,000 [108+16/4], Accrington St. 15.7.11 [44+1/2], Dale 1.7.12 [37+1/1], Chester 21.5.13 [29+2/- Conf], Gap Connah's Quay Nomads 24.7.14*
Honours: England semi-professional international (4 caps), Conference League Cup winners 1999, 2000, Conference champions 2004, League 2 play-off final 2009

After a very brief introduction to the game at Tranmere, Kevin spent several seasons as a regular in the Conference (despite being sent off on his Doncaster debut and collecting 14 yellows and two red cards in 32 games in 1999-2000). Generally playing at left back, though sometimes as a defensive midfielder, he also played for the England semi-pro side. He missed all of 2001-02 through injury before joining Chester City and assisting them to promotion back to the FL in his second season. He played well over 100 times for both Macclesfield, where he was top scorer in 2006-07 with nine penalties and a free kick, and Shrewsbury, breaking his leg in January 2009 but coming back in time to score in the Shrews' play-off semi-final. John Coleman signed him for Accrington in 2011 and then for Dale a year later. Though 34, Kevin was the regular left back for most of his year at Spotland before returning to the new version of Chester, back in the Conference.

Peter Joseph Cavanagh   2012-14

Born: Bootle 14.10.81
5'9" 11st9
Midfield
FL Apps/Gls 47+4/2
Total Apps/Gls 52+4/2
Career: Savio Catholic HS (Bootle), Liverpool jnr, yts 2000, Accrington St. 9.01 to 2009 [88+6/8 Conf, 73+1/6]. Fleetwood 6.10 [38+1/- Conf], Dale 8.6.12 [47+4/2], Altrincham 14.8.14 (also

Liverpool junior coach 9.14), Southport player-coach 5.15. Everton academy coach 2.7.15*
Honours: England 'C' 2004, NPL Cup winners 2002, Lancashire FA Challenge Trophy winners 2002, NPL champions 2003, Conference champions 2006, 2012, League 2 promotion 2014

Attending the same school as Jamie Carragher, Peter was with Livepool from the age of ten. He joined Accrington when they were still in the Northern Premier League and was almost immediately made captain at the age of just 20 as they lifted the NPL Cup and the Lancashire FA Trophy. In all, he was with them for eight years as they made their way up to the FL under John Coleman, making a total of 226 appearances and scoring 22 goals, originally as a right back and later from midfield. A breach of betting rules led to him being suspended by the FA for the whole of 2009-10. Returning to the game with Fleetwood when they, too, gained promotion to the league, he then rejoined John Coleman at Spotland as Dale initially challenged towards the top of League 2 in 2012. Even after Coleman was replaced by the returning Keith Hill, Peter retained his place in midfield and was an important part of the squad that gained promotion, despite lengthy spells out injured. He then returned to the non-league game before becoming a full-time academy coach at Everton.

Ryan Christopher Edwards 2012-13

Born: Liverpool 7.10.93 6'3" 13st12
Centre back
FL Apps/Gls 25+1/0 Total Apps/Gls 28+1/0
Career: Blackburn R. sch 2010, pro 5.12, Dale loan 2.7.12 to 1.13 [25+1/-], Fleetwood T. loan 21.2.13 [9/-], Chesterfield loan 24.7.13 [4+1/-], Tranmere R. loan 28.11.13, Morecambe loan 21.3.14 [8+1/-], Morecambe 20.5.14 [66+2/-]*
Honours: Youth Cup final 2012, FA Academy under-18 league Group C winners 2012, Academy National Cup final 2012, (League 2 champions 2014)

Ryan was captain of Blackburn's academy side that reached the Academy National and FA Youth Cup finals in 2012, scoring one of the goals in the Youth Cup semi-final. Borrowed by Dale for the first half of the following term, he was the third Edwards on the staff along with centre back partner Phil and reserve 'keeper Matty. He was a first choice throughout his stint at the club and then had shorter loan spells with other lower league sides before signing permanently for Morecambe in 2014.

George John Donnelly 2012-15

Born: Liverpool 28.5.88
6'2" 13st
Striker
FL Apps/Gls 43+35/13 Total Apps/Gls 48+38/13
Career: Brookfield HS (Kirkby), Liverpool jnr 2004, Skelmersdale U. 2007, Plymouth A. 3.09 [+2/-], Luton T. loan 28.8.09 [+4/-Conf], Stockport Co. loan 29.1.10 [16+3/4], Stockport Co. loan 7.10 [23/8], Fleetwood T. 6.1.11 £50,000 [15+10/5 Conf], Macclesfield T. loan 9.9.11, signed 1.1.12 £ [28/6], Dale 6.12 £ [43+35/13], Tranmere R. 9.14 £ [4+7/-], Southport loan 30.1.15 [14+2/1 Conf], Skelmersdale U. 28.8.15*
Honours: England 'C' 2011, (Conference champions 2012), League 2 promotion 2014

George worked in a warehouse while scoring 36 goals in only 45 games for Skelmersdale. Signed by Plymouth he only made a couple of substitute appearances but had two useful spells at Stockport. He was signed by Fleetwood for their record fee, but had moved on before they won promotion to the league. He was the subject of a bid by Stockport after the chairman had asked fans on twitter to vote for whether they would prefer to sign George or Halifax's Jamie Vardy (the future England international!) but was sold to Macclesfield instead. Soon on the move again he was bought by Dale in 2012. He figured in 48 games in his first season, though a number were from the bench. Appearing less frequently thereafter, he nevertheless scored on the opening and closing days of Dale's promotion campaign. He was sold to Tranmere just after the start of 2014-15 but was back at his original club Skelmersdale by the start of the following campaign.

Bamberdele Osusegun (Dele) Adebola
2012-13

Born: Lagos, Nigeria 23.6.75
6'3" 12st8
Striker
FL Apps/Gls 22+4/6 Total Apps/Gls 25+4/6
Career: Crewe A. yts 1992, pro 21.6.93 [98+26/39], Bangor C. loan 1993-94, Northwich Victoria loan 1993-94 [18/7 Conf], Birmingham C. 6.2.98 £1M [86+43/31], Oldham A.loan 20.3.02 [5/-], Crystal Palace 15.8.02 [32+7/5], Coventry C. 2.7.03 [115+48/31], Burnley loan 25.3.04 [+3/1], Bradford C. loan 13.8.04 [14+1/3], Bristol C. 30.1.08 [48+8/16], Nottingham F. 30.6.09 [17+45/5], Hull C. 29.6.11 [2+8/-], Notts Co. loan 20.3.12 [3+3/1], Dale 7.8.12 [22+4/6], Wrexham loan 2.13 [10+3/2 Conf], Rushall Olympic 8.13 to cs.15
Honours: Division 2+ play-off winners 1997, League Cup final 2001, Championship play-off final 2008, Conference play-off final 2013, Staffordshire Senior Cup winners 2014

Brought up in Liverpool, Dele turned down the chance of a YTS place at Anfield as he was in the same year group as Robbie Fowler and reasoned that he was unlikely to get in the team ahead of him. Making his debut at 17, he played 150 times for Crewe, scoring nearly 50 goals – 16 of them when Crewe were promoted - before being transferred to Birmingham for £1 million. Figuring in their League Cup Final penalty shoot-out defeat by Liverpool, the big target man again passed 150 appearances and 40 goals before moving on. He subsequently had five seasons with Coventry playing 180 times, his last game being their Championship play-off final defeat in 2008. After shorter stints with other clubs, almost all in the second tier, Dele arrived at Spotland just as the 2012-13 season got underway. He played regularly as Dale faded after a promising start, but when Keith Hill replaced John Coleman, Dele was loaned to Wrexham (where he added another play-off final appearance). He totalled 741 appearances for his FL clubs (a remarkable 226 of them from the bench), scoring 168 goals, but still hadn't finished with the game and was figuring with Rushall Olympic when almost 40. Back in 1998, he had been selected for N. Ireland, but was injured, and was also included in Nigeria's preliminary World Cup squad the same year, and their African Cup of Nations squad two years later.

Raymond Francis (Ray) Putterill 2012-13

Born: Wirrall 3.2.89
5'8" 12st2
Winger
FL Apps/Gls 1+17/1
Total Apps/Gls 3+19/2
Career: Liverpool jnr, sch 2005, pro cs.07, Halewood T. 10.09, Accrington St. 7.10 to cs.11 [11+13/-]. Southport 2.3.12, Vauxhall Motors loan 3.12, Dale n/c 9.8.12 [1+17/1], Hyde U. 22.1.13 [+1/- Conf], Waterloo Dock 28.2.13, Formby cs.13, Waterloo Dock 2014, Marine 22.2.16
Honours: England Schoolboys, England under-16s 2004, FA Youth Cup winners 2007

A member of their 2007 Youth Cup winning side (scoring in the penalty shoot out), Ray played in pre-season games for Liverpool and got as far as being on the bench in a League Cup game despite a horrendous catalogue of injuries including a fractured spine playing for England schoolboys and a total of seven operations. Even after joining Accrington his luck did not improve as Stanley were removed from the JPT for playing him while he should have been serving a six week suspension from his time at Halewood. He was also sent off in his second (and last) game for Southport. John Coleman gave him another chance at Spotland and he appeared regularly from the bench, mainly on the left flank, until leaving the club the same week as his manager and soon returning to non-league football on Merseyside.

Ian Thomas William Craney 2012-13

Born Liverpool 21.7.82
5'10" 12st7
Midfield
FL Apps/Gls +6/0
Total Apps/Gls 1+8/0
Career: Everton jnr 1995, yts 1999, Altrincham 2001, Accrington St. 22.6.04 £17,500 [68+9/23 Conf, 18/5], Swansea C. loan 23.9.06, signed £150,000 9.1.07 [24+4/-], Accrington St. loan 28.9.07, signed £25,000 1.08 [36/8], Huddersfield T. 8.08 £ [23+11/5], Morecambe loan 22.7.09 [16/2], Fleetwood T. cs. 10 [19/3 Conf], Accrington St. loan 25.11.10, signed 31.1.11

[29+15/8], Dale n/c 8.12 to 1.13 [+6/-], AFC Telford 5.2.13 [10+1/1 Conf], Stockport Co. 31.5.13, Stafford R. loan 17.1.14, Conwy Borough 7.7.14 to cs.15
Honours: England National Game XI 2005 (7 caps), Conference champions 2006, (League 1 champions 2008)

Ian was yet another former Accrington player recruited for Dale by John Coleman. He had originally made a mark with well over 100 games at Altrincham as a goal scoring midfielder, before joining Stanley for their last two seasons in the Conference. He also figured for the England non-league side. Soon after Stanley reached the FL he was sold to League 1 Swansea for a sizeable fee. Returning to Accrington after only one league game in 2007-08, they sold him again, to Huddersfield. A third spell at Accrington ended in 2012 and his old boss offered him a short term contract at Spotland. An almost permanent substitute, he started only in the JPT and left for non-league football in the January.

Craig Curran   2012-13

Born: Liverpool 23.9.89 5'9" 11st9
Striker
FL Apps/Gls +4/0
Total Apps/Gls 1+5/0
Career: Liverpool Blue Coat School, Tranmere R. sch 2005, pro 29.8.06 [48+49/14], Carlisle cs.10 [38+19/8], Morecambe loan 22.3.12 [6+1/1], Dale 8.12 [+4/-], Chester loan 9.11.12, Limerick loan 2.13, signed 1.7.13, Nuneaton T. 29.8.14 [11+2/1 Conf], Ross County 2.1.15 [32+6/12 ScL]*
Honours: (Conference North champions 2013), Johnstone's Paint Trophy winners 2011

Craig scored with his first touch at Prenton Park in April 2007 and netted a treble against Brentford in the first 36 minutes a month later, beating the legendary Dixie Dean's record as Tranmere's youngest ever hat-trick scorer. He never became a regular starter, though – he came on as substitute 34 times in 2007-08 - and following a spell at Carlisle was a free agent when picked up by Dale five years later. Like Ian Craney used only from the bench in league games, when he did start in the JPT he was sent off. Loaned to Chester in the Conference North, he scored a hat-trick when coming on as substitute, but his only further involvement at Spotland was as an unused sub just after Keith Hill's return. He later figured both in

Ireland and Scotland, remarkably leaving the Conference's bottom side to play in the Scottish Premier League (one of seven former Dale players in the SPL). Craig missed the second half of 2015-16 following a serious concussion.

Benjamin James (Ben) Smith   2012-13

Born: Whitley Bay 5.9.86
6'1" 12st11
Goalkeeper
FL Apps +0
Total Apps 2
Career: Whitley Bay HS, Newcastle U. sch 2004, Middlesbrough loan 10.05, Leeds U. trial 12.05, Stockport Co. n/c 23.3.06, Doncaster R. 4.8.06 [14+1], Lincoln C. loan 11.07 [9], Morecambe loan 16.10.09 [3], Shrewsbury T. 29.7.10 [36], Dale n/c 10.8.12 to 1.13, Southport 21.3.13 [2 Conf], Stevenage B. n/c 8.13
Honours: (Johnstone's Paint Trophy winners 2007), (League 1 play-off winners 2008), League 2 promotion 2012

The son of Simon Smith, who kept goal for Gateshead in a mammoth 501 games before becoming the Newcastle and England under-19 goalkeeping coach, Ben joined the Magpies as a scholar but did not make his senior debut until signing for Doncaster (twice being unused substitute in Wembley finals). He had a couple of seasons at Shrewsbury and was signed by Dale as backup to Josh Lillis in 2012, playng in two Johnstone's Paint Trophy games. He subsequently opened a health spa back in Shrewsbury.

Rhys Gordon Bennett   2012-16

Born: Manchester 1.9.91 6'4" 14st5
Defender/midfield
FL Apps/Gls 89+21/6
Total Apps/Gls 104+25/7
Career: Bolton School, Radcliffe Borough 2007, Bolton W. jnr 2008, pro 2009, Falkirk loan 6.7.11 [8+10/- ScL], Dale 1.7.12 [89+21/6] Mansfield T. 6.16*
Honours: (Ramsdens Cup winners 2012),

League 2 promotion 2014, Lancashire Senior Cup final 2015

Rhys was with Bolton Wanderers from junior level, but made his first senior appearances for Falkirk, scoring on his debut at Brechin in the Ramsdens Cup, which Falkirk went on to win. He signed for Dale in 2012 and made his debut in midfield when Peter Cavanagh was injured. Returning to his previous defensive role, either at centre back or right back, he was a regular for the rest of the season. He was less used in the promotion campaign, though he did play in the crucial end of season victories over Bristol Rovers and Cheltenham. Up in League 1, he reclaimed a more regular place, again playing in several positions, but was little used in 2015-16 before being released.

Joseph Gerard (Joe) Rafferty 2012-16*

Born: Liverpool 6.10.93 6'0" 11st11
Right back
FL Apps/Gls 108+6/2* Total Apps/Gls 119+3/3*
Career: Marincourt HS, Liverpool jnr, sch 2010, Dale 2.7.12 [108+6/2]*
Honours: Republic of Ireland under-18s (2 caps) 2010, under-19s 2011, League 2 promotion 2014

Joe had been a junior with Liverpool, captaining their under-18s side and also featuring for the Republic at youth level, and was the tenth Liverpudlian signed by fellow 'scousers' John Coleman and Jimmy Bell in the summer of 2012. In the matchday squad for virtually every game, he started at right back in about half the matches in his first season, when he was only 19, and became the usual choice during the promotion campaign. Although challenged for the right back slot by first Rhys Bennett and then Andy Cannon, Joe continued as the most regular choice as Dale established themselves in League 1 and was also sometimes chosen in midfield.

Luke David Watson 2010-13
Born: Knowsley 30.7.94
Midfield
FL Apps/Gls +0/0 Total Apps/Gls +0/0
Career: Dale jnr 2009, sch 2010, pro 1.5.12 to cs.13, Droylsden loan 1.3.13
Honours: Youth Alliance (North West) champions 2011

Coming through Dale's junior sides, playing regularly when only 15, Luke earned a professional contract at the end of his scholarship. He played in the 2012 pre-season friendlies, but missed the start of the campaign injured. Rumoured to be in contention for international selection by Malta, his one appearance in Dale's match day squad for a league game came against Morecambe in the October and he was later loaned to Droylsden, bottom of the Conference North.

Joel Alexander Logan 2011-16

Born: Manchester 25.1.95 5'11" 11st
Winger
FL Apps/Gls 4+9/0
Total Apps/Gls 5+10/0
Career: Dale sch 2011, pro 4.13 to 5.16 [4+9/-], Southport loan 22.11.13 [4/- Conf], Stalybridge Celtic loan 27.3.14, Carlisle U. trial 29.6.15, Wrexham loan 8.15 [+3/- Conf]
Honours: Lancashire YC winners 2013

Joel joined Dale as a scholar and scored in their Lancashire Youth Cup final success, also playing in the Lancashire Senior Cup semi-final the same week. His first senior involvement was as substitute at Plymouth in October 2012 and he was substitute several times before the end of the season. He didn't play at all the following season, though, spending most of his time out on loan. He figured in the League Cup in August 2014, but remarkably - not even having been on the bench for some time - his first start came in the FA Cup victory over Notts Forest. He finally made his first league start the following month but was placed on the transfer list at the end of the season and did not figure thereafter.

Terence Michael (Terry) Gornell 2012-13

Born: Liverpool 16.12.89 5'11" 12st4
Striker
FL Apps/Gls 16+3/5
Total Apps/Gls 16+3/5
Career: Tranmere R. jnr 2007, pro 2.7.08 [25+15/3], Accrington St. loan 19.9.08 [10+1/4], Accrington St. 27.8.10 [40/13], Shrewsbury T. 4.7.11 £ [37+16/9], Dale loan 8.11.12, signed 10.1.13

[16+3/5], Cheltenham T. 12.7.13 [39+20/6],
Accrington St. 2.2.15 [22+13/7]*
Honours: League 2 promotion 2012

John Coleman's final signing for Rochdale, Terry was another who had played for Coleman at Accrington, where he had netted 13 times in the run to the play-offs in 2010-11. Initially on loan from Shrewsbury, he signed for an undisclosed fee and netted twice against Exeter – unfortunately when Dale were already three goals down – before being sent off. On his return from suspension he scored two more in a 4-2 win at Bradford but did not manage any further goals before being released. In 2015 he returned to Acrington and figured in the side which missed promotion on goal difference the following year.

Stephen Philip (Steve) Collis 2012-16*
Born: Harrow 18.3.81 6'2" 13st
Goalkeeper
FL Apps +0 Total Apps +0
Career: Barnet jnr 1998, pro 27.8.99, Nottingham F. 11.7.00, Yeovil T. 6.8.01 [2 Conf, 41+2], Tiverton loan 2002-03, Aldershot loan 2002-03 [3 Conf], Southend U. 3.7.06 [20+1], Crewe A. 1.7.08 [19], Bristol C. 25.1.10, Torquay U. loan 6.5.10 [1], Peterborough U. 6.8.10, Northampton T. loan 8.3.11 [3+1], Macclesfield T. 23.9.11, Buxton cs.12, Dale n/c 29.1.13, player-coach cs.13*
Honours: Conference champions 2003, League 2 champions 2005

Steve joined Yeovil before they gained promotion to the FL and remained with them for another three seasons as they went on to reach League 1. He was used as number two 'keeper for a couple of seasons each at Southend and Crewe, but hardly figured for any of his clubs from 2010 onwards. When Keith Hill wanted a second string goalkeeper in January 2013 he signed Steve on a short term contract. He was appointed goalkeeping coach that summer but retained his playing registration and continued to appear on the bench as necessary, also playing in pre-season games, and was again the regular substitute 'keeper in 2015-16.

Jamie Paul Allen 2012-16*

Born: Rochdale 29.1.95
5'11" 11st
Midfield
FL Apps/Gls 90+8/9*
Total Apps/Gls 98+12/9*
Career: Matthew Moss HS, Dale jnr, sch cs.11, pro 4.13 [90+8/9]*
Honours: Alliance League (North West) champions 2011, Lancashire YC

winners 2013, League 2 promotion 2014

Jamie started out with Dale at the age of eight and was already in the youth team before becoming a scholar. Unused substitute in Keith Hill's second game back, he was in the first team squad a few times towards the end of 2012-13, also skippering the Lancashire Youth Cup winning side and appearing in the Lancashire Senior Cup semi-final. He was short listed for League 2 apprentice of the year. Elevated to the senior squad for the new season, he made his debut in the JPT and started in midfield in the following league game. Quickly establishing himself during Dale's run to promotion he was voted League 2 player of the month in March 2014. Oddly enough he also became their first player to score against all three Devon clubs. Again central to Dale's successful return to the third tier, when they finished in a best ever 8th position, he was appointed skipper in 2015 when still only 20, leading the side to their highest points tally in League 1.

Michael Charles Rose 2012-16

Born: Salford 28.7.82 5'11" 11st2
Left back/midfield
FL Apps/Gls 101+17/8 Total Apps/Gls 112+20/9
Career: Swinton HS, Manchester U. jnr, yts, pro 9.9.99, Chester C. 7.7.01 [33+1/4 Conf], Hereford U. 4.7.02 [78+1/6 Conf], Yeovil T. 14.5.04 [38+4/1], Cheltenham T. loan 25.8.05 [3/-], Scunthorpe U. loan 2.1.06 [15/-], Stockport Co. 8.7.06 [94+11/8], Norwich C. loan 29.1.10 [11+1/1], Swindon T. 30.6.10 [27+8/3], Colchester U. 16.5.11 [34+2/2], Dale 14.2.13 to 5.16 [101+17/8]
Honours: England 'C' 2002 to 2003 (4 caps), League 2 champions 2005, play-off winners 2008, promotion (2006), 2014, League 1 champions 2010, PFA League 2 team of the year 2005, 2014

Signed by Keith Hill soon after he returned to the club, Michael had recently been released by Colchester. He had originally spent three years at Conference level, figuring for Chester with his brother Stephen, and appeared for England 'C'. He joined Yeovil the year they won League 2 and was voted into the PFA team of the year. Another member of Stockport's side from the 2008 Wembley defeat of Dale, he was still with County when they went into administration and had the odd experience of being loaned out by the bottom side in the league to League 1 champions Norwich. He was a regular member of Dale's promotion side in 2014, missing only four games playing either in his usual position at left back or in midfield, and was again voted into the PFA select side. Despite a couple of lengthy spells out of the side, he continued to be an important member of the side - not least for his expertise at free kicks - in either of his two roles, as Dale made their mark in League 1, before being released when he was nearly 34. As a youngster, Michael had been Greater Manchester under-16 judo champion.

Richard Glyn (Ritchie) Jones   2012-13

Born: Manchester 26.9.86 6'0" 11st Midfield
FL Apps/Gls 2+1/0
Total Apps/Gls 2+1/0
Career: Manchester U. sch 2003, pro 4.11.04, Royal Antwerp (Belgium) loan 1.06, Colchester U. loan 27.10.06 [+6/-], Barnsley loan 12.2.07 [1+3/-], Yeovil T. loan 14.8.07 [7+4/-], Burnley trial 3.08, Hartlepool U. 23.7.08 [58+11/7], Oldham A. 7.7.10 [21+10/1], Bradford C. 13.7.11 [33+3/1], Dale n/c 20.2.13 [2+1/-], San Jose Earthquakes (USA) trial 13.6.13, Grimsby T. 11.9.13 [4+2/- Conf], Edmonton (Canada) 15.1.14*
Honours: England under-16s (6 caps) 2002, under-17s (7 caps) 2003, under-18s (9 caps) 2004, under-19s (11 caps) 2005, under-20s (1 cap) 2006, Nordic (under-17s) championship winners 2003, UEFA under-19s European championships final 2005, Milk Cup youth tournament winners 2003, Central League champions 2005, Premier Reserve League winners 2005, (League 2 promotion 2013)

With United from the age of nine, Ritchie was in their all-conquering reserve sides of 2005 and 2006 who won seven trophies. He also figured for England at all levels from under-16s to under-20s, scoring the winner when the under-17s won the Nordic tournament and playing in the European championships final for the under-19s. However, he made only five appearances for United's first team, all in cup ties, and in 2010 – having just moved from Hartlepool to Oldham - was cited by FA Director of Football Development Trevor Brooking as an example of upcoming English players not given a chance by top clubs. He figured in Bradford City's famous League Cup victory over Arsenal (though he actually had his penalty saved in the shoot-out), but was released only a month or so later and signed non-contract terms at Spotland. He made only three appearances though

and subsequently headed for soccer on the other side of the Atlantic.

Ian Henderson   2012-16*

Born: Bury St Edmunds 24.1.85 5'10" 10st10 Forward
FL Apps/Gls 137+3/49*
Total Apps/Gls 152+4/50*
Career: Methwold HS (Thetford), Norwich C. sch 2001, pro 3.2.03 [26+42/6], Rotherham U. loan 12.1.07 [18/1], Northampton T. 17.7.07 [9+17/1], Luton T. 2.1.09 [14+5/1], Ankaragucu (Turkey) cs.09, Colchester U. 7.1.10 [89+28/24], Dale 14.2.13 [137+3/49]*
Honours: England under-18s 2003 (3 caps), under-20s 2005, Lisbon Trophy winners 2003, Scotland under-19 squad (Milk Cup) 2003, Division 1+ champions 2004, League 2 promotion 2014

Ian followed his brother Tommy – who had been tragically killed in a car crash – to Norwich as a scholar and might have become their youngest ever debutant but remained on the bench. He did break into the first team in October 2002 and was chosen for England under-18s, scoring against Spain in the Lisbon Cup final. He was then called up for Scotland under-19s (qualifying through his father) and also figured for England under-20s. Though scoring four times in 20 games on the flanks when Norwich were promoted to the top flight, he never became a regular starter and moved on after five seasons. Even then, he still didn't really make a mark until reaching Colchester via a brief stint in Turkey. Despite being sent off (by Mike Dean) 45 seconds after coming on as substitute on his debut, he accumulated well over a hundred appearances, mostly playing in midfield, and was everpresent in 2011-12. Joining Dale in 2013, he played a big part in their promotion run the following year, missing only one game (a result of being sent off in the televised game against Bury). He scored 12 goals in partnership with Scott Hogan, including a brilliant volley in the cup victory over Championship side Leeds. Up in League 1, he partnered new found striker Matt Done and after Done was sold, Ian assumed the role of leading the attack, netting a remarkable 22 league goals – his first two full seasons at Spotland having produced more goals than his previous career total. Top scorer again in 2015-16 despite being red carded twice, he joined the small band of Dale players with 50 senior goals to their credit.

Wayne Junior Robert Thomas 2012-13

Born: Gloucester
17.5.79 5'11" 11st12
Defender
FL Apps/Gls 2/0
Total Apps/Gls 2/0
Career: The Crypt
School (Gloucester),
Torquay U. yts 1995,
pro 4.7.97 [89+34/5],
Stoke C. 5.6.00
£200,000 [188+1/7],
Burnley 4.7.05
[46+4/1],
Southampton 16.8.07 £1.2M [39+6/-], Stoke C.
trial 7.10, Doncaster R. 10.8.10 [17+4/-],
Atrometos Athens (Greece) 8.7.11, Veria (Greece)
21.8.12, Luton T. 4.2.13 [2/- Conf], Dale loan
28.3.13 [2/-], AFC Tamworth 9.8.13 [22/1 Conf],
(also Stoke C. junior coach 7.13 to 5.14), Worcester
C. 28.1.14 (also Broadheath JFC coach 9.14, Wigan
A. junior coach 10.14), New York Red Bulls
academy coach 3.15, Worcester C. 10.15 (also
Wigan A. academy coach 10.15)*
Honours: Division 3+ play-off final 1998, Division
2+ play-off winners 2002

Wayne made his Torquay debut as a 16 year old
YTS lad and went on to play 140 games, being
everpresent in 1998-99, before being sold to Stoke
for £200,000. Playing well over 200 games in all
competitions as a centre back or right back, Wayne
was Stoke's player of the year in 2002 when they
reached the new Division 1 via the play-offs.
Burnley signed him on a free and two years later
netted a huge profit when he moved to
Southampton for £1.2 million. Restricted by
injuries at St. Mary's – he missed the whole of
2008-09 - he did play in both legs of the JPT
southern section final in 2010, but missed the final
itself. He later spent a couple of years in Greek
football, returning to play a few games for Luton
before they loaned him to Dale at the end of 2012-
13 as defensive cover. In the event, he played in
just the final two games after Dale's survival had
been ensured. In 2014 he made the news when he
played virtually a whole game in goal for
Worcester City, when their 'keeper was injured in
the first minute, and kept a clean sheet. Doubling
up as a player and a junior coach, in 2015 he
obtained a coaching position with New York Red
Bulls.

Callum Camps 2012-16*

Born: Stockport
30.11.95 6'0" 11st11
Forward
FL Apps/Gls
34+12/6* Total
Apps/Gls 40+14/6*
Career: Dale sch 2012,
pro 28.9.13
[34+12/6]*
Honours: N. Ireland
under-18s 2012,
under-19s 2013,
under-20s squad in
Milk Cup 7.13, under-
21s (1 cap) 2015,
(League 2 promotion
2014)

Coming to notice when Dale reached the fourth
round of the Youth Cup, Callum was called up for
the N. Ireland under-18s while a scholar at
Spotland, qualifying via his grandmother. He came
on as substitute in two of Dale's last three games of
2012-13, also figuring for a reserve side in the
Lancashire Senior Cup semi-final. He only
appeared once, as a substitute in the FA Cup tie
against Sheffield Wednesday, the following term,
and oddly enough finally made his full debut in the
FA Cup victory over Forest in 2015, one of six
youth team products in the squad. After the cup
run, the Telegraph named him as one of the best
seven young players outside the Premier League.
He scored the opening goal of the following
campaign – the youngest player to do so for
Rochdale – and established himself in the senior
side, also making the Irish under-21s.

D'arcy Christopher O'Connor 2011-14

Born: Oldham
21.12.94 5'11"
Defender
FL Apps/Gls 1/0
Total Apps/Gls 1/0
Career: Failsworth
Dynamos, St Martin's
School, Hathershaw
College, Oldham A.
jnr, Dale jnr, sch
2011, pro 4.13 [1/-],
Hyde loan 23.11.13
[9+1/- Conf],
Workington loan
24.3.14, Hyde 8.14,
Ashton U. 3.15, Bacup
Borough cs.15*
Honours: Oldham Schools under-14s 2008-09,
under-15s 2009-10, Alliance League (North West)
champions 2011, Lancashire Youth Cup winners
2013

A Dale scholar, D'arcy played in the Lancs Senior Cup semi-final and Dale's winning Lancashire Youth Cup side in 2013, and made his FL debut in the final match of the season. He was given a professional contract, but almost immediately left the club, subsequently turning out for Hyde with whom he had spent time on loan.

Scott Tanser 2011-16*

Born: Blackpool 23.10.94
6'0" 10st3
Left back
FL Apps/Gls 33+5/1*
Total Apps/Gls 43+5/2*
Career: Foxhall Juniors, St Mary's Catholic College, Lytham Juniors, Blackpool jnr, Burnley jnr, Dale sch 2011, pro 4.13 [33+5/1]*
Honours: Blackpool Schools, Lancashire County Schools under-16s 2010-11, Lancashire Youth Cup winners 2013, (League 2 promotion 2014), Lancashire Senior Cup final 2015

Scott was another scholar to appear at the end of the 2012-13 season, coming on for D'arcy O'Connor against Plymouth and setting up the winner for fellow debutant Joe Bunney. He also scored a hat-trick from left back (two of them penalties) in the Lancashire Youth Cup final. Like several of the other youngsters, he then had to wait until 2014 for further involvement, excellent performances in pre-season being rewarded by a starting place at centre back before reverting to full back. He also figured in the Lancashire Cup final but injury cost him much of 2015-16, all his league appearances coming in October and November.

Joseph Elliott (Joe) Bunney 2012-16*

Born: Gorton, Manchester 26.9.93
6'2" 11st
Striker
FL Apps/Gls 36+37/15* Total Apps/Gls 40+40/15*
Career: Manchester C. jnr, Macclesfield T. jnr 2007 to 2009, Wright Robinson Sports College (Gorton), Myerscough College, Lancaster C. 2011-12, Kendall T. 2012, Northwich Victoria 29.11.12, Stockport Co.

trial 12.12 [+1/- Conf], Dale n/c 29.3.13, pro cs.13 [36+37/15]*
Honours: England Schools under-18s 2011-12, England Colleges under-19s 2012, League 2 promotion 2014

Joe's grandfather Allan Grafton was a Dale amateur and non-league player who played for England Schools in 1962. Joe did likewise in 2011 and also played for England while at College, where he was spotted by Rio Ferdinand for Nike's 'The Chance' global talent search. It was Dale who picked up on this and Joe had a dream start with the winning goal against Plymouth on the final day of 2012-13. Signing pro, he was in the Dale squad from the start of the following campaign and also scored on his full debut against Wycombe. He played up front with the goalscorers Hogan and Henderson in the famous FA Cup victory over Leeds and netted a crucial equaliser in the win at Bristol Rovers which enabled Dale to seal promotion the following week. After spells away from the side, he bounced back in 2016, scoring four goals in three games and ending the season with nine.

Ashley Thomas J. Eastham 2013-16

Born: Preston 22.3.91
6'2" 12st4
Central defender
FL Apps/Gls 74+2/3
Total Apps/Gls 91+2/3
Career: Carr Hill HS (Preston), Blackpool sch, pro 5.09 [+1/-], Hyde U. loan 8.09, Cheltenham T. loan 26.11.09 [18+2/-], Carlisle U. loan 25.11.10, Cheltenham T. loan 6.1.11 [8+1/-], Bury loan 25.8.11 [22+2/3], Fleetwood T. loan 29.8.12 [1/-], Notts Co. loan 5.10.12 [3+1/-], Bury loan 21.1.13 [18+1/-], Dale 20.6.13 [74+2/3], Fleetwood T. 5.16*
Honours: Blackpool & District schools, Lancashire Schools, Championship promotion 2010, League 2 promotion 2014, Lancashire Senior Cup final 2015

Ashley spent four seasons with Blackpool, but his only two starts came in the League Cup, the second ending when he was sent off. He did have a number of loan spells though, playing in Cheltenham's astonishing 6-5 win at Burton when they scored three times in the last four minutes. He turned down a further contract at Bloomfield Road to sign for Dale in 2013 and though not a regular in the promotion season, the centre back played in more games than anyone apart from Ian Henderson as Dale established themselves in League 1, finishing 8th. Kept out of the side the following term, Ashley re-established himself as Dale launched a late challenge for the play-offs in 2016, losing only three of the last 17 games, but decided to sign for Fleetwood in the close season.

Oliver James (Olly) Lancashire 2013-16

Born: Basingstoke 13.12.88 6'1" 12st8
Central defender
FL Apps/Gls 88+5/3
Total Apps/Gls 103+5/4
Career: Robert May's School (Odiham), Aldershot as, Crystal Palace jnr, Southampton sch, pro 2006 [11+2/-], Grimsby T. loan 22.10.09 [9/-], Grimsby T. loan 1.2.10 [15+1], Walsall 14.7.10 [45+4/1], Aldershot T. 14.6.12 [10+2/-], Dale 14.6.13 [88+5/3], Shrewsbury T. 5.16*
Honours: Premier League under-18s Group A champions 2005, League 2 promotion 2014

Despite his name, Olly was born in Hampshire and became a scholar at Southampton. He managed a dozen or so games for the Saints even though he was red carded after only 29 minutes on his debut against QPR and was sent again the following month. Indeed, including his loans at Grimsby he was sent off four times in his first 21 FL games. He also had the misfortune to be relegated out of the league both with Grimsby and later with Aldershot. Despite two more red cards, Olly was otherwise a fixture at centre back in the Dale side which won promotion in his first season. His second year was dogged by injuries, but he did score his first Dale goal, a last minute winner in the cup against Northampton. (Oddly enough, none of Dale's centre backs had managed a goal in 2013-14). He was then a regular performer again in Dale's second season in League 1, but turned down a contract extension to join Shrewsbury.

Peter Vincenti 2013-16*

Born: St Peter, Jersey 7.7.86 6'3" 11st13
Forward/midfield
FL Apps/Gls 93+24/26* Total Apps/Gls 110+26/31*
Career: Grainville College, First Tower U. jnr 2003, St Peter jnr 2004, pt 2005, Millwall trial 7.07, signed 29.9.07, Stevenage B. 4.1.08 [23+36/5 Conf, 1+4/1], Mansfield T. loan 22.10.10 [3/- Conf], Aldershot T. 14.1.11 [90+14/14], Dale 10.5.13 [93+24/26]*
Honours: Jersey FA schools, Jersey (Island Games) 2007, Jersey Footballer of the Year 2007, FA Trophy winners 2009, Conference champions 2010, League 2 promotion (2011), 2014

Peter's father, Peter snr, managed the Jersey 'national' side, and Peter jnr played for them in the Island games in Rhodes in 2007. Voted Jersey's footballer of the year 2007, he then left to take a Business Studies degree at Liverpool University, but was signed up by Millwal after a trial. He scored four times for Stevenage's reserves against Southend and appeared regularly in their Conference side, also netting in their FA Trophy semi-final win. He went on to score Borough's first goal in the FL (in fact the first FL goal anywhere that season) but was left out for next game. He became a league regular at Aldershot, though, figuring over 100 times, generally in midfield, before they were relegated in 2013. Like Olly Lancashire he then signed for Dale, and generally playing out wide in midfield or up front was an integral part of Dale's promotion side, being in the squad for every game bar one (when he was suspended for a red card against Bury). Often surprising teams with his prowess in the air for a wide man, he had by far his best goal scoring campaign since turning pro with a total of 16 in 2014-15, including the winner from the spot in the cup victory over Notts Forest. Early the following term, he had a purple patch in front of goal, scoring seven times in nine games, but managed only one more and had to settle for a place on the bench as the season progressed.

Matthew Charles (Matty) Lund 2013-16*

Born: Manchester 21.11.90 6'0" 11st13
Midfield
FL Apps/Gls 77+6/11*
Total Apps/Gls 89+6/12*
Career: Crewe A. sch 2007, Stoke C. 7.09, Hereford U. loan 23.11.10 [1+1/-], Oldham A. loan 28.7.11 [2+1/-], Bristol R. loan 30.1.12 [9+4/2], Bristol R. loan 26.7.12 [14+4/2], Southend U. loan 14.2.13 [10+2/1], Dale 21.6.13 [77+6/11]*
Honours: N. Ireland under-21s (6 caps) 2011-13, N. Ireland squad 2014-15, League 2 promotion 2014

Matty joined Stoke from Crewe's academy and scored a hat-trick for their reserves against Portsmoouth. He was unused sub once for the PL side but otherwise his only experience came from several loan spells prior to signing for Dale. Another of the new signings who immediately had a big part in Dale's promotion, he missed only a handful of games and netted nine goals from central midfield – it would have been 10 but he had a penalty saved at Newport on the final day. The following year he twice suffered a dislocated shoulder, and he also suffered with injuries in 2015-16, but when fit remained an automatic choice. He was also selected for the senior N. Ireland squad, flying back overnight from Romania to be part of the Dale side the following day.

Jack William O'Connell 2013-14, 2014-15

Born: Liverpool 29.3.94 6'3" 13st5
Central defender
FL Apps/Gls 66+1/5
Total Apps/Gls 75+1/5
Career: Poeta Salvador la Rueda (Benalmadena, Spain), Cardinal Heenan HS (Liverpool), REMYCA U. 2010, Blackburn R. sch 2011, pro 5.12, Rotherham U. loan 22.11.12 [1+2/-], York C. loan 24.1.13 [18/-], Dale loan 22.7.13 to 5.14 [38/-], Dale loan 1.9.14 to 3.1.15 [17/3], Brentford 2.2.15 [9+7/1]*, Dale loan 10.2.15 to 28.3.15 [11+1/2]
Honours: England under-18s v Poland 2012, under-19 (8 caps) 2012-13, FA Youth Cup final 2012, FA Academy under-18 league Group C winners 2012, Academy national final 2012, League 2 promotion (2013), 2014

Despite attending the same school that Steven Gerrard went to, Jack became a scholar at Blackburn, figuring in the Youth Cup final alongside Ryan Edwards (q.v.) and was selected for England at under-18 and under-19 level. After shorter loans elsewhere, he joined Dale for 2013-14 and starred in central defence alongside Olly Lancashire as they earned automatic promotion. After he made his Rovers' debut in the League Cup, Dale borrowed him again and, now mostly partnering Ashley Eastham, he helped establish them back in League 1. He returned to Blackburn at the end of his loan in January and was then transferred to Brentford. However, the Bees allowed him to rejoin Dale and he was a key part of the challenge for a play-off spot until recalled in March. He eventually played his first league game for a club he actually belonged to in September 2015, making 16 Championship appearances for the Bees during the season.

Bastien Charles Patrick Hery 2013-15

Born: Brou-sur-Chantereine, France 23.3.92 5'9" 10st3
Midfield
FL Apps/Gls 16+17/2
Total Apps/Gls 24+18/2
Career: US Torcy (France) jnr, Paris Saint-Germain (France) jnr 2006, pro 2010, Sheffield W. 6.12, Dale 8.5.13 [16+17/2], Carlisle U. 24.6.15 [16+4/-], Accrington St. 6.16*
Honours: France under-18 (2 caps) 2009, League 2 promotion 2014

Bastien was a junior with French giants Paris Saint-Germain and played 17 times for their second string, PSG II. He then spent a year at Sheffield Wednesday before signing for Dale. Sparsely used in midfield for most of the season, he came into the side to great effect in April, giving a final boost to Dale's promotion run. He figured a number of times as Dale started well in League 1, but fell behind other youngsters such as Camps and Cannon and was allowed to leave, joining Carlisle in 2015. He made the news playing for the Cumbrians against Liverpool, not so much for laying on the League 2 side's surprising equaliser (unfortunately he then failed in the penalty shoot-out), as for his even more surprising bright red hairstyle.

Robert Scott (Robbie) Thomson 2013-14

Born: Dundee
7.3.93 6'2" 13st3
Goalkeeper
FL Apps 1 Total
Apps 1
Career: Celtic jnr,
pro 1.12,
Stenhousemuir
loan 9.12 [7 ScL],
Airdrie U. loan
14.2.13 [11 ScL],
Carlisle U. trial
6.13, Oldham A.
trial 7.13, Dale trial
7.13, pro 26.7.13 [1],
Cowdenbeath
8.7.14 [32 ScL],
Queen of the South
7.15 [30 ScL]*

Honours: Scotland under-15s, under-16s (3 caps),
under-17s (9 caps), under-19s 2011

Son of Scott Thomson, formerly of Forfar and
Raith, the Hibs goalkeeping coach, Robbie started
out with Celtic and appeared in goal for Scotland
at all levels from under-15s to under-19s. His first
senior games were during a loan spell at
Stenhousemuir and after being released by Celtic
he signed for Dale. He appeared just once, when
Lillis was ill, otherwise occupying the bench. In an
earlier spell at Airdrie as backup to Kenny Arthur
(q.v.) he had conceded 32 goals in 11 games from
which Airdrie garnered just two points, and things
were equally hard at his next club Cowdenbeath
who were beaten 10-0 by Hearts in February 2015.
However, the following week Robbie was the star
as they held out for a goalless draw against
Rangers.

Javan Noel Vidal 2013-14

Born: Manchester
10.5.89 5'10" 10st
Right back
FL Apps/Gls 2/0
Total Apps/Gls 3/0
Career: Manchester C.
jnr 2005, pro 7.08 to
cs.11, Grimsby T. loan
9.08 [2+1/-], Aberdeen
loan 16.1.09 [9+4/-
ScL], Derby Co. loan
1.2.10 [+1/-],
Chesterfield loan
20.1.11 [5+1/-],
Panetolikos (Greece)
1.12, Stockport Co.
15.3.13 [4/- Conf], Dale trial 7.13, n/c 9.13 to 1.14
[2/-], Port Vale trial 7.14, Tamworth 29.8.14,
Wrexham 19.5.15 [20+3/2 Conf]*

Honours: England under-19s, under-20s (2 caps)
2009, (League 2 champions 2011, promoted 2014)

An England under-19 and under-20 cap, Javan
played just once for City, in a League Cup tie, and
had several spells out on loan. A move to Greece
was unproductive and after some time away from
the game, Javan played a few games for Stockport
prior to a trial at Spotland. He was signed on non-
contract terms, but appeared in only three games
at right back (making a total of just nine career FL
starts despite his international appearances). He
later gained more regular football at Conference
level.

Graham Rickard Cummins 2013-14

Born: Cork 29.12.87
6'2" 11st11
Forward
FL Apps/Gls
15+12/4 Total
Apps/Goals 16+15/4
Career: Tramore Ath,
College Corinthians,
Cobh Ramblers
2006, Waterford U.
2009, Cork C. 2010,
Preston NE 31.1.12 £
[18+16/4], Dale loan
2.9.13 to 5.14
[15+12/4], Exeter C.
trial 7.14, signed
14.8.14 [26+8/7], St. Johnstone 7.15 [23+9/8
ScL]*

Honours: Republic of Ireland under-23s 2010,
League of Ireland division 1 champions 2007,
2011, Munster Senior Cup winners 2009, PFAI
division 1 team of the year 2008, 2009, division 1
player of the year 2010, 2011, League 2 promotion
2014

An experienced League of Ireland player at an
early age, Graham had already played 77 games for
Cobh Ramblers – he was in the PFAI first division
team of the season when he was 19 - before prolific
spells at Waterford (17 goals in a season) and Cork
(42 goals in 62 games). He hit a club record 24 for
the latter in 2011 and was voted the division's
player of the season in both 2010 and 2011.
Transferred to Preston, he found goal scoring
harder, netting just two in each of the next two
seasons. Dale borrowed him for most of the 2013-
14 campaign and he proved a useful back-up to the
main strikers. He next joined Exeter, once their
transfer embargo ended, and in 2015 headed for
St. Johnstone where he scored in each of his first
three SPL games and also netted in a surprise
defeat of champions Celtic.

Gary Richard Perry Dicker 2013-14

Born: Dublin 31.7.86
6'0" 12st
Midfield
FL Apps/Gls 10+2/1 Total
Apps/Gls 13+2/1
Career: Bishop Galvin School
(Dublin), St Mac Dara's
Comm. Coll., Templeogue U.,
Cherry Orchard, UCD 2004,
Birmingham C. loan 2006-07,
Stockport Co. 29.5.07
£40,000 [54+4/-], Brighton & HA loan 26.3.09
[9/1], Brighton & HA 25.6.09 [100+29/6],
Blackpool trial cs.13, Dale 13.9.13 [10+2/1],
Crawley T. 23.1.14 [9+2/-], Carlisle U. 27.6.14
[29+10/1], Kilmarnock 1.2.16 [12/- ScL]*
Honours: Republic of Ireland under-19, under-21,
League of Ireland 1st division champions 2004,
League 2 play-off winners 2008, (promotion
2014), League 1 champions 2011, SPL/Scottish
Championship play-off winners 2016

Like Graham Cummins, Gary started out in the
League of Ireland, having previously played Gaelic
sports. He joined Stockport in 2007 and was yet
another player with future Dale connections to
play in their play-off victory over Dale. He also
gained promotion from League 1 with Brighton
and accumulated around 150 appearances in four
years despite missing much of 2011-12 through
injury after appearing in every match the year
before. A free agent in 2013, he signed a short term
contract with Dale and figured in midfield while
Cavanagh was injured, then moving back to Sussex
with Crawley. He spent eighteen months in League
2 with Carlisle but then switched to Scottish
Premier League side Kilmarnock, helping them
preserve ther top flight status in the play-off final.

Lee Robert Molyneux 2013-14

Born: Liverpool
24.2.89 6'1" 12st9
Midfield
FL Apps/Gls +3/0
Total Apps/Gls +3/0
Career: Whiston
Juniors, Everton jnr,
sch 2005, pro 3.3.06,
Southampton 2.1.09
[4/-], Port Vale loan
25.3.10, Plymouth A.
3.8.10 to 1.11 [7+2/-].
Accrington St. 8.12
[33+6/8], Crewe A.
7.13 [6+4/-], Dale loan 20.11.13 to 12.13 [+3/-],
Accrington St. loan 23.1.4 [14+3/6], Accrington St.
loan 3.10.14 [7+3/1], Tranmere R. 13.1.15 [7+4/-],
Morecambe 4.7.15 [18+16/3]*

Honours: England under-16s (10 caps), under-17s
(6 caps) 2006, under-18s, Staffordshire Senior Cup
final 2010, (League 2 promotion 2014)

Lee worked his way through the junior ranks at
Everton, playing left back for their reserves at 16
and being on the subs bench for the first team
several times in 2007-08. He also won England
caps at the various youth levels. All four of his
Southampton appearances came in the month he
joined them (he was sent off in the last one). After
his Plymouth contract was cancelled, he resumed
his career at Accrington, where he scored two long
range efforts against Dale - his first senior goals.
He then remarkably netted a hat-trick from full
back against Barnet, subsequently being played
further forward. Dale borrowed him briefly from
Crewe but he appeared only from the bench and
after further loans back at Accrington left Crewe
for Tranmere just before they lost their league
place, Lee quickly moving on to Morecambe.

George Edwards Porter 2013-14

Born: Sidcup 26.7.92
5'10" 12st6
Forward
FL Apps/Gls 1+1/0
Total Apps/Gls 1+1/0
Career: Cray
Wanderers 2009,
Leyton Orient 5.10
[9+25/1], Lewes loan
29.10.10, Hastings T.
loan 1.11, Burnley
3.7.12, Colchester U.
loan 1.1.13 [13+6/1],
AFC Wimbledon loan 18.7.13 [17+4/-], Dale 31.1.14
[1+1/-], Dagenham & Redbridge 8.14 [7+12/1],
Maidstone U. 1.2.15, Welling U. 20.7.15 [23+6/1
Conf]*
Honours: League 2 promotion 2014, Isthmian
League premier division champions 2015

Cray Wanderers' player of the year in his first
season, George moved to Orient but was unable to
secure a regular place despite scoring a hat-trick
from the wing on a summer tour. The majority of
his league starts actually came during loan spells at
Colchester and Wimbledon and his Dale carer was
very short. Substitute in a televised game at Bury,
he started the next game in place of the suspended
Henderson but wasn't seen again. He helped
Maidstone win the Isthmian League title in 2015
and was included in the England C squad.

Sean Andrew McGinty 2013-15

Born: Maidstone 11.8.93 6'2" 11st9 Defender
FL Apps/Gls +1/0
Total Apps/Gls +1/0
Career: Charlton A. jnr 2006, Manchester U. yts 7.09 £1M, pro 2011, Morecambe loan 27.2.12 [4/-], Oxford U. loan 17.7.12, Carlisle U. loan 6.11.12 [+1/-], Tranmere R. loan 28.3.13 [3/-], Sheffield U. 25.6.13 [2/-], Northampton T. loan 1.14 [2/-], Dale loan 23.3.14, signed 20.5.14 [+1/-], FC Halifax T. loan 10.11.14 [2/- Conf], Aldershot T. loan 20.2.15 [13/- Conf], Aldershot T. 5.15 [24/1 Conf], Torquay U. 6.16*
Honours: Republic of Ireland under-17s (7 caps) 2009-10, under-19s (11 caps) 2010-2012, under-21s (10 caps) 2013-14, Youth Cup winners 2011, League 2 promotion 2014

Sean had a somewhat chequered career after being snapped up by Manchester United, who paid £1M to take him from Charlton's junior sides. He appeared in their Youth Cup winning side, at left back or centre back, but never made United's first team and only ever started 11 FL games anywhere. A loan at Morecambe was ended by a dislocated shoulder and both Oxford and Tranmere sent him back early, the latter after a breach of discipline which resulted in him being sacked by Sir Alex. (He was the last player to leave Old Trafford during Ferguson's long reign). Sean was also a regular for the Republic's under-17s to under-21s. Signed by Sheffield United, he managed only a couple of games and was loaned to Dale just a couple of weeks after being sent off in his last game for the Republic under-21s. He played in the last few minutes of the game at Bristol Rovers which almost guaranteed Dale promotion and was given a contract for the following term. However, after an unconvincing pre-season he never came close to first team selection and was loaned out to Halifax and then Aldershot, joining the latter permanently at the end of the season.

Craig Thomas Lynch 2013-14

Born: Chester-le-Street 25.3.92 5'9" 10st1 Forward
FL Apps/Gls +1/0
Total Apps/Gls +1/0
Career: Sunderland jnr, sch 2008, pro 2010 [+2/-], Hartlepool U. loan 8.9.12 [2+4/1], Dale 18.2.14 [+1/-], Gateshead trial 7.14, Spennymoor U. 8.8.14, Blyth Spartans 5.2.15, Durham C. 9.6.15*
Honours: League 2 promotion 2014

Like McGinty, Craig made just one substitute appearance for Dale, in the final game of the promotion campaign, at Newport. Then 22, he had previously been with Sunderland from the age of seven and been substitute in a couple of first team games in 2011. His only FL starts were during a month's loan at Hartlepool in 2012.

Calvin Hyden Andrew 2014-16*

Born: Luton 19.12.86 6'2" 12st11 Striker
FL Apps/Gls 19+43/11* Total Apps/Gls 24+52/12*
Career: Luton T. jnr, pro 25.9.04 [26+29/4], Grimsby T. loan 8.05 [3+5/1], Bristol C. loan 30.1.06 [1+2/-], Crystal Palace 7.08 £80,000 [17+36/2], Brighton & HA loan 30.1.09 [3+6/2], Millwall loan 18.11.10 [3/-], Swindon T. loan 11.3.11 [9+1/1], Leyton Orient loan 1.3.12 [2+8/-], Crawley T. trial 8.12, Port Vale 26.11.12 [7+15/1], Mansfield T. 8.8.13 to 6.1.14 [11+4/1], York C. 24.3.14 [5+3/1], Dale trial, signed 25.7.14 [19+43/11]*
Honours: League 1 champions 2005, League 2 promotion 2013

Calvin's whole hearted contribution to Dale's cause elevated him in the fans' standing after initially being the butt of comments about his goal scoring – he had, admittedly, scored just 13 in 10 years in the FL. He actually became the first Dale player to score when coming on as substitute in three successive league games, indeed all six of his goals in his first season were scored as a substitute, including a last seconds winner against Port Vale, one of his earlier clubs. His previous main contributions, mostly playing in a target man role, had been at Luton in 2007-08, when he appeared in 48 games in all, albeit a majority of them as a sub, and Palace in 2009-10 when he played in 28 Championship games.

Jonathan (Johny) Diba Musungu   2014-16*

Born: Mbuji-Mayi, DR Congo 12.10.97
6'0" 11st9
Goalkeeper
FL Apps +1* Total Apps +1*
Career: St Cuthbert's HS, Dale jnr, sch cs.14, pro 18.11.14 [+1]*
Honours: Greater Manchester Schools, ESFA under-16 Inter-County trophy winners 2014, (Lancashire YC winners 2013),

Lancashire Senior Cup final 2015

Johny was brought up in Rochdale and was with Dale from the age of 11. He was already in the youth team by his 15th birthday in 2012 (along with the equally young Kisimba Kisimba, Nyal Bell, Connor Martin, later of Accrington, and Connor Ronan who moved to Wolves) and was called up for England under-15 and under-16 goalkeepers' training camps, reportedly attracting interest from Chelsea. He was also in the Greater Manchester Schools side which beat Lancashire Schools in the ESFA trophy final. Given a place on the first team bench from the start of 2014-15, he was unexpectedly called upon in only the third game of the season when Lillis was injured. He subsequently signed a pro deal just after he turned 17 but has yet to make a further appearance.

Stephen John Dawson   2014-15

Born: Dublin 4.12.85
5'9" 11st9
Midfield
FL Apps/Gls 27+3/0
Total Apps/Gls 33+3/0
Career: Portmarnock, Leicester sch, pro 2003, Mansfield T. 8.05 [106+11/4], Bury 3.7.08 [87+1/6], Leyton Orient 4.6.10 [59+1/3], Barnsley 31.1.12

[67+14/5], Dale 12.8.14 [27+3/-], Scunthorpe U. 20.5.15 [22+1/-]*
Honours: Republic of Ireland under-21 (2 caps) 2005-06

Another of the Dubliners to sign for Dale in recent years, Stephen was already an experienced lower league campaigner when he arrived at Spotland. He made over 100 appearances for Mansfield, representing the Republic at under-21 level while at Field Mill, but when they were relegated to the Conference joined Bury and made 97 apearances in midfield in just two seasons. Signed by Keith Hill when he was at Barnsley, Stephen was released after two and a half years and joined Hill again at Spotland. A first choice when fit, he helped Dale re-establish themselves in League 1 before moving on to Scunthorpe who, like Dale, just missed the play-offs. Stephen's brother Kevin was also a youth international and played for Shelbourne and Yeovil, while another brother, Brendan, was with Shamrock Rovers.

Conrad Joseph Logan   2014-15

Born: Ramelton, Co. Donegal 18.4.86
6'2" 14st
Goalkeeper
FL Apps 19 Total Apps 25
Career: St Mary's School (Ramelton), St Eunan's College (Letterkenny), Swilly Rovers 2000, Leicester C. academy 2001, pro 7.04 to cs.15 [21+2], Boston U. loan 24.12.05 [10], Boston U. loan 20.4.06 [3], Stockport Co. loan 9.8.07 [34], Luton T. loan 20.8.08 [22], Stockport Co. loan 27.3.09 [7], Bristol R. loan 18.2.11 [16], Rotherham U. loan 5.8.11 [19], Dale loan 18.8.14 to 12.14 [19]. Hibernian 3.16 [2 ScL]*
Honours: Republic of Ireland youth international, under-17s 2002-03, under-18s 2003, under-19s 2004, League 2 play-off winners 2008, (Championship winners 2014), Scottish FA Cup winners 2016

The son of Joe Logan, who played for Sligo and Finn Harps, Conrad originally played Gaelic football, but was inspired to beome a soccer goalkeeper by watching Celtic and Republic of Ireland legend Packie Bonner. Joining Leicester's academy, Conrad figured for the Republic at all levels up to the under-19 side and played his first FL games during loan spells at Boston. He made his Leicester debut in 2006, figuring in a total of

20 matches during the season, but after returning to the reserves went out on further loans, playing for Stockport in their Wembley victory over the Dale. He was unused substitute in every Leicester game in 2012-13 and was a non-playing member of the squad which reached the top flight in 2014. Indeed he figured in just ten games in his last eight years at Leicester. He was signed by Dale to cover for the injured Josh Lillis and made a big impression as Dale comfortably handled the step up to League 1. Unfortunately, he too was injured in a game against Notts County and ruled out for the rest of the season. Leicester did not then renew his contract, his next game remarkably coming in the Scottish Cup semi-final, when his two penalty saves took Hibs through to Hampden, where they defeated Rangers. A big AP McCoy fan, Conrad is a keen follower of the horses.

Shamir Daniel Sanchez Fenelon [aka Goodwin] 2014-15

Born: Brighton 3.8.94 6'1" 12st8
Striker
FL Apps/Gls +4/0
Total Apps/Gls +4/0
Career: Brighton &HA sch 2010, pro 5.12 [1+1/-], Tonbridge Angels loan 2012-13, Torquay U. loan 11.1.14 [11+1/1], Dale loan 29.8.14 to 29.9.14 [+4/-], Tranmere R. loan 21.11.14 [9+1/2], Dagenham & Redbridge loan 27.2.15 [3+1/-], Crawley T. 22.6.15 [9+21/2]*, Whitehawk loan 8.15
Honours: Republic of Ireland under-21s 2015

Known as Shamir Goodwin until 2014, he scored 20 goals for Brighton's youth team in 2011-12. One of his several loan moves took him to Dale in August 2014, but with the side going well, his only game time was in a few cameos from the bench and he only stayed a month. He also had the unfortunate record of spending time with both Torquay and Tranmere in the seasons they lost their league places. Despite being called up for the Republic of Ireland under-21s in 2015, he was released by Brighton and joined neighbours Crawley.

Nyal Aston Nathanial Bell 2013-16

Born: Manchester 17.1.97 6'2" 11st
Striker
FL Apps/Gls +3/0
Total Apps/Gls +3/0
Career: Dale jnr, sch 2013, pro 6.15 [+3/-], Droylsden loan 18.9.15 to 21.11.15, Chester loan 29.1.16 [+3/-Conf], Gateshead 6.16*
Honours: Lancashire Senior Cup final 2015

In Dale's youth team when he was 15, Nyal hit a hat-trick against Nantwich in the Youth Cup the following term. (He had also been the Olympic torch bearer through Burscough in 2012). He made his FL debut as substitute in the victory over Coventry in September 2014, and was selected for the League Football Education XI the following month, based on performances for academy sides. After figuring in the Lancashire Cup final, he spent most of 2015-16 out on loan, being named on the bench just once, and was then released.

Andrew Francis (Andy) Cannon 2012-16*

Born: Ashton-under-Lyne 14.3.96 5'9" 11st9
Right back/Midfield
FL Apps/Gls 38+5/0* Total Apps/Gls 43+6/0*
Career: Stockport Co. jnr, Dale sch 2012, pro 5.14 [38+5/-]*
Honours: Lancashire Youth Cup winners 2013

Signed by Dale when Stockport's academy closed down, Andy played in the Lancashire Youth Cup winning side and played in midfield for the reserves in the Lancs Senior Cup semi-final the same week. He made his senior debut as substitute, playing at right back, as Dale came back from a goal behind to win 3-2 at Orient in September 2014. Despite some injury problems, he figured more prominently the following year, picking up nine yellow cards in the process.

Jonathan Jack Lyndan Muldoon 2014-15

Born: Scunthorpe 19.5.89 5'10" 10st12
Striker
FL Apps/Gls 2+1/0
Total Apps/Gls 3+3/0
Career: St Bede's School, Pepperells (Scunthorpe SL), Scunthorpe U. jnr, sch 2006, Doncaster R. sch 12.07, Sheffield Hallam University 2008, Brigg T. 2008, Sheffield FC 12.08, Glapwell cs.09, Alfreton T. 19.1.10, Stocksbridge Park Steels 1.7.10, North Ferriby U. cs.12, Sheffield FC loan 15.2.13, Worksop T. 5.7.13, Dale 5.14 [2+1/-], Halifax T. loan 13.2.15 [8+4/2 Conf], Lincoln C. 28.5.15 [45+1/9 Conf]*

Jack had been on the books of Scunthorpe and Doncaster before taking a sports science degree and at the same time turning out in non-league football. Also working as a plasterer, he played alongside Scott Hogan at Stocksbridge Park Steels and after scoring 21 goals in a season at Worksop followed Hogan to Spotland. Unfortunately injured in pre-season, he was unabe to make the impact that Hogan had and after a handful of apearances he was loaned out to Halifax, scoring twice in their only victory in the last 15 games of the season. He subsequently signed for Lincoln where he was everpresent in the National League (formerly the Conference) in 2015-16.

Kisimba Kisimba 2014-16*

Born: 23.10.97 5'9" 11st11
Defender
FL Apps/Gls 0/0
Total Apps/Gls +0/0
Career: St Cuthbert's HS, Dale jnr, sch cs.14*
Honours: Greater Manchester Schools, ESFA under-16 Inter-county Trophy winners 2014, Lancashire Senior Cup final 2015

Kisimba was a schoolmate of Johny Diba (and future Wolves player Connor Ronan) and played with them for Dale's youth team and for the inter-county cup winning Greater Manchester Schools, originally as a central midfielder and then a

defender. He was named as substitute for the JPT tie against Walsall in 2014 when still a first year scholar and figured in a reserve line-up in the Lancashire Cup final but has yet to make a senior appearance.

William David (Billy) Hasler-Cregg 2013-16
Born: Accrington 11.9.96 5'8" 9st8
Midfield
FL Apps/Gls +0/0 Total Apps/Gls +0/0
Career: Burnley jnr, Dale sch 2013, pro 6.15, Droylsden loan 9.15, Altrincham 5.16*
Honours: Lancashire Senior Cup final 2015

Though a scholar, Billy trained with the first team in 2014-15 and was twice named as substitute. He also scored four goals in a 9-0 defeat of Nantwich in the Youth Cup. He signed a professional contract the following summer and played in the delayed Lancs Cup final but spent most of the season out on loan successfully at Droylsden, before signing for Altrincham. Prior to concentrating on his football, Billy was a useful junior triple jumper for Hyndburn Athletics Club.

Reuben Courtney Noble-Lazarus 2014-16
Born: Huddersfield 16.8.93 5'11" 13st5
Forward
FL Apps/Gls 9+20/2 Total Apps/Gls 10+24/3
Career: Newsome HS, Barnsley as, sch 2009, pro 2011 [10+36/3], Scunthorpe U. loan 12.11.13 [2+2/-], Dale loan 27.10.14, signed 13.1.15 to 5.16 [9+20/2]
Honours: (League 2 promotion 2014)

Reuben's primary claim to fame is as the youngest ever FL player at 15 years and 45 days, coming on as substitute for Barnsley against Ipswich on 30 October 2008. He had scored a hat-trick for their under-18s the previous week, and manager Simon Davey stated that he would have selected him for a League Cup tie earlier in the season, but the rules did not permit a 14 year old to play. He made further substitute appearances over the next few seasons, making his first start in April 2011. He appeared in a few games when Keith Hill was boss at Oakwell and Hill signed him for Dale in 2014 to give another alternative up front, but he was able to make little impression over the next 18 months.

Tomasz Wojciech Cywka 2014-15

Born: Gliwice, Poland 27.6.88 5'11" 11st8 Forward
FL Apps/Gls 1+2/0
Total Apps/Gls 1+4/0
Career: Polonia Bytom (Poland), Zantka Chorsow (Poland) 2003, Gwarek Zabrze (Poland) 2004, Wigan A. trial 3.06, signed 5.7.06, Oldham A. loan 31.10.06 [+4/-], Derby Co. loan 25.3.10 [4+1/-], Derby Co. 1.7.10 [24+15/5], Reading 26.1.12 [1+3/-], Barnsley 6.8.12 [35+24/9], Blackpool 28.7.14 [5+1/1], Dale loan 11.14 [1+2/-], Wisla Krakow 7.15*
Honours: Poland under-18s, under-19s, under-20s World Cup 2007, under-21s (2 caps) 2006 and 2009, Polish under-19s league champions 2006, Championship winners 2012

Making a mark with Gwarek Zabrze, the feeder club to Gornik, Tomasz was in their side which won the Polish under-19 championship in 2006, before deciding to move to England to join Wigan. He appeared for Poland at various age levels — indeed he is said to be the youngest ever player for their under-21s - but managed just a couple of cup ties for the Latics. A spell with Derby County turned out to be somewhat more productive and he also played quite regularly (under Keith Hill) while at Barnsley. Hill borrowed him for Dale towards the end of 2014, but he had few opportunities, starting just in the defeat by Scunthorpe, when Vincenti was out injured. He returned to Poland to play for Wisla Krakow.

Febian Earlston Brandy 2014-15

Born: Manchester 4.2.89 5'6" 9st13 Striker
FL Apps/Gls 1+3/0
Total Apps/Gls 1+3/0
Career: West End Boys, Manchester U. jnr, pro cs.07 to 30.6.10, Swansea C. loan 18.1.08 [2+17/3], Swansea C. loan 22.7.08 [+14/-], Hereford U. loan 2.2.09 [14+1/4], Gillingham loan 6.11.09 [5+2/1]. Leicester C. trial 1.11, Preston NE trial 2.11, Notts Co. 28.2.11 to 5.11 [5+4/-]. Panetolikos (Greece) 2.12, Walsall 26.7.12 [27+7/7], Sheffield U. 25.6.13 [10+4/-], Walsall loan 13.1.14 [20/4], Rotherham U. 27.6.14 [+1/-], Crewe A. loan 19.9.14 [6+2/1],

Dale 12.1.15 to 4.15 [1+3/-], York C. trial 9.15, Oldham A. trial 9.15 to 10.15, Ubon UMT U. (Thailand) 12.15*
Honours: England under-16s (4 caps), under-17s (2 caps), under-18s (2 caps), under-19s (5 caps), under-20s (4 caps), FIFA under-20 World Cup (Egypt) 2009, Youth Cup final 2007, Champions Youth Cup winners (Malaysia) 2007, League 1 champions 2008, St Kitts & Nevis (2 caps) 2015

Febian won a string of England caps at all youth levels, scoring eight times in 17 internationals, and also netted the only goal for United against Juventus in the Champions youth cup final. Nevertheless, he failed to break into the senior team at Old Trafford and was loaned out to several other clubs, featuring – mainly as substitute – for the Swansea team which won League 1 in 2008. His best spells in the league came after he signed for Walsall in 2012, and then when the Sadlers borrowed him again the following season. He only managed one substitute appearance for Rotherham before signing a short term deal at Spotland and after just a handful of appearances he faded from first team contention. Nevertheless, in June 2015 he played in two World Cup qualifiers for St Kitts & Nevis and then moved to Thailand.

James Lewis (Jamie) Jones 2014-15

Born: Kirkby 18.2.89 6'2" 14st5 Goalkeeper
FL Apps 13
Total Apps 13
Career: Everton jnr, pro 4.7.07, Dale loan c.3.08, Leyton Orient 30.6.08 [151], Preston NE 6.6.14 [17], Coventry C. loan 23.1.15 [4], Dale loan 26.2.15 to 4.15 [13], Colchester U. loan 11.9.15 [17], Stevenage B. 29.1.16 [17]*
Honours: League 1 play-off final 2014, promotion 2015

Jamie was a young professional at Everton when he spent some time at Spotland in 2008. He had six years at Orient, mostly as a regular choice in goal, and accumulated 179 appearances before turning down a further contract. In 2013, he had been attacked by a Swindon fan who invaded the pitch and aimed punches at him. Initially first choice after joining Preston, when he lost his place he joined Dale and replaced Josh Lillis for the last two months of the season. Oddly, he had played against Dale three times earlier in the term, twice for North End and once for Coventry. After leaving Deepdale, he signed for Stevenage Borough.

James Hooper   2013-16*

Born: Manchester
10.2.97 5'10"
Midfield/striker
FL Apps/Gls 1+1/0*
Total Apps/Gls
1+1/0*
Career: Bury jnr,
Dale sch 2013, pro
6.15 [1+1/-]*
Honours: Lancashire
Youth Cup winners
2013, Lancashire
Senior Cup final
2015

A member of the Lancashire youth cup wining side, James netted all the Dale youth team's goals in a 5-4 defeat by Shrewsbury in 2014 and was included as a first team substitute for one game near the end of the season. Given a professional contract in the summer, he was also linked with a move to Norwich. He made a promising debut in mid-season and was retained for another term.

James (Jim) McNulty   2015-16*

Born: Runcorn 13.2.85
6'2" 12st1
Central defender
FL Aps/Gls 46/0*
Total Apps/Gls 52/0*
Career: Liverpool sch
2001, Everton sch
2002, Wrexham cs.03,
Bangor C. loan 2.04,
Caernarfon T. cs.04,
Macclesfield T. 7.06
[28+6/1], Stockport Co.
2.1.08 [39+1/1],
Brighton &HA 2.2.09
£150,000 [10+3/1],
Scunthorpe U. loan 23.3.10 [2+1/-], Scunthorpe U. loan 15.7.10 [5+1/-], Barnsley 24.6.11 [53+3/2], Tranmere R. loan 3.10.13 [12/-], Bury 17.1.14 [43+3/-], Dale 2.6.15 [46/-]*
Honours: Scotland under-17s (6 caps) 2001-02, Scotland under-19s (4 caps) 2003-04, League 2 play-off winners 2008, promotion 2015

Jim was with both Liverpool and Everton as a youngster, also being selected for the Scottish under-17s, but apart from an FRT game for Wrexham, his first senior appearances were in the Welsh League, spending two years as a regular with Caernarfon. Originally a left back, he had

spent a couple of seasons back in the FL – he was yet another of the Stockport play-off team against the Dale at Wembley - when Brighton bought him for £150,000. However, shortly afterwards he suffered a serious injury that required him to have a kidney removed. Rumoured to be a target to replace Craig Dawson at Spotland before Keith Hill and Dave Flitcroft moved to Barnsley he signed for them instead and won their player of the year award in 2012. By now playing as a central defender, Flitcroft also signed him for Bury and after they released him, it was Hill's turn to sign Jim for a second time. First figuring at centre half, he later reverted to left back as Dale lost only three of their last 17 games and gained their best ever points tally in the third tier, Jim completing the season everpresent in all competitions.

Donal Jeremiah McDermott   2015-16*

Born: Dublin
19.10.89 5'10" 12st
Midfield
FL Apps/Gls
32+5/2* Total
Apps/Gls 36+7/3*
Career: Ashbourne
U., Cherry Orchard,
Manchester C. sch
2006, pro cs.08,
Milton Keynes Dons
loan 11.9.08 [+1/-],
Chesterfield loan
7.8.09 [13+2/5],
Scunthorpe U. loan
26.1.10 [4+5/-],
Bournemouth loan
24.3.11 [6+3/1], Huddersfield T. 1.7.11 £ [6+3/-], Bournemouth 31.1.12 [12+8/1], Dundalk 5.7.14, Salford C. 5.1.15, Ramsbottom U. 2.15, Dale trial 4.15, signed 6.15 [32+5/2]*
Honours: FA Youth Cup winners 2008, League 1 promotion (2012), 2013, League of Ireland premier division champions 2014, (Northern Premier League division 1 north champions 2015)

Once scoring in a Manchester Cup game against Dale, Donal played on the wing for City in the Youth Cup final alongside Andrew Tutte and David Ball (q.v.) and netted five times in a loan at Chesterfield. He scored for Bournemouth in the play-off semi-final against Huddersfield in 2011 and then signed for the Terriers. He soon rejoined the Cherries, but was rarely used as they moved up the leagues and left for League of Ireland winners Dundalk. He spent 2014-15 in the Northern Premier League before getting the chance to resurrect his FL career with Dale, a chance he grabbed by becoming a regular in their mdfield.

Lewis Alessandra 2015-16*

Born: Heywood 8.2.89
5'9" 11st7
Forward
FL Apps/Gls 3+5/1
Total Apps/Gls 4+7/2
Career: Roach
Dynamos, Dale jnr,
Oldham A. jnr, pro
cs.07 [34+33/8],
Chester C. loan
21.8.09 [4/- Conf-
exp], Morecambe
23.6.11 [55+27/7],
Plymouth A. 11.6.13
[82+4/18], Dale 8.6.15
[3+5/1], York C loan
8.3.16 [11/2],
Hartlepool U. 6.16*
Honours: Lancashire Youth Cup winners 2007,
Lancashire Senior Cup final 2015

A member of the Latics side which beat Dale in the
2007 Lancashire Youth Cup final (along with the
likes of Kallum Higginbotham, q.v.), Lewis made
around 70 appearances after turning pro that
summer. He netted a hat-trick against Scunthorpe
in 2008 but his spell at Chester was expunged
when they were expelled from the Conference. He
played in a number of positions for Morecambe
but became more of a regular scorer when at
Plymouth (even though Argyle initially used him in
midfield), netting 25 times and missing only a
handful of games during his two seasons. Despite
goals in successive games in September, he had
few opportunities at Spotland and was loaned to
York towards the end of the season. Lewis's
brother Ryan plays for Rochdale Town.

Nathaniel Otis Mendez-Laing 2015-16*

Born: Birmingham
15.4.92 5'10" 11st12
Winger
FL Apps/Gls 18+15/7*
Total Apps/Gls
21+15/10*
Career:
Wolverhampton W.
jnr, sch 2008, pro
27.3.10, Peterborough
U. loan 15.7.10
[8+25/5], Sheffield U.
loan 5.8.11 [4+4/1],
Peterborough U. 6.7.12
£100,000 [22+29/4],
Portsmouth loan
15.11.12 [5+3/-],
Shrewsbury T. loan 30.1.14
[3+3/-], Cambridge U. loan 18.2.15 [10+1/1], Dale
27.8.15 [18+15/7]*

Honours: England under-16s (2 caps) 2008,
England under-17s (7 caps) 2008, Gothia Cup
winners 2009, League 1 promotion 2011

An England youth international, Nathanial's only
first team experience with his initial club Wolves
was in a League Cup tie in 2009 while still a
scholar. He spent a season on loan at
Peterborough, appearing in 40 games in all,
though the majority were as substitute, and in
2012 Posh signed him permanently for £100,000.
He suffered from injuries and lack of fitness,
though, and started only nine league games in his
last two years with the club. He joined Dale just
after the start of 2015-16 and after a remarkable
cup hat-trick against Swindon gradually gained a
regular starting place, reaching double figures in
goals.

Joel Castro Dinis Pereira 2015-16

Born: Boudevilliers,
Switzerland 28.6.96
6'2" 12st12
Goalkeeper
FL Apps 6
Total Apps 7
Career: Le Locle
Sports (Switzerland)
jnr, FC Xamax
(Switzerland) jnr,
Neuchatel Xamax
(Switzerland),
Manchester U. sch
11.7.12, pro 7.14*,
Dale loan 16.10.15 to
29.12.15 [6]
Honours: Switzerland
under-15s (2 caps) 2011, under-16s (3 caps) 2011,
Portugal under-17s (5 caps) 2012, under-18s (3
caps) 2013, under-19s (6 caps) 2014, under-21s
2016, Milk Cup winners 2013, Premier League
under-21 league champions 2015

Capped for Switzerland at under-15s and under-
16s, Joel switched allegiance to his father's country
of origin Portugal when he joined Manchester
United. He figured in their UEFA youth league side
in 2013-14 and was already in the under-21s at the
age of 18. He played only in a JPT tie in his original
loan spell with Dale, but after returning to Old
Trafford surprisingly reappeared a week later and
went straight into the side in place of subsequent
player of the year Josh Lillis, Dale taking ten
points from his six games. He ended the season
playing for Portugal under-21s.

Jean-Christophe Kloblavi (John) Ayina

2015-16
Born: Rouen, France
9.4.91 5'11" 11st11
Striker
FL Apps/Gls 0/0 Total
Apps/Gls +1/0
Career: EA Guingamp
(France) jnr 2007, EA
Guingamp B pro 2008-
09, Paris Saint-Germain
B (France) 7.09 to 7.11,
US Quevilly (France)
trial 10.11, signed 1.12, Cordoba (Spain) 9.7.12,
Ecija (Spain) loan 4.1.13, Racing Santander (Spain)
2.9.13, Inverness Caledonian Thistle trial 7.14,
Getafe B (Spain) 28.8.14, Falkirk trial 9.15, Dale
trial 10.15, n/c 6.11.15, Newport Co. 21.1.16
[10+4/1]
Honours: Coupe de France final 2012, Spanish
division 2B promotion 2014

John played in the French lower divisions with the
second strings of Guingamp and then giants PSG.
He next joined US Quevillaise, a semi-pro third
tier side who remarkably won through nine rounds
to reach the French Cup Final, where they were
narrowly beaten 1-0 by an Lyon side including the
likes of Lloris and Gourcuff. John had made the
headlines in the quarter final when he scored twice
against Marseilles. He then moved to Spain,
playing in the second and third tiers and gaining
promotion with Racing Santander. He had a trial
at Spotland in 2015 and made one substitute
appearance in the JPT as a non-contract player. He
subsequently played a number of League 2 games
for Newport County.

John Anthony James O'Sullivan 2015-16

Born: Birmingham
18.9.93
5'11" 13st1
Midfield
Lge Apps/Gls 2/0
Total Apps/Gls 3/0
Career: Blackburn R.
sch 2009, pro 2012
[1+4/-]*, Southport
loan 9.1.14 [21/3 Conf],
Accrington St. loan
19.9.14 [13/4],
Barnsley loan 18.2.15
[7+1/-], Dale loan
26.11.15 to 12.15 [2/-],
Bury loan 14.1.16
[12+7/-]
Honours: Republic of Ireland under-15s 2008,
under-16s, under-19s (13 caps) 2011-12, under-21s
(4 caps) 2012-13

A Blackburn academy product, John made his
debut for them on the final day of 2012-13. He had
several useful loan spells with lower division clubs,
scoring twice on his Accrington debut in a
remarkable 5-4 win at Northampton, but that at
Spotland didn't prove a success. Withdrawn after
half an hour of his debut when on a last warning
from the referee, he was sent off after just 11
minutes of his only other league game. He spent
the remaner of 2015-16 on loan at Bury; oddly he
played for Dale when they lost to Bury in the cup
and for Bury when they lost to Dale in the league.

David Thomas (Dave) Syers 2015-16

Born: Leeds 30.11.87
6'0 11st9
Midfield
FL Apps/Gls 2+4/0
Total Apps/Gls
2+4/0
Career: Leeds GS,
Ossett Albion, Leeds
University, Harrogate
T. 1.4.09, Farsley
Celtic 17.6.09, Ossett
Albion 2.10,
Harrogate T. 12.3.10,
Guiseley 1.7.10,
Bradford C. trial
15.7.10, signed 10.8.10
[38+17/10],
Doncaster R. 14.6.12 [20+14/3], Scunthorpe U.
loan 5.10.13 [15/5], Scunthorpe U. 10.1.14
[25+8/5], Dale 18.1.16 to 5.16 [2+4/-]
Cricket for Leeds GS, Spen Victoria, Pudsey St.
Lawrence, Collingham, Farsley
Honours: English Universities 2008, League 1
champions 2013, League 2 promotion 2014

Dave was a top class schoolboy cricketer, winning
the Wetherall award for the best allrounder in
schools cricket (previous winners included Derek
Pringle and Chris Cowdrey) and played in the
Bradford League. He also joined Ossett Albion
while at school and played over 150 games, some
of them in goal, around his university studies (he
obtained a first in classics at Leeds). A goal scoring
midfielder, he had a successful start in the
Conference North with Farsley Celtic in 2009, but
they were liquidated mid-season and he agreed to
join Guiseley. Nevertheless, they allowed him to go
on trial at Valley Parade and he signed a
professional contract with Bradford City after
scoring on his debut. He top scored and won their
players' player of the year in his first season, but
after losing his place to Ritchie Jones (one of eight
past or future Dale players in the Bantams' squad)
Dave joined Doncaster in 2012. He played fairly
regularly when Rovers won League 1, but after a

spell on loan, joined Scunthorpe the following season. He hit the first hat-trick of his career against Plymouth during The Iron's run to promotion, but suffered a serious knee injury in the first game of 2014-15 and hardly played before joining Dale on a short contract in January 2016.

Niall David Stephen Canavan 2015-16*

Born: Bramley 11.4.91 6'3" 12st8 Central defender FL Apps/Gls 11/1* Total Apps/Gls 11/1* Career: St Mary's Menston Academy (Leeds), Scunthorpe U. jnr 2004, yts 2007, pro 4.09 [145+9/15], Shrewsbury T. loan 22.3.11 [3/-], Dale loan 15.2.16 to 5.16 [11/1], Dale 5.16* Honours: Leeds City Boys, Republic of Ireland under-21s (7 caps) 2011-2012, League 2 promotion 2014

Niall made his debut for Scunthorpe's youth team towards the end of 2004-05 when still only 14 and skippered the side before turning pro. He made his league debut in August 2009, but only established himself in the centre of the defence three years later, when the Iron were relegated to the fourth tier (despite Niall's personal contribution of six goals). He then missed only one game when Scunthorpe immediately bounced back to gain promotion alongside Dale in 2013-14. He was out of the picture following changes of management when borrowed by Dale in 2016, and Niall's centre back partnership with Ashley Eastham helped turn round a previously disappointing run of form. He signed permanently at Spotland in the summer.

INDEX TO PLAYERS

151

		Page	Season	To	FL	FAC	FLC	AMC	PO	Other	Total
Peter	Cavanagh	129	2012-13	2013-14	47+4/2	3/0	1/0	1/0			52+4/2
Iyesden	Christie	81	2005-06	2006-07	14+5/2		1/0				16+5/2
Darrell	Clarke	84	2006-07		5+7/1					1/0	6+7/1
Jamie	Clarke	72	2004-05	2005-06	53+10/1	4/0	2/0	2+2/0		1/0	61+13/1
Simon	Coleman	47	2000-01	2001-02	13+3/1		1/0		+1/0		14+4/1
Theo	Coleman	82	2005-06	2006-07	1/0						1/0
Steve	Collis	134	2012-13	2015-16*	+0						+0
Charlie	Comyn-Platt	91	2006-07		+0/0						+0/0
Paul	Connor	50	2000-01	2003-04	76+18/28	8+1/3	3/0	+1/0	+1/0	3+1/2	90+22/33
Ernie	Cooksey	73	2004-05	2006-07	64+23/8	6/0	2/0	3+2/0		1/0	76+25/8
Ian	Craney	131	2012-13		+6/0	+1/0	+1/0	1/0			1+8/0
Lee	Crooks	83	2006-07	2007-08	31+9/0	1/0	1/0	2/0		2/0	37+9/0
Graham	Cummins	140	2013-14		15+12/4	+2/0		1+1/0			16+15/4
Craig	Curran	132	2012-13		+4/0		+1/0	1/0			1+5/0
Tomas	Cywka	145	2014-15		1+2/0	+2/0					1+4/0
Chris	Dagnall	79	2005-06	2009-10	124+33/57	5/1	5/0	4+1/2	5/3	1+1/1	144+35/64
Luke	Daniels	117	2010-11		1						1
Stephen	Darby	119	2011-12		34+1/0		3/0	2/0			39+1/0
Simon	Davies	46	2000-01		7+5/1	+1/0	1+1/0	+1/0			8+8/1
Craig	Dawson	104	2008-09	2010-11	84+3/19	3/2	3/0	1/1			91+3/22
Stephen	Dawson	143	2014-15		27+3/0	5/0		1/0			33+3/0
Johny	Diba Musungu	143	2014-15	2015-16*	+1						+1
Gary	Dicker	141	2013-14		10+2/1	1/0		2/0			13+2/1
Liam	Dickinson	118	2010-11		7+7/0						7+7/0
Nathan	D'Laryea	93	2007-08	2008-09	2+4/0	1/0	1/0		2/0	+1/0	6+5/0
Louis	Dodds	90	2006-07		6+6/2						6+6/2
Matt	Done	115	2010-11	2014-15	64+30/15	8+1/3	1+2/0	4/2			77+33/20
George	Donnelly	130	2012-13	2014-15	43+35/13	2+2/0	1+2/0	2/0			48+39/13
Kevin	Donovan	66	2003-04		4+3/0						4+3/0
John	Doolan	80	2005-06	2007-08	75+8/3	1/1	2/1	2+1/0	+1/0	2/0	82+10/5
Matt	Doughty	51	2001-02	2003-04	96+12/1	8+1/1	2+1/0	4/0	2/0	3+1/0	115+15/2
Craig	Dove	83	2006-07							+1/0	+1/0
Julian	Dowe	40	1999-00		1+6/0	1+1/1					2+7/1
Lee	Duffy	52	2001-02	2003-04	20+8/0	3/0	1/0	2+1/0		3+1/0	29+10/0
Matt	Duffy	45	1999-00	2001-02	+0/0						+0/0
Darren	Dunning	55	2001-02		4+1/0						4+1/0
Kieran	Durkan	52	2001-02	2002-03	16+14/1	3/0	2/0	1/0		1+2/0	23+16/1
Ashley	Eastham	137	2013-14	2015-16	74+2/3	10/0	2/0	5/0			91+2/3
Nathan	Eccleston	123	2011-12		3+2/1	+1/0		1/0			4+3/1
Lewis	Edge	85	2006-07		+0						+0
Matty	Edwards	106	2009-10	2012-13	5+3		1				6+3
Phil	Edwards	127	2011-12	2012-13	44+3/0	2/0	1/0	1/0			48+3/0
Ryan	Edwards	130	2012-13		25+1/0	1/0	1/0	1/0			28+1/0
Anthony	Elding	114	2010-11		9+8/3	1/1	1+1/1	1/0			12+9/5
Tony	Ellis	42	1999-00	2000-01	55+4/17	1+1/0	1/1	5+1/0			62+6/18
Kelvin	Etuhu	88	2006-07		3+1/2						3+1/2
Rafale	Evans	96	2007-08	2008-09	1/0						1/0
Wayne	Evans	39	1999-00	2004-05	259/3	18/0	9/1	9/0	2/0	2/0	299/4
Jordan	Fagbola	121	2011-12		+0/0						+0/0
Shamir	Fenelon	144	2014-15		+4/0			1/0			1+4/0
Chus	Fernandez	61	2002-03		+0/0						+0/0
Frank	Fielding	102	2008-09	2009-10	41				2		43
Dave	Flitcroft	39	1999-00	2010-11	141+20/4	7+4/0	5+2/0	8+1/0	2/0	1+1/0	164+28/4
Willo	Flood	69	2003-04		6/0						6/0
Matt	Flynn	107	2009-10	2010-11	7+4/0			1/0			8+4/0
Tony	Ford	39	1999-00	2001-02	81+8/6	4/0	6/1	4+1/0			95+9/7
Tony	Gallimore	73	2004-05	2005-06	64+4/0	3/0	2/0	3/0			72+4/0
Kevin	Gibbins	70	2003-04	2005-06	+0/0						+0/0
Paul	Gibson	43	1999-00		5						5
Bryan	Gilfillan	83	2006-07							+1/0	+1/0
Matt	Gilks	44	1999-00	2006-07	174+2	9	4	7		3	197+2
Danny	Glover	111	2009-10		+2/0						+2/0
Alan	Goodall	71	2004-05	2010-11	113+12/8	4/0	2/0	6/0		1+1/0	126+13/8
Warren	Goodhind	79	2005-06	2006-07	10/0	1/0		1/0			12/0
Terry	Gornell	133	2012-13		16+3/5						16+3/5
Simon	Grand	54	2001-02	2003-04	33+7/2	7/0	1/0	1/0		1/0	43+7/2
Bobby	Grant	117	2010-11	2012-13	40+2/17	1/0		1/1			42+2/18
Reece	Gray	111	2009-10	2013-14	2+11/2						2+11/2

		Page	Season	To	FL	FAC	FLC	AMC	PO	Other	Total
Richard	Green	41	1999-00	2001-02	6/0						6/0
Gareth	Griffiths	51	2001-02	2005-06	176+8/14	8/1	3/0	7/3	2/0	3/0	191+8/18
Ashley	Grimes	120	2011-12	2012-13	54+20/18	1+1/0	4/3	1+2/1			60+23/22
Simon	Hackney	128	2011-12		1+1/0						1+1/0
Phil	Hadland	46	2000-01		12+20/2	1/0	+1/0	1/0			14+21/2
Marcus	Hahnemann	53	2001-02		5			2			7
Gary	Hamilton	47	2000-01		+3/0						+3/0
Billy	Hasler-Cregg	145	2014-15	2015-16	+0/0						+0/0
Andy	Haworth	112	2009-10	2012-13	6+8/0						6+8/0
Greg	Heald	69	2003-04	2004-05	39/3	2/0	1/0			1/0	43/3
Tom	Heaton	110	2009-10		12						12
Ian	Henderson	135	2012-13	2015-16*	137+3/49	9/1	3+1/0	3/0			152+4/50
Bastien	Hery	139	2013-14	2014-15	16+17/2	3+1/0	2/0	3/0			24+18/2
Kallum	Higginbotham	94	2007-08	2009-10	31+38/7	2+2/0	1+1/0	+1/0	3/0	+1/0	37+43/7
Stephen	Hill	52	2001-02	2003-04	10+1/0	2/0				1+1/0	13+2/0
Darren	Hockenhull	62	2002-03		6+1/1						6+1/1
Lee	Hodges	59	2002-03		3+4/0			1/0		2+1/1	6+5/1
Scott	Hogan	111	2009-10	2013-14	29+4/17	4/2	1/0	1+1/0			35+5/19
Dean	Holden	123	2011-12		20+1/0	1/0					21+1/0
Marcus	Holness	95	2007-08	2011-12	93+15/4	4+1/0	6/0	7/0	+1/0		111+16/4
Grant	Holt	67	2003-04	2015-16	78+11/37	4/5	2/1	2/2		1/0	87+11/45
James	Hooper	147	2014-15	2015-16*	1+1/0	1/0					2+1/0
Rene	Howe	97	2007-08		19+1/9				2+1/0		21+2/9
Dean	Howell	49	2000-01		2+1/0						2+1/0
Mark	Jackson	81	2005-06	2006-07	20+4/0	1/0		+1/0			21+5/0
Tommy	Jaszczun	77	2005-06		12+5/0	1/0	1/0				14+5/0
Richard	Jobson	53	2001-02	2002-03	49+2/3	6/0	1/0	2/0	2/0	2/0	62+2/3
Jamie	Jones	146	2014-15		13						13
Mark	Jones	102	2008-09		7+2/0	1+2/0		1/0			9+4/0
Ritchie	Jones	135	2012-13		2+1/0						2+1/0
Ryan	Jones	116	2010-11		+0						+0
Steve	Jones	57	2001-02		6+3/1						6+3/1
Stephen	Jordan	123	2011-12		17+2/0	1/0		1/0			19+2/0
Jake	Kean	119	2011-12		14			1			15
Reece	Kelly	100	2007-08		+0/0						+0/0
Clark	Keltie	100	2008-09	2009-10	26+5/1	2/0	1/0	1+1/0			30+6/1
Jason	Kennedy	106	2009-10	2013-14	170+14/11	6/1	7/2	3/0			186+14/14
Tom	Kennedy	92	2007-08	2015-16*	177+2/9	6/0	6/0	5+1/0	5/0	1/0	200+3/9
Kisimba	Kisimba	145	2014-15	2015-16*				+0/0			+0/0
Ben	Kitchen	76	2004-05	2005-06	3+6/0			+1/0			3+7/0
Peter	Kurucz	124	2011-12		11						11
Kevin	Kyle	48	2000-01		3+3/0						3+3/0
Kyle	Lambert	101	2008-09		+1/0						+1/0
Rickie	Lambert	75	2004-05	2006-07	61+3/28	1/0	1/0	2/0		1/0	66+3/28
Olly	Lancashire	138	2013-14	2015-16	88+5/3	10/1	3/0	2/0			103+5/4
Adam	Le Fondre	88	2006-07	2009-10	65+33/37	3/4	+3/0	2+1/0	2+3/0	1/1	73+40/42
Michael	Lea	113	2009-10		+0/0						+0/0
Christian	Lee	48	2000-01		2+3/1						2+3/1
Tommy	Lee	98	2007-08		11				3		14
Steve	Lenagh	40	1999-00		+0/0						+0/0
Josh	Lillis	109	2009-10	2015-16*	169+2	8	6	4			187+2
Danny	Livesey	68	2003-04		11+2/0						11+2/0
Eddie	Loewen	58	2002-03							1+1/0	1+1/0
Conrad	Logan	143	2014-15		19	4		2			25
Joel	Logan	133	2012-13	2015-16	4+9/0	1/0	+1/0				5+10/0
Kelvin	Lomax	95	2007-08		10/0						10/0
Kevin	Long	126	2011-12		16/0						16/0
David	Lucas	120	2011-12		16	1	2	1			20
Matty	Lund	139	2013-14	2015-16*	77+6/11	8/1	2/0	2/0			89+6/12
Craig	Lynch	142	2013-14		+1/0						+1/0
Steve	Macauley	59	2002-03		6/0			1/0			7/0
Gary	Madine	103	2008-09		1+2/0						1+2/0
Marc	Manga	108	2009-10		+2/0	+1/0					+3/0
Paul	Marshall	121	2011-12		+1/0						+1/0
Rory	McArdle	79	2005-06	2009-10	141+7/5	8/0	3/0	2/0	5/1	1/0	160+7/6
Sean	McAuley	43	1999-00	2001-02	34+3/0	3/0	1+1/0	3/0			41+4/0
Sean	McClare	44	1999-00	2003-04	38+9/0	1/0	1/0	1/0		1/0	42+9/0
Sean	McConville	128	2011-12		2+2/0						2+2/0

		Page	Season	To	FL	FAC	FLC	AMC	PO	Other	Total
Paddy	McCourt	54	2001-02	2004-05	31+48/8	2+4/1	+3/0	1+4/0	+1/0	1+1/0	35+61/9
Donal	McDermott	147	2015-16*		32+5/2	1+1/0	1+1/1	2/0			36+7/3
Lee	McEvilly	57	2001-02	2008-09	62+46/33	5+2/1		1/0	2/1	1+3/2	71+51/37
Sean	McGinty	142	2013-14	2014-15	+1/0						+1/0
Leighton	McGivern	72	2004-05		2+23/1	+2/0	+1/0	+2/0		+1/0	2+29/1
Kevin	McIntyre	129	2012-13		37+1/1	2/0	1/0	2/0			42+1/1
Alan	McLaughlin	56	2001-02		15+3/1				2/0		17+3/1
Jim	McNulty	147	2015-16*		46/0	2/0	2/0	2/0			52/0
Gavin	Melaugh	61	2002-03		17+2/1	5/1					22+2/2
Nathaniel	Mendez-Laing	148	2015-16*		18+15/7	1/3		2/0			21+15/10
Sam	Minihan	128	2011-12	2012-13	1/0						1/0
William	Mocquet	87	2006-07		6+1/1						6+1/1
Lee	Molyneux	141	2013-14		+3/0						+3/0
Lewis	Montrose	99	2007-08		+0/0						+0/0
Clive	Moyo-Modise	77	2005-06	2006-07	2+26/1		+1/0	2/0		+1/0	4+28/1
Ben	Muirhead	90	2006-07	2008-09	30+13/3			2/0	+3/0	1/0	33+16/3
Jack	Muldoon	145	2014-15		2+1/0	1+1/0		+1/0			3+3/0
Glenn	Murray	87	2006-07	2007-08	50+4/25	3/0	2/1	1/0			56+4/26
Kangana	Ndiwa	68	2003-04		+1/0						+1/0
Tom	Newey	104	2008-09		1+1/0						1+1/0
Reuben	Noble-Lazarus	145	2014-15	2015-16	9+20/2	+2/1	1+1/0	+1/0			10+24/3
Temitope	Obadeyi	112	2009-10	2011-12	8+9/2						8+9/2
Jack	O'Connell	139	2013-14	2014-15	66+1/5	4/0	1/0	4/0			75+1/5
D'arcy	O'Connor	136	2012-13	2013-14	1/0						1/0
Chris	O'Grady	108	2009-10	2011-12	88+2/31	3/0	2/0				93+2/31
Vince	O'Keefe	55	2001-02		+0						+0
Chris	Oldfield	117	2010-11		+0						+0
Michael	Oliver	46	2000-01	2002-03	87+16/9	6/1	5/0	3/0	2/0	2+1/1	105+17/11
Brett	Ormerod	125	2011-12		4+1/1						4+1/1
John	O'Sullivan	149	2015-16		2/0	1/0					3/0
Rory	Patterson	60	2002-03	2003-04	5+10/0	+1/0		1+1/0		+1/0	6+13/0
Matty	Pearson	129	2012-13		8+1/0	1/0	1/0	1+1/0			11+2/0
Martin	Pemberton	67	2003-04		1/0						1/0
David	Perkins	89	2006-07	2007-08	54+4/4	1/0	1/1	1/0	2/1		59+4/6
Warren	Peyton	42	1999-00	2000-01	1/0						1/0
Clive	Platt	40	1999-00	2002-03	151+18/30	13/5	5/1	6/1	1/0	2/0	178+18/37
Glenn	Poole	91	2006-07		1+5/0						1+5/0
George	Porter	141	2013-14		1+1/0						1+1/0
Rory	Prendergast	88	2006-07	2007-08	6+13/2	+1/0	+2/1	1/1		1/0	8+16/4
Ashley	Probets	72	2004-05		4+5/0	+1/0	1/0	+2/0		1/0	6+8/0
Ray	Putterill	131	2012-13		1+17/1	+1/0	+1/0	2/1			3+19/2
Joe	Rafferty	133	2012-13	2015-16*	108+6/2	4+1/0	3+1/0	4+1/1			119+9/3
Simon	Ramsden	80	2005-06	2008-09	107+5/6	1/0	4/0	2/0	5/0	2/0	121+5/6
Neil	Redfearn	70	2003-04		9/0						9/0
Jack	Redshaw	115	2010-11		+2/0			1/0			1+2/0
Danny	Reet	91	2006-07		+6/0						+6/0
Reuben	Reid	89	2006-07		+2/0						+2/0
Jordan	Rhodes	102	2008-09		5/2						5/2
Mark	Richards	76	2004-05		4+1/2						4+1/2
Marcus	Richardson	75	2004-05		1+1/0						1+1/0
Lloyd	Rigby	82	2006-07	2007-08	+0						+0
Karl	Rose	55	2001-02					1/0			1/0
Michael	Rose	134	2012-13	2015-16	101+17/8	8+1/1	1+1/0	2+1/0			112+20/9
Adam	Rundle	84	2006-07	2009-10	95+32/17	5+2/0	5/1	3+1/0	5/1	1/0	114+35/19
Sam	Russell	93	2007-08	2008-09	38	4	1	3			46
Morike	Sako	86	2006-07		14+3 3	1+1 0		+1 0			15+5/3
Damon	Searle	41	1999-00		13+1/0						13+1/0
James	Sharp	86	2006-07		12/1	1/0		1/0			14/1
Jon	Shaw	101	2008-09	2009-10	5+2/1	1+2/0	1+1/0		+1/0		7+6/1
Dennis	Sherriff	106	2009-10				+0/0				+0/0
Chris	Shuker	64	2003-04		14/1		1/0				15/1
Michael	Simpkins	63	2003-04		25+2/0	1/0	1/0	1/0		1/0	29+2/0
Paul	Simpson	58	2001-02	2002-03	37+5/15	3+1/1	1/0	1/0	2/1	2/0	46+6/17
Deane	Smalley	117	2010-11		+3/0						+3/0
Ben	Smith	132	2012-13		+0			2			2
Jeff	Smith	68	2003-04		1/0						1/0
Shaun	Smith	69	2003-04		13/0						13/0
James	Spencer	92	2007-08	2008-09	20		2			1	23

		Page	Season	To	FL	FAC	FLC	AMC	PO	Other	Total
Scott	Spencer	107	2009-10		+4/0			+1/0			+5/0
Nathan	Stanton	85	2006-07	2009-10	138+1/0	5/0	3/0	3/0	4/0		153+1/0
Dale	Stephens	107	2009-10		3+3/1						3+3/1
Craig	Strachan	66	2003-04		+1/0						+1/0
Blair	Sturrock	78	2005-06		15+16/6	+1/0	+1/0	1+1/0			16+19/6
Dave	Syers	149	2015-16		2+4/0						2+4/0
Michael	Symes	127	2011-12		14+1/4						14+1/4
Danny	Taberner	109	2009-10	2011-12	+0	1					1
Paul	Tait	71	2004-05	2005-06	31+16/3	3+1/0	1/1	3/2		1/0	39+17/6
Scott	Tanser	137	2012-13	2015-16*	33+5/1	6/0	1/0	3/1			43+5/2
Danny	Taylor	44	1999-00	2000-01	+1/0						+1/0
Jason	Taylor	110	2009-10		23/1						23/1
Michael	Taylor	62	2002-03		2/0						2/0
Scott	Taylor	96	2007-08		2+2/0						2+2/0
Wayne	Thomas	136	2012-13		2/0						2/0
Joe	Thompson	82	2005-06	2012-13	89+58/15	2+1/2	2+3/0	5+1/0	1+1/0		99+64/17
Josh	Thompson	116	2010-11		11+1/1		+1/0	1/0			12+2/1
Robbie	Thomson	140	2013-14		1						1
Lee	Thorpe	97	2007-08	2008-09	23+13/6	2+1/0	+1/0	1+1/1	2/0		28+16/7
Lee	Todd	45	2000-01	2001-02	48+2/3	1/0	3/0				52+2/3
Ciaran	Toner	101	2008-09	2009-10	39+11/1	2/0	+1/0	2/0	2/0		45+12/1
Kevin	Townson	49	2000-01	2004-05	41+61/25	2+4/1	+3/3	4/1	1+1/0	2+3/0	50+72/30
Neal	Trotman	120	2011-12		12/0		1/0	1/0			14/0
Stephen	Turnbull	90	2006-07		2+2/0						2+2/0
Andy	Turner	50	2000-01		2+2/0						2+2/0
Andrew	Tutte	116	2010-11	2013-14	77+18/10	4/0	6/1	3+2/0			90+20/11
Marc	Twaddle	121	2011-12		1+1/0			1/0			2+1/0
Tony	Vaughan	83	2006-07							1/0	1/0
Javan	Vidal	140	2013-14		2/0			1/0			3/0
Peter	Vincenti	138	2013-14	2015-16*	93+24/26	8+2/4	4/0	5/1			110+26/31
David	Walsh	47	2000-01	2001-02	+0/0		+1/0				+1/0
Callum	Warburton	85	2006-07	2007-08	4/0	+1/0				+1/0	4+2/0
Paul	Ware	45	2000-01	2001-02	21+17/2	1/0	2/0	1/0			25+17/2
Scott	Warner	60	2002-03	2005-06	57+16/2	2+3/0		3/0		1+2/0	63+21/2
Luke	Watson	133	2012-13		+0/0						+0/0
Jerome	Watt	94	2007-08		+0/0						+0/0
Paul	Weller	74	2004-05		5/0						5/0
Simon	Whaley	108	2009-10		8+1/2						8+1/2
Ben	Wharton	97	2007-08		+1/0						+1/0
Paul	Wheatcroft	53	2001-02		6/3						6/3
Joe	Widdowson	113	2010-11	2011-12	60+6/0	1/0	5/0	+1/0			66+7/0
Matt	Williams	77	2004-05		+1/0						+1/0
Owain fon	Williams	118	2010-11		22						22
Robbie	Williams	119	2010-11		9/0						9/0
Scott	Wilson	42	1999-00		+1/0						+1/0
Scott	Wiseman	100	2008-09	2010-11	100+5/1	3/0	2/0	2+2/0			107+7/1
Danny	Woodhall	74	2004-05	2005-06	+0						+0

ADDITIONS AND CORRECTIONS TO PREVIOUS VOLUMES

A number of minor additions and typos in details given in previous volumes in this series have been noted.

Volume 1: 1907-1939
Preface: the number of players included is 655, not 665.
Page 15: A. Mills and J.B. Mills are almost certainly the brothers Alfred and James Barlow Mills, born Farnworth OND.1884 and AMJ.1880, respectively.
J. Bowden: born Glossop 8.10.1884, add to career Glossop am 9.10 to 1913-14 [7/-]. He was also a first class cricketer for Derbyshire, playing 231 games between 1909 and 1930, twice scoring 1000 runs in a season.
H. Barnes: born Blackburn JFM. 1886.
Joseph Thorp: born Bury JAS.1882.
T.A. Broome: born 14.1.1892.
W.T. Chamberlain: Dale appearances [16/- CL].
P. Hardy: born Bradford JAS.1892. He emigrated to Canada in 1913 and after serving in their military played for New York Field Club in 1921-22.
J.W. Swann: his game for Manchester C. was in the second division, not first.
J. Hebden: Dorman Long am 8.33.
E. Goodwin: Leeds C. appearances (first spell) [19/3, 13/3 WL].

Volume 2: 1939-1973
Page 14: Arthur Richardson became a photographer at an engineering works, not Alfie Anderson, the previous player in the list.
Alick Robinson: Bury guest appearances [46/- WL].
Jack Robinson: Raith R. guest appearances [1 ScWL].
Samuel Patton: born Newtonards, Co. Down.
Ernie Toseland: add that he was everpresent when Manchester C. won the league title in 1936-37.
Hugh O'Donnell: Celtic appearances [75/20 ScL].
Ossie Collier: Reading appearances [2/- WL], Hibernian appearances [1/- ScWL].
Ron Johnston: Albion R. appearances 1942-43 [5/1 ScWL].
Joe Devlin: Accrington St. appearances, second spell [1/- expunged].
Peter Whyke: add Honours: League Cup final 1962.
Additions and Corrections (p.146): Christopher Wynn born 1889, not 1883.

Volume 3: 1973-1999
Preface: the total number of players in the first three volumes was 1549 not 1559.
Tony Whelan: transferred to Manchester C. 2.73 not 1.72. He played in the Lancashire Cup Final in 1972, not 1971.
John Dungworth: scored 49 goals for Aldershot in two years, not 29.
Jason Smart: near end of text insert "but actually joined Crewe" before "for £50,000".
Alan Reeves: Alan and his brother David were in the 1994 PFA XI, not 1993.
Jackie Ashurst: Dale trial 8.92 to 9.92, not 9.82.
Richard Sharpe: Colorado Rapids add [15/2 MLS].
Stephen Bywater: FL Apps should be +0. Career update: Kerala Blasters (India) 8.15, Burton A. 13.1.16*. In Honours add (League 1 promotion 2016).
Gary Jones: date re-signed for Dale 19.2.04, not 19.2.03. Career update: Southport cs.15 [43/5 Conf]*.
Appearances summary:
  S. Bywater – add FL +0
  P. Dwyer – FL and Total should be 15/1
  A. Reed – AMC should be 2/1, Total 12/1
Additions and Corrections (p.135):
  A. Rawlings should be Division 3N champions
  D. Bain Division 1 champions 1928
  E. Toseland and R. Neilson Division 1 champions 1937
  D. Boxshall Division 3S champions 1948
  H. Rudman should be Division 2 promotion

Any corrections that need to made to this volume will be posted on the Soccerdata.com web site.